T4-AHV-967

WITHDRAWN
The Catholic
Theological Union
LIBRARY
Chicago, Ill.

75.00
90E

THE GARLAND LIBRARY OF READINGS IN

ETHNOMUSICOLOGY

A Core Collection of Important Ethnomusicological Articles in Seven Volumes

Edited by Kay Kaufman Shelemay
Wesleyan University

A GARLAND SERIES

CONTENTS OF THE SERIES

VOLUME 1

HISTORY, DEFINITIONS, AND SCOPE OF ETHNOMUSICOLOGY

◆

VOLUME 2

ETHNOMUSICOLOGICAL THEORY AND METHOD

◆

VOLUME 3

MUSIC AS CULTURE

◆

VOLUME 4

MUSICAL TRANSCRIPTION

◆

VOLUME 5

CROSS-CULTURAL MUSICAL ANALYSIS

◆

VOLUME 6

MUSICAL PROCESSES, RESOURCES, AND TECHNOLOGIES

◆

VOLUME 7

A CENTURY OF ETHNOMUSICOLOGICAL THOUGHT

VOLUME 2

Ethnomusicological Theory and Method

Edited by Kay Kaufman Shelemay

WITHDRAWN
The Catholic
Theological Union
LIBRARY
Chicago, Ill.

GARLAND PUBLISHING
NEW YORK & LONDON
1990

Kay Kaufman Shelemay is Professor of Music at Wesleyan University. Her books include *Music, Ritual, and Falasha History* (winner of the ASCAP-Deems Taylor Award 1987 and the 1988 Prize of the International Musicological Society) and *A Song of Longing*. She has edited the two-volume *Ethiopian Christian Chant, An Anthology* (with Peter Jeffery) and has published numerous scholarly articles. A recipient of fellowships from the National Endowment for the Humanities and the American Council of Learned Societies, Shelemay is a member of the Board of Directors of the Society of Ethnomusicology.

Introduction Copyright © 1990 by Kay Kaufman Shelemay
All Rights Reserved

Library of Congress Cataloging-in-Publication Data
Ethnomusicological theory and method/ edited by Kay Kaufman Shelemay.
p. cm. — (The Garland library of readings in ethnomusicology; v. 2)
Reprint of essays originally published in various sources 1910–1987.
ISBN 0-8240-6470-4 (alk. paper)
1. Ethnomusicology. I. Shelemay, Kay Kaufman. II. Series.
ML3799.G37 1990 vol. 2
780'.89 s—dc20
[780'.89]90-3539

Design: John M-Röblin

Printed on acid-free, 250-year-life paper
Manufactured in the United States of America

GENERAL EDITOR'S INTRODUCTION

Over a century of ethnomusicological research has given rise to a large if widely scattered scholarly literature. The *Garland Library of Readings in Ethnomusicology* presents a selection of distinguished articles on diverse historical, methodological, and theoretical topics dating from the nineteenth century to the 1980s.

All articles have been photographically reproduced as originally printed, each volume incorporating both older contributions and more recent scholarship, arranged for the most part in chronological order. In this manner, a single volume provides insight into individual approaches to common problems or issues over time, while the series as a whole sets forth an overview of the history and nature of a changing ethnomusicological discourse.

Ethnomusicologists have always published in an international and interdisciplinary array of periodicals and collections of essays, rendering many of the publications difficult of access. For this reason, a special effort was made to incorporate here valuable writings that are difficult to locate of out-of-print. Consideration was given to including important older articles from rare or inaccessible sources while also incorporating more recent contributions crucial to the thorough treatment of a particular theme or issue. Approximately one fourth of the entries in this series are drawn from *Ethnomusicology*, reflecting its status as a most important venue for ethnomusicological publication during the second half of the twentieth century. The majority of the articles are in English, with a minority of contributions in French, German, and Spanish.

Articles were chosen with primary consideration for their treatment of major issues or problems that have occupied ethnomusicological thought and practice. While many of the selections contain discussion of a particular musical tradition as part of a more general statement or argument, articles were selected with consideration of their contribution to the methodological and issue-oriented focus of the series. No attempt was made to balance geographical coverage or to provide a representative sample of musical traditions that have been the subject of ethnomusicological research. In some cases, copyright difficulties prevented the inclusion of other entries of choice.

In juxtaposing within a seven-volume collection a number of important articles originally conceived independently, the *Garland Library of Readings in Ethnomusicology* brings together individual scholarly efforts in a new context. The rubrics under which the articles have been organized emerged during the process of bibliographic selection. Each volume unites articles that speak in some way to the common theme or problem reflected in its title, although some of the items in the collection could have fit equally well into more than one volume of the series.

Volume 7 contains contributions that intersect with and overlap the themes of the other six volumes, each entry representing a new perspective, paradigm, or approach at its respective time of publication.

Ethnomusicologists have since early dates been concerned with both the boundaries and mandates of their discipline. Volume 1 includes articles treating the history, definition, and scope of the field. These range from early summaries of ethnomusicological subject matter and state of research to later, comprehensive discussions spanning the discipline at large, its intellectual history, and future prospects.

Ethnomusicologists have always invoked and applied a wide range of theories and methods in their research. Volume 2 incorporates a diverse collection of articles that either make explicit theoretical or methodological statements, or implicitly set forth approaches that transcend their particular case study. Several contributions define the relationship between ethnomusicology and other fields of inquiry, as well as the impact of the methods and theories of other disciplines on ethnomusicological scholarship.

Attention to the role of music in culture and methods for the study of music in context is the theme linking articles included in Volume 3. All articles in this volume explicitly address the cultural aspects of music making—the role of music in human social life, thought, and action.

Articles discussing the philosophy, methodologies, and technologies of musical transcription are found within Volume 4, while the methods and problems of cross-cultural musical analysis are the subject of Volume 5.

Ethnomusicologists have long been concerned not only with music-making, but with music-makers and the processes through which musical materials are generated, transmitted, and documented. Volume 6 contains selected articles on musical instruments and musicians, on the processes of composition and performance, and on the technologies and methods through which these materials have been preserved and studied.

Volume 7 presents articles that signalled new trends or subject of ethnomusicological concern at their time of publication. Their chronological presentation together graphically illustrates the scope and dynamism of ethnomusicological research throughout the first century of its history.

This series is intended to provide a core collection of ethnomusicological articles for libraries that may not own a wide array of periodicals or that may seek to preserve their often fragile originals from heavy use. The volumes can also serve as a convenient resource for teaching and study, a welcome alternative to the dozens of crumpled photocopies that access to these widely dispersed offerings otherwise necessitates. Although no single collection can do justice to the extraordinary diversity of thought that has characterized ethnomusicological inquiry to date, it is hoped that these volumes provide both a balanced overview of the past and a useful resource for readers as they draw upon existing research in their search for new intellectual directions.

Kay Kaufman Shelemay

GENERAL ACKNOWLEDGMENT

I thank

Philip V. Bohlman, Regula Burckhardt Qureshi, Bruno Nettl,

Adelaida Reyes Schramm, and Ruth Stone

for their advice and assistance in compiling this reprint series.

CONTENTS

SUGGESTIONS TO FIELD-WORKERS IN COLLECTING FOLK MUSIC AND DATA ABOUT INSTRUMENTS.

By Helen H. Roberts,
Yale University, New Haven, Conn.

THE writer has been asked several times to formulate a list of suggestions to field-workers in collecting and recording the music of various primitive or simple peoples. The response is made the more willingly because it is becoming increasingly difficult to secure untainted folk-music, and hence it is necessary to enlist the assistance of all who find themselves in a position to gather it, who are willing to make the attempt; also because long experience in transcribing phonograph records made by various explorers who have penetrated seldom-visited regions has shown that they often leave much to be desired.

Musical compositions, and especially musical instruments, because of their complicated construction and non-utilitarian character, afford particularly valuable criteria for tracing culture-connections between peoples whose history is still, and probably will remain, to a great extent, largely a matter of conjecture. Much more could be done with confidence in the matter of comparison if songs, instead of being merely described, were actually noted or taken on phonograph records (as indeed many collectors have already done), and if instruments, instead of being loosely alluded to as " a kind of guitar " or " a sort of fiddle," and so on, were minutely described, along with methods of manipulation, and drawn or photographed. While it is generally true that most uncivilized peoples do not philosophize much about their music, or view it in the abstract to any extent, in some cases they do have definite standards which should be learned if possible.

The present suggestions and instructions are formulated principally to help inexperienced collectors, with the Pacific area and its periphery principally in mind, but most of the remarks are applicable to any region. With the Pacific becoming rapidly more and more opened to the march of civilization, and still too little known—apparently the great cross-roads in a huge stream of ancient life—it is important that data from there be accurate and detailed.

Approaching the Informants.

In collecting folk-material of any sort it should never be forgotten that, added to the usual problems of collecting, such as the botanist, entomologist, geologist, etc., has to face, is the human factor. When this human factor is contrary, the collector's chances of success are small. Suitable methods of approaching informants are best left to the ingenuity of the collector, in which his own personality plays no small part. Much also depends upon the kind of people among whom he is to work, their natural temperament, their open friendliness or suspicion of strangers, and especially of white men, among whom they often do not discriminate the good from the bad, feeling that all are enemies, and against whom they often cherish not unjustifiable resentment.

Frequently the songs of a people, especially their ceremonial songs, contain the most sacred lore they know. A collector in residence among natives who have tried him out and discovered him not lacking, but rather their trusted friend, will find this a sesame, the native deriving as much pleasure from reciting his lore and finding his friend interested in it, as the collector in recording it. But a stranger coming among them seeking songs, myths, and the like, must remember that such requests are often regarded as unwarranted probing into private affairs, and must go about it slowly and tactfully—a most difficult procedure sometimes, when time is limited. Most of what will be valuable for ethnology will come from the old folk, the reactionaries. In the face of the march of civilization even their own children are turning away from old ways, and this often hurts the sensitive pride of the elders so that they become more than ordinarily difficult of approach. Each people has its code of good breeding applying to strangers coming among them. These it is wise to learn in advance, if possible, and to adhere to strictly. Not a few lives have been lost by impertinent investigators who regard their human " specimens " as quite without sensibilities. Nowhere is real consideration more needed than in dealing with natives, and this even to the most minute particulars. I have found that sometimes merely an interest expressed in old-time customs, an admiration for them, a sympathy uttered for the loss of the good old days, a desire to hear about them, will bring a glow to aged faces and a surprising volubility. In the face of the most improbable tales I never flick an eyelash, but simulate belief, if necessary, and amazement.

Among Polynesians, particularly, it has been a time-honoured custom for one visiting, or coming to ask a favor, to offer a gift, and the collector unprepared or unwilling to do this loses in the end far more than he gains. It is not usually possible to appeal to an unenlightened people to divulge their sacred knowledge as a civic or patriotic duty, to be given over to white people and be carried no one can tell where, to be turned against them in no one knows how many disastrous ways. One must first inspire confidence. It has been the almost invariable practice of anthropologists from reputable institutions to pay, and sometimes heavily, for a native's time and store of knowledge. In native society those who wish to learn the secrets of their powerful elders pay handsome prices. Why should not a stranger do so? Not many regions of the earth are left, where the white man's lesson of demanding plenty of compensation for *his* favours has not been dearly learned by defrauded natives, who apply this lesson when they ask to be paid for leaving their cultivating, hunting, and fishing, to sit hours beside a frequently annoying inquisitive stranger to amuse and instruct him. Payment should be made the more readily when it is seen to what levels of poverty most natives are reduced by the invading white, with whom they are not equipped to compete.

But if a collector does pay, he should be careful not to overdo it. Unthinking prodigality on the part of fleeting visitors has, in many regions, not only totally obscured to native intelligence the proper value of money, but of time. Passing strangers have often, therefore, made absurdly difficult the path of the investigator who must linger months in a given region and work slowly. Natives, having been well schooled, are not slow to take advantage of their position as possessors of a wanted commodity. To keep a flow of wealth turned in their direction, some have been known to stoop to ready fabrications; but generally natives are fundamentally honest, and if the collector plays fair himself and is canny and kind, he will win over the better element to his side, and it is usually easy enough to check up on data manufactured to order by asking the informant to repeat in rapid succession what he has given, by cross-questioning, and so on, and by comparing information taken independently from several sources unknown to one another. What might be lost, however, from gathering and paying for spurious material would be small compared to the gain resulting from fair and reasonable dealing, and from exposing and dismissing without rancour a native caught lying.

On the part of the collector, no promise, however small, should be made which cannot be scrupulously fulfilled, even at the cost of great personal inconvenience; or if unforseen events make it impossible, every effort should be made to notify the native and make all as right as possible. Animosity still rankles deeply in some Hawaiians toward a white man, now dead, the author of a book on Hawaiian life, who inveigled them to Honolulu at their own expense, the fruit of their small savings, under the promise to repay the passage, and promptly forgot it as soon as the information was forthcoming. It speaks well for one victim of this duplicity that he received me with courtesy in his humble little home, and expressed his regret kindly that he did not possess the particular sort of information I sought. He offered me much other data, not bearing on my work, which I would gladly have recorded had my own problem not been placed under a time limit for completion (an unfortunate and at times ruinous condition for the folk-lorist to work under), which demanded intense concentration on the data I needed. Impatience, or efforts to curb or "guide" talkative informants, frequently result only in their complete balking.

It may seem that such cautions as have just been given are superfluous preaching, but it is astonishing how many white people, passably presentable at home, show despicable traits when they are where they cannot be observed except by people of a supposedly lower order of intelligence than themselves. Yet dealing with natives frequently brings out abilities for winning them never suspected at home, when one must come down to simple fundamentals, and proves that natives, like children, warm to sincerity and thrive on kindness and honesty.

COLLECTING.[1]

The musical problem divides itself into two parts—vocal and instrumental. Closely allied with these two phases of pure music, especially among the less art-concious peoples, are poetry and dancing. With many peoples they may be said hardly to exist separately, since the songs are little more than intoned words, accompanied by gestures and posturings. Some individuals can give the texts of songs without singing them only with the greatest difficulty, or sing the tune without enunciating the words, and rarely they cannot sing the tune ordinarily produced by an instrument. With the Hawaiians, for instance, so intimately is gesture bound up with all vocal expression that the old people, especially, cannot comfortably recite a chant without the pantomime and facial expressions which customarily accompany it.

Gesture is but one phase of dancing, and though it is perhaps not necessary for the collector to describe minutely every movement, nor is it easy or even possible to note down dance steps except one be specially trained in a system of notation for them, nevertheless accurate and full descriptions of dances accompanying tunes which are collected, aid considerably in understanding the whole subject. For instance, odd shifts in metre, apparently most irrational, may be explained by special momentary dance or ceremonial requirements. Ordinarily, dancing tends to regularize metre, which becomes more or less irregular in simple song. How many of us, singing dance- or march-tunes without bodily movement, observe all the rests accurately and sing without acceleration or retardation? The tendency toward

[1] This paper was written in 1925 but was not published. In 1929 appeared a new edition of *Notes and Queries on Anthropology* from the Royal Anthropological Institute of Great Britain and Ireland, London, in which pages 295-321 deal with the subject of music, and particularly instruments. In some respects it duplicates ideas here set forth, and is an admirable summary to which the reader is referred.

irregularity without the stiffening prop of motor habits is evidently a common psychological phenomenon.

In the Pacific area, especially, certain peculiar types of dances occur, performed either sitting, or, if standing, with little or no movement of the feet and legs, the action being confined to the upper body, with the hands and arms trained to the utmost nicety of expression. These dances are traceable, apparently, directly to the mainland of south-east Asia, and it is highly desirable to have full and accurate description of varieties in the Pacific and on its borders, that relationships, if they exist, may be more closely indicated than has up to now been possible. Other "moving about" dances, where the feet are used, should also be noted and described, together with the dance-costume, the training the dancer undergoes, and the ceremonials involved, if any. It should be determined whether the dances are sacred or secular, and particularly whether a patron deity is invoked who has an altar, and what are the decorations on this altar. The dramatizations involved in such dances should be recorded.

It is absolutely necessary to pay close attention to the poetry or the text of the songs, since the correctness of the analyses of the structure of the tunes, or of the entire song from the standpoint of lines, refrains, verses, and so on, often depends entirely on the divisions of the text. A record of a song without accompanying texts written out is reduced in value at least fifty per cent., since the delimitation and arrangement of parts are fully as important as the mere tonal content of a melody. This is especially true of more or less limited or monotonous melodies, where the delimitations of parts might be arbitrarily placed at various points with no text to guide the analyst, and where melodic curves are irregular.

Vocal Music.

In collecting vocal music several points should be kept in mind. Songs of almost any people divide into sacred and secular, and this distinction is particularly important for ethnologists. Under these two heads other classifications may usually be made. It is necessary to learn what kinds of songs are known to the people. It might be imagined, for instance, that all peoples would have lullabies and love-songs, but some groups do not. An effort should be made to obtain a list of the various kinds of songs known, and to ascertain all native classifications, names, and general musical terminology, if it exists. Analogies in musical situations are doubly important for ethnology where terms are similar. Some peoples classify their songs according to the mode of instrumental accompaniment, others according to the manner of singing, others according to the text-content, others according to the purpose of the song, etc.; some have several classifications. As full information as possible on these points should be gathered. It is important to take not one, but several, examples of the songs of each type, to see if there is actually any uniformity of style, or musical structure, for songs of any given class, and to have the songs sung, not merely once, but, if possible, several times by the same singer, or different singers, in order to be able to gauge the limits of variation—individual, as regards any song as rendered by different singers, and personal, as regards the habits of any singer carrying through several songs. Only by such means can the norms of tonal material and forms be measured and the true identity of tunes be established. Rare songs, however, or indeed any which the collector has reason to believe valuable, should not be passed by merely because all these methods of check cannot be applied to them. Songs are frequently individual property, and none but the owner may sing them or will even know them. Obviously, in such cases, it would be impossible to have them sung by more than one person.

Religious and Secular Songs.

While topical songs—that is, the songs of the moment—are frequently found to contain unconscious, and therefore reliable and valuable, pictures of tribal psychology which might be obtained in no other way, such songs are apt to be shorter-lived than the more sacred. They are also more likely to undergo local tampering to fit temporary conditions, especially if they are humorous and have taken the popular fancy and travelled rather widely. A humorous incident loses half its charm if the characters figuring in it are unknown, hence it not uncommonly happens that names of characters and places will be changed so that the humorous or dramatic feature that appealed in the song will apply more aptly to a new locality to which it has been diffused.

Changes of name and incident bring about melodic and rhythmic variation in the accompanying tune. Therefore, from a historical standpoint, the local topical tunes are apt to be less valuable, less carefully preserved, and, unless particularly attractive, more quickly forgotten. If a collector must concentrate, or confine himself to a few songs, he should by all means seek the most ancient songs the old people can sing, and particularly religious and ceremonial songs, which are likely to be transmitted for generations unchanged, because of their associations. They may contain genealogies, prayers, eulogies to long-dead rulers, incidents of history and the like, invaluable to ethnologists who seek to put together surviving fragments into wholes which may reveal lost history and forgotten connections. The religious songs, also, do not lack those faithful representations of modes of life and thought, the more valuable because the more archaic.

Dance Songs.

Dance songs may be either religious or secular. The distinction should be ascertained in all cases and, if the song is religious, the ceremony and place of the song in it should be described. It is often useful to have a whole set of songs belonging to a given ceremony, rather than a mere sample, in order to see if a ceremonial musical pattern pervades them, or whether they are heterogeneous. In these cases it is better to concentrate on types of ceremonies likely to be found widely scattered, such as those connected with curing disease, with death, marriage, weather, crops, and the like. With sets of such songs available for comparison, it is now and then possible to trace the diffusion of religious ideas, as in the corn-ceremonies of the ancient Aztecs, which have apparently spread northward as far as the Plains Indians in North America. Ceremonials, like topical songs, may lose much of their original character in a new locality at the hands of another group, who, however, may re-adapt the tunes with comparatively little change, or in other ways still leave some traces for the musicologist to follow. On the other hand, to secure only ceremonial songs when collecting is to obtain only a partial view of the musical range of a people, so to speak; for if ceremonial sets do exist, more or less prescribed in character of tune, rhythm, or certain other purely structural features, and more or less alike in ritual, samples of only these might give a very incomplete idea of what, musically speaking, the people were capable of. In topical songs fancy has full range. There are no religious restrictions, no traditions to follow, hence (although in some regions they exist even for secular songs) the topical songs are usually apt to be more developed, from a purely musical standpoint, than the more ancient, even archaic hymns, because music, like all else, unless fettered by tradition, tends to change and usually to progress.

Music and poetry may be recorded in two ways—by direct notation, or by phonograph records. If the collector is a well-trained musician with an accurate ear and sense of time, and the conditions are either very favourable or, paradoxically very unfavourable, direct notation may have to serve. Under favourable conditions the music may offer few complexities, and informants may prove to be willing singers, patient with the slow process of writing, and to all intents and purposes excellent teachers. Many negroes are such. Under these conditions it is hardly necessary to go to the expense and trouble of conveying a phonograph and fragile records, or the much more expensive talking film outfits, unless it is desired to procure audible records.

Under unfavourable conditions the region may be so inaccessible, the opportunity to record so unexpected, the reluctance to sing so hard to overcome, that all that can be obtained must be noted in passing, without appearing to get down to serious work. But scraps, if well selected, are better than nothing. Longhand notation is, of course, very much slower than record making, and requires patience in all concerned. On the other hand, it has many merits. It affords excellent opportunities to the recorder for observing the musical intelligence and ability of the singer, his variability from repetition to repetition in melody, form, text, etc., as would not be noted under the rather more strenuous and rapid recording by phonograph. It also affords an excellent chance for conversation by the way, for questions are bound to arise which would never occur to the collector in the more perfunctory process of making records, and would only too late be put by the transcriber. Moreover, in this more leisurely pursuit, an informant may appeal to a bystander for assistance in recollecting, or arguments may arise which, to the alert collector, may furnish valuable additional data. Longhand notation is the best method possible for checking up on impromptu composing and frauds. Phonograph records and longhand notations of the same song may be compared with advantage.

Apparently many singers take almost as great an interest in the process of notation as in that of making records, and are particularly delighted when the collector, reading from the music, is able to reproduce, not only the text, but the melody of their own songs on so short an acquaintance. In my experience, most primitive singers seem not so meticulous in observing mistakes in melody as in text, but now and then there are exceptions. One Jamaican informant was remarkable in this respect. He picked out the minutest flaws in renditions, soon learned about the place on the page where they occurred, and in performing very quickly grasped the necessity of stopping instantly on signal, so that I could write down all my memory retained without the distraction of having the melody continuing, and was able to resume, when I was ready, at the point where he had stopped, without loss of a fraction of a beat.[2] When a collector observes such an informant, he is the one to select for intensive work.

The above remarks about recording apply equally well to the music of instruments. Notation also has the advantage here over phonograph records in that all pitches may be noted for any kind of instrument (not always possible to record with phonographs available) and there is a fine opportunity to observe methods of manipulation and to question informants. Noting by hand has one more advantage—it is less likely to draw an unmanageable crowd of curious onlookers than is the phonograph, or, if these gather, their interest soon wanes and they depart, leaving the collector and informant in peace.

Usually, the best method is to record the song on a phonograph record, waiting to transcribe it into notation until quiet and leisure are available. This saves putting

[2]Another, an Indian, beat a clapper in rhythms utterly at variance with those of the tune he was singing. He was vastly entertained by my efforts to imitate him, the training of faculties for imitation being much more difficult than, and certainly distinct from, the faculties of observation. He patiently illustrated again and again, not aware that my faulty execution lay in lack of practise.

natives to the trouble of endless repetitions and starting over again. I have found them very restive and soon wearied under the direct notation method, not being able to understand why it was necessary, after having given a song once, to sing it again and again, while their memories are badly upset by working piecemeal.

Before taking a song on a record, a number should be scratched with a pin on the record itself, as well as written on its container, to correspond with one in a stenographic notebook, under which should be noted all data relevant to the song—the place where it was collected, the name and age of the informant, his tribal affiliations, birthplace, and where he learned the song, the composer if known, and its probable age, as well as whether it is religious or secular, its title, class, and so on, and the use to which it is put. Having the informant sing over a song first gives the collector an idea of its length, and whether it is likely to fit the record without being curtailed. If it has endless repetitions of theme, some of these may be cut down, after explaining to the informant that the record will not take them all and asking him to make it shorter, describing where he omits " doubling," and making note of these in the book. Natives are quick to catch such points if they are clearly explained.

It is simply a matter of expediency whether, after the first trial at singing the song, it should be taken immediately on the record, or the text written out first. This is the longest and most tedious part of the proceeding, and is best over with while the singer is fresh and not excited by singing. Emotions become strangely stirred just in singing before the horn. Then, too, informants will almost invariably wait to sing into the horn and to hear a record of themselves, when, this curiosity being satisfied, they might not wait to recite in tedious fashion what they have already given and heard; nor do they appreciate why the collector cannot distinguish words on the record as they can.

By writing out the texts first, the collector familiarizes himself with them somewhat, and is in a position to check up on subsequent alterations in singing (which, to a limited degree, almost invariably occur). Having them written before him, he can prompt the singer if, in the excitement of making a record, he forgets at a crucial moment, especially when he pauses for breath and looks about, catching a glimpse of a bystander, or something that diverts him. Without such prompting many a record would be ruined, the needle travelling on and on, the singer becoming more and more embarrassed and chagrined at his failure. Moreover, by writing out the text first, the collector soon learns how much text will fit an available space, and may thus dispense with the initial singing when working with an experienced informant. Surprisingly soon some natives learn how much space a song would require, and hunt about in their minds for songs of the right length to fit available blank spaces.

Much tact is needed in prompting embarrassed singers, and caution should be exercised about hurrying the singer, or betraying annoyance. Likewise, in taking dictation from feeble old informants who are subject to lapses, care should be taken to wait patiently and not to tire them too much. With such people, morning is the best time, and it is safer to stop too soon and come another day than to be regarded as a pest by one who has become over-tired.

The texts[3] should first be written along, without comment, in exactly the form in which they are sung, including all the filler and nonsense syllables and distortions of spoken words incident to setting them to melody. If they cannot be recited in this way, they should be sung line for line. Often the word-forms will not correspond to spoken forms in current use. The collector may be mistaken about what groupings of syllables constitute single words, but attempts to isolate these later will bring responses, and with an intelligent informant, corrections. Having secured the chanted form, each word and line should be taken up in order.

Frequently a native will say, "That is not the way we talk it, but the way we sing it," and the spoken form, shorn of its embellishments, should be taken down with

[3] Collectors recording linguistic material would do well to familiarize themselves with the phonetic systems adopted by students of language. Perhaps the best, because most practical from the standpoint of printing, is set forth in *Phonetic Transcription of Indian Languages*, being a report of a committee of the American Anthropological Association on this subject, published as no. 6, vol. 66, of the *Smithsonian Miscellaneous Collections*, Washington, September, 1916.

careful regard for phonetics, with sufficient interlinear space to premit of writing translations directly under the elements pertaining to them. Attempts to divide words into grammatical elements are apt not to be successful, however, unless both collector and informant are quick-witted and observing. Some informants learn word-analysis quite quickly, others never, and many are nonplussed by the problem of recasting their language into another medium so remote in grammatical processes from their own. Translations should be as exact as possible, with the word-order of the original followed literally, as well as the sense. Freer translations may be appended, if they can be ascertained. The informant should be asked to designate natural divisions of lines and verses as a help in later musical analysis. The same words may sound differently on occasion, but no attempt at standardization should be made by the collector on the basis of snap judgments. It is better to preserve individual peculiarities and variations which may be due to momentary phonetic situations.

It is almost impossible to transcribe records later, with their texts, without the aid of the written lines, for even the best records are far from satisfactory in an exotic language, and consonants in records always tend to be obscured. Where the difference between a *k* and a *t* may not be clear on a record, reference to the notes will settle the matter. Amateurs almost never obtain excellent records immediately. In singing it is a common practice, particularly in Pacific languages, to mutilate or mouth texts, so that, even if the phonetics used should be clear on the record, words might hardly be recognizable. Archaic words are often preserved in song-texts that have been lost in modern common speech, and frequently they provide clues to older linguistic forms, and to historical connections now forgotten. Hence, for many reasons, texts are almost invaluable, apart from the additional fact that they tend to convey much information about tribal customs and psychology which might otherwise be overlooked, or impossible to secure from direct questioning. To collect tunes without texts is to do only half of the work and to reduce the value of that half to practically nothing.

When the words are all secured, it is well to ask the informant to recite or even sing them at the customary speed, before attempting to make a record. This is one very good way of checking up on spurious material, since one who is making up as he goes cannot give the material again and again in the same manner, as can one who knows his song. Usually, dishonesty detected and the privilege of singing into the horn being refused, is punishment enough, especially if it is done before an audience. This second complete recitation gives the collector a chance also to detect inadvertent omissions, or to cut out lines that have crept into the song in hazy association which do not belong and are apt not to appear in rapid recitation. Informants are often delighted and astonished if, after this is accomplished, the collector reads off the words. His cleverness at remembering (!) them and getting them all in order and pronouncing them correctly (if he does), always excites their wonder and admiration. Score one for the collector! Frequently, on hearing the text read, informants will detect errors they have made which might have passed unnoticed when reciting it themselves. It is always well to read the text and ask for corrections.

A final reason for securing the text first, which has already been hinted, is that an informant is always under some strain in singing into the horn, and once that is accomplished—especially if the informant be old—the strain being removed, there is a decided lapse. I well recall losing the text of a very valuable old chant beyond recall, in Hawaii, by letting the old man sing it first. When it came to reciting it afterward, he was about halfway through when suddenly his memory failed him and he could not recall the rest. I had no more records, and hesitated to play again the one record of it that I had, which I hoped to have cast, and trusted to being able to make out the words later when playing the record; but it proved a false hope, since the style of chanting involves a curious mouthing of syllables which renders them unintelligible even to natives who do not know the chant. Until he sang the song, the old man knew it perfectly; but, as his embarrassment at forgetting it increased, so did his hope of recalling it decrease.

MAKING RECORDS.

In making records the machine should rest solidly on a table, chair, or the floor, indoor-recording being preferable to outdoor. Any shaking such as that set up by a chair standing unevenly, or a floor vibrating to the movements of dancers, should be avoided. The singer should not be allowed to touch the machine or the horn. Placing him properly before the instrument and getting correct tone-production depends largely on experience and conditions. Ordinarily, his face should be about three inches from the horn, directly in front of it, but if his voice is very resonant or naturally loud, the distance should be increased, unless he can be made to reduce the volume. It is surprising how often a singer, hearing his record played over, will recognize its defects himself, criticize his own performance very well, and strive for better effects on his own initiative, once he knows what to expect.

Timid people usually sing in very low tones, and this condition is sometimes very difficult to overcome. It requires tactful handling, an ability to set the informant at his ease with exchange of pleasantries, and so on. The collector, once he has heard a line or so of the tune, may be able to correct the difficulty by illustrating a higher pitch himself. Natives who have trouble in taking the initiative in transposing to higher levels will often be found easily able to follow example. Timidity is as often the result of fear of being overheard singing by his fellows as of shyness before a stranger, and I have had to take people miles away from home to put them completely at ease. It is important to proceed leisurely, to give natives time to think, and to put themselves " in the mood," and, above all, to allow them ample rest-periods, with time for smoking and walking about. This sort of work is new to them, and though they can concentrate and work very hard for hours at accustomed tasks, they find long sessions before the horn extremely irksome.

Sometimes it is necessary to sacrifice records in order to inspire confidence and a spirit of emulation in prospective informants. The collector may need to sing into a record and reproduce it for his audience. Finding a willing singer, it often pays to have him make extra records for the sole purpose of playing for natives, who take the greatest pleasure in hearing their own music and in recognizing the voices of their fellows. In fact, they usually demand a hearing of other records at once, when they find they can be rendered audible. Now and then I have met quite stubborn refusals to sing, with a remark that such and such a person gave me a certain song, and, to dispel all doubt, I have produced the record and played it. If the stubborn one knew the first singer, he was usually astonished and delighted to recognize the voice, and, in fact, was astonished anyway to hear a record, forgetting his own determination to give nothing in a desire to hear the effects of his own voice. His vanity was also appealed to in the prospect of preserving his voice to posterity, or in sending his song abroad. For such concert-practices several good records were reserved, and rarely failed to bring results. The delight of unschooled natives in listening to themselves knows no bounds. They thoroughly enjoy hearing their own little mannerisms reproduced, since no other singer can imitate them. Frequently they completely forget their surroundings and ogle and smile into the horn and join in the singing in sympathy. Usually informants want to hear every record which they make, but when the necessity of keeping one record unplayed is explained to them, they acquiesce.

Although the equipment will presently be discussed in full, a few remarks at this point about the records themselves are pertinent. Records should never be touched with the fingers on the polished outer surface to be engraved, since moisture may damage the surface, or the oil from the hands cause the needle to slip. They should be removed from and returned to their boxes by bracing two fingers inside the cylinder, and placed on and removed from the mandrel of the machine by pressure on the record ends.

When the record is in position, the recorder in place, and the singer prepared with the necessary instructions, the machine is wound up and the lever controlling the motion of the mandrel is released. After the record is revolving at normal speed, the needle should be gently placed on it and *allowed to run several threads* before the singer is permitted to begin, which he does upon a signal. Before beginning, however, it is a good idea to blow into the horn with a pitch pipe the pitch *a* (435 vibrations). Having a definitely-known pitch at the beginning of the record will enable any transcriber to adjust a machine later for playing the record at the original speed and pitch. After the singer has ceased, the needle should be allowed to run a few threads.

Raising it while the sound continues should be avoided, and the machine should never be stopped during recording until the needle is raised from the record.

While a record is being cut, the minute wax shavings should be blown away from the needle point continually, care being taken not to use such force as to deflect the path of the cutter; otherwise the shavings not only tend to clog the way, but to accumulate in grooves already made, from which it is difficult to remove them, especially in warm weather. A finished record should immediately be brushed with a soft, broad, camel's hair brush to remove any particles adhering to it before placing it in its box.

As far as practicable, and funds, number of blanks, and the time of the collector and informant allow, duplicate records should always be made of the songs which appear to be worth while. As an excuse, or explanation, of this (and one is often needed) the fragility of the record and its liability to breakage, as well as its tendency to wear when played, should be made plain, for I have found most informants quite interested in such matters and ready to listen to reason if one is given which satisfies them. After two are made, the best should be selected, from its clean-cut appearance, freedom from pauses and mistakes, etc., and although the two are given the same number, the preferred should be marked *A*, for instance. Deep indentations on a record do not necessarily indicate clarity. More often they denote over-singing, or blasting. Such records are very difficult to transcribe. The best impression should not be played at all, but reserved for casting, if an indestructible record is desired, or for the transcriber to work with, who at best labours under the greatest difficulties in taking off music and text. If both casting and transcribing are intended, the transcriber may work from casts if a delay is feasible. No record which has been played even once should be offered for casting.

In recording two or more voices it is rather difficult to make a good record with a small-mouthed horn, and awkward to carry a larger one about. If the informants can be made to hold their heads close together in front of the horn, or if those with shriller or heavier voices stand directly behind the others, a small horn may suffice. In this way I have recorded quartet-singing and even choruses, by having the principal singers directly in front of the horn.

Instrumental Music.

The development of instrumental pieces is controlled, to a considerable extent, by the type of instrument on which they are played. If the instrument is archaic, limited in range and power, untunable, and with a purely individual scale, the music can expand only in certain directions. Musical compositions played by instruments are highly desirable to have, as specimens of a people's musical inventiveness, but such pieces are not likely to be handed down any length of time without the memory-props of words or notation, or unless instruments are exactly duplicated. Certain styles of instrumental accompaniment, however, may become stereotyped for certain dances or ceremonies, and should be taken in sufficient number to afford a clear conception of their character, particularly of their rhythms.

The old-fashioned machines, and indeed any machine until those of most recent types were perfected, will record only indifferently, or not at all, sounds of low pitch and intensity. Instruments of wood or vegetable material, which are made to vibrate by striking, whether solid or having an air cavity, are not likely to make an impression on the record unless the material is unusually resonant or the pitch is relatively high. Informants are rather apt at making substitutions for these instruments, however, such as a tin pan or any metal receptacle of large dimensions for a drum, beaten with a stick or knife; smaller and lighter-toned vessels of metal for smaller drums; and cans with pebbles or shot in them, or bells, for rattles. Only one Hawaiian rebelled at making what he called *Paki* (Chinese) music. It is next to impossible to have the singer's mouth and the instrument which accompanies him both directly in front of the horn, so that the instrument should be struck rather heavily in order to be recorded in the position in which it must be held. Flutes, however, and most wind instruments record beautifully, and unless stringed instruments are too faint in tone, like the musical bow, they will also record well.

Data about Instruments.

In the Pacific the most primitive types of instruments imaginable still exist. Their crudeness, together with their enormously wide distribution, should, generally speaking, be one of the strongest arguments for their age, especially as some are not readily suggested by the material entering into their manufacture, and would not be easily conceived without precept and example. In fact, many appear to be, not crude copies of more developed instruments which have come in with civilization, but ancestral forms of types now much more highly developed on the mainland of south-eastern Asia and elsewhere. There, through existing modern forms and back through older ones found in isolated districts, pictured in ancient illustrations, described in old tales, are to be traced instruments like those still found in the Pacific. Since in isolation all culture tends toward specialization, if not slowing down, there are local developments in musical instruments in the Pacific which are no longer archaic or even very similar to the ancestral forms; but on the whole, excepting modern importations, the majority of the instruments are exceedingly simple and widely distributed. Under these considerations, the cruder the instrument the more important it is likely to be for ethnology. All instruments should be minutely described, drawn or photographed, and, if possible, a specimen secured. Among those which might be thought beneath notice is the pit in the ground, covered with a slab of wood, on which dancers stamp to mark time with their bare feet, such as that used by the Maidu and Pomo of California, some Solomon Islanders, the Easter Islanders, and the New Hebrideans (who, however, strike the board with sticks). Closely related to this are little concavo-convex "shield-like" pieces of wood, placed on the ground with one end propped on a stone so as to enlarge the resonance chamber, and stamped with the foot, such as was an ancient Andaman and Hawaiian instrument. In the Andamans this is known to be derived from the warrior throwing his shield on the ground after a successful encounter with his enemy and stamping on it in a wild and joyful war-dance. No doubt such a dance, apart from being very primitive, is very ancient.

Another insignificant-looking little instrument, giving rise to much speculation, is the whistle or horn improvised from a spirally-twisted ribbon of a leaf, or grass, or strip of bark, blown into at the smaller end. This is apparently an exceedingly ancient device. Its wide but scattered distribution as reported, means, apart of course from several possible independent origins, that it evidently has dropped out of memory in many regions, also probably that it has been overlooked by collectors in others. It occurs in Hawaii, in remote West Africa, in ancient rural England and among peasants of the lower Rhine and in Galicia in its simplest form, varied somewhat in size, shape, and material. In England it had almost passed out of memory more than half a century ago, and its use then was confined to a commemorative hunt performed annually by only three villages, which preserved the tradition from the days of King John or thereabouts. In Hawaii its use goes far back before foreign invasion, for it is described in old legends. The English horn is of bark, and large, while the Hawaiian is made of a torn ribbon of the *ti*-leaf, and minute, but both the method of manufacture, and the shapes, are very similar in the two places. The African type flares into a lip at the lower end, while apparently those from Central Europe are simple like the English. Horns made in the same fashion, but more developed, with mouthpieces of cane (which the English horn had made of bark), with finger stops in them, are found in the region of Sumatra and Java, and are intermediate in size, while very large ones occur among the peasants in Northern Europc.

Conch-shell trumpets are not musical instruments, strictly speaking, but should be included with them. They seem important in tracing culture-connections. The position of the mouth-hole should not be overlooked, as has frequently been the case when such trumpets have been mentioned by various writers. It is desirable to know, also, whether a mouthpiece is attached to the shell, and by what means the horn is carried (as in a netted cord bag, for instance), the species of shell used, and whether it is found alive in the region where the horn is used.

No detail of description, even as to ornamentation, is too unimportant to be mentioned. A good illustration of this point is the Ainu stringed instrument, the *tonkari* or *mukko.* While in shape it closely resembles the crocodile harps of Burma and Siam, called *takhay* or *megyoung* (compare the names), the perfectly useless or unnecessary carving (that is, not necessary to the functioning of the instrument) which has become wholly conventional and even in part omitted on Ainu instruments, establishes beyond doubt the identity of the history of the two in the light of the more realistic carving on the Burmese and Siamese harps. These still resemble the crocodiles that first suggested the carving, which belong to the fauna of Burma and Siam but not to that of northern Japan. Without the Burmese and Siamese instruments as bases for comparison, the carvings on the Ainu instruments, reduced as they are, would be meaningless. In the light of the fact that these instruments are practically identical in the two regions, the dark element in the Ainu race is readily understood, and a study of their features, which are markedly those of the more southern races, confirms the assumption that the Ainu are a mixed people and that some of them, as their own legends and linguistic evidence would indicate, came from the south-west.

From these instances it is readily seen how important a part such objects as musical instruments, which are unnecessary to the maintenance of life of a people, and in form not usually controlled by environmental conditions, may play in helping to unravel the mystery of man's prehistory.

Equipment.

Numerous devices for recording sound mechanically and electrically have been produced in recent years, but nearly all must be discarded by the collector of folk music, since they are not practical for the conditions under which he must usually work, for the ends which he is seeking, or for his pocket-book. Most of the latest devices on the market depend upon electrical current for their operations, and though electric recording is much more satisfactory than mechanical recording, current is likely not to be obtainable where the best ethnological material is to be found; but even where it is, or with the aid of dry batteries, the weight of such apparatus makes it highly impractical for use in the field and for constant moving about. Such mechanisms are frequently quite complicated and delicately adjusted, affording extra hazards for amateur operators, and necessitating the constant attendance of a skilled mechanic. Nothing on the American market is well adapted to the problem; specially constructed apparatus is very expensive, with the disadvantage of the likelihood that repairs will be equally costly. For some regions heavy equipment may be carried in an automobile and allowed to remain, if it is possible to reach informants by this means, but in other places natives live far from roads which can be travelled by cars, and equipment must be carried by hand.

Certain types of portable apparatus such as that devised by Metfessel at the University of Iowa, while recording sufficiently well, are expensive to operate, and the transcribing of the records is not only very laborious but costly, making a collection of even so small a number as a hundred songs prohibitive for the average collector. Hence, at present, the most satisfactory solutions are still the old-fashioned portable phonographs with cylindrical records devised by the Columbia graphophone and Edison companies years ago. These machines, unfortunately, are no longer being manufactured, and the Edison company, at least, no longer has them in stock, but both companies still manufacture cylinder records, and the machines may still be picked up in phonograph shops and others handling second-hand goods. They are, however, becoming less and less common.

Edison machines of various models are somewhat easier to find than Columbia graphophones, but have several disadvantages. So many different models were made that the chances of finding two alike are more remote than with other makes, and the parts of different models are not in the main interchangeable, hence repairs to damaged machines might be less readily effected. Edison points cut and wear the wax more than those of the Columbia graphophones or the dictaphones, therefore the records do not stand up so well. Edison produced some models on which four-minute records could be made, of the same size as two-minute records, by means of finer grooves and cutters, but these are not satisfactory, since the walls between the grooves are so thin that with wear they soon become obliterated. Two-minute records are much to be preferred, and a still better result may be obtained by using a four-minute cutter (and reproducer) with two-minute grooving. For convenience in transporting, no machines equal the Edison and Columbia phonographs and graphophones, and, if the records are carefully made, the results are sufficiently good for most ethnological and folk-lore purposes, although they are far from being ideally accurate or adequate for the minute researches of the sort demanded by psychologists.

The spring-motor dictaphone, also no longer made, is a product more recently and more widely in use. It is excellent for recording, except for its weight. It can be carried about like a portable sewing machine, but is too heavy for long distances or much climbing about, or for any lifting except by robust and muscular individuals. Dictaphone records seem to be of better material and to withstand wear from repeated playing better than either of the other types of American cylinder record, and have the added advantage of being thick, and so less easily broken, and shaved with better results if a record has been spoiled. It is comparatively easy to obtain the loan of a shaving machine in any city of fair size where there are government administrative offices or large business houses, for dictaphones and Ediphones are rather widely used. In Honolulu such a machine was found in the Territorial Court, the use of which was courteously permitted. I believe the records of all makes will fit sufficiently well on the mandrels of the shaving machines to accomplish efficient shaving. The loan of such a machine occasionally will save a purchase for which the collector ordinarily would have but little use. I have been told that records may be quite well shaved on an ordinary phonograph by holding a razor blade steadily against them at the proper angle, but I have not had occasion to experiment with the success of this method, and, as a general procedure, think it of doubtful value.

The length of dictaphone and Ediphone records is a distinct advantage, as it offers more recording surface at proportionately less expense. But Ediphone records will not fit Edison phonographs, and the Ediphone is electrically driven. Dictaphone records will fit either the old-fashioned spring-motor dictaphone or the modern electrically-driven ones.

Dictaphone recorders and reproducers are excellent, and some are so fitted in the machine that both remain *in situ*, being brought into alignment with the record by a small lever, instead of being completely removed and substituted, one for the other. This is a great convenience in field-work, for it renders quick shifts perfectly feasible. There is no danger of points being dropped and broken during transference, or from insufficient packing when being carried about, or of one being inadvertently left behind when both have been out and in use during a collecting-session. The Dictaphone company could provide, on a special order, a more sensitive diaphragm for recorder and reproducer, and even assemble a more easily-portable machine, but it would necessarily be costly, especially in a reversion to a spring-driven machine. Were it not for the weight of the old types, I would unhesitatingly recommend them above all others.

Wira, of Berlin, Germany, manufactures a small portable phonograph and supplies spare parts and 100 cylinders in a kit specially packed for field work, as low as around $100, including shipment to a port as remote from Berlin as one of the Ellice Islands, via Fiji.* This is only about a quarter more expensive than a second-hand Edison, which brings from $15 to $35, depending on the shop and the condition of the machine, plus 100 records at $45, without shipping charges. I have neither used nor examined a Wira machine, hence cannot evaluate it, but from all reports it works well, and is used by many German explorers.

For various reasons, portable phonographs using disc records with attachments for recording are not desirable, although the discs are less bulky to handle than cylinders, and the machines lighter in weight. They are not as accurate, and the discs tend to warp.

A paper horn, straight, made of thin glazed cardboard, is better both for recording and reproducing than the metal horns usually sold with machines, since it eliminates extraneous noises to a greater degree. Such horns are not easy to carry about, but could be made so as to unroll, though some device must be used to fasten them to the collar used for holding horns above the recorder or reproducer.

It is particularly desirable when using Edison machines to procure, if possible, spare arms which follow the thread bar and carry the needle along the record. These are of soft metal, and if the needle is not fully lifted from the record when it is desired to carry it back and forth, this

* The consignee was Mr. D. G. Kennedy, whose work at Vaitupu is being published by this *Journal.* The machine was secured through the generous co-operation of Miss Roberts and Dr. Clark Wissler, of the American Museum of Natural History, New York.—EDS.

arm may be drawn along the bar with disastrous results to the threads on the arm. Those on the bar are more durable, being of harder metal. Spare belts are sometimes needed for spring-driven machines, and one or two should be included in the outfit. Extra recorders and reproducers are essential, more of the former than the latter, for, if necessary, playing the records can be omitted. A spare crank may prove indispensable, and even a spare spring. An oil-can and some fine-grade machine-oil should not be overlooked. The graphite in the spring may become hardened if one is long in the field, and to overcome this a little melted vaseline is a satisfactory lubricator, poured in through the vent and given time to soften the graphite. Screw-drivers of two sizes, very small and medium, should be taken, but ingenuity may create screw-drivers from surprising material at times.

Cylinder-records should be packed in their individual containers in wooden boxes fitted with partitions of corrugated cardboard like egg containers. I have had many records cracked and broken in the less resistant cartons recently substituted for wooden boxes, even by the companies shipping the records. Aside from the packing-boxes needed for apparatus, a light basket with a lid and handle which can be passed over the arm is very handy for carrying a few records about for a half-day's trip. Being stiffer than a bag, lighter and more easily carried than a box, it may be taken on horseback, and the records will be fairly well protected from jolting. A flat canvas bag, such as children use for school books, with a zipper fastening at the top, or a flap which fastens down, is needed for notebooks, pencil, pitch-pipe, and other small articles and tools.

List of Equipment.

Columbia graphophone, Edison phonograph, Dictaphone, or Wira phonograph, with spring motor. Electrically-driven machines if current is to be available in field work, which is unlikely. Machines should be easily portable, yet heavy enough to be durable.

Horn, made of thin glazed cardboard.

Spare belts and other easily destructible parts, especially recorders and reproducers. At least three recorders and two reproducers. A spare crank.

Machine-oil and small oil-can. Small screw-driver.

Flat camels' hair brush about an inch and a half wide.

Blank cylindrical wax records, number depending upon proposed amount of work. 150-200 a good average. A cylinder with two-minute recording will hold one long song, on the average, or two or three quite short ones, always allowing a short space between them.

Pitch-pipe which will give *a* (435 vibrations).

Blank music-notebooks having closely-ruled staves so that note-heads need not be much enlarged to fill spaces and can thus be made rapidly, with considerable space between staves to allow room for writing texts and drum-rhythms of the accompaniments beneath the notes. I allow four to six 80-page notebooks for a season of six months.

Stenographer's notebooks.

Pencils, knife, and good eraser.

Suitable container for records, horn, machine, for shipping as well as for short trips in the field. Bags and baskets for field-trips.

A rope and strap, handy for securing the horn and tying up boxes.

[The phonographic record of the human voice was discussed by Professor A. Lodewyckx, University of Melbourne, in his paper, "Linguistic Problems of the Pacific," published in *J.P.S.*, 32 (1923), p. 215.—Eds.]

6.

Uber einige Panpfeifen aus Nordwestbrasilien.

Von Erich M. von Hornbostel.

Auf Veranlassung von Herrn Dr. Koch-Grünberg habe ich an einer Anzahl von Blasinstrumenten seiner nordwestbrasilischen Sammlungen die Tonhöhen bestimmt. Zu solcher Untersuchung eignen sich natürlich nur Instrumente mit fester Abstimmung, von Blasinstrumenten also solche, deren Töne möglichst unabhängig sind von der Art und Stärke des Anblasens. Am besten ist diese Bedingung bei Panpfeifen erfüllt: ihre Stimmung hängt nahezu ausschließlich von den Maßen der Rohre ab. Zudem darf man erwarten, die musikalische Absicht des Verfertigers gerade bei Panpfeifen am getreuesten verwirklicht zu finden; es bedarf weder großer Geschicklichkeit noch besonderer Übung, um ein Rohr durch allmähliges Verkürzen auf die gewünschte Tonhöhe zu bringen, und hat man einmal zu viel abgeschnitten, so kann man das verpfuschte Rohr mit leichter Mühe durch ein anderes ersetzen. Bedeutend schwieriger schon ist die Herstellung von Flageoletts, bei denen die Tonhöhen außer von den Maßen des Rohrs auch von den Dimensionen des Mundstücks und der Verteilung der Fingerlöcher abhängen. Auch bei bedeutender Handfertigkeit wird hier das Gelingen in hohem Maße vom Zufall abhängen. Den verändernden Einfluß der Windstärke kann man durch möglichst gleichmäßiges Anblasen unschädlich machen, so daß auch diese Instrumente für Tonhöhenmessungen brauchbar sind. Die offenen Längsflöten aus Röhrenknochen setzen eine besondere Technik des Anblasens voraus; die ganz zufälligen, schwer regulierbaren Dimensionen, die unregelmäßige Gestaltung des Hohlraums, die mühsame und zeitraubende Arbeit des Löcherbohrens in so hartem Material machen es überdies unwahrscheinlich, daß die Verfertiger und Bläser hohe Anforderungen an die Stimmung von Knochenflöten stellen. Man kann daher auf ihre genauere Untersuchung wohl ohne großen Verlust verzichten. Da leider auch die Flageoletts keine theoretisch verwertbaren Resultate gaben, soll sich die folgende Mitteilung auf die wichtigsten Befunde an den Panpfeifen beschränken. Zur Vergleichung mit den nordwestbrasilischen Instrumenten, die jetzt — mit zwei Ausnahmen — im Besitz des Königlichen Museums für Völkerkunde in Berlin sind, habe ich gelegentlich auch einige andere Stücke dieses Museums herangezogen.

I. Schon bei oberflächlicher Untersuchung muß es auffallen, daß manche Instrumente paarweise zusammengehören. Dies zeigt sich nicht nur an dem gleichen Aussehen, sondern auch an der identischen Stimmung. So unterscheiden sich die beiden großen, sorgfältig gearbeiteten Panpfeifen der Uanána (Rio Caiarý-Uaupés, Inv. Nr. V. B. 6322 und

6323)[1]) nur in den letzten drei von ihren 17 Rohren; alle andern stimmen absolut genau miteinander überein. Die kleine Panpfeife der Siusí (Rio Aiarý, Inv. Nr. V. B. 6318) — 7 Rohre — scheint dem Aussehen nach eine neuere Nachbildung von Inv. Nr. V. B. 6320 — 8 Rohre — mit Hinweglassung des tiefsten Tons zu sein. Bei dem älteren und darum wohl als Modell wertvollen Exemplar hat man das kürzeste Rohr, das gesprungen ist, durch eine Fadenumwicklung repariert. V. B. 6317 (Tukáno, Rio Tiquié)[2]) mag nach dem großen zusammengehörenden Paar V. B. 6324 und 6325[3]), dem sie auch äußerlich ähnlich ist — 10 Rohre, Art der Verknüpfung —, als Kinderspielzeug gebildet worden sein. Absolut identisch sind auch zwei fünfrohrige Panpfeifen der Pareçí (Zentralbrasilien, Sammlung v. den Steinen, Inv. Nr. V. B. 2010 und 2011); auf den beiden Flageoletts der Auetö (Zentralbrasilien, Sammlung v. den Steinen, Inv. Nr. V. B. 2776 und 2818) stimmen die Töne mit Ausnahme des tiefsten mit großer Annäherung überein; (2776 steht im ganzen ein wenig tiefer als 2818). Daß Instrumentenpaare von identischer Stimmung zu dem Zweck hergestellt werden, um gleichzeitig geblasen zu werden, ist schon a priori nicht unwahrscheinlich. Das Bild auf Tafel VIII (Bd. I, S. 254) zeigt, wie je zwei Bläser nebeneinanderstehend die Panpfeifen in symmetrischer Lage am Munde halten. Genau ebensolche Paare von Panpfeifenbläsern finden sich auf altperuanischen Vasenbildern. Die beiden Pfeifen haben hier stets die gleiche Anzahl von Rohren (meist 5) und sind auf manchen Darstellungen durch eine lange Schnur verbunden; die Spieler blasen entweder beide das längste, oder beide das kürzeste Rohr an.[4])

Man wird kaum fehlgehen mit der Annahme, daß nicht nur die zusammengehörenden Instrumente, sondern gerade die korrespondierenden Rohre gleichzeitig angeblasen werden; mit anderen Worten, daß man auf den Panpfeifenpaaren unison musiziert, oder dies wenigstens ursprünglich der Fall war. Nicht um polyphones Zusammenspiel zu ermöglichen, sondern offenbar um die an sich schwachen Pfeifentöne zu verstärken, werden die Tonreihen verdoppelt.

Bemerkenswert ist die außerordentliche Sorgfalt des Kopierens. Daß man sich dabei nicht nach dem Augenmaß, sondern nach dem Gehör richtet, geht schon daraus hervor, daß Länge, Weite und Wanddicke der gleichgestimmten Rohre zwar in den meisten, aber doch nicht in allen Fällen gleich ist. Daß tatsächlich akustisch verglichen wird, wurde mir von Dr. Koch-Grünberg ausdrücklich bestätigt. Auf optischem Wege würde auch kaum eine so große Genauigkeit zu erreichen sein. Es wäre interessant zu erfahren, ob die Indianer die Schwebungen, die beim gleichzeitigen Erklingen wenig verschiedener Töne auftreten, beobachtet haben; ob sie etwa beim Abstimmen sich nach dem Fehlen der Schwebungen richten, wie wir, und ob sie sie vielleicht als unschön vermeiden wollen. Jedenfalls beweist die Genauigkeit der Übereinstimmung, wie sorgfältig die Leute, hörend

[1]) Vgl. Bd. I, S. 299, Abb. 178, rechts.

[2]) Vgl. dieselbe Abb., Mitte.

[3]) Vgl. dieselbe Abb., links.

[4]) Vgl. Ch. W. Mead, The Musical Instruments of the Inca, Supplement to American Museum Journal, Vol. III, No. 4, July, 1903, Plate I, Fig. 2. Ebenso Berliner Museum für Völkerkunde V A. 12005 (Chimbote, coll. Bolivar), V. A. 4676 (Trujillo, coll. Macedo) und viele andere.

und schnitzend, bei der Herstellung ihrer Panpfeifen zu Werke gehen; ferner, daß ihre Unterschiedsempfindlichkeit für Tonhöhen nicht geringer ist, als die unsere[1]). Und man darf vertrauen, daß auch bei der Herstellung der Tonreihen (auf Panpfeifen) nicht technisches Ungeschick oder mangelhafte Bildung des „Gehörs" die Ausführung der Absicht behinderten.

II. Wer solche Feinhörigkeit für ein Zeichen von musikalischer Begabung zu halten geneigt ist und einen der Unterschiedsempfindlichkeit entsprechend ausgebildeten „Intervallsinn" zu finden erwartet, der wird enttäuscht sein, wenn er z. B. die ersten 12 Rohre von V. B. 6322 (oder die identischen von V. B. 6323) anbläst: er wird eine mehr als zwei Oktaven umspannende Tonreihe finden[2]), in der keine Oktaven, keine Quinten, ja, außer ein paar leidlichen Quarten überhaupt keine Intervalle vorkommen, die uns musikalisch brauchbar scheinen. Dennoch scheint man versucht zu haben, auf den übrigen Rohren Töne dieser Leiter in der höheren Oktave zu „verdoppeln". So sind Rohr XIII und XIV auf beiden Instrumenten sehr annähernd die Oktaven von VIII und IX; XV, XVI und XVII auf 6323 die Doppeloktaven von V, VI und VII; XV auf 6322 (wahrscheinlich) die Oktave von X, und XVII die Tripeloktave von II. (XVI ist auf diesem Exemplar leider zerbrochen.) Wie mag diese wunderliche Tonleiter entstanden sein?

Aus den Messungen ist zwar unmittelbar ersichtlich, daß je zwei durch ein zwischenliegendes getrennte Rohre (zu große) Quarten geben, die durch die Zwischenstufen (ungefähr) in zwei gleichgroße Intervalle geteilt werden; daß die Größe der Einzeltonschritte also zwischen Ganztönen und kleinen Terzen etwa die Mitte hält. Aber hierauf allein ließe sich schwer eine theoretische Hypothese aufbauen. Die Lösung des Rätsels bringt erst eine genauere Untersuchung der Instrumente selbst. Einseitig geschlossene Röhren geben bekanntlich bei stärkerem Anblasen anstatt des Grundtons dessen Teiltöne von ungerader Ordnungszahl. Ist die Schwingungszahl des Grundtons n, so sind die seiner Obertöne 3 n, 5 n usf. Auf den längeren Rohren der großen Panpfeifen erhält man die Obertöne außerordentlich leicht, bei den längsten Rohren sogar leichter als die Grundtöne. (So konnte ich auf Rohr I von V. B. 6325 noch den 9. Teilton erhalten.) Die Messung von V. B. 6322 ergab nun folgende Schwingungszahlen[3]):

Tabelle I.

Rohr Nr.	I	II	III	IV	V	VI	VII	VIII	IX	X	XI
Grundton	420	481.6	560.5	651.3	374.4	439.5	516	598.5	699	397.4	461.6
3. Teilton	622.5	357.2	414.3	478.5	553	651.3	376.5	445.7	517.5	—	—
5. Teilton	519	602	699	397.4	464	—	—	—	—	—	—

[1]) Das Gegenteil wird für sog. Primitive meist angenommen und schien sich auch bei eigens zur Prüfung dieser Frage angestellten Versuchen (Ch. S. Myers an Murray-Insulanern, Frank G. Bruner an verschiedenen Stämmen) zu bestätigen; man muß aber damit rechnen, daß nicht eine Minderwertigkeit des Sinnesorgans, sondern Ungeübtheit oder Unvermögen, die Aufmerksamkeit auf die Reize und die gestellte Aufgabe zu konzentrieren, die Erhöhung der Schwelle bedingt.

[2]) Siehe Tabelle II.

[3]) Der bequemeren Vergleichbarkeit halber sind alle Töne in dieselbe Oktave

Man sieht auf den ersten Blick, daß die 3. Teiltöne von III bis IX mit den Grundtönen von I bis VII, und die 5. Teiltöne von I bis V mit den Grundtönen von VII bis XI sehr annähernd übereinstimmen. Hieraus geht aber ohne weiteres hervor, daß sich die Indianer beim Abstimmen nach den Obertönen gerichtet haben. Den tatsächlichen Vorgang der Konstruktion kann man sich etwa folgendermaßen vorstellen: Man geht von Rohr I als gegebener Länge (und Tonhöhe) aus und schneidet Rohr III so, daß sein (dritter) Teilton „wie ein hohes Rohr I klingt", d. h. gleich wird der Doppeloktave von I; ebenso geht man dann von III nach V, von V nach VII usf. (Das umgekehrte Verfahren, bei dem man, von III ausgehend, I nach dem dritten Teilton von III stimmen würde, würde uns a priori plausibler scheinen; dennoch wäre es unnatürlicher, da man von den höchsten Pfeifen ausgehen müßte, die nur schwer — oder gar nicht — zum „Umschlagen" zu bringen sind[1]). Wie von I zu den Rohren mit ungerader, so gelangt man von II zu denen mit gerader Ordnungszahl. Man erhält so zwei in sich gleichgebaute, aber voneinander unabhängige Systeme, die es zu verknüpfen gilt.

Als Prinzip für diese Verknüpfung möchte ich kein mechanisches, sondern ein psychologisches als wahrscheinlich annehmen. Durch das Zurückverlegen des 3. Teiltons (Quinte) unter den Grundton erhält man natürlich die „Umkehrung" des Intervalls, d. h. seine Ergänzung zur Oktave: die Quarte. Die Quarten des einen Systems (I—III—V usf.) dürften als melodische Schritte zu groß wirken, und bei dem Versuch, sie unterzuteilen, liegt es nahe, den Zwischenton (etwa II) so zu wählen, daß er von den Nachbarn durch gleichgroß scheinende Intervallschritte getrennt ist. Dieses Prinzip der ‚distanzgleichen" Teilung spielt ja in der nichtharmonischen Musik der verschiedensten Völker eine große Rolle und ist auch bei andern der hier besprochenen Instrumente offenbar angewendet worden.

Auch die Beurteilung von Tondistanzen muß man zu dem rechnen, was man gewöhnlich „Intervallbewußtsein" nennt. Für die ursprünglichere und wichtigere Grundlage des Intervallbewußtseins nicht nur bei Zusammenklängen, sondern auch bei Tonfolgen wird aber meist die bevorzugte Stellung der „konsonanten" oder „natürlichen" Intervalle (d. h. solcher von einfachem Verhältnis der Schwingungszahlen) gehalten. Dieser Faktor, so könnte man zunächst glauben, habe die Benutzung von Obertönen, da sie mit den Grundtönen konsonante Intervalle bildeten, veranlaßt oder wenigstens begünstigt. Aber diese Meinung wird gerade durch die Obertöne und die Art ihrer Verwendung widerlegt. Betrachtet man die Koinzidenzen der Grundtöne unserer Pfeifen mit den — bisher nicht berücksichtigten — fünften Partialtönen, so findet man, daß je drei der nach den dritten Teiltönen gebildeten Intervalle (z. B. I-III-V-VII zusammengenommen genau zum fünften Teilton des Ausgangstons — eigentlich zu dessen tieferer Oktav — führen. Wenn man aber von irgendeinem Ton durch drei verbundene Quarten aufwärts schreitet (z. B.

---

transponiert. Um die wirklichen absoluten Tonhöhen zu erhalten, muß man die Zahlen der Grundtöne I bis IV mit 0.5, X und XI mit 2 multiplizieren; die Zahlen der 3. Teiltöne von II bis VI mit 2, von VII bis IX mit 4; die der 5. Teiltöne von I bis III mit 2, IV und V mit 4.

[1]) In einzelnen Fällen dürfte aber auch dieses Verfahren angewendet worden sein, vgl. S. 385).

$c-f-b-es_1$), so gelangt man zur k l e i n e n Terz (über der Oktav) des Ausgangstons, während der 5. Teilton die g r o ß e Terz (über der Doppeloktav) des Grundtons ist! Wie erklärt sich nun dieser scheinbare Widerspruch der Beobachtungen gegen die einfachsten akustischen Gesetze? Die Tonhöhe einer Pfeife hängt nicht bloß von der Länge sondern auch von der Weite des Rohrs ab. Der Ton ist tatsächlich etwas tiefer, als er der einfachsten, bloß die Rohrlänge berücksichtigenden Berechnung nach sein müßte; diese Depression der Tonhöhe infolge des Einflusses der Rohrweite findet aber auch bei den Obertönen statt. Die dritten Teiltöne werden also alle etwas zu tief, die Quinten zwischen ihnen und den Grundtönen zu klein, und, wenn man die Obertöne unter die Grundtöne verlegt, die Quarten zu groß. Fügt man drei solcher Quarten zusammen, so addieren sich die — an sich geringen — Vergrößerungen des reinen Intervalls, und man gelangt zu einer schon recht erheblich zu großen kleinen Terz des Ausgangstons. Andrerseits wird natürlich auch der 5. Teilton infolge des Einflusses der Rohrweite zu tief, die große Terz, die er mit dem Grundton bildet, zu klein. Daß diese verkleinerte große Terz mit jener vergrößerten kleinen Terz — also z. B. der fünfte Teilton von I mit dem durch (verstimmte) Quarten erreichten Grundton von VII — (fast) genau zusammenfällt, ist jedenfalls eine merkwürdige und auffallende Tatsache[1]).

Es ist kaum anzunehmen, daß dieser Zusammenhang den Indianern ganz entgangen sein sollte; wenn sie sich auch über ihn, als etwas von der Natur Gegebenes, nicht besonders gewundert haben mögen. Es wäre sonst nicht recht einzusehen, warum man die künstlichere Prozedur der Quartenketten, bei der man den Oberton des neuen (höheren) Rohrs nach dem Grundton des alten (tieferen) orientiert, dem offenbar näherliegenden Vorgang des sog. pythagoreischen Quintenzirkels vorgezogen hätte, bei dem man das neue Rohr einfach dem Oberton des tieferen gleichmacht[2]).

Eine andere Frage wäre, ob man die fünften Teiltöne zur Bildung der höheren Pfeifen (hier etwa von VII an) an Stelle der dritten Teiltöne benützt, oder ob man sie zur Kontrolle der durch die dritten Teiltöne gewonnenen Stufen verwendet hat. Das erstere wenigstens ist deshalb wahrscheinlich, weil man mit Hilfe der fünften Partialtöne noch weiterkommen kann (hier zu X, XI und — vielleicht — XII), wo die dritten wegen der Kürze des Rohrs schon versagen.

Durch die zunehmende Schwierigkeit, bei kürzeren Rohren die Obertöne zu erhalten[3]), ist denn auch der Ausdehnung des Quarten- und Terzen-Systems nach der Höhe eine natürliche Grenze gesetzt; die Erweiterung des Umfangs geschieht dann (von XIII an, vgl. oben S. 380) nach Oktaven. Nach der Tiefe zu wird es umgekehrt immer schwerer, das Umschlagen in den Oberton zu vermeiden; man muß die größten Rohre (hier z. B. I) ganz schwach und vorsichtig anblasen und die (Grund-) Töne bekommen

---

[1]) Es ist hier nicht der Ort für eine eingehende Erörterung des physikalischen Problems, das nicht ohne Schwierigkeiten ist.

[2]) Ein diesem zweiten analoges Verfahren, aber mit Terzen statt Quinten, würde angewendet, wo man mit den fünften Teiltönen operiert.

[3]) Wieweit es mir selbst geglückt ist, ersieht man aus Tabelle I. Wahrscheinlich wäre mit größerer Anstrengung noch der 5. Teilton von VI, nach dem wohl XII gebildet ist, zu erblasen gewesen.

dann etwas Dumpfes, Breites, Unscharfes, das die genaue Vergleichung der Tonhöhe mit den höheren Oktaven erheblich erschwert[1]). So wird auch nach unten der Umfang durch die Natur des Instruments beschränkt.

Außer einer einzigen distanzgleichen Teilung ist also die Oktavenvergleichung — die Wiederholung „desselben" Tons in verschiedener Höhenlage — das Einzige, was der Mensch bei der Konstruktion dieses Instruments an musikalischer Kunst aufzuwenden hatte. Alles andre wurde ihm sozusagen von der Natur geliefert. Die Anhänger der älteren naturphilosophischen Musiktheorie hätten also hier — wenigstens in den noch unverbundenen Systemen der Rohre von gerader bzw. ungerader Ordnungszahl — einen Fall von einer „natürlichen" Stimmung; einer Stimmung, deren physikalische (hier auch ein wenig botanische) Basis letzten Endes das Wohlgefallen an den Intervallen begründen soll. Wie aber sehen diese Intervalle aus! In der nebenstehenden Tabelle II sind die Schwingungszahlen (der Grundtöne), wie sie die Messung ergeben hat, zusammengestellt mit den Zahlen, die unter der Annahme berechnet sind, daß die Erniedrigung der Obertöne konstant, und zwar gleich dem arithmetischen Mittel der beobachteten Depressionen wäre. Darunter findet man die Intervalle zwischen je zwei benachbarten Tönen, ausgedrückt in Hundertsteln des temperierten Halbtons (Cents); endlich die Intervalle in Cents, von II als Grundton aus berechnet[2]), und zum Vergleich die nächstliegenden Intervalle der reinen Stimmung.

Man sieht zunächst, daß für die Töne VII, VIII und IX die aus den 5. Partialtönen berechneten Werte sich den Messungsresultaten noch enger anschließen, als die aus den 3. Partialtönen gewonnenen

Tabelle II.

Tonhöhe (a_1 = 440)		gis	b-h	des	es-e	ges	a	ces	d	$\bar{f}$	$\overset{+}{g}$	$\underline{b}$	c-cis	d
Schwingungszahlen	beobachtet	I 420	II 481.6	III 560.5	IV 651.3	V 374.4	VI 439.5	VII 516	VIII 598.5	IX 699	X 397.4	XI 461.6	XII 538.5	XIII 594.8
	aus dem 3. Teilton	414.5	481.6	559.6	650.4	378	439.2	510.5	593.4	689.6	400.8	465.8	541.5	593.4
	aus dem 5. Teilton	—	—	—	—	—	—	515	598.5	695.4	404.1	469.8	545.8	598.5
Intervalle in Cents	beobachtet		237	262	260	242	278	277	257	269	222	259	267	172
	aus dem 3. Teilton		260	260	260	260	260	260	260	260	260	260	260	160
	aus dem 5. Teilton		—	—	—	—	—	—	260	260	260	260	260	160
Summen in Cents	beobachtet	- 237	0	262	522	764	1042	119	376	645	867	1126	193	365
	aus dem 3. Teilton	- 260	0	260	520	780	1040	100	360	620	880	1140	200	360
	aus dem 5. Teilton	—	—	—	—	—	—	116	376	636	896	1156	216	376
rein	Cents	—	—	267	498	(814)	(996)	112	(386)	(702)	884	(1088)	204	—
	Verhältnisse	—	—	6:7	3:4	(5:8)	(9:16)	15:16	(4:5)	(2:3)	3:5	(8:15)	8:9	—

[1]) Bei der ersten Messung hatte ich I zu 420 (× 0.5) bestimmt, bei einer zweiten Messung zu 409; der Berechnung nach (s. u.) wäre der genaue Mittelwert (414.5) das Richtige.

[2]) Die Wahl dieses Grundtons wird später (**Abschnitt V**) gerechtfertigt werden. Auch bei der Berechnung der Zahlen aus den Obertönen wurde von 481.6 ausgegangen.

Zahlen. Aber auch die Übereinstimmung mit den letzteren (mit Ausnahme von IX) ist hinreichend genau. Der vorgefundene Tatbestand nähert sich also dem einfachen Idealfall einer gleichstufigen („temperierten") Leiter an, die sich über zwei Oktaven plus einem Ganzton erstreckt und im Umfang jeder Oktave 5 Stufen enthält. Das System enthält (und zwar, da die Leiter temperiert ist, von j e d e m beliebigen Ton als Grundton ausgehend) folgende Intervalle: In der ersten Oktave ein Intervall zwischen Ganzton und kleiner Terz; eine zu große Quarte; ein Intervall zwischen Quinte (rein 702 Cents) und kleiner Sext; ein Intervall zwischen kleiner (rein 996 Cents) und großer (rein 1088 Cents) Sept; — in der zweiten Oktave[1]) einen Halbton, ein Intervall zwischen kleiner (rein 316 Cents) und großer Terz (u. zw. näher der großen), ein Intervall zwischen Tritonus (rein 590 Cents) und Quinte, eine (fast reine) große Sext, ein Intervall zwischen großer Sept und Oktave (näher der Sept); — endlich in der dritten Oktave einen Ganzton. Von diesen zehn Intervallen wären also — bei geringen Ansprüchen an die Reinheit — in unserer Musik höchstens vier brauchbar, alle andern wären verpönt, da sie „neutral" sind, d. h. zwischen den „musikalischen" liegen.

Dennoch klingt auch uns diese merkwürdige Tonreihe, als R e i h e, gar nicht so übel. Wir vertragen eben in strengem Nacheinander so manches, was uns im Zusammenklang äußerst mißtönend wäre. Dem Indianer aber dürfte es nur darauf ankommen, daß die Intervalle ungefähr einer bestimmten Größe (Distanz) entsprechen, etwa von „Ganztonwirkung", wenn man den Begriff nicht zu eng nimmt; und daß sie untereinander ungefähr gleich (die Töne aequidistant) sind. Auch liegt es ja in der Natur der Panpfeife, daß Folgen benachbarter Töne bequemer zu blasen und darum häufiger sind, als größere Intervallsprünge.

Das fehlende Bedürfnis nach festbestimmten größeren Intervallen würde es aber begreiflich machen, daß man beim Verfertigen des Instruments mangels

[1]) Die Intervalle der zweiten Oktave sind auf die Oktave des Grundtons bezogen; der „Halbton" ist also eigentlich eine kleine None usf.

Tabelle III.

Tonhöhe (a_1 = 440)		ges		g+		a+		b-h		c-cis		d		ē		f+		
Schwingungszahlen	1. Oktave	I 376.5		II [402]		III 442		IV 481.6		V 545.7		VI 579.3		VII 651.3		VIII 704.3		
	2. Oktave	—		IX 402		X 444.5		XI 487.8		XII 533.5		XIII 598.4		XIV 647.7		XV 718.8		
	3. Oktave	XVI 378.7		XVII 406.8		XVIII 447		XIX 481.6										
	Mittel	377.6		404.4		444.5		483.7		539.6		588.9		649.5		711.6		(755.2)
	berechnet	V 378		X 400.8		VI 439.2		II 481.6		XII 541.5		VIII 593.4		IV 650.4		[O 713]		(756)
Intervalle in Cents	Mittel		119		163		147		189		151		170		158		103	
	berechnet		100		160		160		200		160		160		160		100	
Summen in Cents	Mittel	771		890		1053		1200 0		189		340		510		668		(771)
	berechnet	780		880		1040		1200 0		200		360		520		680		(780)
rein	Cents	814		884		(996)		1200		204		(316) (386)		498		702		
	Verhältnisse	5:8		3:5		(9:16)		1:2		8:9		(5:6) (4:5)		3:4		2:3		

bestimmter Intervallvorstellungen sich an das klammert, was man vorfindet: die Obertöne. Und diesen Wegweisern treu zu folgen, bringt noch einen weiteren Vorteil mit sich: der Mitspieler kann auf einem zweiten, dem ersten gleichgestimmten Instrument (fast) jeden Ton nach Belieben auch durch seine Oktave (bzw. Doppeloktave) verstärken und so die Fülle des Gesamtklangs erhöhen. Ob dieser und ob den andern angedeuteten Möglichkeiten die Tatsachen entsprechen, das kann nur durch erneute Beobachtung an Ort und Stelle sichergestellt werden. Es ist aber zu bemerken, daß eine große Anzahl südamerikanischer Panpfeifen (Peru, Bolivien) aus z w e i aufeinandergebundenen Serien von Rohren bestehen, von denen die einen an beiden Enden offen sind und daher die höheren Oktaven der andern geben.

III. Das Prinzip der Quartenketten kann, anders angewendet, auch ohne Zuhilfenahme der Distanzteilung zu stufenreicheren Leitern führen. Das Panpfeifenpaar der Tukáno V. B. 6324/25 gibt ein Beispiel davon. Die beiden Instrumente (von je 10 Rohren) sind nicht gleichgestimmt, vielmehr so eingerichtet, daß die Tonhöhen des einen Systems zwischen die des anderen fallen. Eigentlich handelt es sich um e i n System, dessen Töne umschichtig auf zwei Instrumente verteilt sind; dies zeigt sich schon an den — eben verteilten — Oktaven. Wenn man, von den verschiedenen Oktavlagen absehend[1]), die Mittel der Schwingungszahlen nimmt und sie mit denen vergleicht, die den 3. Teiltönen der Pfeifen V. B. 6322/23 entsprachen (siehe die ersten fünf Reihen der Tab. III), so läßt schon die gute Übereinstimmung[2]) verwandte Systeme vermuten.

Die Art des Zusammenhangs der beiden Tonsysteme möge folgendes Schema veranschaulichen.

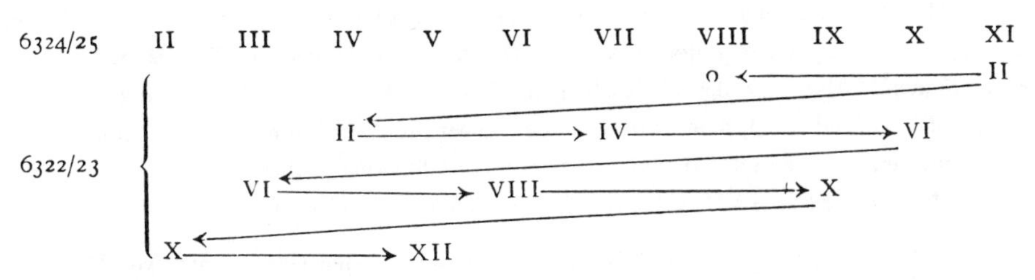

Bei 6322/23 bildeten je zwei, durch eine zwischenliegende getrennte Pfeifen eine (zu große) Quarte. Das Schema stellt das Konstruktionsprinzip von 6324/25 durch die Ordnungszahlen der entsprechenden Pfeifen von 6322/23 dar. Man geht wieder von II aus um eine Oktave zurück, dann zwei Quarten vorwärts, wieder eine Oktave zurück und zwei Quarten vor, noch ein drittes Mal eine Oktave zurück und eine Quarte vor. So erhält man alle Töne des neuen Systems (6324/25) von II bis XI mit Ausnahme von VIII. Diesen Ton, der auf 6322/23 fehlt, erreicht man durch einen Quartenschritt vom Ausgangston abwärts. (Er ist mit O bezeichnet, weil er auf 6322/23 unmittelbar vor I liegen müßte, wenn dieses Instrument nach der Tiefe zu um ein Rohr erweitert würde). Die

---

[1]) I bis VIII sind mit 0.5, XVI bis XIX mit 2 zu multiplizieren.

[2]) Die Übereinstimmung der Centszahlen würde noch erheblich besser, wenn man statt des Mittelwerts 483.7 den „Häufigkeitswert" 481.6 als Grundton annähme, was sich wohl rechtfertigen ließe.

übrigen Töne von XII (6324/25) aufwärts sind, mit Ausnahme von XVI und XX, die Oktavenwiederholungen von II bis XI. Das System basiert also auf dem Prinzip des Quartenzirkels, das demjenigen des bekannten pythagoreischen Quintenzirkels vollkommen analog ist; nur werden für die Fortschreitungen die (unreinen) Quarten benützt, die von den Obertönen geliefert werden. Dies geht nicht nur aus der Übereinstimmung der Töne mit denen von 6322/23 hervor, sondern natürlich auch aus der Koinzidenz der gemessenen Obertöne selbst mit den Grundtönen. Die in Betracht kommenden Werte sind in der folgenden Tabelle zusammengestellt [1]).

Tabelle IV.

	IV	V	VI	VII	VIII	IX	X	XI	XII	XIII
Grundtöne	481.6	545.7	579.3	651.3	704.3	402	444.5	487.8	533.5	598.4
3. Teiltöne	361.6	392.5	414.3	478.5	504 6	584	654.9	704.3	392.5	436.7

Man erhält durch den Quartenzirkel eine siebenstufige Leiter, deren Stufen durch Dreivierteltöne (der Theorie nach 160 Cents) und Ganztöne (200 Cents [2])) gebildet werden. [Die von III und IV als Grundtönen ausgehenden Reihen würden uns vielleicht als — recht verstimmte — „Dur"tonleitern erscheinen; die Terzen und Septimen sind neutral. Selbstverständlich kann der subjektive Eindruck des Europäers nichts für die Intentionen der Indianer beweisen.]

Den 17 Tönen, zu denen der Quartenzirkel allein geführt hat, werden noch drei weitere, vermutlich wieder unter Benützung einer Distanzteilung, hinzugefügt: Halbierung des Ganztons XV bis XVII oder (wahrscheinlicher) der Quarte XIV bis XVIII ergibt den Ton XVI (= 6322 V).

Um die Stufenzahl zu vermehren, ohne allzu kleine Intervalle zu erhalten, hätte man auch einen der andern Ganztöne (IV bis V, VIII bis IX, XI bis XII) unterteilen können. Aber nur der eingeschlagene Weg führt zu einer Erweiterung des Umfangs der Tonreihe. Indem man von dem neuen Ton XVI um eine Doppeloktave abwärts geht, erreicht man I; und ein Quartenschritt aufwärts führt zu XX (Schwingungszahl = 508; theoretisch = VII auf 6322, Schwingungszahl 510.5 [3])).

[1]) Die 3. Teiltöne von VII bis XIII entsprechen den Grundtönen von IV bis X; nur Grundton V und Oberton VIII differieren wesentlich, was eben zu dem Schluß führt, daß VIII nicht von VI, sondern von XI aus gewonnen wurde (s. o.). In dem Schema S. 385 wurden der Übersichtlichkeit halber die Schritte IX bis XII und X bis XIII durch die theoretisch gleichwertigen II bis V bzw. III bis VI ersetzt.

[2]) Dieses (theoretische) Intervall ist zufällig dem europäischen temperierten Ganzton genau gleich. Die empirischen Werte sind indes abwechselnd kleiner und größer (189 bzw. 222 Cents).

[3]) Da XX schon bedeutend zu hoch ist, um Obertöne zu geben — schon bei XI wird das Anblasen der Obertöne schwer — kann es de facto nicht von XVI aus gebildet worden sein. Möglicherweise ist XX gleich dem 5. Teilton der (zerbrochenen) Pfeife II, wie XIX tatsächlich gleich dem 5. Teilton von I ist. Doch mag auch letzteres Zufall sein. Als Kuriosum sei noch erwähnt, daß die Töne XVI bis XX auf 6324/25 gerade den höchsten Tönen von 6322/23 entsprechen, in denen sich die Pfeifen dieses sonst gleichgestimmten Paares unterscheiden (s. S. 379 oben).

Endlich ist die Serie von 20 Pfeifen, wie oben erwähnt, umschichtig auf zwei Instrumente verteilt worden. Daß dies bloß zu dem Zweck geschehen sein soll, um die einzelne Panpfeife handlicher zu machen, ist nicht gut anzunehmen, da ja auch 6322/23 je 17, andere südamerikanische Panpfeifen noch mehr Rohre haben (z. B. die aus Pebas — vgl. S. 388 — 311[1])). Andrerseits wäre die Möglichkeit, Oktavenzweiklänge zu blasen, statt durch Verteilung ebensogut (oder besser) durch Verdoppelung der ganzen Serie (wie bei 6322/23) zu erreichen gewesen. Vielleicht sagten die Tonschritte dem Intervallgefühl der Indianer nicht zu: wie die Quarten zu groß, so mögen ihnen die Dreivierteltöne zu klein sein. Dort erhielt man durch Einschaltung neuer Pfeifen ein Intervall zwischen Ganzton und kleiner Terz; hier durch Ausschaltung jeder zweiten Pfeife Intervalle, die zwischen dem Ganzton (204 Cents) und der großen Terz (386 Cents) liegen. Es ergeben sich nämlich folgende zwei Reihen:

Tabelle V.

V. B. 6325		I	III	V	VII	IX	XI	XIII	XV	XVII	XIX
Intervalle in Cents	becbachtet	277	365	306	365	334	354	317	214	292	
	Mittel	282	336	321	380	310	340	328	222	310	
	berechnet	260	360	320	360	320	360	320	200	320	
V. B. 6324		**II**	**IV**	**VI**	**VIII**	**X**	**XII**	**XIV**	**XVI**	**XVIII**	**XX**
Intervalle in Cents	beobachtet	[313]	318	338	403	315	336	270	288	221	
	Mittel	310	340	328	385	336	321	261	282	229	
	berechnet	320	360	320	360	360	320	260	260	260	

„Große Terzen" finden sich, wie man sieht, mit einer einzigen Ausnahme (VIII bis X) überhaupt nicht. Schon aus diesem Grunde wäre es ganz verkehrt, in den Tonreihen etwa „zerlegte Dur- und Mollakkorde" im Sinne unserer europäischen Musik finden zu wollen. Aber auch die übrigen Tonschritte würden eine solche Interpretation als unzulässig erweisen: 7 [8] „kleinen" stehen 6 „neutrale" Terzen gegenüber. Man müßte, wenn man überhaupt europäische Intervallbegriffe hier anwenden will, auch eine ganze Anzahl der halbierten Quarten (auch in 6322/23) als kleine Terzen gelten lassen. Dem Indianer aber sind gewiß sowohl solche Kategorien ganz fremd, als auch präzise Vorstellungen idealer Intervalle — „reiner" Intervalle irgendwelcher Art. Und so mögen ihm auch die durch Quartenhalbierung und die durch den Quartenzirkel gewonnenen Tonreihen nicht gar so (voneinander) verschieden vorkommen[2]).

[1]) Auch hätte man zwei Panpfeifen machen können, von denen die zweite die Tonreihe der ersten fortsetzt. Diese Einrichtung hat z. B. ein Panpfeifenpaar der Nahuquá (V. B. 2554 a, b, Samml. v. den Steinen): das letzte (6.) Rohr der größeren ist gleichgestimmt dem ersten Rohr der kleineren und zugleich die tiefere Oktave des überhaupt letzten Tons (V auf 2554 b).

[2]) Hierin liegt durchaus kein Widerspruch zu der Fähigkeit, Intervalle distanzgleich zu teilen, also Distanzgleichheiten zu beurteilen. Denn es ist etwas anderes: eine Tonreihe als Melodie, also als Ganzes, auf sich wirken lassen, und etwas anderes: zwei isoliert gegebene Tonschritte miteinander vergleichen.

IV. Die Tonreihe, die auf die beiden Panpfeifen V. B. 6325 und 6324 verteilt worden ist, ist auf dem kleinen Exemplar V. B. 6317 ungeteilt geblieben. Dieses als Kinderspielzeug bezeichnete Instrument ist offenbar eine — mit Ausnahme der Töne III, V und VIII recht gute — Nachbildung der Töne X bis XIX des für Erwachsene bestimmten Panpfeifenpaares.

Tabelle VI.

	I	II	III	IV	V	VI	VII[1])	VIII	IX	X
V. B. 6317	444.5	495.5	557	602	670	721	384.5	414	438	478.5
V.B. 6324/25 (X–XIX)	444.5	488	533.5	598.5	647.5	719	378.5	407	447	481.5

Daß man hier die Reihe zusammenhängend reproduziert hat, ließe sich vielleicht (so paradox dies klingt), ähnlich motivieren, wie im anderen Falle die Zerteilung. Möglicherweise wirkt nicht die geringe Tondistanz an sich unbefriedigend, sondern ihr Gefühlscharakter. Wie hohe Töne dünn, klein (gelegentlich sogar lächerlich), so erscheinen kleine Intervalle u. U. leicht, spielerisch; wie tiefe Töne breit, groß, so weite Tonschritte fest, feierlich. Es möchten daher für die kleinen Pfeifen der Kinder mit ihren hohen Tönen auch kleine Intervalle nicht so schlecht passen. Auch die kleinen Panpfeifen der Siusiknaben (V. B. 6320, 6318; 6319, 6321) haben zwar den großen verwandte Tonsysteme[2]) (vgl. Tab. VII, Seite 389), aber durchwegs kleine Intervalle, oft sogar solche, die offenbar durch Unterteilung größerer Schritte entstanden sind.

V. Selbst wenn, wie es den Anschein hat, die auf den Panpfeifen verkörperten Töne in sich völlig geschlossene Systeme bilden, so bleibt doch noch eine Frage offen, die Frage nach den absoluten Tonhöhen. Denn wie immer ein Tonsystem beschaffen sein mag, es kann nur die Verhältnisse der Töne zueinander, die Intervalle, bestimmen, oder, anders ausgedrückt, die relative Lage der Töne zu einem Grundton. Die absoluten Tonhöhen (die sich in den Schwingungszahlen ausdrücken), hängen also von der Wahl des Grundtons (Ausgangstons) ab. Daß der Ausgangston von der Willkür des Verfertigers oder vom Zufall bestimmt sein sollte, wird schon durch die recht gute Übereinstimmung der auf den Panpfeifenpaaren V. B. 6322/23 (Uanána!) und V. B. 6324/25 (Tukáno!) gefundenen Schwingungszahlen unwahrscheinlich. Noch auffallender sind die Koinzidenzen der Tonhöhen, wenn man V. B. 6324/25 mit einer großen, vortrefflich gearbeiteten Panpfeife aus Pebas (V. B. 417, coll. Staudinger)[3]) vergleicht. An diesem Exemplar läßt sich auch der Hauptton des Systems sicher erkennen. Während man bei V. B. 6324/25 noch im Zweifel sein konnte, ob II, III oder IV als Ausgangston anzusehen sei, da alle drei Töne sich in

---

[1]) Von VII an sind die Werte mit 2 zu multiziplieren.

[2]) In der Tabelle VII sind auch noch zwei Exemplare aus Dr. Koch-Grünbergs Privatsammlung, sowie das später erwähnte Instrument aus Pebas mit aufgenommen, deren Tonreihen ebenfalls mit den hier besprochenen zweifellos in Zusammenhang stehen. Eine ausführliche Analyse würde indes hier zu weit führen.

[3]) Dieses Instrument hat 31 Rohre; davon geben nur die ersten 18 meßbare, Rohr XIX bis XXII sehr hohe, schrille, die übrigen überhaupt keine Töne mehr. XXIX bis XXXI sind, da die Tiefe des Hohlraums geringer wird als seine Weite, eher als Näpfchen denn als Rohre zu bezeichnen. Vielleicht hat irgendwelche Zahlensymbolik diese merkwürdige Bildung veranlaßt, vielleicht wollte man der Panpfeife einfach die Gestalt eines rechtwinkligen Dreiecks geben.

Tabelle VII.

Gruppe	Instrument														
Peru, antik	Thonpanpfeife Ica	402	—	—	—	484.7	—	—	—	606	—	—	—	746	775
	coll. Gretzer	—	—	—	—	483.2	513	545.7	—	—	—	[704.5]	—	744.6	—
		—	—	436.7	456.8	481.6	—	—	—	—	—	—	—	—	—
	V. A. 8589 Steinpanpfeife	—	—	—	—	—	—	—	—	—	671	—	—	—	773•
	Cuzco	—	413°	432.4•	467.5°	—	—	526.7	—	604•	662°	—	—	—	773
	V. A. 15901 Thonflöte	—	—	—	—	494	—	—	—	614	—	707	—	—	(785)
	San Ramon	402	—	444.5	—	488	—	—	(553)	—	—	—	—	—	—
Nordost-peru, modern	V. B. 417	—	—	—	—	—	—	—	—	—	—	718	—	—	—
	Rohrpanpfeife	—	409	—	—	482	—	547	—	—	643.4	709.4	—	—	784
	Pebas	—	—	—	—	478.6	—	528	—	604	—	677	—	754.8	—
	coll. Staudinger	—	—	—	450	486.5	—	—	—	577.4	643.4	—	(734)	—	—
		—	(413)												
Nordwestbrasilien, modern	Rohrpanpfeife	—	—	—	—	—	—	—	—	—	—	—	—	—	790
	Tukáno	—	—	—	454.4	—	—	542	—	—	622.5	707	—	—	—
	coll.	—	409.1	—	469.8	—	—	528.4	—	612.2	—	701.6	—	—	785
	Koch-Grünberg	—	—	444.5	—	484.7	—	—	—	584	647.7	—	732	—	766.2
	V. B. 6324/25	—	—	—	—	—	—	—	—	—	—	—	—	753	—
	Panpfeifenpaar	[402]	—	442	—	481.6	—	545.7	—	579.3	651.3	704.3	—	—	—
	Tukáno, R. Tiquié	402	—	444.5	—	487.8	—	533.5	—	598.4	647.7	718.8	—	757.4	—
		406.8	—	447	—	481.6	507.8	—	—	—	—	—	—	—	—
	V. B. 6322/23	—	420	—	—	481.6	—	—	560.5	—	651.3	—	—	749	—
	Panpfeifenpaar	—	—	439.5	—	—	516	—	—	598.5	—	699	—	—	—
	Uanána	397.4	—	—	461.6	—	—	538.5	—	594.8	—	684	—	(753)	780
	R. Caiarý-Uaupés	—	—	(442)	—	478.5	(522)	—	—	—	—	—	—	—	—
	V. B. 6320, 6318 Zwei Panpfeifen Siusí, Rio Aiarý	—	—	439.5	—	491.9	—	545.7	—	606	658.5	701.6	723.2	—	770.6
	V. B. 6317 Panpfeife	—	—	444.5	—	495.5	—	—	556.8	602	670.2	—	721	—	769.4
	Tukáno, R. Tiquié	—	414.3	438	—	478.5	—	—	—	—	—	—	—	—	—
	V. B. 6319	—	—	—	—	—	—	—	—	595	662.4	—	723.2	740.4	770.6
	Panpfeife Siusí	—	—	442	—	494	—	—	—	—	—	—	—	—	—
	V. B. 6321 Panpfeife Siusí	—	—	—	—	—	510	—	567.6	—	637	707	—	—	775
	Panpfeife	—	—	—	—	—	—	(549)	—	—	—	690.4	—	—	—
	coll.	—	419.9	—	—	—	—	547.5	—	—	—	690.4	—	—	—
	Koch-Grünberg	—	419.9	—	—	—	513	—	—	—	637	—	—	—	—

den beiden höheren Oktaven wiederholen, ist auf V. B. 417 nur e i n Ton dreifach (in verschiedenen Oktavlagen) repräsentiert. Eben dies ist aber auch bei der Tonreihe der Fall, die in der ersten (Horizontal-) Rubrik — (den ersten 3 Zeilen) — der Tabelle VII verzeichnet ist, und auch die absolute Höhe dieses durch Verdreifachung ausgezeichneten Tons ist genau dieselbe, wie die der Grundtöne von V. B. 417 (III und seine Oktaven) und V. B. 6324/25 (IV und seine Oktaven). Die eben erwähnte Tonreihe stammt aber von einer Panpfeife aus glasiertem roten Ton, die in I c a (P e r u) ausgegraben worden ist (Sammlung Gretzer, noch nicht inventarisiert), und deren Größe (13 Rohre)[1]) und außerordentlich schöne und sorgfältige Faktur sie sowohl zu einem seltenen, wertvollen Fundstück als zu einem besonders vertrauenerweckenden Untersuchungsobjekt macht. Auch die anderen Töne dieser Pfeife, ferner die Stimmung einer kleinen Panpfeife aus schwarzem Talkstein („Huayra Puhura" aus C u z c o , V. A. 8589, Sammlung Centeno)[2]) und einer eigentümlich geformten tönernen Vertikalpfeife (aus S a n R a m o n , V. A. 15901, Sammlung Bolivar)[3]) möge man untereinander und mit den Rohrinstrumenten der heutigen Indianer vergleichen. Aber schon der „Hauptton" allein möchte als Beweismittel genügen. Um Mißverständnissen vorzubeugen, möchte ich nochmals ausdrücklich hervorheben, daß hier nicht Tonhöhen v e r h ä l t n i s s e , sondern a b s o l u t e T o n h ö h e n in Rede stehen. Gleichheit von Intervallen, ja von ganzen Tonsystemen kann immer als zufällige Konvergenzerscheinung gedeutet werden; sie können, nach gleichen oder nach verschiedenen, aber zum selben Resultat führenden Prinzipien da und dort und immer wieder voneinander unabhängig entstehen. Für die Wahl der absoluten Tonhöhe dagegen gibt es nur zwei Möglichkeiten: man folgt dem Zufall oder man kopiert ein Modell. Daß man in allen besprochenen Fällen zufällig dieselbe Tonhöhe sollte getroffen haben, das ist, wie man wohl zugeben wird, äußerst unwahrscheinlich.

Man wird also zu der Vermutung geführt, daß trotz der zeitlichen und räumlichen Trennung e i n e n g e r Z u s a m m e n h a n g d i e m o d e r n e n n o r d w e s t b r a s i l i s c h e n B l a s i n s t r u m e n t e m i t d e n a l t p e r u a n i s c h e n v e r b i n d e.

Mit andern Kulturerzeugnissen mögen aus dem Inkareich auch Panpfeifen in die Diaspora gelangt sein, vielleicht durch Vermittlung weit vorgeschobener Zweigniederlassungen oder befreundeter Kulturzentren, mit denen man in Handelsbeziehungen stand.[4])

---

[1]) Die Tonhöhe des einzigen zerbrochenen Rohrs (IX) wurde aus den Dimensionen erschlossen.

[2]) Die Rohre II, IV und V haben kleine Fingerlöcher und geben bei geöffnetem Loch die mit ° bezeichneten Werte.

[3]) Das Instrument hat fünf Fingerlöcher vorn und eins (etwas oberhalb V) hinten; ist dieses geöffnet, so erhält man die eingeklammerten Werte. Es sei besonders darauf aufmerksam gemacht, daß auch hier wieder — bei geschlossenem hinteren Fingerloch — der e r s t e u n d l e t z t e Ton der Reihe dem „Normalton" entspricht.

[4]) Solche wurden von den deutschen Conquistadoren noch vorgefunden. Vgl. K o n r a d H a e b l e r , Die überseeischen Unternehmungen der Welser und ihrer Gesellschafter (Leipzig, 1903), namentlich pp. 257, 308; H e r m. A. S c h u m a c h e r , Die Unternehmungen der Augsburger Welser in Venezuela. Hamburgische Festschrift zur Erinnerung an die Entdeckung Amerikas (Hamburg, 1892), Bd. II. S. 73 ff.

Eine streng beobachtete, vielleicht durch religiöse Vorstellungen lebendig erhaltene Tradition mag bei den primitiveren Barbaren die kostbaren Modelle oder ihre ersten Nachbildungen ängstlich behütet und durch die Jahrhunderte hindurch den Nachfahren vererbt haben. Wie sorgfältig und genau der Indianer Tonhöhen kopiert, das haben schon die identisch gestimmten Instrumentenpaare gezeigt. Und auch das paarweis Blasen der Panpfeifen schon im antiken Peru ist erwähnt worden[1]). Endlich würde ein so künstliches Konstruktionsprinzip, wie der Quartenzirkel, das bei einem „Naturvolk" überrascht, als zugleich mit dem Ausgangston importiertes Kulturgut wohl verständlich sein. In der Tat ist es wahrscheinlicher, daß man dem ganzen Modell nahe zu kommen versucht, als daß man ihm bloß einen einzigen Ton entnommen hat. Wenn so aber wirklich die wesentlichen Grundlagen altperuanischer Tonkunst bis in unsere Zeit erhalten geblieben sind, so dürfen wir vielleicht hoffen, daß mit ihnen auch einiges von den melodischen Formen sich vor der Conquista in das schwer zugängliche Hinterland gerettet habe.

---

[1]) Man vergleiche auch die Pfeife, die Mead, l. c. Plate III. Nr. 6 abbildet. Sie scheint eine tönerne Nachbildung eines Tierschädels zu sein, wie ihn auch die Nordwestbrasilianer als Pfeife benützen (vgl. Abb. 184 S. 302 im I. Band dieses Werks).

AROUND VON HORNBOSTEL'S THEORY OF THE CYCLE OF BLOWN FIFTHS

A. The hypothesis. When, on the 25th of November 1935, ERICH MARIA VON HORNBOSTEL died, his brilliantly-conceived theory concerning the structure of a large number of exotic scales, commonly called the „theory of blown fifths", seemed to have found pretty general agreement. It was expounded in various stages of its development, now concisely, now in greater detail, by its author in **Anthropos** 1919/'20 (p. 569 **et seq.)** and in Vol. 8 of GEIGER and SCHEEL'S **Handbuch der Physik** (1927), and further by ROBERT LACHMANN in his **Musik des Orients** (1929); by CURT SACHS in his **Vergleichende Musikwissenschaft** (1930); by FRITZ BOSE in the **Atlantisbuch der Musik** (1934) p. 960 **et seq.**; by MARIUS SCHNEIDER in his article **Ethnologische Musikforschung** (in PREUSS, **Lehrbuch der Völkerkunde** p. 135 **et seq.)**, 1937; by GEORG SCHÜNEMANN (**„Archiv für Musikforschung"** Vol. I fasc. 3 and 4), 1936; by HEINRICH HUSMANN in his article **Marimba und Sansa der Sambesikultur** (in the **Zeitschrift für Ethnologie,** Vol. 68, p. 197 **et seq.),** 1936, and by the present writer in **De Toonkunst van Bali,** Vol. II (1925), in the article **De l'origine des échelles musicales javano-balinaises (Journal of the Siam Society** XXIII) (1929) p. 111 **et seq.,** in **De Toonkunst van Java,** Vol. I (1934) p. 19—31, and in **A musicological argument for cultural relationship between Indonesia — probably the isle of Java — and Central Africa (Proceedings of the Musical Association,** Session LXII) (1936).

The broad outline of this theory of blown fifths may be stated as follows:

From somewhere in Central Asia — probably from the territory called today Chinese Turkestan — the legendary Chinese musician LING LUN, by the order of the mythical emperor HUANG TI, imported a tone-sequence which may be obtained — starting from a fundamental tone of 366 v.d. (the so-called **huang chong,** yellow bell), produced on a bamboo tube closed at the bottom end by a node, about 230 mm long and 8.12 mm in diameter - by taking the twelfth of this fundamental tone (produced by overblowing), transposed an octave lower, as the second tone in the sequence; the twelfth of this second tone, again transposed an octave lower, as third tone, etc., etc.

Now according to VON HORNBOSTEL, these twelfths obtained by overblowing (and, therefore, also the corresponding fifths, called by him „blown

— 3 —

fifths" (Blasquinten)) are on the average (within the register in question here) just over one-tenth of a tone (i.e. **24 cents**) [1]) smaller than the natural intervals of that name, with the result that the series of fifths obtained thereby does not — like the cycle produced from the pure fifths of **702** C. — after twelve jumps of a fifth each, finish up approximately (allowing for octave-difference) on the same tone from which it started, but does not reach this point until after 23 jumps; then, however, with greater exactitude, as the following figures show:

12 pure fifths of **702** C = **8424** C
7 octaves of **1200** C = **8400** C

Difference: **24** C = the „comma" of PYTHAGORAS;

23 blown fifths of **678** C = **15594** C
13 octaves of **1200** C = **15600** C

Difference: **6** C = ¼ „comma" of PYTHAGORAS.

Now by „condensing" the entire series of 23 blown fifths within one and the same octave, we obtain, starting from the **huang chong** of 366 v. d. (O = XXIII), the following sequence of tones[2]):

O	I	II	III	IV	V	VI	VII	VIII	IX	X
366	541	400½	593	438	648½	480½	710	525	387½	574

XI	XII	XIII	XIV	XV	XVI	XVII	XVIII	XIX	XX	XXI
425	628½	465	688	509	376½	557	412	609	450½	667

XXII	XXIII = O
493½	366

Granting that VON HORNBOSTEL correctly interpreted the above-mentioned legend, the conclusion must be that, before ancient China began to base its scales — as is still the custom today — on „Pythagorean" tonal sequences obtained from string-measurement and constructed on the principle of pure fifths, it must have known another type of scales, derived from the cycle of blown fifths described above.

---

[1]) The „cent" as metrical unit for the measurement of musical intervals was suggested by the English musicologist A. J. ELLIS, and first applied by him in his foundational treatise **Tonometrical Observations on some existing non-harmonic scales (Proceedings of the Royal Society** 1884). The **cent** is equal to one-hundredth part of the tempered European semitone. This method accordingly permits of the immediate comparison of the intervals of exotic scales with those familiar to us from childhood.

[2]) Some of the vibration figures given here deviate a little from those originally taken by VON HORNBOSTEL. The values computed by the present writer with the aid of the cents-table published later by VON HORNBOSTEL (**Zeitschrift für Physik**, Vol. 6, 1921) doubtless approximate the pure cycle of blown fifths slightly more accurately still. Only the last blown fifth has been taken greater by **6 cents** in order to round off the cycle as a whole.

Now as far as I am aware, no instruments producing this latter type of scale have yet come into our possession or to our knowledge from prehistoric China itself; indirectly, however, their existence at some time or other may be inferred from the fact that, as von Hornbostel discovered, a large number of exotic scales found in use among peoples widely separated both historically and geographically, as well ethnologically, may be derived **in some regular manner** from that cycle of blown fifths. As investigations by von Hornbostel and a few other musico-ethnologists have shown, this is the case, for example, with the tunings of pan-pipes originating from Oceania, pre-Colombian Peru, modern Ecuador, Columbia and N. W. Brazil, and with xylophone tunings from Siam, Birma, Java, Bali and Central Africa. Now it is a matter of general agreement among musicologists that scales with definitely fixed, as it were „objectivated", intervals **must** be products of a high culture level; there are various indications pointing to the probability that the cultural influence manifested in the tunings here referred to originally emanated from China. [1]).

To elucidate the above argument it may be useful to give a number of examples of scales examined by the writer in the course of many years. The Roman figures indicate the steps of the cycle of fifths; the encircled Arabic numerals, the degrees of the scale measured; those underneath either the Roman or the encircled numerals, the vibrations figures (v.d.), and the Arabic numerals in heavy type, the intervals expressed in **cents.**

It will be seen that the scales compared are identical not only relatively (i.e. with regards to the intervals), but also in the absolute sence (i.e. with regard to pitch).

It appears that the scale-types, called, in Java, **pélog,** make use of two different selections of blown fifths:

(a) one type is formed by 7 consecutive cycle steps, resulting — when arranged in scale-sequence — in a series of intervals which, expressed in **cents,** presents the following aspect:

156 156 156 210 156 156 210,

or, in certain cases, some inversion of this sequence.

Here follow a few examples of this type, from Bali, Java and the Congo territory, respectively:

---

[1]) About the reason why scales of this type have been handed down unchanged from generation to generation for so many centuries, vide von Hornbostel, **Die Maassnorm als kulturgeschichtliches Forschungsmittel (Pater Wilhelm Schmidt-Festschrift** 1928), p. 305; Maurice Courant, **Essai historique sur la Musique classique en Chine** (in Lavignac, **Histoire de la Musique,** Vol. I, p. 77 **et seq.**) (1912), p. 80; J. Combarieu, **La Musique et la Magie** (1909), and **Histoire de la Musique,** Vol. I (1913), first two chapters; J. Kunst, **De Toonkunst van Java** (1934), Vol. I, p. 30, and **De Inheemsche Muziek en de Zending** (1948), p. 6—8.

Blown fifths X-XVI incl.	XII 314½	XIV 344	XVI 376½	XI 425	XIII 465	XV 509	X 574	XII 628½
Gam. Saih pitu from Ksatria, Dén Pasar (South Bali)	① 312½	② 341½	③ 375	④ 430	⑤ 470	⑥ 510	⑦ 576	①' 625
	153	162	237	154	142	210	142	
Deviations in cents:	—9	—13	—7	+20	+18	+4	+6	—9

Blown fifths XII-XVIII incl.	XII 314½	XIV 344	XVI 376½	XVIII 412	XIII 465	XV 509	XVII 557	XII 628½
Bamboo gambang from Batu bulan (South Bali)	① 315	② 343½	③ 378	④ 415½	⑤ 465	⑥ 508	⑦ 556	①' (630)
	150	171	162	202	153	165	197	
Deviations in cents:	+4	—3	+7	+14	0	—3	—3	+4

Blown fifths XVII-XXI incl.	XVII 557	XIX 609	XXI 667	XVIII 824	XX 901	XVII 1114
Gam. Gong from Padangtegal, distr. Ubud, (South Bali)	① 555	② 606	③ 670	⑤ 828	⑥ 894	①' 1110
	152	174	366	133	375	
Deviations in cents:	—6	—8	+8	+8	—14	—6

Blown fifths VI-XII incl.	XI 425	VI 480½	VIII 525	X 574	XII 628½	VII 710	IX 775	XI 850
Hindu-Jav. demung, excavated in Banjarnegara (Mus. R. Bat. S. No. 1051a)	① 427	② 475	③ 518	④ 576	⑤ 628½	⑥ 710	⑦ 768	①' (854)
	184	150	184	151	211	136	184	
Deviations in cents:	+8	—20	—24	+6	0	0	—16	+8

— 6 —

Blown fifths	II	IV	VI	I	III	V	VII	II
I-VII incl.	200¼	219	240½	270½	296½	324¼	355	400½
Gam. Kyahi								
Munggang	①	②	③	④	⑤	⑥	⑦	①¹
(Paku Ala-	199½	217	237	273	298	326	357	399
man, Jogja)		**146**	**153**	**245**	**151**	**155**	**158**	**192**
Deviations								
in cents:	**—7**	**—16**	**—23**	**+16**	**+9**	**+9**	**+10**	**—7**

Blown fifths	XVI	XVIII	XX	XV	XVII	XIX	XIV	XVI
XIV-XX incl.					139¼	152¼	172	
	188¼	206	225¼	254½	278½	304½	344	
	376½	412	450½	509	557	609	688	753
Marimba of	①	②	③	④	⑤	⑥	⑦	①¹
the Bakwese					140½	152½	171½	
SW Belgian						**145**	**201**	**122**
Congo (Congo	189	205	227	252	276	302	338	
Mus. No.		**141**	**176 ·**	**181**	**157**	**156**	**195**	**106**
15862)	368	411	456	510	572	604	692	(736)
		192	**180**	**194**	**198**	**94**	**236**	**106**
Deviations					**+15**	**+ 3**	**— 6**	
in	**+ 7**	**— 8**	**+ 8**	**—13**	**—16**	**—14**	**—31**	
cents:	**—40**	**— 4**	**+16**	**+ 4**	**+46**	**—14**	**+10**	**—40**

Blown fifths	XVI	XVIII	XX	XV	XVII	XIX	XIV	XVI
XIV-XX incl.					139¼	152¼	172	
	188¼	206	225¼	254½	278½	304½	344	
	376½	412	450½	509	557	609	688	753
Marimba of	①	②	③	④	⑤	⑥	⑦	①¹
the Bakubu					141½	151	172	
S. Belgian						**112**	**226**	**131**
Congo	185½	205½	228	248	281	309	332	
(Congo-Mus.		**177**	**180**	**146**	**215**	**165**	**124**	**215**
No. 15861)	376	412	458	516	568	620	688	(752)
		158	**184**	**206**	**166**	**152**	**180**	**154**
Deviations					**+28**	**—14**	**0**	
in	**—25**	**— 4**	**+21**	**—44**	**+ 9**	**+26**	**—62**	
cents:	**— 2**	**0**	**+29**	**+24**	**+34**	**+32**	**0**	**— 2**

(b) It is probable that another pélog sequence represents an older form than the preceding one; we might conveniently call it „primitive" pélog. It consists of 8 steps of the cycle at intervals of 12 fifths between each other; arranged according to height of pitch, these tones produce a series of intervals formed from steps of a blown semi-fourth (**261** C) [1]) and of the following sizes:

105 156 261 156 105 156 261.

In this, however, the second step — to be reached in the manner indicated (i.e. the 13th fifth including the starting point) — is always skipped, because, if it were gathered into the scale, it would split the seventh pélog-interval (of **261** C.) into two smaller intervals of **105** and **156** C. respectively, which would alter the scale from being a heptatonic one into an octotonic one:

Part of the cycle of blown fifths in semi-fourths arrangement	XII 314½	I 541	XIII 465	II 400½	XIV 344	III 296½	XV 509	IV 438
Gam. Kyahi Kanyut Mèsem pélog (Mangku Nagaran)	② 317	—	⑥ 465	④ 399	③ 345	① 295	⑦ 512	⑤ 439
Deviations in cents:	**+15**	—	**0**	**—7**	**+5**	**—8**	**+10**	**+4**

---

[1]) i.e. 7 octaves of **1200** C each = **8400** C
12 blown fifths of **678** C each = **8136** C

Difference: **264** C.

We should bear in mind, however, that the cycle of blown fifths — which in fact, does not „round off" exactly, but with a minus discrepancy of **6** C — has to be run through nearly four times in order to obtain this type of scale; so that we have to reckon with an „error" of about 4 × **6** = **24** C., i.e. a reduction of about **3** C per step, as a result of which these degrees are, theoretically, only **261** C, or exactly a semi-fourth ($\frac{522}{2}$ C.)

Cf., in regard to semi-fourth scales (which have also been found elsewhere, notably in Melanesia, NW Brazil and ancient Peru): VON HORNBOSTEL in GEIGER and SCHEEL **Handbuch der Physik** VIII, p. 431.

Part of the cycle of blown fifths in semi-fourths arrangment	XIX 304½	VIII 525	XX 450½	IX 387½	XXI 333½	X 287	XXII 493½	XI 425
Gam. Kyahi Bermara (kraton Jogja)	② 308	—	⑥ 450	④ 387½	③ 332½	① 290	⑦ 496	⑤ 425
Deviations in cents:	**20**	—	**—2**	**0**	**—6**	**+18**	**+9**	**0**
Gam. Kyahi Pengasih (kraton Solo)	② 308	—	⑥ 450	④ 392	③ 335½	① 286	⑦ 500	⑤ 421
Deviations in cents:	**20**	—	**—2**	**+20**	**+10**	**—6**	**+22**	**—17**

Arranged according to pitch, the tones of these three semi-fourths pélog scales form the following series of intervals:

	①		②		③		④		⑤		⑥		⑦		①[1]
Kyahi Kanyut	295		317		345		399		439		465		512		590
Mèsem:		**125**		**146**		**252**		**165**		**100**		**167**		**245**	
Kyahi	290		308		332½		387½		425		450		496		580
Bermara:		**104**		**132**		**265**		**160**		**99**		**169**		**271**	
Kyahi	286		308		335½		392		421		450		500		572
Pengasih:		**128**		**148**		**270**		**123**		**116**		**182**		**233**	

Nothwithstanding the fact that scales of this **b**-type (or, at any rate, those unmistakably deriving from this type, i.e. those whose I-II and V-VI steps are considerably smaller than their II-III, IV-V and VI-VII steps, while their III-IV and VII-I[1] steps are about a semi-fourth) are at the present time more numerous than those of the previously described **a**-type, it is precisely the latter that have given us an insight into the structure of the entire pélog system; it is these scales which have supplied the answer to the question why pélog, in playing practice, possesses only three different paṭets. [1]).

* * *

[1]) Cf. **De Toonkunst van Java**, Vol. I, p. 33.

Of the scales classed in Java among the group of **sléndro**-scales, there are also a number of types, each of which can be derived from the cycle of blown fifths, each in its own way, **but always according to a fixed, regular principle.** On the ground of a large number of scale measurements, I am inclined to distinguish three phases of development, to which I propose to give the names of **primitive** (or **semi-fourths-), medium,** and **modern** sléndro, respectively.

(c) Primitive sléndro makes use of 5 cycle-steps which, again, lie at distances of 12 fifths from each other. Assuming this scale to close on the octave, we get in this way a series of intervals of the following type:

261 261 261 261 156

Some examples of this, from the Congo territory and from Java, respectively, are:

Part of the cycle	(O)				XXII				XXI		(O)
of blown fifths	183				246¼				333½		366
in semi-fourths	366				493½				667		732
arrangment [1]			XI				[X [2]]				
			212½				287				
			425				574]				
							III				
							296½				
							593				
Marimba from the	①		②		③		④		⑤		①'
Yakoma-tribe,	185½		210½		247		298		338		
Belgian Congo		**218**		277		**325**		**218**		**147**	
(Congo-Mus.	368		428		494		596		676		(736)
No. 34939)		**262**		**248**		**325**		**218**		**147**	
Deviations	+24		—17		+ 1		+ 9		+23		
in cents:	+ 9		+12		+ 1		+ 9		+23		+ 9

---

[1]) To be read from right to left, because of the fact that the tones of this scale **go up** in the **descending** sequence of fifths.
[2]) Step X has been replaced by a step III which lies 7 fifths (one **saptaka**) higher in the cycle.

Part of the circle of blown fifths in semi-fourths arrangment	IV 438		XV 509		III 593		XIV 688		II 801		(IV) 876
Gam. miring of Musadikrama, désa Katur, Bajanegara	⑤ 434	230	① 510	252	② 590	246	③ 680	259	④ 791	163	⑤ 868
Deviations in cents:	—16		+ 4		— 8		—20		—22		—16

We see, therefore, that primitive pélog and primitive sléndro are closely akin: both they are semi-fourths scales and they differ only as regards the number of intervals within the octave: in the case of primitive pélog there are 7, and in the case of primitive sléndro, 5.

(d) Medium sléndro employs 5 cycle-steps which lies at distances of 6 fifths from one another, which produces, when arranged according to pitch, a sequence of intervals of the following type:

264 204 264 204 264

Here are a few examples of this type of scale:

Series of blown fifths	XIX 304½	II 400½	VIII 262½	XIV 344	XX 450½
Gam. miring from Bajanegara	② 308	④ 399	① 262	③ 347	⑤ 450
Deviations in C:	+20	— 7	— 4	+15	— 2
Gam. miring from Ngumpak, Bajanegara	② 310	④ 405	① 266	③ 348	⑤ 455
Deviations in C:	+32	+19	+22	+20	+17

It will be seen that the latter of these two gamelans is pitched, in its entirety, about **20** C higher than the absolute norm; relatively, however, it is purer than the former, since its intervals hardly deviate at all from the theoretical ones (in playing practice the discrepancy would not be noticeable):

Gam. miring from Bajanegara	① 262		② 308		③ 347		④ 399		⑤ 450		①' 524
		280		**207**		**241**		**209**		**263**	
but											
Gam. miring from Ngumpak	① 266		② 310		③ 348		④ 405		⑤ 455		①' 532
		266		**200**		**262**		**202**		**270**	
Theoretical scale:		**264**		**204**		**264**		**204**		**264**	
Deviations in cents:		**+2**		**—4**		**—2**		**—2**		**+6**	

In regard to these medium sléndro scales I should remark that its tones, when arranged in the position which they occupy in the cycle, are known in Bali by names whose vowels form a „spectral" sequence from light to dark:

①	③	⑤	②	④
ding	**dèng**	**dang**	**dong**	**doong**

This is a significant point, in a race like the Balinese, which is so fond of relating the pitch of a tone, the size of an instrument or part of an instrument (key, sound-kettle), on the one hand, and the tone-colour of the instrument's name, on the other hand.

(e) Modern sléndro, the third type, employs, for the two even, or the three uneven tones of its scale, cycle-steps again lying at distances of 6 fifths from each other; for the three (or two) remaining intermediary tones, however, tones are used which lie half-way between the third and fifth of the cycle-steps missed; together they constitute a sequence presenting f.i. the following picture:

I III/V VII IX/XI XIII I',

which, when expressed in cents, results in the following scale:

234 234 234 234 264

There are plenty examples of this; I content myself with a few of the most striking instances:

Scale derived from the cycle of blown fifths	XVII/XIX 291		XXI 333½		O/II 383		IV 438		VI/VIII 502		XVII/XIX 582
Kyahi Kanyut mèsem sléndro (Mangku Nagaran Solo)	① 291		② 331		③ 383		④ 439		⑤ 500		①' 582
		223		**253**		**236**		**225**		**263**	
Deviations in C:	**0**		**—13**		**0**		**+ 4**		**— 7**		**0**

Scale derived from the cycle of blown fifths	III 296½		V/VII 339		IX 387½		XI/XIII 444½		XV 509		III 593
Kyahi Pengawé sari (Paku Alaman, Jogja)	① 295		② 341		③ 390		④ 446		⑤ 511		①' 590
		251		233		234		233		249	
Deviations in C:	— 8		+10		+11		+ 5		+ 7		— 8

Scale derived from the cycle of blown fifths	XIII 232½		XV/XVII 266½		XIX 304½		XXI/O 349½		II 400½		XIII 465
Gam. sléndro of R. M. Jayadipura, Jogja	⑤ 231		① 266		② 304		③ 349½		④ 399		⑤' 462
		245		231		239		231		254	
Deviations in C:	—12		— 2		— 2		+ 2		— 7		—12

Scale derived from the cycle of blown fifths	I/III 283		V 324½		VII/IX 371		XI 425		XIII/XV 486½		I/III 566
Gam. sléndro, Rancha iyuh, Tanggerang, res. Batavia	① 282½		② 323		③ 371		④ 427½		⑤ 486		①' 564½
		232		241		245		222		260	
Deviations in C:	— 5		— 7		0		+10		— 2		— 5

Scale derived from the cycle of blown fifths	XIX 304½ 609		XXI/O 349½ 698½		II 400½ 801		IV/VI 458 916		VIII 525 1050		XIX 609 1218
Gendèr wayang from Pliatan, South Bali	① 611		② 350 700		③ 397 794		④ 459 918		⑤ 522 1044		①' 611 1222
		236		218		251		223		272	
Deviations in C:	+ 6		+ 4		—15		+ 3		—10		+ 6

— 13 —

This modern sléndro-scale often seems to be tempered to form an equigrade tone-sequence with the structural formula:

240 240 240 240 240

This equigradity, however, is never reached perfectly, but the remaining imperfections have no **functional** significance anymore, with the result that one and the same nuclear melody, when played on one gamelan, may sometimes produce a totally different (tonal) effect on the western ear than when it is played on another gamelan.

(f) Finally, we come across scales employing 7 consecutive **even** („feminine", or **yin**) or **uneven** („masculine", or **yang**) cycle-steps, i.e., for example, the steps:

I III V VII IX XI XIII

or, for instance,

VI VIII X XII XIV XVI XVIII

which sequences, when expressed in **cents,** give the following theoretical scale:

156 156 156 156 156 156

and which, therefore, assuming them to have seven steps, and to finish on the octave, must contain one larger interval, of **1200** — (6×**156**) = **1200** — **936** = **264** C, unless — as von Hornbostel appears to have found in NW Brazilian scales — they just ignore the octave altogether.

Von Hornbostel inclined to the supposition that, of these „Umschichtreihen" („alternating series"), as he called them (each of which missed the interval of approximately a fifth, so important for melody-building: blown fifth =678 C; pure fifth = 702 C; tempered fifth =700 C; whereas 4 × 156 =624, and 5× 156 =780 C), a „masculine" and a „feminine" sequence were played each time on two complementary instruments, in order to provide for this missing fifth-interval; further, that in view of the difficulty of this roundabout method, some tones (ultimately three) from each set of seven were changed over [1]), as a result of which tone-sequences were obtained by means of which the desired fifths could be produced, i.e. scales which are nothing more or less than the modern pélog-scales described above sub (a). For with the aid of these it is possible to play all sorts of fifths, since (3 × **156**) plus **210** = **678** C, which represents the blown fifth.

---

[1]) These substitute-tones are those which have their place 7 steps (a **saptaka**) earlier or further in the cycle, which amounts to a tone either 52 C higher or 52 C lower, respectively, than the tone to be replaced.

It appears, however, that many of the modern pélog-scales have got stuck in a kind of transition-stage between a real pure pélog- and an „alternating" scale.

First an example from South-America, an Andean pan-pipe. It is a double-instrument with one series of 8 stopped tubes, extending over two octaves, and an other series of 8 open tubes, intended (at least as far as they could be made to sound, which was no easy matter) to produce exactly the same scale, one octave higher. The complete instrument, therefore, covers three octaves.

The series of stopped tubes gave the following sequence of tones. They form, as we shall see, a „feminine" alternating series, of which one tone is replaced by another, one **saptaka** further in the cycle — the first of the three steps that lead to real pélog:

Blown fifths VI-XVIII	VI	VII	VIII	IX	X	XI	XII	XIII	XIV	XV	XVI	XVII	XVIII
	240½	360	262½	387½	287	212½	314½	232½	172	254½	376	278½	206
	480½	720	525	775	574	425	628½	465	344 688	509	752	557	412
Pan-pipe from La Paz, Bolivia (Mus, de l'Homme, no. 30.44.32).	⊙		③ 262½		⑦ 578		④ 313	⑥ 467	① 171 ①¹ 683		⑤ 380		② 206½
Deviations in C:			**0**		**+12**		**—7**	**+5**	**—10** **—13**		**+16**		**+4**

When arranged according to pitch, the tones of this scale form the following sequence of intervals:

①		②		③		④		⑤		⑥		⑦		①¹
171		206½		262½		313		380		467		578		683
	326		**416**		**304**		**336**		**357**		**369**		**286**	

The next scale, this time one from the isle of Bali, has already set two of the three steps in the direction of real pélog:

Blown fifths VI-XVIII incl.	VI	VII	VIII	IX	X	XI	XII	XIII	XIV	XV	XVI	XVII	XVIII
	480½	710	525	387½	574	425	628½	465	688	509	367½	557	412
Gam. Semar pegulingan, Ubud (S. Bali)	⑦ —	④ 714	① 527	⑤ 389	② 568		③ 636		⊙		⊙		⑥ 416
Deviations in C:		**+10**	**+6**	**+6**	**—18**		**+23**						**+17**

This originally a „feminine" scale, too, has replaced the „alternating" cycle-steps XIV and XVI by the steps VII and IX, both one saptaka earlier in the cycle, but not yet the step XVIII by the step XI, which would give this scale a pure pélog-structure.

When arranged according to pitch, the tones of this scale form the following sequence of intervals:

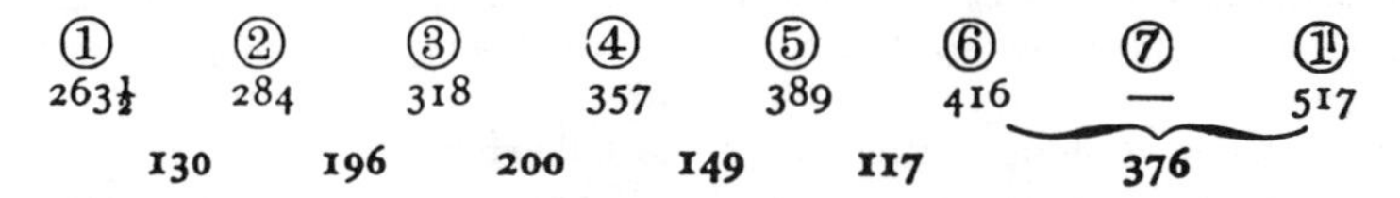

Such transitional forms do exist also between (d) medium and (e) modern sléndro. The following scale is an example of this. As will be seen, only the tone ④ occupies a fresh position; tone ② through whose displacement from cycle step IX or II to XVI/XVIII this scale would have been completely converted into modern sléndro, is still in the medium-sléndro position:

Scale derived from the cycle of blown fifths	VIII	X/XII	XIV	XVI/XVIII	XX	XXII/I	III	V/VII	IX	XI/XIII	XV
	525	574/628½ 600½	344	376½/412 394	450½	493½/541 516½	593	648½/710 678½	387½	425/465 444½	510
Gendèr wavang from Ubud (S. Bali)	⊙		① 347		⑧ 452	④ 516	⑤ 590		② 388		⊙
Deviations in C:			+15		+5	—1	—8		+2		

When arranged according to pitch, the tones of this scale form the following sequence of intervals:

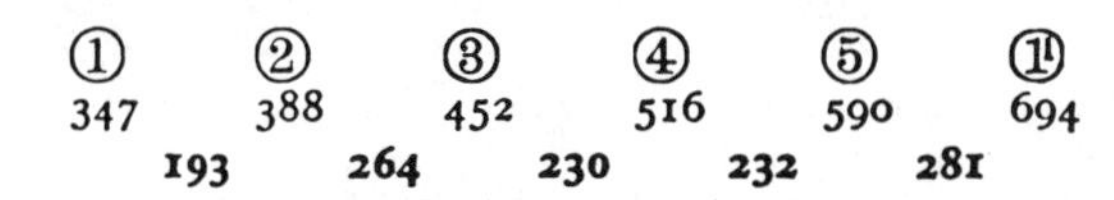

It might just be possible that the „coupling" of two instruments, which is still found today in the musical practice of different peoples, is reminiscent of the primitive stage, i.e. the simultaneous playing of a **yang**- and a **yin**-instrument. One example of this might be the Sundanese pan-pipes **(hatong),** which are always blown in duplicate during harvest festivals, and called **indung** (= mother) and **anak** (= child). The double-row pan-pipes used by some South American Indian tribes might perhaps be explained in the same way.

In the case of African marimba's too, „male" and „female" tone-sequences are also occasionally combined in one and the same instrument. Such a combination of a masculine and a feminine scale of the type referred to here is shown, for example, by a marimba from the Bayanzi-tribe (Belgian Congo):

Male series	XIV	XVI	XVIII		VI		VIII	X			XII
of blown fifths								143½			
VI-XVIII	172	188½	206								
	344	376½	412		480½		525	574			628½
Female series				XIII		XV			XVII	XIX	
of blown fifths						127½				152½	
XIII-XIX				232½		254½			278½	304½	
Marimba of the	①	②	③	④	⑤	⑥	⑦	⑧	⑨	⑩	⑪
Bayanzi (Congo-						127		143½		151	
Museum no.	171½	191	210	233		255			282½	306	
31354)	346	381½	420		472		526	570			624
Deviations						—3		0		—14	
in cents:	—5	+25	+33	+4		+4			+24	+9	
	+10	+20	+33		—29		+3	—12			—12

And the same combination we find realized on a marimba from the Kasai district:

Alternating series of bl. fifths	XVIII	XIX	XX	XXI	XXII	(O)	(I)	II	III	IV	V	VI	VII	VIII	X
	206	1218	225¼	333½	246	366	270½	400½	296½	438	648½	480½	355	525	1148
Marimba Kasai distr. (Mus. du Cons. Brussels no. Prov. 128)	①	⑭	②	⑤	③	—	—	⑦	④	⑧	⑪	⑨	⑥	⑩	⑬
	205	1232	226	330	246			397	302	440	652	473	360	526	1160
								⑫							
								808							
Deviations in cents:	—8	+20	+5	—18	0	—	—	—15	+32	+8	+9	—27	+24	+3	+18
								+15							

This remarkable correspondence and kinship between scales, both as regards their structure and as regards their absolute pitch, is not an isolated phenomenon; it appears that there also exists — if we are to accept VON HORNBOSTEL's argument on the subject in his above-mentioned paper **Die Maassnorm als kulturgeschichtliches Forschungsmittel** — a similar connexion in the field of metrical standards. For in this treatise the author brings forward a plausible argument to the effect that the length of the bamboo tube on which the basic tone of the cycle of blown fifths, the **huang-chong,** is sounded — i.e. 230 ± 3 mm [1]) — was adopted as sacred norm and served, as such, as basis for the length-measurements valid not only in ancient China, but also, it seems, in the territory of the Sumerian priest-prince Gudea (2600 B.C.), as well as in pre-Columbian South America. In other words, it would appear that we are here confronted with two inseparably connected phenomena — one metrical, the other musical — which constitute irrefutable evidence of the existence of an early contact between cultures covering an astonishingly extensive, in fact, almost world-wide area. It will be admitted that this would be a discovery of the very first importance; indeed, a discovery almost too grand to be accepted without scepticism or criticism. In effect, objections were duly raised to the theory; it is to be regretted that they were not put forward until after the death of him to whom we owe this hypothesis.

B. Objections to Von Hornbostel's theory.

Criticism of the theory of the cycle of blown fifths, partly amounting to complete rejection, has been published chiefly by two musicologists, Miss KATHLEEN SCHLESINGER and Dr. MANFRED BUKOFZER; while CURT SACHS, in his more recent writings, also gives the impression of discountenancing it. [2])

Now it had already been remarked on previous occasions that one could hardly credit the assumption that such an extremely complicated structural form as that embodied in a cycle of blown fifths of 23 steps could possibly have been conceived and realized as early as the third millennium B.C.; nay, it was affirmed that it was utterly impossible to arrive at construing a cycle of this kind by purily experimental means.

But are we sure that this view is correct? One feels inclined to doubt it, in view of the existence of structures such as those of the scales reproduced above (p. 6, 8, 9, 12 and 13), and still more strongly, in view of that of a pan-pipe from Ecuador in possession of the Musée de l'Homme, Paris, under No. 41.39.1. The tonal sequence of this latter instrument — which counts as many as 26 tubes — uses no less than 16 out of the 23 steps of the cycle — they are, moreover, 16 **consecutive** steps — covering the latter with truly remarkable accuracy, as the following table shows:

---

[1]) This norm has not remained precisely the same through the centuries; it has fluctuated somewhat, around 230 mm as a central value, but with a deviation of a few millimetres at most. About the magical significance of this norm for the dynasties and the empire of China I may refer the reader to VON HORNBOSTEL, **op. cit.**; MAURICE COURANT, **Essai historique sur la musique classique en Chine,** p. 80, and CURT SACHS, **The Rise of Music in the Ancient World, East and West** (1943), p. 11.

[2]) Cf. also W. APEL, **Harvard Dictionary of Music** (1944, 3rd ed. 1945), p. 374a.

No. of tube	Vibration-figure	Interval in cents	Step of the cycle of blown fifths		Deviations in cents
1.	682		XIV	688	—16
		708			
2.	453		XX	450½	+ 9
		311			
3.	542		I	541	+ 4
		287			
4.	461		XIII	465	—19
		469			
5.	604		XIX	609	—14
		323			
6.	728		O	732	—10
		231			
7.	832		XVIII	824	+17
		324			
8.	690		XIV	688	+ 4
		521			
9.	932		XIII	930	+ 4
		391			
10.	746		XVI	753	—16
		704			
11.	1120		XVII	1114	+ 9
		303			
12.	940		XIII	930	+18
		491 (709)			
13.	1248 (624)		XII	1257 (628½)	—12
		326			
14.	1034 (517)		XV	1018 (509)	+27
		657 (1857)			
15.	1512		XVI	1506	+ 6
		298			
16.	1272		XII	1257	+21
		502			
17.	1700		XI	1700	0
		250			
18.	1472		O	1464	+ 9
		524			
19.	1992		XXII	1974	+15
		397			
20.	1584		II	1602	—22
		697			
21.	2368		III	2372	— 2
		300			

No. of tube	Vibration-figure	Interval in cents	Step of the cycle of blown fifths		Deviations in cents
22.	1992		XXII	1974	+15
		508			
23.	2672		XXI	2668	+ 2
		508			
24.	1992		XXII	1974	+15
		686			
25.	2760		XIV	2752	+ 4
		489			
26.	2232		XVII	2228	+ 3

This pan-pipe uses, therefore, the following steps of the cycle:

XI	XII	XIII	XIV	XV	XVI	XVII	XVIII	XIX	XX	XXI	XXII	O	I	II	III
17	16	4	1	14	10	11	7	5	2	23	19	6	3	20	21
	13	9	8		15	26					22	18			
		12	25								24				

On examining sequences of tones such as the above, we must indeed be led to wonder whether it was so impossible, after all, even in those remote times, to attain to the construction of a cycle such as we are dealing with, for the construction of the proto-type of a pan-pipe like this Andean one is hardly feasible without the preliminary knowledge of the complete cycle of fifths.

For that matter: even if there had been unsurmountable difficulties of a practical nature in the way of tuning the tones by way of overblowing and then lowering them each time by one or two octaves — seeing that there were such a large number of steps to run through — then there was still a second method to arrive at an equivalent result: we possesss data which show that, in addition to the acoustical method discussed, there existed another, metrical method, which consisted of giving each subsequent tube either 3/4 or 4/3 of the preceding one's length. In this way, too, a chain of fifths was obtained each slightly smaller than a pure fifth.

This possibility has been taken in consideration also by VON HORNBOSTEL, towards the end of his life. In a letter dated May 12, 1935, we read:

„Ich glaube jetzt eigentlich, dass es im alten China den in der Litteratur ausschliesslich beschriebenen **metrischen** Quintenzirkel auch in der Praxis gegeben hat. Wenn man nämlich Röhren (von konstantem Durchmesser) nach dem Rezept 1, × 3/4, × 4/3 usw. schneidet, so werden die Quinten ebenfalls zu eng und zwar (wie ich einmal durch einen flüchtigen Versuch überzeugt habe) etwa im gleichen Verhältnis wie beim überblasen. Für das Verhältnis des metrischen zum Blasquintenzirkel (BZQ) sind verschiedene Annahmen möglich: 1°. der BZQ ist älter, der metrische Zirkel erst von den Theoretikern eingeführt und dann neben oder statt den BQZ verwendet; 2°. der metrische Quintenzirkel ist älter, und erst in der Praxis durch den bequemeren BZQ ersetzt worden (dies könnte sogar erst ausserhalb Chinas bei Völkern geschehen sein, die keinen Maassstab und keine Längenmessung kannten); 3°. = 1°. plus 2°., d.h., der BQZ hat zu allen Zeiten bei den Praktikern vorgeherrscht, ist nur zeitweise in den gelehrten Kreisen durch den metr. QZ. ersetzt worden, ganz analog wie es mit den bequemen Körpermaassen (Fuss, Fingerbreite, Spanne usw.) und den normierten Maassen der Fall war. Diese letzte Hypothese ist mir persönlich die wahrscheinlichtste." [1])

However this may be, Father P. Rozing S.V.D. came forward, in 1946, with a rather plausible argument in support of the theory that it would be quite possible to construe at least the majority of the scale-structures referred to above, without having a complete cycle of blown fifths at one's disposal at all.

Father Rozing's reasoning is as follows:

We may regard the existence of the octave-interval as a primary fact, since it arises in a natural way from the simultaneous singing by men and women, whose voices usually move at an octave's distance:

I	I'
0	1200 C.

By overblowing a stopped flute one obtains the — too flat — twelfth of the tonic (1878 C), which, when brought back into the octave, yields the blown fifth of 678 C. We then obtain the following tone-sequence:

I		II		I'	
0		678		1200 C.	
	678		522		=1200 C.

1) „As a matter of fact, I now believe that, in ancient China, the **metrical** cycle of fifths which alone is described in the literature, must also have existed in musical practice. For, if we cut down tubes (of constant diameter) according to the recipe 1, × 3/4, × 4/3, etc. etc., the fifths also become too small, and, in effect — as I discovered one day by a more or less superficial experiment — in approximately the same proportion as by overblowing. Different assumptions are possible in regard to the relation between the metrical cycle and the cycle of blown fifths (CBF): (a) the CBF is older, and the metrical one was introduced only by theorists, when it was used either in the place of, or side by side with, the CBF; (b) the metrical cycle is older, and was replaced only in practice because the CBF was easier (this, indeed, might well first have been the case with peoples outside China, who lacked standards by which to measure lengths); (c) = (a) plus (b), i.e. the CBF has prevailed at all times amongst practical musicians, being replaced only as time went on, in learned circles, by the metrical CF in a way quite analogous to the simpler measurements based on the body (foot, span, finger-width, etc.) relatively to normalized ones. This latter hypothesis appears the most probable to me personally."

When applying the same process again, but starting, this time, from tone II, we get the blown fifth of the first blown fifth, and this, within the scale-compass, will be placed between tones I and II, at a distance of 156 C from tone No. I (for, 678 + 678 — 1200 = 156 C)::

I		II		III		I'	
0		156		678		1200 C.	
	156		522		522		=1200 C.

So long as these tones were used only for the purpose of giving signals, or to accentuate dance-steps, they were quite adequate as such. For the purpose of melody-forming, however, the two distances of a blown fourth (522 C.) are rather too great. There was every reason, therefore, to fill up these fourths by means of an intermediate tone. This filling up of structural intervals may still be observed to this day among primitive peoples, e.g. the North Papua tribes. [1])

The smaller intervals aimed at may be obtained in two ways, **i.e.** either on the „consonance-principle" (the intervals already obtained came into being in this way) or on the „distance-principle" — in this case, by halving both fourths. Instances of the halving of fourths have also been found — as we saw above (p. 8, footnote) — among primitive peoples in our own time.

When halving the two fourths in question we obtain the following scale:

I		II		III		IV		V		I'	
0		156		412		678		939		1200 C.	
	156		261		261		261		261		=1200 C.

which is the very scale referred to above (p. 10) under the name of **primitive slendro,** and which, as we have seen, is still found on certain **gamelans miring** in Bajanegara and in Central Africa.

The heptatonic scale may also be explained by means of the course of development described above. We begin at the stage where the following tone-distances were available:

I		II		III		I'	
0		156		678		1200 C	
	156		522		522		=1200 C.

Now instead of following, from this point, the „distance-principle", as we did in the case of sléndro, we adhere to the „consonance-principle". On overblowing a stopped tube with a pitch equal to tone No. II, we obtain

---

[1]) Cf. Kunst, **A Study on Papuan Music** (1930).

a tone which, when lowered by an octave, yields a blown fifth lying 156 C above step No. III (678). In the same way, another blown fifth may be derived from this newly-obtained tone (834 C. above step No. I), whose position will be 312 C (i.e. 834 + 678 — 1200 C) above tone I. From the latter, in its turn, a blown fifth may be derived, which will take its place in the sequence at 990 C. above step No. I (for 312+678 =990 C); and finally, from the last-named blown fifth, a step whose position will be at a distance of 468 (=990+678—1200 C) from step No. I. In other words, in order to obtain this new tone-sequence we simply apply the overblowing process another four times, i.e. six times in all. The result, then, will be the following scale:

I	II	III	IV	V	VI	VII	I'	
0	156	312	468	678	834	990	1200 C	
156	156	156	210	156	156	210		= 1200 C.

i.e. the pélog-scale which, as we have seen, is constructed out of seven succeeding fifths of the cycle of blown fifths.

It is, of course, possible to carry on with this method of generating fifths, as has been done here six times, still further. The result will then be a series of intervals of 156 C. If we hold on to the principle of „limitation to the octave" — which was the initial idea in this line of thought — we shall get a series of seven steps of 156 C, followed by one of 108 C. And this is the „Umschichtreihe" (alternating series of tones) in the purest form which, therefore, in this line of reasoning, is a **younger** scaleform than either real pélog or sléndro (miring).

Modern sléndro may also be derived in a similarly simple manner, namely, from the „Umschichtreihe" just mentioned:

156 156 156 | 156 156 156 | 156 108

468 | 468 | 264

234 234 | 234 234 | 264

which amounts, after all, to a halving of two intervals which are too large for melodic construction (distance-principle), in the same way as we supposed it to be the case in the construction of the **sléndro miring** scale.

The generation theory expounded above has the following advantages as compared to that given previously:

(1) it is simpler, more feasible psychologically, and substantiated by examples from present-day musical practice;

(II) both the fifth-interval and the octave are present from the start, and are not obtained, as in the case of the pélog-fifths, only afterwards by means of the interchange of male and female tones. Father ROZING is of opinion that one may well conceive the existence, in higher forms of culture, of tone-sequences constructed without the aid of these two fundamental intervals; but in the case of more or less primitive peoples this is less probable, and still less in this particular case in which the fifth-interval, according to our supposition, constitutes the foundation of the entire tonal system;

(III) finally there is the most important point that this presentation of the evolution of the scale does not require any previous acqaintance with a complete cycle of blown fifths, which is too complicated a structure to assume it to have been present when these tonal systems were first generated. It is, however, quite possible that, later on, when all these different tonal sequences were available, the construction of such a cycle was próceeded to, just as the Chinese, and the Greeks, came to the construction and calculation of the Pythagorean cycle.

At the same time, however, we should remark that no explanation is given in Father ROZING's line of thought for the structure of medium sléndro, with the following steps:

264 204 264 204 264,

which, in our exposition of the matter, is the result of bringing together into a single octave five tones lying at distances of six blown fifths each time (**vide** above, p. 11).

We may draw attention to the fact that, both in the course of development described by Father ROZING and in our explanation, sléndro and pélog were correlated in the beginning, i.e. before they became individualized into the sequences indicated by their respective names. Sléndro — both in one of its pre-stages and its modern form — assumes its typical structure by transferring at a given moment from the consonance- to the distance-principle, whereas pélog (as well as the „Umschichtreihe") is typified by the fact that it remains true to the consonance-principle.

Now what are the objections raised during the last few years against VON HORNBOSTEL's theory?

Dr. BUKOFZER's criticism [1]) may be summarized as follows:

---

[1]) a) **Präzisonsmessungen an primitiven Musikinstrumenten** („Zeitschrift für Physik" Vol. 99, p. 643 et seq.), 1936;
b) **Kann die „Blasquintentheorie" zur Erklärung exotischer Tonsysteme beitragen?"** („Anthropos" Vol. 32, p. 241 et seq.), 1937.

(I) the blown fifth is a variable magnitude and does not always measure **678** C. It is now a pure fifth, now too large or too small. This depends on the length of the tube and its diameter. The manner of blowing may also make difference.

(II) The **huang chong**, says Dr. B., produces a tone of about 357 v. d., and **not** one of 366 v. d.

(III) It is not possible to realize a cycle of blown fifths in the manner indicated.

(IV) The course of development of sléndro is much too complicated.

(V) When, as is the case in modern sléndro, the distance between the theoretically possible steps is taken so small, that the octave is made to contain no fewer than 46 tones (i.e. the 23 blown fifths-degrees and the same number of intermediary tones — see above p. 12), while a deviation of circa **13** C., in both directions is allowed for, not only all the tones of a sléndro-, but of **any** scale whatsoever are bound to find their equivalent in such a theoretical sequence of tones. For, in this case, the distance between the respective theoretical tones would then be no more than **1200** : 46 = **26** C = **2** × **13** C.

Against this reasoning I would submit the following arguments.

Ad (I). Although the blown fifth is admittedly variable, and, broadly speaking, decreases in range according as the fundamental tone is a higher one, I have recently found, when measuring those of several pan-pipes, that the majority of the blown fifths produced on stopped tubes of average length (i.e. between 20 and 30 cm) were definitely smaller than the pure fifth (**702** C), and generally ranged roundabout **670—690** C; in other words, that VON HORNBOSTEL, in fixing the blown fifth of these tubes, in the middle register, at an average of **678** C, perfectly well knew what he was doing.

Ad (II). My own experiments showed further that the **huang chong** (366 v.d.), produced **by oral blowing** into a stopped tube with a wall-thickness of 1 mm and **with an inside diameter of 8.12 mm, as indicated by prince Chai Yü,** [1]) requires an air-column length of exactly the Chinese metrical norm of 230 mm (while its blown fifth turned out to be **689** C). Until, therefore, my own measurements are proved to have been incorrect, I feel compelled to adhere to my conviction that VON HORNBOSTEL was right, and that some error must have crept into Dr. B.'s experiments and calculations, however seemingly accurate they may have been.

And, indeed, there **are** mistakes to be found in his treatise **„Präzisionsmessungen** etc.". First and foremost: the experimental tubes measured by him to test the relation between the metrical norm and the fundamental tone, have a too large diameter, i.e. of 11—19 mm (mostly

---

[1]) **Vide** MAURICE COURANT, **Essai historique sur la musique classique des Chinois** (in LAVIGNAC, Encyclopédie de la Musique, Vol. I), p. 91.

12 mm) instead of 8.12 mm. No wonder, therefore, that the results obtained do not coincide with VON HORNBOSTEL's theory and my own experiments.

[Apart from this cardinal error, I noted one more small inaccuracy — such as slip through now and then in everybody's work — viz. on p. 661 of his treatise, where Dr. B., in the second column of the table erroneously mentions the vibrationnumbers obtained **by calculation,** instead of the intended numbers obtained **by means of blowing with the mouth** (cf. p. 649 op. cit.)].

Ad (III) and (IV). It should be clear that the objections raised under these numbers are for the most part satisfactorily dealt with by Father ROZING's approach to the problem, while, for the rest, the existence of pan-pipes of the type which we have described on p. 19/20 shows that the said objections are not perhaps so unsurmountable as Dr. B. appears to believe.

Ad (V). Finally, as regards the argument under this number, Dr. B.'s remark is admittedly quite justified, but he forgets an other, in this connection far more important, element, which to my mind invalidates his argument, viz. **the regularity** with which the tones of the sléndro-scale fit into the theoretical sequences. By this I mean that, in a large number of cases, the tones of the scales compared do **not** coincide **at random** with certain tones here or there in the theoretical sequence, but, as we have seen, invariably with such tones as are placed **at equal mutual distances from each other** (for primitive sléndro **vide** p. 10; for medium sléndro p. 11, and for modern sléndro p. 12, above).

The same applies **ceteris paribus** to the pélog-scales (cf. p. 5—9).

With this I believe that also this objection, so weighty at first blush, has been set at nought.

I may add in this connection that (a) although it is doubtless possible, theoretically and in a laboratory, to get tubes such as are described here to produce musical sounds by different methods, in actual playing practice a tube was made to sound exclusively **by the mouth,** while there was **only one particular position of the lips** that allowed of the sound being produced well on any particular tube; (b) that the tones obtained in this manner are susceptible only between extremely narrow limits to being driven up by means of increased pressure of breath before jumping up to the twelfth, and (c) that, once the fundamental tone of a tube has been blown, it is **not** necessary (as Dr. B. pretends it is) to alter the position of the mouth in order to produce this twelfth.

* * *

Whereas, therefore, BUKOFZER's criticism in both his articles mentioned was purily negative — for he merely contends that the theory of blown fifths can never have been the foundation of the scales in the respect of which VON HORNBOSTEL imagined to be able to show it to be — Miss SCHLESINGER goes further.

In her stout volume [1]) she gives a wealth of material from which she concludes that a large number of exotic scales are identical with different ancient Grecian **auloi**-tunings **(harmoniai).** Miss SCHLESINGER's argument — although rightly criticized on some points by the Dutch physicists Prof. Dr. A. D. FOKKER and Dr. E. J. DIJKSTERHUIS — gives the impression of being very thorough and learned, and — it must be admitted — the parallelism between the Greek **harmoniai,** as reconstructed by her and the exotic scales measured, is apparently quite as convincing as that between the same tonal sequences and the hypothetical cycle of blown fifths. But when, after this, she comes to the conclusion that the Grecian scales are **foundational** to the other ones [2]), one is inclined to wonder why the relation between the different musical systems should necessarily be of this nature. Is it not more feasible to assume, as VON HORNBOSTEL does, that both the Greek and those other scales have their common origin in a primitive system whose genesis lies hidden in ages long past? For, is this not also the explanation of the correlation between other ancient Grecian and f.i. ancient Hindu-,,Aryan" cultural phenomena, such as religious and philosophic notions, the structure of the language, etc.? [3])

This, however, is to say that, also after Miss SCHLESINGER's discovery, we have not got much further as regards finding an other explanation of the correspondence (both relative and as regards absolute pitch) between the scales of races and peoples so different and living so far apart.

* * *

In another treatise, however, which, owing to war conditions, did not come to my notice until quite recently, Dr. BUKOFZER attempts to give, indeed, such another explanation of the genesis and development of Javanese tonal systems. [4])

He summarizes his argument in the following six points:

(1) The fourth has been shown to be the structural interval in the Pélog and Munggang systems. Thus, the older stratum of Javanese music has something in common with ancient Greek, Japanese, and (to some extend) even American music.

---

[1]) **The Greek aulos** (London 1939).

[2]) Ibid. p. 291: ,,the harmoniai of ancient Greece, as a survival or a rebirth, in the music of the folk of many nations";

p. 334: ,,the harmoniai as origin of the musical system of Java and also of Indonesia generally".

[3]) Cf., amongst others, H. G. RAWLINSON, **India and Greece** in ,,Indian Art and Letters", Vol. X, p. 57; CURT SACHS, **The Rise of Music in the Ancient World East and West,** p. 209.

[4]) **The evolution of Javanese tone-systems** (in ,,Papers read at the Intern. Congress of Musicology, held at New-York Sept. 11th to 16th, 1939", p. 241 et seq.) (1944).

(II) If we explain the Sléndro system as being derived from the Pélog scale we must conclude that some of the tone names were transferred from the older system to the younger. This is confirmed by the fingering of the **suling.**

(III) The size of the steps selected from Pélog fits in with a regular sléndro scale.

(IV) The tones in Pélog and Sléndro often coincide even in pitch.

(V) This coincidence is partly known to the Javanese under the term of **tumbuk.**

(VI) The etymology of the word Sléndro enables us to determine the age and the chronology of the Sléndro system.

I must confess that Dr. B.'s argument has failed to convince me.

In the first place I cannot agree with Dr. B. in his derivation of pélog from the three-tone munggang scale. He argues that these munggang scales vary in range between a fourth and a major third, and that, providing one leaves out of consideration the lowest tone of the present pélog scales, one may represent those scales as consisting of the doubling of a munggang tonal sequence, i.e. by two conjoint munggang-„tetrachords". which would then represent, from high to low, the two sets of three tones **bem-nem-lima** and **lima-ḍaḍa-gulu,** respectively.

Dr. B. bases his argument on the measurements, as known to him, of the interval-sequences of munggang-scales, of which he asserts that there are **thirteen** in all. I wonder by what road Dr. B. arrives at this number. I believe I am acquainted with the whole of the existing literature dealing with Javanese music; Dr. B. was never in Java; and in the fifteen years during which I had the privilege of investigating Javanese music on the spot I never came across more than **six** three-toned munggang-scales, either optically, or auditively. Neither do I believe that there are any more; but there do exist a number of other three-toned orchestras, viz. **six** gamelans Koḍok ngorèk, and **one** so called gamelan Patalon. Only by including these can we bring the number up to thirteen. The scale-intervals of ten of these gamelans may be found in Table XVI of my „Toonkunst van Bali", Vol. II, and in „De Toonkunst van Java", Vol. I, pp. 197, 199 and 200.

Now, if we examine the steps of the ten three-tone sequences, of which I noted the vibration-numbers — the same from which Dr. B. derives his argument — we shall see that there are only **two,** or, if we stretch a point, **three,** of them which may be said to supply more or less the interval distances which Dr. B. needs for substantiating his explanation of the pélog scale. For it is only in the case of the gamelan Koḍok ngorèk in the Jogja kraton, in that of the Munggang in the Solo kraton, and, at a pinch, in that of the gamelan Koḍok ngorèk in the Jogja kepatihan, that a conjoint doubling as referred to by Dr. B. leaves room for a lower tone **bem** lying at the right distance; i.e. the tone with which the pélog octave — looked at from low to high — begins, and without which the pélog sequence would not be a pélog sequence at all; which amounts to saying that only in the three cases named above does this tone **bem** form, with the next higher tone **gulu,** an interval of about normal size (**110—120** C). In these three cases we get the following pélog octave structure:

	bem[1]	**gulu**	**bem**
Munggang, kraton Solo,	2×**558** C	+**124** C	=**1200** C
Koḍok ngorèk, kraton Jogja	2×**532**	+**136**	„
Koḍok ngorèk, kepatihan Jogja	2×**520**	+**160**	„

In three other cases the „residue"-interval **gulu-bem** turns out much too great:

	bem[1]	**gulu**	**bem**
Patalon, kraton Solo	2×**510**	+**180**	=**1200** C
Munggang, kraton Jogja	2×**494**	+**212**	„
Munggang Sèngkang turunan from the Mangku Nagaran, Solo	2×**490**	+**220**	„

whilst in the remaining four there is not even any question of a residue-interval; nay, in three of these four cases the doubling of the three-tone scale **itself** already reaches above the close of the octave!:

	bem[1]	**gulu**	**bem**
Koḍok ngorèk II, kraton Solo	2×**600** C	**0** C	=**1200** C
Munggang Segara windu, Mangku Nagaran, Solo	2×**608**	—**16**	
Munggang, Madiun	2×**613**	—**26**	
Koḍok ngorèk, kraton Solo	2×**621**	—**42**	

The structure of the three-tone scales which have thus far become known, therefore, does not justify any attempt to base upon it, in the way Dr. B. has indicated, the genesis of the pélog scale.

But even if the measurements of the interval-sequences of the three-tone ensembles mentioned should have yielded a majority of intervals of the size required to support Dr. B.'s presentation of the case — **quod non** — even then his theory would not, in my opinion, hold water. For, what are the facts?

In order to make acceptable the genesis of the pélog scale from two conjoint munggang-„tetrachords", the lowest tone of the pélog scale (the **bem**), as we have already mentioned, is represented as having been added later, and this notion is supported by the contention that, in many pélog tone-sequences, the (second) tone **gulu,** and not the **bem** „actually dilimits the scale". I am at a loss to understand how Dr. B. arrives at this pronouncement. The tone **bem** is quite as essential to the pélog scale as all the other tones, more especially the **gulu, ḍaḍa, lima** and **nem.** It should also not be forgotten that the other name for **bem** is **penunggul,** i.e. „head". This is not a name for a tone that has been added, as it were, on second thought! Moreover, I have never, as far as I can remember, come across any pélog-instruments or -scales delimited by the tone **gulu** in all the fifteen years of my sojourn in Java.

On the single-octave pélog instruments, on the other hand, the tone **bem**[1], finishing the octave at the „top" (and indispensable if the pélog sequence should actually have arisen from two conjoint munggang-tetrachords), hardly ever occurs; only a single case of this is known to me, namely in the Madurese gamelan, whose tuning I was able to measure at the time at Kedawung in East-Java. [1])

To say the least it gives one to think, before accepting Dr. B.'s theory as correct, that, for the sake of his argumentation, he disavows as it were the tone **bem** as a pélog scale-tone, but is evidently, at the same time, unable to do without it for the construction of his tetrachords, which, according to him, are foundational to the pélog-scale.

Ad (III) and (IV). Without any doubt there exists a certain interrelation between pélog and sléndro, namely, as may have become clear from the above, between their respective semi-fourths phases (cf. p. 8 **sub** (b) and p. 10 **sub** (c)). We shall find that it is the 6th and 7th step which the semi-fourths pélog **does** and the semi-fourths sléndro **does not** use, that actually take the position of **gulu** and **lima,** respectively, when put in their proper places in the pélog tone-sequence.

As long as this semi-fourths sléndro — now become so rare, and, it appears, confined to a few „islands" in East-Java [2]) — was the generally used form, the playing of a suling pélog whose 2nd and 5th stop was kept closed, would result in a perfectly satisfying sléndro scale. This is, of course, no longer to today, because another form of sléndro has taken the place of the semi-fourths form, which latter, having consequently been degraded to sléndro **miring,** „deviating" sléndro, has fallen in decline.

The result if this is that, when — at any rate in the Principalities — a sléndro tone-sequence is imitated today on a suling pélog in the manner indicated, this is only done for the purpose of obtaining a comical effect.

In the Sunda districts — where the people are not unduly particular, at any rate instrumentally speaking, and where ancient forms and customs are blessed with a longer life than elsewhere in Java, notably in Central Java with its much greater cultural creativeness — this type of sléndro scale, played on a suling pélog is taken more seriously today; nevertheless it is admitted there too, that only an **approximation** to the now customary sléndro scale is thereby obtained.

But **tumbuk,** mentioned in point (v), in my opinion cannot be adduced

---

[1]) Cf. **De Toonkunst van Java,** Vol. I, p. 208, scale No. 1.
[2]) **Ibid.** Vol. I, p. 18 and 19.

in support of the theory that sléndro must have been derived from pélog, better: that there is a genetic connexion between both systems. For **tumbuk** is favoured nearly exclusively [1]) for the sake of the considerable saving of bronze resulting from it. It occurs, besides, comparatively rarely, and then, moreover, far more frequently in the form of tumbuk **lima** (this effecting a still greater saving of bronze) than of tumbuk **nem** — the only form Dr. B. mentions — (or, for that matter, tumbuk **jongga**). [2]) Moreover: in the **case** of tumbuk no more than one single tone is ever involved; and surely it is plain that the common possession of **one** tone is in itself no evidence whatsoever of any relationship existing between two scales!

The author's argument on p. 242 of his paper is not quite clear to me. He there speaks of **three** sorogan, although he states just before that there exist only **two**; the tone **pélog** as a substitute for **ḍaḍa,** and the tone **barang** for **bem.** (In reality there are **two** sorogan **in each paṭet,** namely in P. 6 the tones **pélog** and **barang**; in P. barang the tones **bem** and **pélog**; in P. 5 (originally) the tones **ḍaḍa** and **barang).** As third sorogan, however, Dr. B. adds the tone **bem,** and then he states that the relative position of these three sorogan have been interpreted by me as tonic, dominant and subdominant, respectively. I am unable to find any place in my writings where I could have represented the relation between those sorogan-tones and, for that matter, between any sorogan-tones, in a way justifying such an interpretation. It may be that Dr. B. had in mind the schematic representation of the pélogscales, given on p. 32 of „De Toonkunst van Java"; but in that case it is not the tones **pélog, barang,** and **bem,** which would seem to play the role of tonic, but the tones **pélog (a+), bem (e)** and **lima (b),** respectively.

Neither is Dr. B.'s representation of the three principal pélog paṭet-scales (p. 242) quite accurate.

When we reproduce them, in the usual European way, from low to high, [3]) we do not obtain the sequences named by Dr. B., but the following (and with the sorogan-tones placed in brackets):

in paṭet barang:	b	c	d–	(e)	f+	g	(a+)
in paṭet nem:	e	f+	g	(a+)	b	c	(d–)
in paṭet lima:	a+	b	c	(d–)	e	f+	(g).

And these scales definitely lie — irrespective of Dr. B.'s view — at distances of a (pélog-)**fifth** from each other:

[1]) Perhaps, in some rare cases, also for „modulation" from sléndro to pélog, or **vice versa.** Cf. **De Toonkunst van Java,** Vol. I, p. 66 sub C.

[2]) Ibid. Vol. I p. 113, footnote. The three forms of **tumbuk** which I have mentioned, i.e. **nem, lima** and **jongga** are the only existing ones.

[3]) They ought really to be given, in the proper Javanese manner, from high to low, and starting with the most important tone, the **dasar** (the „pivotal" tone), being the tone **ḍaḍa (g)** in P. barang, the **nem (c)** in P. nem and the **gulu (f+)** in P. lima.

P. barang: b c d^- (e) f^+ g (a^+)
P. nem: e f^+ g (a^+) b c (d^-)
P. lima: a^+ b c (d^-) e f^+ (g)

The same applies, **ceteris paribus,** to the three sléndro-patet's.

It therefore appears to me that the construction which Dr. B. puts on the matter is far from being supported by the facts which the study of Javanese music has revealed.

Having regard to all this, I believe I am justified in affirming that we are not allowed to speak of any structure of **fourths** as being the basis of the Javanese tonal systems, and that we may well adhere to a presentation of the facts in which the **fifth** is regarded as the generative element **par excellence** [1]). This is also in complete accordance with the view of Javanese musicians themselves, as is evident, for example, from the writings of Radèn MACHYAR ANGGA KUSUMADINATA [2]).

But perhaps we must distinguish here, in some cases at least, [3]) between pélog as a mere tone-sequence, and pélog as it is used melodically. Prof. Dr. J. HANDSCHIN, the Basle musicologist, who read my objections against the theory of Dr. BUKOFZER, wrote to me in this connexion:

„Ich glaube, ich würde hier mehr unterscheiden zwischen Pélog als Material-Tonleiter and Pélog als musikalischer Tonleiter. In letzterer Hinsicht ist es doch oft so, dass der Ton **f** (entschuldigen Sie, wenn ich **gulu** so vereinfacht bezeichne) die untere Grenze der Melodie bildet und dass die Melodie quartenmässig aufgebaut ist...... Darum akzeptiere ich aber doch auch die konkrete Ableitung von BUKOFZER nicht, oder vielmehr: ich brauche es nicht zu tun. Es ist durchaus nicht nötig, dass die Pélog Material-Leiter durch Aneinanderfügung von zwei Munggang-Quarten entstanden ist, und doch kann musikalisch (musikalisch nicht nur vom europäischen sondern auch vom javanischen Standpunkt aus) die Quart hier grundlegend sein. Auch die Ableitung von Sléndro aus Pélog durch Weglassen von Tönen ist wahrscheinlich zu mechanisch, und doch tritt auch in Sléndro musikalisch ein Einfluss der Quarte entschieden in die Erscheinung" [4]).

---

[1]) See, about fifth-relation, f.i. **De Toonkunst van Java,** Vol. I, p. 37, 47/8 (finales), 58/9 (patet's), 284 (melodic structure) and 327/8 („pivotal" tones).

[2]) **Djadjar mamaos** (rakitan pèlog), Vol. I (1929), II (1930); (rakitan slèndro), Vol. I (1930); **Sarining Gentra Murangkalih** (pèlog sarèng salèndro) 1935).

[3]) For, without doubt, the melodic structure is based far more often on the fifth-relation. Cf., f.i., **De Toonkunst van Java,** Vol. II, Appendix 53.

[4]) „I think I would prefer, in this case, to distinguish between pélog as „tone-material", and pélog as a name for a musical scale. For, if one looks at it from the latter angle, one often finds that the tone *f* (excuse my using this simplified designation of the tone **gulu**) forms the lower limit of the melody, and that the melody is constructed on the basis of fourths.... For this reason I do not accept, however, BUKOFZER's too direct deduction, or rather, I do not need to accept it. There is absolutely no need for the pélog scalar material to have originated from the joining together of two munggang fourths; musically speaking (not only from the European, but also from the Javanese standpoint), the fourth can just the same be the fundamental structural principle. Moreover, the derivation of sléndro from pélog by omitting certain tones is probably also too mechanical a procedure; nevertheless, in sléndro melodics, too, the influence of the fourth is quite apparent".

Ad (vi). Now granting that both pélog and sléndro are based on the cycle of blown fifths, and granting, further, that the word **sléndro** may actually be said, on etymologically incontestable grounds, to derive from **Çailéndra** (the name of the princely dynasty ruling in Central Java during the 8th century A.D.), then this **cannot** mean that sléndro only **came into being** in Java during the period, and at the instigation of these Çailéndras (as Dr. B. endeavours to demonstrate), but only that it was **imported** there by them, and subsequently — through their influence — attained musical hegemony. [1])

There are, however, still other possibilities to be examined in this connexion.

There is first of all Dr. STUTTERHEIM'S suggestion that sléndro might possibly be the specifically **Javanese** tonal system, and pélog that of the **Sundanese,** who very probably arrived in Java at an earlier period (and of the Balinese and different other archipelago peoples). In that case the derivation of the name sléndro from Çailéndra, which Dr. STUTTERHEIM also considers probable, would have its origin in the circumstance that the central sléndro territory was one and the same as that over which the Javanese Çailéndras ruled during the period of its greatest prosperity and influence. It would then be only the **name** sléndro that arose in the eighth century.

In the third place I must also make mention here of the view of Dr. NYESSEN concerning the racial composition of the population of Java, which, according to this anthropologist, differs in the mountain districts from that in the plains. Dr. NYESSEN comes to the conclusion, based on an examination of more than 10.000 men, that the population of Java consists of:

I. earlier arrivals: a mesophalic, low browed, Proto-Malay mountain population, also characterized by shorter stature, broader nose and light brown eyes, and

II. later arrivals: a brachycephalic, Deutero-Malay lowland population, characterized by taller stature, higher brow, thinner nose and dark brown eyes.

The above division cuts across the other, usual division of the Javanese population into a Sundanese group, a Javanese proper, and a Madurese.

It would seem to me, then, that pélog (which, today, is chiefly limited

---

[1]) And in that case the other (and, in my view, genetically younger) sléndro forms — distinguished in the above as „medium" and „modern", respectively — must also have been known in Java as early as the 8th century A.D., side-by-side with the semi-fourths form. For the structure of these forms, too, presupposes a knowledge either of the cycle of blown fifths or of the corresponding **metrical** cycle of fifths (cf. above, p. 20/21); and it is hardly safe to assume that this ancient Java, only the merest superficies of which had been touched by Hindu culture by that time, could have been familiar with these typical forms of high culture.

to the mountain districts [1]), having been pressed back by the invaders), belonged originally to group I, and sléndro to group II.

(According to this notion too, the priority of pélog in Java is not affected).

Finally there are some minor points:

1°. Dr. B.'s remark that sléndro contains no minór seconds (p. 243) applies exclusively to the sléndro system as played on the majority of Javanese gamelans. The two other sléndro modes — chiefly used vocally— **madenda** and **degung,** quite definitely do make use of such semi-tone steps. [2])

2°. **Pélog bem** is not identical with **pélog nem**; by the former name the paṭet's **nem and lima** are denoted collectively, in contradistinction to paṭet **barang.** The reason for this distinction is, that Central-Javanese gamelans use to-day, both in the paṭet's nem and lima, as principal scale, the same tonal sequence, which deviates from the principal scale, as used in paṭet barang.

3°. Why does not Dr. B. give the correct vibration values (bottom of p. 247) for the tuning of the gendèr Kyahi Udan riris in the Mangku Nagaran, namely 340, 394, 448, 513 and 587, respectively? If he had done this, then the correspondence between this sléndro sequence and five tones of the scale of the Kyahi Kadok manis pélog of the Solonese kraton, which he compares with it, would have looked even more convincing. [3])

4°. The statement that the term **paṭet** is derived from the Sanskrit word **pat** (more correctly, **path)** definitely must be refuted.

Our linguistic co-worker, Drs. R. MELLEMA, whom I consulted in regard to this question, informed me as follows:

The word **paṭet** makes the **prima facie** impression of being of purily Javanese origin, which impression is further strengthened by the fact that it occurs as a verb in the form of **maṭet (dipaṭet),** meaning:

(I) holding on (tightly) to a rope;

(II) (colloquially): to stand taut, to pull at a rope;

(III) (obsolete): to restrain, to contain (also figurative);

(IV) (in certain districts only): to shorten, cut down. [4])

The word would not seem to occur in ancient Javanese; at any rate neither JUYNBOLL, **Oud-Javaansch Woordenboek,** nor VAN DER TUUK, **Kawi-Balineesch Woordenboek,** mentions it.

Sanskrit knows the following:

(I) the root **paṭ (paṭati)** =to split, to burst open;

(II) the root **pat (patati)** =to fall, to drop down, to collapse;

---

[1]) Cf. **De Toonkunst van Java,** Vol. II, Appendices 58A and B.

[2]) **Vide De Toonkunst van Java,** Vol. I, p. 41 and 42.

[3]) The source of those tone-sequences is not **De Toonkunst van Java,** but **De Toonkunst van Bali.**

[4]) Cf. PIGEAUD, **Javaans-Nederlands Handwoordenboek,** p. 264.

(III) the root **path,** with the substantives **pathi** and **patha** =path, road, method, manner.

Of these three roots, the first two are obviously ineligible for our purpose. The root **path,** which Dr. B. has in mind, does not exist in ancient Javanese. But even if it did, it would not bring us any further, because it is phonetically impossible for an aspirated **tenuis (th)** to be converted into a lingual **ṭ** (indicated, in our system of transcription, for convenience sake and from lack of suitable symbols, by **ṭ,** but in reality a totally different sound from **th).**

Moreover, the first syllabe of the Javanese **paṭet** can never function as root, since it would be impossible to explain the rest of the word. The only part of the word which, as Javanese root, could possibly represent the most ancient part, is **ṭet**; and it is obvious that this cannot have anything in common with the Sanskrit **path.**

Thus far Mr. MELLEMA.

As the reader must no doubt have concluded by this time, I am, however regrettably, compelled to disagree with almost every argument on the above subject that my friend and colleague BUKOFZER advances in his three treatises (and in the article on this subject, written by him in APEL's Harvard Dictionary of Music). My only excuse is: **amicus Plato, magis amica veritas.**

For the rest, far be it from me to contend that all the mysteries surrounding the scales at issue and their interrelation are to my mind swept away by VON HORNBOSTEL's theory, nay, it is, indeed, not entirely to be excluded that really this theory is founded on an error, be it a brilliant and fascinating one. But this, however, will then need to be demonstrated with other and stronger arguments than those, stated above.

And further, this cannot be gainsaid: **if** VON HORNBOSTEL's theory one day should turn out to be untenable, it will nevertheless have the great merit of having clarified certain very thorny problems relative to the structure and the correlation of the instrumental scales of various peoples living far apart in time and space. The fate of this theory will then be similar to that of the famous epicycle-theory of PTOLEMY, which gave an adequate explanation of the apparent movements of the heavenly bodies, and which was nevertheless shown later on to be completely false. Sometimes, indeed, scientific knowledge is increased more by means of the error committed by a genius, than by irrefutable truths.

Amsterdam, February 3rd., 1948.

SOME REFLECTIONS ON AUTHENTICITY IN FOLK MUSIC

by

MAUD KARPELES (London)

THE title of my paper, "Some Reflections," is intended to be taken literally because in it I shall be thinking aloud rather than presenting you with well reasoned arguments and conclusions. This is not out of disrespect to my distinguished audience, but on account of the extreme complexity of the subject. Most of us have a general sense of what is and what is not a genuine folk song or folk dance, but there are many border-line cases that are hard to classify, and personally I should find it difficult to state categorically what are the particular musical elements that can be said to constitute authenticity. In any case I think that authenticity must always be a comparative rather than an absolute quality. I hope, however, that I may be able to suggest certain methods of approach, which others better qualified than myself may be tempted to explore further. My aim is to be practical and to discuss what we in the Council can do towards preserving the purity of the folk music that has come down to us.

In discussing the problem we must pre-suppose that there is such a thing as folk music: that it does exist as a specific genre, in spite of the incidence of border-line cases, because otherwise there is no problem to discuss. We must therefore agree on a definition of folk music, so that we have some point of departure. I will not weary you by going over the well-worn ground of controversy relating to origins, or enter into a discussion on the rival merits of the production and reception theories or the validity of the ***versunkenes Kulturgut*** contention. But I will ask you to accept as a working definition, at any rate for the time being, the one that has been so well expounded by Cecil Sharp, Gordon Gerould and many other scholars. That is, "Music that has been submitted through the course of many generations to the process of oral transmission." I am aware that this definition is not completely cast-iron. It has its weak spots which call for qualifying re-inforcement, but in the main, it does allow for the classification of folk music as a specific type and it enables us to draw a distinction between folk music and so-called popular music. Assuming that we accept this definition, we must proceed to examine the manner in which oral transmission operates.

We must first remind ourselves that folk music, although it is a distinctive genre, is nevertheless a branch of the general art of music and it cannot be entirely divorced from it. It differs from art or composed music because of the different manner of its conception. Art music, although it owes something to tradition, is in the main the product of an individual. A musical thought comes to the composer, whether from his inner consciousness or from some extraneous source, no matter. He makes it his own, consciously works on it, develops it and gives it expression. It may take a few hours or a number of years before the composition attains its final form, but its evolution is dependent upon one man (or woman) and the duration of its conception is restricted to the period of the composer's life. Folk music, on the other hand, develops mainly unconsciously. Its evolution is dependent not on one person but on many; its conception is a matter of many generations; and, strictly speaking, it never attains a final form. Folk music has been generated by a different process from art music, and it is by virtue of this process, i.e. oral transmission, that it acquires its distinctive characteristics. But it is not wholly unrelated to art music (composed music is perhaps a better phrase). There have always been mutual borrowings and influences, and folk music that has borrowed from or been influenced by composed music does not necessarily cease to be folk music, provided, of course, that it has been submitted to the process of oral transmission.

Yet when we hear a folk song or see a folk dance that has been subjected to modern influence, the purists amongst us protest that it is not authentic. Are the purists right, and if they are, is there anything that can be accepted as absolute folk music, that is to say, is there any traditional music that has not at some time or other been subject to extraneous influence, whether it be liturgical music, secular composed music, the music of another level of society or of a foreign culture? The point is this: can we accept as genuine and authentic, a song in which we can detect a phrase of music that was composed many years ago, or one which uses the musical idiom of art music of a bygone age, and at the same time exclude songs which are based on modern present-day popular songs?

Let us take a concrete example. Should we or should we not classify as authentic folk song that type of song that is commonly called "hill-billy," and should we admit as authentic the banjo or guitar accompaniment that nowadays so often accompanies folk song—an innovation of probably the last thirty years or so? These songs answer the definition of folk song in that they are acquired by oral transmission, and yet the purists would, I think, say that they are not as authentic as the folk songs that were sung by the people of the southern mountains (as I heard them thirty years ago) without any accompaniment and before they came into touch with modern civilisation, and, above all, before the days of radio. And I think the purists are right. But why? Is there some special virtue in the past that we have lost, so that the evolution of folk music no longer operates as it did formerly? The answer is Yes and No.

Every age has it special problems, and it is perhaps difficult to see things in their right perspective when we are close to them. Had there been folk music experts and folk music societies in the Middle Ages one can imagine that in certain countries they might have gathered together and seriously discussed whether modal tunes cast in the heptatonic scale were not less authentic than pentatonic tunes. But there were no folk music societies then and the fact that there are now is part of the problem.

The point we have to consider is whether oral transmission now works as effectively towards the evolution of folk music as it did formerly. Evolution, I need not remind you, is dependent on continuity, variation and selection: continuity which preserves the tradition; variation which springs from individual creative impulse; and selection which pronounces the verdict of the community. It will, therefore, help us to assess the folk music of the present day if we consider it in relation to the operation of these three factors.

First, continuity, which preserves the tradition. There can be no question that the continuity of the musical life of peasants and country people in many parts of the world has been very seriously disturbed in the last few generations and particularly in the present one. (I speak of peasants and country people. I know that the singing of folk songs is not limited to them, but in the main it is they who are responsible for upholding the tradition.) There has been industrialism which has uprooted people from their accustomed ways of life and severed their association with the land; then general education which has persuaded them to look down on their traditional modes of expression and incidentally has impaired their memories; and lastly there has been the radio, and this perhaps has had the most destructive effect of all, musically, because it has swept like a tide through the lands into the farthermost corners and has submerged the people's traditional art. In former times, folk music was undoubtedly influenced to some extent by the popular music of the day. We know, in fact, of many instances in which popular composed tunes have passed into tradition. But the difference is, I think, that formerly the traditional musician did not take on more than he could assimilate. He was so steeped in the tradition that he had the power of converting extraneous material into his own idiom. But of recent years there has been too great and too sudden a break in the tradition, and the extraneous material has to a great extent acted as a destructive instead of a fructifying force upon traditional forms of expression.

Individual creative impulse, the second element of evolution, which I have termed variation, still operates. Creative impulse is natural and inborn and the untutored artist of to-day will adapt indiscriminately from traditional and from composed sources what he requires for his own needs. And it may be that his adaptations will provide the seeds of future development. There are, I think, signs that this is the case.

Finally, there is the process of selection—the verdict of the community—which accepts or rejects the many variations and deviations and ultimately determines the course of tradition. But we have to remember that the process of selection, as applied to oral transmission, operates in time as well as in space. Oral transmission in space, which may be merely an indication of ephemeral popularity, does not in itself fulfil the qualifications of what, for want of a better word, I will call "folkiness." For that, we have to have oral transmission in time. In other words, folk music is the product of many generations of singers, dancers or instrumentalists. Given the right conditions, it is possible that "hill-billy" and other popular music of to-day might in time become folk. But are the right conditions likely to be fulfilled? That is the question. As far as we can see, modern conditions are such that natural selection cannot operate freely, because it is continuously subjected to interference. In the past, we have seen the damaging effect of interference by the broadside on traditional verse, and in this connection I would refer you to the illuminating chapter on broadsides in Evelyn Wells's recent publication, *The Ballad Tree.** But the influence of the broadside is a very small thing compared with the effect of modern methods of transmitting popular music.

However, we cannot look into the future, and no one can say definitely what the next stage in the evolution of folk music will be.

In the meantime, what of the present? Can we in the Council influence the course of events? We, i.e. the individual members and the folk music societies that we represent, may not be able to do as much as we should like, but we can at least recognise our responsibilities. In these days, folk music, like many other more mundane aspects of life, is not free from planning and organisation; whereas formerly the evolution of folk music was an unconscious matter, there are now conscious agencies at work. There are the many folklore societies that are actively engaged in bringing the songs and dances before the public by means of instruction, social gatherings, performances, festivals and so on. There are the schools that include folk song and folk dance in their curriculum. There are the entertainers of various kinds, including the radio. And finally, there are the individual collectors who publish their material. All this is excellent, of course, provided that it is done with discrimination and a full sense of responsibility. William Allingham, a nineteenth-century collector of ballads, has described the publication of traditional songs as "the quick work (good and evil) of a despotism compared with the gradual result of an old constitutional government." This is an apt analogy which applies not only to publication but to all the other agencies that I have enumerated. Folk music that appears in print, that is heard over the radio, or on the gramophone, or that is taken into the repertoire of an organised society no longer rests entirely on its own merits as it would were it dependent merely upon oral tradition, but it acquires, as it were, a seal of authority which gives it a fictitious value.

We have therefore a great responsibility. Those who have themselves collected from the old generation of singers and dancers and know how much the songs and dances have meant to them will, in particular, appreciate the solemn trust that has been laid upon us. An old Morris dancer from Lancashire, long since dead, once wrote me: I have given to you dances that I have given to no one else, not even my own son, for I know that you will treasure them as much as I do." It goes without saying that we must not falsify the material that we receive from traditional sources. But I think we have a further duty to perform and that is to exercise discrimination in the selection of the material that we present to the public. For, by selecting the best and most authentic folk music, we may in some measure counteract the damaging effects produced by modern conditions.

But here we come back to where we started. On what basis is our selection to be made and what is to be our test of authenticity?

* See review on p. 117.

In this matter, the scholars and experts will be able to give guidance, for a scientific analysis of folk music will to a certain extent show what elements in it are old and what are of recent date; what are indigenous and what come from external sources. But this in itself is not enough. Certainly, it is right that we should pay respect to what has stood the test of time. On the other hand, it would be a mistake to make a fetish of maturity. After all, one of the characteristics of folk music is its agelessness, because it is in its very nature the accumulated expression of all ages including our own. And this brings me to my final reflection.

I think that the ultimate test should be based on artistic grounds. The purest folk music is that which has been submitted to the crucible of tradition, and which emerges as a complete artistic unity. If the modern ingredients in folk music do not stand out as misfits but merge with the older elements so that together they make a satisfying whole, then I think we can be confident that this music has as much claim to authenticity as the music produced by the peasants of some isolated region who have had no contact with modern ways of life.

Dr. Albert Lord (Harvard University), whose interest lay mainly in oral texts, thought that the principles of the study of texts might be transferred to the study of music. He suggested that possibly the essential difference between folk music and composed music was a question of oral composition rather than oral transmission, that is the difference of method between a composer and singer who thinks in terms of notes that have already been fixed and set down and the one who has no fixed pattern in his mind but is going entirely by ear.

Professor Saygun said that the comparative method could be used both with texts and with music.

Professor George Herzog (Indiana University) believed that the most useful criterion of folk material, whether of music, texts or other art forms, lay in the manner of its fashioning through the special techniques of folk tradition; variability, flexibility and constant re-creation. If the material had been subjected to this treatment, then it was "authentic." Were one to restrict the term "authentic" to material which is indigenous to and in the style of the locality, one would meet with overwhelming difficulties. There was no pure race or pure culture, and there were, therefore, no pure folk music styles or traditions. In all folk music there had always been innumerable extraneous influences bringing new material into the repertory of the folk group. Sometimes this new material had been successfully absorbed and sometimes not.

Mr. Lord had offered a stimulating and challenging idea in suggesting that oral composition and its extensive use of formulas is the mark of the technique of an authentic folk tradition. We must bear in mind, however, that composition plays a more prominent role in heroic epic poetry (for instance that of Yugoslavia, which Mr. Lord has investigated) than in folk song at large. We could not with certainty generalise about folk song on the basis of the heroic epic tradition.

Dr. Herzog, commenting on Miss Karpeles' paper, said that she had given a concise and lucid statement on authenticity in folk music and on the whole he was in agreement with her. We had, however, to admit that this view of authenticity was dependent on the exercise of our own taste and sense of values and it implied a subjective judgment. This was not necessarily wrong, but we must be aware of the implications.

Miss Karpeles said that Dr. Herzog had put his finger on the weak spot of her argument. It was perfectly true that the assessment of artistic merit was largely a matter of taste, and that, it might be argued, was an individual matter. To a certain extent that was true. On the other hand, taste could be acquired by soaking oneself in the tradition It was important that those who were responsible for disseminating folk music should have an extensive knowledge of it, and that they should be familiar with its particular idiom so that they would be able to feel, perhaps almost intuitively, when the modern elements had merged with the older elements and had amalgamated to form a satisfying whole. If, at the same time, these persons were likewise scholars or were, at any rate, willing to listen to the scholars' words of wisdom, they would immeasurably strengthen their positions.

Professor CHERBULIEZ said that we had to consider not only the taste of the scholar but that of the singer or dancer. Our great task was to bring the conscious taste of the scholar and the unconscious taste of the folk musician into line.

Mr. OLCUTT SANDERS (Austin, Texas), referring to Professor Saygun's emphasis on the background of folk music, made the suggestion that the real problem of transmission and evaluation at the present time was that there was a lack of relation between the presentation of folk music and its setting. He said: The gramophone and the radio give us a disembodied folk expression. They give only the music that we hear, but we do not hear it in any particular relation to anything else and so we have no sound basis for judgment. One of the reasons why people like a particular thing (and it is all a matter of taste, unconsciously) is that they associate it with a total experience that is pleasing. In other words, we keep on singing a song, not merely because it is lovely (it may not be particularly lovely), but because we continue to associate it with an original lovely experience.

Mrs. SIDNEY ROBERTSON COWELL (Shady, New York) said that the role of the music critic was important. He must try to be a musicologist on the one hand, and a philosopher or professor of aesthetics on the other. People who were responsible for the selection of folk music must take some such middle road, and the combination of subjectivity and objectivity was a hurdle that could not be escaped.

Professor MARIUS BARBEAU (Ottawa) explained the methods and conclusions which had been derived from the experience of collecting French-Canadian folk songs. He said: In the Gaspé and other places we have folk singers who know as many as 300 songs. We have so far collected, since 1915, over 12,000 versions of 5,000 or 6,000 traditional songs. The repertory is mixed, for the singers were apt to take all that comes to them, good and bad. There are, however, regions in Canada where natural selection is very good, because the singers have not undergone the influences to which others, say, those near Montreal, have been submitted. We have found through long experience, through study and analysis of the texts, a sure method of judging what is and what is not authentic, that is the knowledge of the *ars poetica*, the composition of the texts and their relation with the melody. There are two big repertories in connection with the texts. There is a popular repertory that goes back to the *jongleur*, and is an old romance tradition, purely oral, that derives from the early days of the French language in France. On the other hand, there is the repertory of the troubadours—the higher class composers, the learned, the writers, etc. These two repertories are, on the whole, incompatible with each other, although there are exchanges between the two. The *ars poetica* of the *jongleur* is most complicated. It has lines varying from four to sixteen syllables with caesuras of all kinds. Assonance prevails everywhere. A masculine ending usually alternates with a feminine caesura or "césure épique." There might be as many as 40 or 50 different classifications. The structure of the melodies is essentially dependent upon the text. If you know the *ars poetica* of the French folk songs of the past, then you know what is authentic and what is not. If you have a short stanza, which is characteristic of the *ars poetica*, then you know that you have authenticity; whereas long and complicated stanzas, with "rimes" and "rimes croisées," are a modern development, belonging to the written repertory of the upper class. Once you have learned how to depend on the spoken word in close relation to its melody, then you can detect further distinctive traits of authenticity in the melody itself. Here you will find the old modes, the old style of singing, rhythms with an interesting lilt and syncopation. Upon reaching this stage, you no longer depend upon vague impressions, but upon analyses and true experience.

Mr. CHARLES SEEGER (Washington, D.C.) said we must be careful, in our use of the term "tradition," not to limit its meaning to the idiom of folk music. There were traditions not only in the fine art of music, but in the popular art as well. If anyone had any doubt about this he should ask himself what it is that a young student in any conservatory studies. It was, surely, the traditions of harmony, counterpoint and form of the Occidental fine art of music. And not only these, but the traditions of conformity and unconformity with which they may be followed, the traditions of performance, of criticism, of concert attendance, and even of publishing and library service, that would allow him to read scores and to read about composers and their works.

There were also the traditions relative to the use of folk music by professional and popular composers—the traditions that found their supporters in the trends of "folklorism" or "anti-folklorism"—and in those of "universalism" and "nativism," colonialism and autochonism.

No less important, but more difficult to survey and study, were similar trends in folk music itself—the resistance to urban influences and the seduction by them.

Professor BEN LUMPKIN (University of Colorado) concurred with Miss Karpeles' opinion that it was obligatory for the Council to distinguish between the genuine and the spurious elements in folk tradition. Miss Karpeles had mentioned various agencies, through the influence of which the spontaneity of the folk song had been undermined. He would like to add another—not so much a single agency as a tendency. He referred to the political parties and propagandists, people with causes, who used folk song, a harmless-sounding term, for propaganda purposes and thus brought folk songs into bad repute.

Dr. STITH THOMPSON (Indiana University) related the opposing views of two collectors of folk songs, one of whom was always seeking for the ideal version of a song, and the other who accepted every song he heard as equally good, regarding it as the song of a particular old man or old woman. The question, said Dr. Stith Thompson, is: "Are there aesthetic values that we can apply to authenticity in folk songs?"

Mr. JASIMUDDIN (Dacca, E. Pakistan) affirmed that everything sung by the unlettered should be collected and afterwards classified.

The CHAIRMAN said that the subject was too wide and too difficult for a final decision to be announced, but he proposed to close the discussion.

The HONORARY SECRETARY asked leave to read a communication from Dr. Paul Brewster which had a bearing on the subject.

*The Use of Music in the Study of a Problem of Acculturation**

ALAN P. MERRIAM
University of Wisconsin (Milwaukee)

IN RECENT years the acceptance of comparative musicology, or ethnomusicology, as a recognized branch of anthropological investigation has increased considerably. The result has been a number of studies of the music of nonliterate people, but as yet little theoretical application for such studies has been shown. The present paper will attempt to indicate one way in which musical investigation can be used to support anthropological theory, with the hope that its broader ramifications will become apparent by implication.

For purposes of discussion let us state a hypothesis in the field of acculturation studies as follows: When two human groups which are in sustained contact have a number of characteristics in common in a particular aspect of culture, exchange of ideas therein will be much more frequent than if the characteristics of those aspects differ markedly from one another. In order to test this hypothesis let us examine the musical acculturative situation which exists, first, between Western culture and the Flathead Indians of western Montana and, second, between Western culture and urban Africa south of the Sahara with special reference to the Belgian Congo.

Among the Flathead Indians the evidences of acculturation with respect to music are by no means pronounced, and those changes which can be documented appear in areas of activity surrounding the music rather than in the actual music itself, that is, in such matters as the construction of musical instruments or the use of song texts as opposed to vocal quality or scale structure.

Flathead musical instruments at present include the war drum, hand drum and end-blown flageolet, a reduction in number from that indicated in earlier sources. Turney-High, for example, speaks of the whistle "made of bird bones" which was used in courting and, more specifically, in arranging trysts, as well as "rattles made by stringing deer hoofs on thongs tied to sticks," which were used both by shamans in the Camas Dance and by laymen in less esoteric dancing (Turney-High 1937:39, 83). Teit further indicates the presence of the rasp which, however, he mentions only in passing and without description (Teit 1927–28:386). The whistle and rasp are nowhere found in use today while the modern sleighbell has been substituted for the original rattle; these bells

* This paper was first presented at the meetings of the American Anthropological Association at Tucson, Arizona, Dec. 29, 1953. The author wishes to acknowledge with thanks the support of the Belgian American Educational Foundation, the Wenner-Gren Foundation for Anthropological Research and l'Institut pour la Recherche Scientifique en Afrique Centrale, which made research in the Belgian Congo possible, and the Music Foundation of Montana State University, which supported field work among the Flathead Indians.

are fastened together in chains which may be wrapped around the legs of the dancers or fastened at one end to the ankle, the other end being held in the hand.

A number of changes have been made by the Flathead in those instruments which are still in use. The war drum was originally made from a hollowed section of tree trunk or sturdy bark, covered with skin or hide to form a double-headed instrument; the two heads were tied together by a thong which ran back and forth between the two pieces of hide. At present, the Flathead war drum has been replaced by the European bass drum with the original drum-head left on as long as possible and later replaced with deerhide. One informant —the tribe's outstanding singer by common acknowledgment—further argued for the merits of an inner tube stretched over a washtub, saying in fact that it was superior to the instrument of traditional manufacture because the rubber would not loosen in wet or cold weather.

Similar changes have taken place in the construction of the hand drum. Under earlier conditions the hand drum was constructed of thin strips of wood, preferably fir, which were soaked and bent, or occasionally of a hollowed tree stump; at present a circular cheese crate serves as the basic frame. A hand drum made especially for the author used the metal speaker frame from an old radio; the virtues of this instrument were extolled on the basis that it would "last a lifetime." In former times the hand drum was headed with deerhide which was wetted, allowed to dry in place and secured with thongs; at present if a wooden frame is used the single head is fastened with thumbtacks. The drumstick used with both the war and hand drums was formerly of wet wood and, specifically, of wild cherry, padded at one end with soft hide. Today the selection of the stick is often carefully made but almost any stick may be used, the tip padded with cloth.

The third instrument of Flathead manufacture, the flageolet, has undergone changes similar to those found in the drums, although the change is perhaps not quite so extensive. The instrument was formerly made of elderberry or fir, the finger holes burned into the material with fire. At present most flutes are still constructed of wood, but a piece of metal tubing is considered completely adequate and, indeed, recommended by some musicians for its permanence.

It is apparent, then, that the musical instruments of the Flathead have sustained considerable actual physical change attributable for the most part to contact with products of European manufacture. The change from deer hoof rattles to sleighbells, from wooden war drums to European bass drums, from wooden hand drum frames to those of metal, and from wooden to metal flageolets all point up this fact. But while the form of the instruments has undergone change there is nothing to indicate that the musical function has changed at the same time. The war drum still takes its accustomed place in the dance circle, providing a basic beat for the dancers; the hand drum accompanies the individual singer, and the flageolet is still used to play love songs. Thus while the materials or method of manufacture have changed among the Flathead, the instruments serve their accustomed and traditional musical purposes.

Certain pressures have been instituted, moreover, in urging the Flathead to accept and learn to use European instruments. The earliest established mission schools included the study of music and the formation of musical organizations based on the European pattern, and such training is still offered in reservation schools. While many fine Indian instrumentalists in the imposed pattern are to be found, they have become musicians in the Western sense playing European music on European instruments, not Flathead music on European instruments or European music on Flathead instruments. Again the separation is clear; while new techniques have been learned they are kept separate from traditional music.

In the use of song texts some rather remarkable changes have apparently taken place in the last fifty years. Teit, throughout his section entitled "Ceremonies and Dances," constantly intimates that Flathead songs in the early part of this century had definite texts which varied in content not only from song to song but among the various types of songs as well (Teit 1927–28: 286–94). In 1931, Lewis published a complete text of a Sinka kaa, or Canvas Dance song, which was not only extensive in actual length, but which sustained a consistent and developing line of poetic thought (Lewis 1931:379). In view of these facts, it is surprising to find that in contemporary singing nonsense syllables, beginning usually with the consonants "h" and "y," are used almost exclusively. In those few songs in which texts do appear, the translation most often proves to be meaningless both to the collector and to the singer; exceptions are very infrequent. This loss of song texts cannot as yet be satisfactorily explained, but for our purposes it is again significant to note that this change has taken place not in the actual production of musical tones themselves, but in word usage; thus the musical system, in its literal sense, has not been affected to any great extent.

A distinctly intrusive element incorporated into Owl Dance songs is the use of a four-line English text interpolated between nonsense syllables. These verses typically have a love connotation, such as:

If you'll marry me
Then I will love you.
If you know me once
Then I'll never go.

These short texts, a widespread phenomenon among North American Indians, have had some effect upon the melodic line in Flathead Owl Dance songs. While the basic melodic rhythm is not broken, the line itself tends to be flatter, or more level, where English texts are interpolated than the usual pattern which is most often markedly descending in character. In this respect, then, an acculturative process has taken place which has had some direct effect, though relatively minor, on the music itself.

A second musical change concerns the ending of the War Dance songs. At present the drum pattern is steady until the last few bars of the song are approached at which point it is suddenly halved in tempo and increased in volume; this new pattern continues to the end of the song. After a brief pause of perhaps two to three seconds the drumming is recommenced and the identifying phrase of the song repeated. This coda is used exclusively in War Dance songs. Flathead musicians, however, say that the coda is absent in the original and "true Flathead War Dance songs" and, using this to differentiate the two types, sing the few "original" songs which are still remembered as a more or less academic exercise. Here, then, is an actual musical change which has demonstrably taken place within the memory of living musicians; at the same time the change is clearly attributable to borrowing from other Indian tribes rather than to the impact of European culture.

Finally it may be noted that fewer young men are today learning to be musicians, and fewer new songs are being created from the Vision Quest simply because this practice is becoming increasingly more infrequent. Most of the functional situations to which music contributed its part are gone, but the music itself is still important to the people, serving functionally in some cases as in the practice of sweating, and functioning psychologically in enhancing the self-respect of the individual as a member of his group.

The changes which have been noted in Flathead music are for the most part changes of situation, of construction of musical instruments, or of loss of song texts, but they are not changes in actual musical performance, in the production of certain tone qualities, the melodic line or the rhythmic accompaniment. While European instruments have been mastered and cowboy songs sometimes adopted as popular entertainment, these forms are kept distinct from traditional music.

The musical situation among various groups of the Belgian Congo, on the other hand, presents striking differences from that among the Flathead. Indeed, music in urban centers throughout almost all of Africa south of the Sahara shows such a widespread picture of change that examples can be drawn from wide areas rather than necessarily from a single culture. The aspects of musical acculturation are, further, of much broader pattern than those discussed in connection with the Flathead; the question is not so much that of the adoption of new materials in the construction of traditional instruments as it is the taking over of European instruments to the exclusion of those of native manufacture, not so much the loss of song texts or the inclusion of brief lines of English as the changeover of text material from traditional subjects to those dealing with European ways and material culture, not so much a musical change of a four-bar coda as the adoption of European formal structures in composition of melodic lines and harmonic backgrounds, although these changes continue to be expressed in African ways.

In Leopoldville in the Belgian Congo, for example, traditional music has been subordinated to new forms similar to European folk melodies. The leader-chorus pattern, so widely used in Africa, has been modified in favor of male quartets in which a solo voice appears infrequently in comparison to its former importance. The quartet itself is built around the harmonies provided by the guitar, and percussion instruments have moved away from the use of the traditional three-drum choir of the area and are now frequently represented by a beer bottle struck with the back of the blade of a pocket knife. Soloists accompany themselves with the guitar instead of native instruments, singing in European ballad form. Hymns taught by the missionaries have reached such an influential estate that casual and informal singing in the home or in the fields often tends to be expressed in this form.

The radio and the phonograph have contributed much to the rapid expansion of these changes. A remarkable number of Congolese own portable mechanical phonographs, and records are supplied by at least three firms established in Leopoldville, whose libraries are aimed directly toward the modern popular African market.

The spread of the modern idioms which are based largely on European instruments and forms has brought some rather striking changes to the musical face of Africa. In Nigeria among the Ibo and Yoruba, tin whistles originally introduced in Cracker Jack boxes, are prominent in modern popular recordings. In Zanzibar, and along the upper east coast in general, cowboy music from America as interpreted by Africans ranks high as a popular musical form. It is no longer startling to hear a Gold Coast African police band tear into Duke Ellington's "Rockin' in Rhythm" or a Zulu group present a repertoire of songs ranging from ballads accompanied by a concertina, through four-part songs strongly reminiscent of American Negro spirituals, to a Calypso-Jazz combination featuring trumpet, clarinet and guitar.

But the lines of influence do not travel a one-way street. In recent years, for example, at least five different Catholic masses have been scored which go under the generic name of the "Bantu mass." These masses have been written by Europeans with the express intention of incorporating African melodies into the liturgical chants; in some cases drums have even been played as accompaniment during the services. In another area, we may point to many of the so-called "South American" rhythms, the conga and samba, for example, which have successfully been adopted into European musical literature; to a great extent these rhythms were originally African. It must be noted further that these "Latin-American songs," which changed considerably over a period of years, are returning now to Africa by means of the radio and the phonograph, to be received enthusiastically as a new mode of expression for popular song.

These examples indicate fusions of musical style rather than necessarily wholesale borrowing, for no matter what the form exchanged it is always modified in the new situation. Further, this by no means indicates that traditionally African musical expression has disappeared. The greatest change is taking place in urban centers; in large areas in the bush where contact has not been sustained Western influences are of no importance.

It is clear from this discussion that markedly dissimilar results have emerged in the acculturation situation brought about by contact with Western culture. While the Flathead have clearly neither incorporated Western musical traditions into their own music nor contributed distinctively musical traits to it, the musicians of Africa have both absorbed and given to a very considerable extent. The problem here under discussion, then, is whether in the musical systems themselves there are factors which prevent or accelerate, as the case may be, exchange of musical traits—not whole musical systems, of course—between the cultures. The evidence points strongly toward the fact that this is indeed the case.

Let us first consider points of difference or similarity between Western and Flathead music. Music in the Western tradition is based essentially upon the diatonic scale which consists of five whole tones and two semitones arranged in the order represented by the white keys on the piano keyboard from *C* to *C*. The Western minor keys represent the same system but in different order. Among the Flathead the single scale of most importance is the pentatonic, a combination of three whole steps and two steps of a minor third—on the piano keyboard *CDEGAC*. This scale is a device sometimes used in Western music for special effects, but in general it is considered a restricting scale construction and is relatively infrequently used.

Again, Western music is based upon a harmonic system to the extent that even unaccompanied singing infers a harmonic basis automatically supplied by the listener. Western academic music, indeed, has focused its attention upon harmony, and composers constantly seek new harmonic devices to give added color in composition. Flathead songs, on the other hand, never use harmony, nor is implied harmony part of the tradition.

The melodic movement of Flathead songs is characterized in many cases by a sharp descent from initial to final tones of each phrase, followed by a wide upward skip and a repeated descent. Western music, on the other hand, tends to be more level in melodic line, and where sharp descents are used they are ordinarily not repeated over and over again. Flathead music is also mainly vocal in character and, further, unaccompanied by any instrument other than percussion; Western music is almost always accompanied by instruments which give a strong harmonic background for the vocal line, and instrumental so os are by no means uncommon. There is virtually no polyphony in Flathead music; in Western music polyphony plays a very important role. Finally, the criterion of good voice production in Western music is based upon the controlled relaxation of the muscles used in singing. The Flathead, on the other hand, strive for a voice quality that is nasalized, strained and penetrating, produced through a tight, though open, throat. This particular vocal quality alone prevents the Western singer from imitating Flathead voice production without considerable readjustment of vocal habits.

The case of African music as compared to the folk music traditions of the Western world, on the other hand, is quite different. Musically speaking, the western one-third of the Old World land mass is homogeneous and set off from the Indo-Arabic and Sino-Mongolian areas (Waterman 1952:207). This homogeneity is based upon the use of the diatonic scale and of harmony present in both European and African music and absent in the other areas for the most part. Two strong points of contact for mutual exchange of musical traits are thus immediately established.

Closely allied with the use of harmony in African music is the tradition of accompaniment of the voice not only with percussion instruments but with stringed instruments. These instruments may produce chords as with the *lokombi* of the Ekonda in the Belgian Congo, or at least single tones which produce a distinct harmonic effect as with the *lulanga* of the Bashi. The melodic lines of Western and African music are both more level than that of the Flathead; polyphony is strong in both musical systems. While the African criterion of voice production differs in certain ways from that of Western music, the differences are much less marked in quality than those which differentiate Flathead music from either.

Let us turn back now to our original hypothesis. In its terms we should expect an interchange of musical traits and ideas between two cultures in which the systems have a considerable number of characteristics in common, while we should not expect interchange between two cultures in which the musical systems have little in common. Such has been shown to be the case in respect to music; Western and Flathead musical systems, having little in common, have in fact exchanged virtually no ideas. Flathead music is little affected by Western traditions, and Western music has borrowed virtually nothing from the Flathead, for the two systems are simply not compatible. On the other hand, African and Western music, having a great deal in common, are mutually influential upon one another; we have borrowed much from Africa and Africa has borrowed much from us.

This, of course, disregards the grosser aspects of the acculturative situation and considers only that single aspect which is of direct concern here—music. However, the hypothesis, which could be leveled in consideration of other aspects of culture, applies to music, and music applies to the working out of the hypothesis.

BIBLIOGRAPHY

Lewis, William S.

1931 Red man's farewell song as he went forth to battle. Frontier 11:378–80.

Merriam, Alan P.

1951 Flathead Indian instruments and their music. Musical Quarterly 37:368–75.

1953 African music reexamined in the light of new material from the Belgian Congo and Ruanda Urundi. Zaire 7:244–53.

Teit, James A.

1927–28 The Flathead group. *In:* The Salishan Tribes of the Western Plateaus, by James A. Teit. Bureau of American Ethnology (Forty-Fifth Annual Report). Washington, D. C.

Turney-High, Harry Holbert

1937 The Flathead Indians of Montana. American Anthropological Association Memoir No. 48.

Waterman, Richard A.

1952 African influence on the music of the Americas. *In:* Acculturation in the Americas, ed. Sol Tax. Chicago, University of Chicago Press.

SOME NOTES ON A THEORY OF AFRICAN RHYTHM ADVANCED BY ERICH VON HORNBOSTEL

by

JOHN BLACKING

In an article on African Music written in 1928, Hornbostel offered an explanation of certain features of African rhythms which may puzzle Western ears (Hornbostel '28, p. 52):—

"African rhythm is ultimately founded on drumming. Drumming can be replaced by hand-clapping or the xylophone; what really matters is the act of beating; and only from this point can African rhythms be understood. Each single beating movement is again twofold: the muscles are strained and released, the hand is lifted and dropped. Only the second phase is stressed acoustically; but the first inaudible one has the motor accent, as it were, which consists in the straining of the muscles. This implies an essential contrast between our rhythmic conception and the African's; we proceed from hearing, they from motion; we separate the two phases by a bar line, and commence the metrical unity, the bar, with the acoustically stressed time-unit; to them, the beginning of the movement, the arsis, is at the same time the beginning of the rhythmical figure; up-beats are unknown to them. (i.e. *up-beats as weak beats, in the way Western musicians use them.* J.B.) To us the simple succession of beats 𝄾 ♪ 𝄾 ♪ appears as syncopated, because we only attend to its acoustic aspect. In order to understand African rhythms as they really are, therefore, we must thoroughly change our attitude; and in order to write them down adequately we must place the bar-line before the rest or the up-beat . . . the elementary form of African 3/4 rhythm is not | 𝅗𝅥 ♩ | (3) but | ♩ 𝅗𝅥 | (3) . . ."

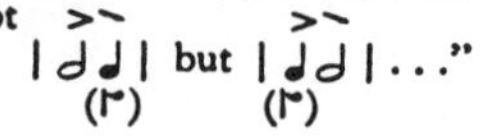

A. M. Jones refers to these remarks in his article "African Drumming" (Jones '34, p. 49):—

"Hornbostel with considerable ingenuity justifies these (marks of emphasis) on the ground that it is the *raising* of the arm rather than the actual sound of the strike, that carries the strong accent in African percussion rhythms. If our version be accepted, note that these accented notes practically all fall naturally into position, counting the strike as the accent. My African informant repudiates Hornbostel's notion. In this example, at any rate, it is entirely irrelevant."

These are the only references to motor concepts of rhythm in African Music that I have been able to find. Hornbostel does not say whether he deduced the theory himself or whether he had gotten it from some educated African or European enquirer. If his theory is correct then it deserves more attention than it has so far received, since it would be fundamental to the proper understanding of much African music. Although Hornbostel implies that *all* African peoples conceive their rhythms physically from motion rather than musically from hearing, it is more likely that the generalization applies, if at all, only to certain groups. Jones' African informant repudiates the notion; and this suggests that at least one group of Africans may not think of rhythm in this way.

Until Hornbostel's theory has been hammered out and proved true or false—or perhaps true *and* false, according to its application in different parts of Africa—accurate research into African music is seriously impeded. His proposition raises many problems and offers some solution to others:—

(1) *What is the precise nature of this suggested contrast between African and European concepts of rhythm?*

If one watches Chopi musicians playing their xylophones, they appear to be "attacking" their instruments with all the force they can muster. The only movement downwards that could be interpreted as a release of muscular tension is that which follows the raising of one arm in the air (see photo below), and this movement appears to be done only by a leader; it is a sign for the beginning of a new section of the music. Already an indictment of Hornbostel's theory? . . . .

High-speed photograph of the leader of a Chopi *timbila* orchestra preparing to begin a new section of the music. (*Photo*—J.B.)

Two high-speed photographs of Chopi musicians playing in the arena of a Johannesburg Mine Compound. Note the looseness and turning of the wrists, especially of the bass players (top). If they were hitting their instruments they would not be holding the beaters in that way. The pictures also show how the wrists are suspended from the shoulders. In the second photo (bottom) the leader has just jerked his beret on to the xylophone of the man behind. *(Photos—J.B.)*

One has a similar impression of downward "attacking" movements when one watches the performance of a virtuoso pianist. If in fact he were pounding his instrument the tone would be unpleasantly harsh (It sometimes is!). Closer analysis of his movements will usually reveal that there is constant upward lift, which makes the downward "thrust" more of a downward "drop" Some piano teachers insist that all the muscular effort must be made when *preparing* to play each tone, so that the note is actually struck during a moment of muscular relaxation. The fingers are allowed to fall on to the keys rather than compelled to hit them: thus, contrary to what may seem natural, the louder one plays the more relaxed one is. In playing groups of tones, or chords, which succeed each other slowly it is possible to emphasize the periods of effort between the relaxed sounding of the tones. Obviously this is impossible when the tones are sounded in quick succession, as in fast semiquaver runs; and here the muscular effort is made theoretically before the beginning of each musical *phrase*, each "moment of relaxation" covering several quickly-changing tones.

Thus when African xylophonists or drummers play successions of notes or beats quickly and appear to be beating downwards they may still be adhering to Hornbostel's theory, with the same modifications that a pianist would have to make to his theory of effort and relaxation when playing fast passages. The clue to the technique which underlies their performance, whether conscious or unconscious, is to be found in the movements of the trunk, and more particularly the shoulders. In the same way one often learns more by watching a pianist's arms and shoulders rather than his hands and fingers. The Chopi play their xylophones with a loose wrist which is supported directly from the shoulder; if the wrist were supported by the forearm rather than the shoulder, so that they *hit* the keys forcefully with the beaters, I do not think that they could possibly play almost continuosly and as vigorously as they do for more than an hour at a time, while the *Ngodo* dance is performed.

The procedure of both European and African performers appears to be virtually the same: an African drummer raises his hand prior to letting it fall on to the instrument, and a European pianist must prepare a chord both mentally and physically before producing the musical sound. In both cases the performer is a step ahead of his audience; in a sense the pianist proceeds as much from motion as the African drummer. Similarly a violinist must make a muscular effort before sounding a musical tone; a wind player must "strain" and take a breath before he releases the air and plays.

The contrast which Hornbostel suggests is therefore not so much one of procedure as of *attitude* towards movements and the production of musical sounds. He claims that Africans think of the sounds as a bi-product of rhythmical movement, whereas Westerners pay more attention to the sounds than to the movement which causes them.

(2) *Comparison of Hornbostel's theory with dancing and the ethos of much African music.*

"In Africa, the music of the dance and the dance itself are one indivisible whole." (Jones '52, page 1).

This fact has been corroborated by so many other observers that there seems little reason to doubt its truth. Since music for dancing must be related to the dance movements and in many cases in Africa might be considered subordinate to them, one might expect to find musical concepts derived from the physical pattern of the movement. (Sachs dwells on this point in Sachs '37, page 181 ff., giving several examples of the correlation between styles of music and dancing.)

A large number of African dances might be described as extrovert (see Sachs '37); the tendency is to achieve emotional release by straining the body upwards and outwards. The *Ndhlamu* stamping dance of the Nguni group in Southern Africa might appear at first to be an obvious contradiction of this: but in fact the tense winding-up of the body is a longer and more significant movement than the stamping release. The pattern is one of Tension—Relaxation, Tension—Relaxation. This is the pattern of many African melodies (see for instance Hornbostel '28, p. 34 ff.); Sachs calls this type of melody "pathogenic" (Sachs '43, p. 41).

The general pattern of Western music is one of Relaxation-Tension-Relaxation.[1] The tendency is to sing up the scale, whereas in Africa the tendency is to do the opposite: some instruments are even tuned from the highest to the lowest note—or, as African musicians say, from the smallest to the largest.

Telescoping these larger physical patterns into the space of a bar of four beats we find that the African up-beat should be the strong beat, equivalent to the Western down-beat. Physically the sensations are similar; the first beat is the strong beat: but in one case it is a movement upwards and in the other a movement downwards. Musically, as Hornbostel suggests, the results are not the same: the Western music runs 1 - 2 - 3, 1 - 2 - 3 etc., whereas the African music runs 1 - 2 - 3, 1 - 2 - 3 etc.

I have noticed a similar contrast expressed in the overall movements of ballroom dancing and jiving. However well one waltzes, dances the Foxtrot or the Quick-Step, one tends to come *down* to the ground on the strong beats:—1 - 2 - 3, 1 - 2 - 3, 1 - or 1 - 2 - 3 - 4, 1 - 2 - 3 - 4. In jive dancing, however, one tends to *lift* the body off the floor. I have checked this point recently at some European night clubs in Johannesburg. During the playing of waltzes, steady and sentimental numbers the couples danced or slouched around the floor in the normal Western fashion: but as soon as the band played a semi-hot number several dancers would indulge in a pseudo-jive style of bounce-dancing. With hardly a single exception amongst all those whom I observed, they lifted their bodies on the strong beats of the music (Beats 1 and 3, since all the tunes were in duple time), and let them drop on the weak beats.

The syncopations of Jazz are often regular and monotonous, and it may be that this is due to a different conception of up-beats and down-beats. The upward lift, as opposed to the downward beat, is surely what gives Jazz its bounce. On the few occasions when I have played jazz on the piano I have found that bouncing up and down on the piano stool or lifting the shoulders in time to the music is very helpful to good rhythmic playing. It might well be shown that the fundamental innovation in Jazz was the replacement of the down-up movement found in most Western music and dances, by the up-down movement, a concept apparently derived from African dancing.

(3) *How far is Hornbostel's theory likely to apply to the rhythmic foundations of all African vocal and instrumental music?*

Although I have suggested that, in line with Hornbostel's hypothesis, the taking in of the breath for singing and playing wind instruments is equivalent to the raising of the arm prior to the beating of the drum (Section I of these Notes), it is more likely that the actual moment of exhalation coincides with the strong upward movement of the body. Although further tension, that of taking a breath, precedes it, the beginning of a pathogenic line of melody is really the climactic moment of tension. (When Chopi dancers sing they wind themselves up, moving their heads forwards, backwards and sideways left and right before bursting into the melodic phrase with tremendous vigour. The leader of the *Makwaya* dance of the Shangaan of Portugese East Africa sizzles

[1] See, for instance Hindemith '47, p. 115 etc. Most Western music is shaped like a curve or a rising plane; very few works could be called pathogenic in outline. One might perhaps stretch a point and say that Vaughan Williams' 6th Symphony in E minor follows a pattern of Tension—Relaxation.

ominously like the fuse of a thunderflash before putting every ounce of effort into the first explosion of his speech-song.) Hornbostel deduces that theoretically the emphasis of the vocal line (and presumably that of melodies played on wind instruments also) should run at loggerheads with the audible beat of the percussion:—

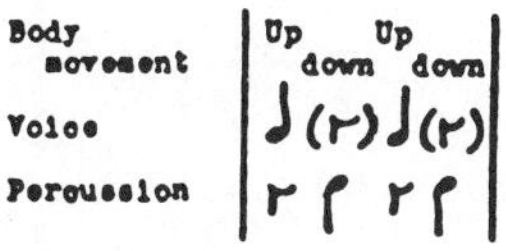

Body movement — Up down Up down
Voice
Percussion

If the whole body is strained and lifted in order to accentuate the melodic line, it cannot be expected to beat downwards at the same time. Perhaps this is why handclaps often occur systematically on the off-beats of a sung melody: the raising of the arms and the spreading of the hands is an act of tension resolved by the clap. Though these explanations of syncopation may be shown to apply in some areas of Africa, it must not be thought that they can be applied universally: for instance, in the areas in Northern Rhodesia and Southern Congo where polyrhythmic technique is commonly used the syncopation may perhaps be explained in a different way. In a pounding song of Tonga girls from Northern Rhodesia, analysed by D. K. Rycroft (Rycroft '55 ,p. 21), the down-beat of the pestles coincides with the strong beats of the vocal line. (This does not of course mean that all work songs will contradict Hornbostel's hypothesis: I can think of many cases where it is best for the physical movement to follow the vocal effort rather than synchronize with it. For instance, if a group of men are pulling a rope to the shout of "heave", the pulling will be more effective if the effort is made just after the shout rather than with it.)

Similar rhythmic features may be found in Jazz music, according to a recent definition of F. H. Garner and A. P. Merriam. Under the heading, "Continual off-beat phrasing of melodic accents", they list:—

"a. Phrase patterns in which melodic accents fall between dominant percussive beats.

b. Melodic cycles of three beats superimposed on a fundamental rhythm of two or four beats, the beats themselves remaining equal in value."

Both these features are often loosely called "syncopation". (b) may be explained on the basis of polyrhythmic technique (see Jones '34 etc.); while (a) may perhaps be explained on the basis of the elaboration of Hornbostel's theory which I have discussed.

Quite recently I came across some African music which seemed to combine both these features at the same time. I give below a diagram of the rhythmic foundations of the *ngeniso* movement of a Chopi *Ngalanga* dance from the Zavala district of Portuguese East Africa.[3]

[3] Special dubbings of this recording can be obtained by arrangement from the International Library of African Music. It was collected on 4.x.55, (Research No. HIM-4), during a short expedition led by Mr. Tracey.

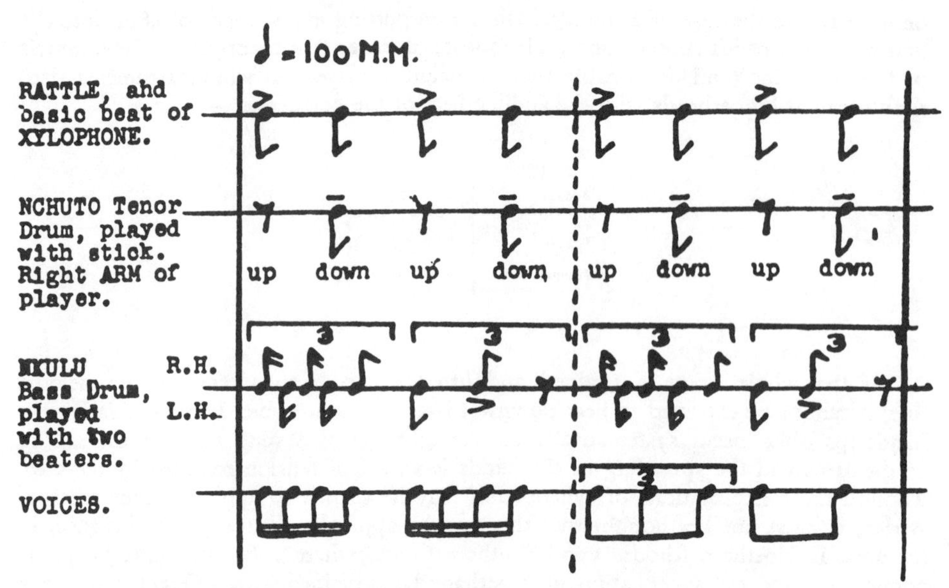

Rhythmic foundations of *ngeniso* movement from a Chopi *Ngalanga* dance.

The notation of the voice part must not be taken too literally, since the rhythm was governed by the words; nevertheless the tendency was to slow down over the course of each two-bar phrase, as indicated above. A solo xylophone begins the dance, the other two join in with the rattle player, and then the two drummers: the voices enter when the rhythm is well under way. I checked my notation of the drum rhythms by playing them myself: when I emphasized the first of each triplet group in the *Nkulu* part I was corrected: only when I tested Hornbostel's theory and played with the accent on the last note of each group (as indicated above), was my performance approved. I tried playing the *Nchuto* drum as if it was the second of a group of triplets; that was also corrected. There is further use of polyrhythmic technique which I have not indicated above; the xylophones were often played with the left hand in duple time and the right in triple time. I was told by our Chopi interpreter, himself a musician, that the triple time is regarded as a variation within the basic duple time, and that it is important that the player should maintain the duple time in the left hand part. (cf. Drum technique described in Jones '52 ,p. 36 ff.)

Here, then, is evidence of off-beat accents apparently produced by polyrhythmic technique and the application of Hornbostel's theory at the same time. It is worth mentioning that when I first heard the play-back of part of this recording I was tempted to think that the beat of the *Nchuto* drum was in fact the main beat. When they performed it a second time however, it was quite clear that the main beat was set by the rattle player and the xylophonists; I noticed also the body movements of the two drummers, how the *Nkulu* player seemed to take each phrase in one downward swaying movement, and the *Nchuto* player stressed the upward lift of his drumstick almost as much as the downward beat. I could never have guessed what was happening by listening to the recording alone.

(4) *Further evidence in support of Hornbostel's theory.*

The other day a local boy sang us a song with guitar accompaniment. There was no hint of polyrhythmic technique in the rhythmical structure of the music (polyrhythm does not appear to be used extensively by Africans in the Union of South Africa); both accompaniment and melody were in duple time, arranged in 4-bar periods and with simple European-influenced harmonies. The player beat time with his foot; the upward beat of his foot coincided with the strong, apparently syncopated accents of the melodic line; but the downward beat of his foot coincided with the strong beats of his strumming on the guitar. Being accustomed to European music, I regarded his down-beat as the main beat and his up-beat as the weak beat, so that the vocal line seemed excessively syncopated to me, almost monotonously so. If on the other hand the up-beat was to him the strong beat, then his conception of the syncopation would have been entirely different; in fact none of the music would have on him the physical effect of syncopation if it were perfectly normal for him to accent the voice on the up-beat and the percussive sound on the down-beat.

(As Hornbostel points out, the motor concept of rhythm poses certain problems in transcription. Are we to place the bar-line in accordance with the sound or with the physical movement that causes the sound? Written music should of course indicate the sound intended, not the methods of producing that sound; on the other hand, if we are to analyse music thoroughly it seems that we should try to express it in the terms in which it was conceived. Ideally every transcription of African music should be accompanied by some indication of the physical movements which produce the musical sounds. Transcriptions of drumming, for instance, which do not indicate the hand used to play each note, are not very enlightening.)

In listening to some items of African music, and trying to beat time with my foot, I have often found that I wanted to lift not only my foot but my whole body on what should be the first beat of the "bar"; only in this way could I feel the rhythm of the music. An excellent example of this sort of tune is *Mwana aboyi mama* (Ngoma 1378. 78 r.p.m., also on Decca LP 1224, No. 10 in the "Music of Africa" Series).

There is, moreover, evidence that African drummers *feel* their rhythms rather than listen to them. A typical example of this occurs in A. M. Jones' book on the Icila Dance (Jones '52): Mr. Kombe, an African musician, gives demonstrations on the drum; when he makes a mistake it is significant that he says not that he HEARS he has gone wrong, but that he FEELS that he has gone wrong. (p. 36 op. cit.)

I witnessed some of the most striking evidence in support of Hornbostel's theory at the Third African Eisteddfod in Bulawayo (described elsewhere in this issue in the Section 'Notes and News'). All the Choirs had to sing set pieces of European composed music, arranged either for part- or unison-singing. These songs where conducted by the African teachers who coached the choirs: I was astonished to see that several of them gave vigorous up-beats on all the strong beats where I should have given a down-beat. An excellent example of this occurred in the song, "The Lass of Richmond Hill", where eight out of nine African conductors beat thus:—

On Rich - mond Hill there lives a lass,

Conductors' beat: down - UP down UP down UP down UP etc.

The average European conductor would have done the exact opposite. (It must be said that this upward thrust to the strong beat of the bar is considerably more lively than the downward beat common in European conducting). I discussed the matter with some of the African teachers afterwards, and they said that they definitely felt the up-beat to be the strong beat.

These then are some of the thoughts which have occurred to me and some of the evidence I have been able to muster since I was struck so forcibly by the methods of conducting employed by some African teachers at the Bulawayo Eisteddfod. Hornbostel, I discovered, had drawn attention to the 'motor concept' in African rhythms as long ago as 1928; the full significance of what he said does not seem to have been appreciated.

I have written these notes in the hope that they will stimulate correspondence and views both for and against Horbostel's notion from observers and research workers, and above all from African musicians themselves—for the last word in this matter must inevitably come from them.

WORKS QUOTED

Paul Hindemith: 1937—"The Craft of Musical Composition", Book I—Theoretical Part. Associated Music Publishers Inc., New York.

E. M. von Hornbostel: 1928—"African Negro Music", *Africa*, Vol. I, No. 1.

A. M. Jones: 1934—"African Drumming", *Bantu Studies*, the Journal of the University of the Witwatersrand, Vol. 8, No. 1: reprinted 1949, No. 4 of the Occasional Papers of the Rhodes-Livingstone Museum.

A. M. Jones: 1952—"The Icila Dance, Old Style" (with L. Kombe), African Music Society.

D. K. Rycroft: 1955—"Tribal Style and Free Expression", *African Music*, Vol. 1, No. 1.

Curt Sachs: 1937—"World History of the Dance".

Curt Sachs: 1943—"The Rise of Music in the Ancient World East and West".

The Reliability of Oral Tradition*

By MANTLE HOOD

In the evolution of many musical cultures oral tradition has served as a regulative principle. It is not yet widely understood in the West that the cultivated arts of the Orient, referring here to countries east of the Mediterranean, have attained an advanced stage of development through centuries of change, adaptation and growth.[1] The notion of *preservation* as the primary function of an oral tradition is misleading and carries the static or negative connotation of protection and safe-keeping, a process which inhibits change and consequently obviates development. Even the relatively naïve music and text of folk songs exist (by definition) in a number of variants created in accordance with unconscious laws of selection by the community.[2] Therefore in a discussion of the reliability of oral tradition we must in the first place distinguish between *ingenuous* music and *cultivated* music and then realize that the viability of each is determined by a number of contributing factors: (1) the latitude of change and adaptation allowable within the regulations of a particular musical tradition; (2) the interdependence of music and the related arts; (3) the role of social institutions and customs; (4) the effect of compatible and incompatible foreign influences; and (5) the especial impact of Western technology in contemporary times. Although each of these factors deserves an extended and systematic examination, it will be necessary in the limited space available to focus attention on certain musical considerations with only occasional reference to other pertinent factors.

The terms "primitive music," "folk music," "popular music," and "art music," in general usage by the Western scholar, are conceded to be something less than categorical in their applicability; and it has been shown elsewhere that such terms are almost meaningless when applied to music in the Orient.[3] For the sake of clarity in the present discussion it should be noted that the term "ingenuous music" refers to an artless and relatively naïve expression lacking in its development the idea of *conscious* improvement, therefore *unstudied*. "Cultivated music," on the other hand, refers to an expression which has evolved through a conscious effort to improve and refine the various attributes of its disciplines. This dual classification does not discriminate according to function, usage, popularity, social class, utility or

* Read at the 25th annual meeting of the Society, at Chicago, Ill., December, 1959, at a joint session with the Society for Ethnomusicology, as part of a panel discussion on the general topic "The Oral Tradition in Music."

1 See further: Mantle Hood, "Changing Patterns in the Arts of Java," *Bulletin of the Institute of Traditional Cultures*, Part II (Madras, 1959).

2 "Definition of Folk Music," *Proceedings of the 7th Conference of the International Folk Music Council held at Sao Paulo, Brazil* (1954), p. 23; *cf.* Maud Karpeles, "Definition of Folk Music," *Journal of the International Folk Music Council* VII (1955), pp. 6-7.

3 Mantle Hood, "Folk Imitations of the Javanese Gamelan," *Viltis* (Summer, 1956), *passim.*

commercialism, because any of these considerations may apply to either type of music. For the subject under discussion the most important difference between ingenuous music and cultivated music lies in their relative degree of "defensive power," as Jaap Kunst has put it.

Discussing the day-by-day degeneration of native music in Indonesia he states: "As one of the rare exceptions to this unfortunate tendency we may mention, in the first place, Central Java, which would appear to have become gradually, and just in time, conscious of its own cultural values; whilst also in Bali . . . whose population . . . is essentially healthy and of great creative strength, the native music seems to succeed in maintaining itself in its original purity. . . . But in those regions where the ancient musical art is of an ingenuous and semi-conscious character, and consequently lacking in defensive power, it is, quite evidently, irrevocably doomed to die out."[4]

The continuity and development of ingenuous music is largely dependent on extra-musical aspects of the indigenous culture, *e.g.*, on custom and ritual associated with magic, superstition, myth and religion; on dance, poetry and drama; on specific forms of work and play. As long as these interdependencies remain reasonably undisturbed or are constructively affected by outside influences not too dissimilar in kind, the process of oral transmission will maintain traditional musical practices and accommodate adaptation and change. Methods of imitation and rote will assure the continuation and development of musical instruments, traditional tuning systems and scale pitches, modal practices, local and regional niceties of style, musical and poetic forms, etc. But ingenuous music cannot withstand the pressure of complex societies. Traditional music and dance have vanished from Nias, a small island off the west coast of Sumatra, under the restrictions of a Christian mission which forbid the performance of native music because of its association with heathen religion.[5] Among the Lushai tribe and some of the Naga tribes of northeast India similar pressures in recent times have also silenced their traditional music; and even though it is still alive in the minds of the people, they refuse to perform their songs for All-India radio in fear of eternal damnation.[6] Some years ago missionary zeal in Polynesia all but extinguished authentic song and dance.[7] Native music in south and east Sumatra and in South Borneo was replaced by Javanese cultivated music when labor crews were imported by the Dutch.[8] Attempts in Franco Spain to suppress the Basque language ultimately pose a threat to the survival of the indigenous vocal music.[9] English domination finally broke the tradition, dating from the Middle

[4] *Music in Java* (2nd ed., revised and enl.; The Hague: Martinus Nijhoff, 1949), Vol. I, p. 4.

[5] Jaap Kunst, *De inheemsche Muziek en de Zending* (Amsterdam: H. J. Paris, 1947), pp. 11-16.

[6] According to an oral communication from Robert Brown.

[7] Barbara B. Smith, "Folk Music in Hawaii," *Journal of the International Folk Music Council* XI (1959), pp. 51-52; *cf.* E. S. Craighill Handy and Jane Lathrop Winne, *Music in the Marquesas Islands* (Honolulu: Bishop Museum, 1925), p. 5.

[8] *Cf.* Jaap Kunst, *Music in Java*, Vol. I, p. 4.

[9] "The present Government of Spain has closed down the Basque press, has forbidden the teaching of Basque in the schools, and is moving non-Basques into the heart of the country."—Eduardo Torner and Alan Lomax, notes for the LP recording (SL-216) "Spanish Folk Music," *Columbia World Library of Folk and Primitive Music*, Vol. XIV.

Ages, of imaginative, cultivated poetry written by Irish bards in Gaelic; and eventually this tradition was replaced by ingenuous songs with inferior texts in *English,* a foreign language to Gaelic-speaking peoples.[10] In South Africa Hugh Tracey, alarmed by the cultural indifference resulting from Western economic pressures, wrote a little book which explains African music to Africans and thereby, barely in time, instigated a renascent interest among the people.[11]

These few representative examples, chosen at random from among countless others, indicate that the defensive power of ingenuous music is weak, that religious, economic and other pressures quickly overpower it, and that the oral tradition in this type of music is reliable only while the culture of which it is a part remains reasonably undisturbed.

One of the examples cited above showed that Javanese music has ousted native music in Sumatra and Borneo,[12] an illustration not only of the weak defensive power of ingenuous music but also of the strong *offensive* power of cultivated music, the tradition of a simple society being replaced by that of a more complex one. But what about the *defensive* power of cultivated music? What happens when one complex society challenges another? Are we to conclude that the relative complexity of a society determines whether its cultivated music shall survive? If social institutions and customs are forcefully supplanted by those of a foreign culture, must the autochthonous music die out? There is historical evidence to the contrary.

Java has known several successive waves of powerful outside influences: from India, from the advent of Islam, from 350 years of Dutch domination, and recently from the pressure of Western technology.

Beginning in the 6th and 7th centuries Hindu colonization resulted in the development of a written language, the use of a calendar, the widespread adoption of Brahmanism and Buddhism, the establishment of new principles of government, the enforcement of rules of architecture and sculpture,[13] the flowering of musical concepts.[14] During this rich acculturation in the Hindu-Javanese period, lasting until the rise of Islam in the 16th century, Javanese society did not become Hindu[15] but retained its own identity and integrity, notwithstanding the fact that in the beginning of this development its Hindu progenitors represented a much more complex society.

Architectural reliefs and inscriptions on bronze and stone, dating from as early as the 7th century through the 14th century, indicate that a wide variety of Hindu instruments, some of them still found in India today, was in current usage. The same bas reliefs and inscriptions, supported by archeological discoveries of bronze instruments from about

[10] Donal O'Sullivan, "Folk Music: Irish," in *Grove's Dictionary of Music and Musicians* (5th ed., 1954), Vol. III, pp. 291-292, 294.

[11] *Ngoma; an introduction to Music for Southern Africans* (London: Longmans Green, 1948); see further Hugh Tracey, "The State of Folk Music in Bantu Africa," *Journal of the International Folk Music Council* VI (1954), pp. 32-36.

[12] Gamelan music in South Borneo is quite different from that heard in the other islands; a certain ingenuous quality indicates that the indigenous music has affected the music imported by the Javanese.

[13] H. J. de Graff, *Geschiedenis van Indonesië* (The Hague: W. van Hoeve, 1949), pp. 21-29.

[14] Mantle Hood, *The Nuclear Theme as a Determinant of Patet in Javanese Music* (Groningen: J. B. Wolters, 1954), pp. 246-248; and *cf.* Jaap Kunst, *Music In Java,* Vol. I, p. 383.

[15] de Graff, *loc. cit.*

the same period, also depict prototypes of almost all of the instruments of the modern Javanese and Balinese gamelan. This evidence, together with inscribed references to the "chief drummer," the "orchestra leader," the "chief lute player," etc., and descriptions found in Hindu-Javanese and old Chinese literature document the existence of a flourishing musical activity among the nobility of the courts and among the people.[16] It is important to note that none of these sources, however, furnishes evidence that the musical instruments of those ancient times were combined into an ensemble resembling the gamelan of today.[17] The dance reliefs of the famous Borobudur (8th century) and particularly those of Tjandi Prambanan (late 9th or early 10th century) depict a passionate and lively style of dance which suggests a musical accompaniment quite different from that associated with the controlled and stately dances of modern Java. Contemporary music and dance in Bali, characterized by more dynamic contrasts and livelier movement, might represent a transition somewhere between the ancient and modern forms known in Java.

Originally there were two separate types of gamelan, one ensemble composed of loud-sounding instruments used for outdoor functions and one composed of soft-sounding instruments appropriate for indoor use. Probably the combination of these two ensembles was permanently achieved by the end of the Hindu-Javanese period,[18] but it is interesting to note that today Javanese musicians distinguish between loud and soft styles of playing, featuring instruments proper to each. In loud playing the soft instruments are silent, and in soft playing all or only part of the total ensemble may be used.

The contemporaneous existence of distinctly Hindu instruments and distinctly Javanese instruments and the development of the latter to the modern form of complete gamelan provides organological evidence that the defensive power of Javanese cultivated music is strong and that oral tradition has provided reliable regulative principles in the course of its evolution. The nature of these principles will be considered presently.

As Hindu religion had superseded tribal-hero worship, so by the 16th century the Muslim faith, with its unwritten disapproval of music, replaced Brahmanism in Java. The constant association of music with Hindu religious ceremonies, still very much in evidence in Bali today, was an untenable practice in connection with Islam. Certain places revered as the burial grounds of one or another of the Islamic saints were declared sacred, and the performance of gamelan was forbidden in the area. Choosing to interpret this prohibition in a most literal sense local villagers constructed complete sets of gamelan instruments (retaining the same individual names) out of bamboo,[19] reasoning that a real gamelan was composed of metal instruments. Some of the princes were so pleased by the sound of this new ensemble that they had bamboo gamelan made for the pleasure of the royal courts. A general prohibition against the performance of music on Fridays or during the month of fasting was circumvented in the palaces by substi-

[16] Jaap Kunst, *De waardeering van exotische muziek in den loop der eeuwen* (The Hague: Martinus Nijhoff, 1942), p. 9.

[17] Jaap Kunst, *Music in Java*, Vol. I, p. 109.

[18] *Ibid.*, Vol. I, p. 114.

[19] Mantle Hood, "Folk Imitations of the Javanese Gamelan," *passim*.

tuting the *gong kemodong* for the *gong ageng*,[20] in other words the omission by substitution of one gong in an ensemble composed of approximately 75 instruments. Of course the royal courts were considered above the law anyhow. The extent to which the Muslim faith had to accommodate Javanese cultivated music may be realized from the importance of the holy *gamelan sekati*. Every year since the time of the devout religious leaders (the Wali) of the 15th and 16th centuries these ancient gamelan are played throughout the days and nights of the Islamic holy week and are especially housed just outside the mosque.

There are numerous other evidences that the oral tradition in Java was strong enough to adopt and modify cultural manifestations of Arabic-Persian origin according to its own dictates, *e.g.*, the development of the *rebab* as the leader's instrument in the gamelan; a repertoire of Arabic songs sung in Javanese and accompanied by a combination of Arabic and Javanese instruments (called *Santiswaran*); Javanese puppetry and dance based on the stories of the conquests of the Muslim Prince Menak; the retention of the Javanese version of the Hindu Mahabharata as the dominant literature of puppetry and dance but with the token recognition of Batara Settungal, the one God, as being above the Brahman gods and heroes still regarded by the Javanese as their ancestors.

More than three centuries of Dutch colonization, following a slow, systematic exploitation of Indonesian resources, had the passive effect of assuring cultural insularity. Western influences during this period were superficial and interfered little with the regulative principles which governed cultivated music. Up to the present time Christianity has made only slight inroads among the Javanese people. It is germane to our discussion, however, to note that recently in one of the Catholic churches in Central Java a Mass composed in *pélog patet nem* was sung partly in Latin, partly in Javanese, and was accompanied by the gamelan.

The strength and independence of cultivated music fostered by oral tradition may be shown in another way. It was mentioned earlier that prototypes of almost all of the modern Javanese and Balinese instruments were known from the beginning of the Hindu-Javanese period. Today there are three distinctly different developments of gamelan music within a very small geographic area: one in Central and East Java, one in West Java (which is peopled by the Sundanese) and one in Bali. Within each of these divisions a further differentiation may be made by region and by villages within a region. Yet all three basic types—Javanese, Sundanese and Balinese—use the same tuning systems and fundamentally the same kinds of instruments. Marked differences occur among the three musical traditions in the quality of the singing voice and the *rebab*, the usage of drums and the extent to which these may or may not be featured.

Different regulative principles have also guided the refinement of instrumental practice in each of the three ensembles. The Javanese gamelan is larger than the Sundanese and, following the principle of stratification, produces a rich texture of fifteen or more layers of independent melodic-rhythmic lines. Stratification is less developed in the Sundanese gamelan,

[20] Jaap Kunst, *Music in Java*, Vol. I, pp. 266-267.

and the instrumental style is simpler. But the prominence of the voice and the *rebab* and their frequent use of microtonal deviations from the fixed tuning system of the bronze instruments have developed a complicated refinement (*surupan*) of the *patet* (modal) system. Four drums played by one musician are predominant in a highly-varied display of rhythmic patterns. In Balinese gamelan the voice and the *rebab* have almost disappeared. Most of the instruments, including two drums, are tuned in male and female pairs (the female being slightly lower in pitch) which perform rapid interlocking figurations around and above a simple melody. Characterized by sudden contrasts in tempo and dynamics, this ensemble of 30 to 60 players maintains a standard of performance which, in my opinion, surpasses any other orchestra of similar size.

In spite of the common heritage of the Hindu-Javanese period and centuries of constant intercourse up to the present time, and in spite of the ubiquitous Hindu literature of the Mahabharata and the Ramayana with its inseparable musical accompaniment in puppetry, drama and dance, the Javanese, Sundanese and Balinese peoples have maintained and developed their individual oral traditions. The evolution of each of these musical expressions has been determined by the reliable oral transmission of a particular set of regulative principles. The nature of these principles can be more clearly understood by a brief examination of the primary musical concepts which have governed the most complicated of these three traditions—the music of Central Java.

The gradual development of the shape, size, number and quality of the bronze instruments has achieved a balanced ensemble of three distinct families: the *sarons*,[21] the *bonangs*[22] and the gongs.[23] The timbres of these loud-sounding instruments blend into one homogeneous quality of sound, the idea of contrasting orchestral color apparently being foreign to the guiding aesthetic. A comparison of the ancient three-tone *gamelan Munggang*, the younger *gamelan Sekati* (itself more than 400 years old), and the modern gamelan reveals that some of the bronze instruments have been reduced in size but increased in range and number, perhaps to accommodate the union of loud- and soft-sounding instruments and to allow a more flexible ensemble. The soft-sounding instruments of the gamelan also can be divided into three families: (1) the *gendèrs*;[24] (2) the *gambang* (xylophone) and *tjelempung* (plucked zither); and (3) the *rebab*, voice and flute. This group too is characterized by a uniform quality of sound, one which blends easily with the timbre of the bronze instruments when they are playing softly. The shape and size of the drums and their playing style have developed through the years to conform with the governing principle of achieving a homogeneity of sound in the total ensemble.

Another primary regulative principle has fostered the development of reliable modal practices. The main melody of the orchestral piece

21 Four sizes of instruments having six or seven thick, bronze keys mounted over a trough resonator.

22 Occurring in three sizes: an instrument with two rows of bronze, inverted kettles mounted over crossed cords.

23 There are two types occurring in several sizes: one type is suspended vertically and the other mounted horizontally on crossed cords, therefore an inverted kettle.

24 Three sizes of instruments having thin, bronze keys suspended over bamboo resonators.

is composed in accordance with the following considerations: the particular function of each tone of the mode, the special importance of three so-called "gong tones," the use of melodic and cadential formulas with careful regard to the manner in which they are elaborated, the handling of the so-called "enemy tone," the proper approach to and resolution of modulations, the correct usage of exchange tones (*sorogan*), the proper transposition from one mode to another and from one tuning system to another (*e.g.*, *sléndro* to *pélog*), the organic relationship between thematic development and the melodic germ stated in the introduction, rules of melodic movement, delayed cadences, and sundry other disciplines characteristic of cultivated music wherever it may be found. Creative freedom in this instance appears to be no more and no less restricted than in some of the written traditions of Western music. Special consideration is also given to the association of the different modes and the two tuning systems with the particular requirements of the all-night puppet plays and the dance.

The main melody of the piece, having been composed in accordance with these modal practices, becomes in turn the basis of elaboration for the entire ensemble. The form of the piece is determined by the periodicity of strokes on several sizes and types of gongs. The particular pitches played by these gongs is determined by a "structural melody" (the *balungan*) extracted from the main melody, but theoretically half of these structural points may be represented by a choice of one of three different pitches. Other local practices, such as melodic anticipation, permit even this simple melody a high degree of independence from the main melody of the piece.

One of the gongs may sound only once to every eight or more notes of the principal theme. The busier lines of stratification reverse this relationship, so that the *gendèr panerus* or the *gambang*, for example, may be playing 16 or 32 notes to every note of the main melody. The rapid activity of these instruments, however, is not in agreement with all the pitches of the principal theme but instead is also guided by the structural melody or *balungan* mentioned above. For example, in the course of the long melodic phrase (the *gongan*) the principal melody may contain 32 notes, and in the same time span the *gambang* plays 512 notes in a "two-handed" part with some independence between the two hands. Only 8 of these 512 notes must agree with those of the principal melody. This melodic independence is characteristic of all the soft-sounding instruments and to some degree of some of the loud-sounding instruments. The term "heterophony," sometimes used in connection with this and other cultivated musical practices of the Orient,[25] has either lost its Platonian meaning altogether or must be stretched to include works by Dufay, Obrecht, or Ockeghem which employ a cantus firmus in long note values. The absurdity of applying this term to Javanese cultivated music can be more fully appreciated if some of the manifold rules governing improvisation are pointed out.

The specific principles pertaining

[25] *Cf.* "Heterophony," *Harvard Dictionary of Music* (1946), p. 330; see further, "Javanese Music," p. 373: *N.B.*, although its source is not indicated, the transcription in Western notation would bring a smile to the face of any Javanese musician were he to hear it played by the gamelan as written.

to modal practice (mentioned above) form a basis for the art of improvisation. To these must be added: the proper usage, approach and resolution of the various harmonic intervals available on "two-handed" instruments, polyphonic independence between the two hands on some instruments, appropriate places for rhythmic variation, the approach, elaboration and resolution of cadential formulas, the finesse of melodic invention, which will reflect consistently the character of the individual piece, the realization of a part which is harmonious with those of other elaborating instruments, the execution of these and other regulative principles within the idiomatic articulation of a given instrument.

One might wonder how "set" an "improvised" part becomes. This varies somewhat with the type of instrument and with the individual player. On some instruments and with some players once a part has been "worked out" it remains more or less the same for repeated performances. More skilled players, however, manage a flexible and expert improvisation under the guidance of the *rebab* player. The multiple responsibilities of the *rebab* player as the leader of the gamelan have been explained elsewhere. We may mention here, however, that he ". . . leads the female soloist, indicates rhythmic and melodic variations for some of the elaborating instruments, directs changes of tempo and even tessitura—in short, he not only has the responsibilities of the Western orchestral conductor (fulfilled aurally rather than visually) but also guides the flow and direction of the improvisation."[26]

[26]Mantle Hood, "The Javanese Rebab," *Proceedings of the First Congress of the Galpin Society* (in press, 1959).

From the foregoing remarks we might too hastily conclude that the oral tradition in cultivated music is completely reliable, that historical and contemporary evidence suggests an eternal continuity. Unfortunately this is not so. Even the written traditions of Western music have been no stronger than the oral tradition which supported them. Polynomial and binomial systems of notation stretching round the world and back through all the centuries of recorded musical history depend on oral tradition for significant interpretation.[27] Even our modern monomial notation, including such polynomial vestiges as symbols for the trill and turn, must be interpreted in the appropriate stylistic tradition. One is tempted to ask, "How reliable is *written* tradition?" and to answer, as indicated above, "As reliable as the oral tradition on which it depends." We are also likely to forget that in the immediate past of our own written tradition an important part of the measure of the musician was his ability to improvise. The loss of the aesthetic which governed this type of creativity in performance should sharpen our awareness of similar impending losses in other parts of the world.

Blaring forth today on the radios of Iran or in the motion pictures of India is the venal product of commercialized ingenuous and cultivated musics. The impact of Western technology poses a threat which may prove too strong for cultivated music dependent on oral transmission. Although this subject has been examined elsewhere, I should like to quote a few pertinent passages here.

The success of an oral tradition is predicated on a lifetime of devotion by its

[27] Thurston Dart, "Notation," in *Grove's Dictionary* (5th ed.), Vol. VI, pp. 108ff.

practitioners. It has some merits over a written tradition in the development of tonal memory and quick aural perception. But the refinements of a highly developed art can be taught by this method only through months and years of painstaking imitation, until finally the student himself becomes the master; and having learned all that has preceded him—or at least all that his contemporary environment and society caused him to select—he in turn brings to his art an individual contribution that enriches the whole process. . . . In imitative methods of instruction a mistake made by the student is instantly corrected by the teacher, but on the basis of an almost-intuitive knowledge. The mistake is likely to occur and re-occur in different contexts because the teacher himself is not able to explain *in principle* what is wrong. By this method after years of corrective imitation the student finally develops a reliable "feeling" or intuition but no conscious understanding.[28]

In Java the Japanese occupation during World War II and the troubled revolutionary years that followed interrupted the flow of the oral tradition. Today the demand for general education among the younger generation precludes the re-establishment of the old, time-consuming methods of oral training in music. Unless the regulative principles which have guided the oral tradition become consciously known to the young Javanese musicians before the present generation of skilled players dies out, the finest attributes of their tradition will be lost.

University of California at Los Angeles

[28] Hood, "Changing Patterns."

THE CHALLENGE OF "BI-MUSICALITY"*

Mantle Hood

In the world of music one occasionally hears of the highly-skilled mechanic who fancies himself a performer, the clever inventor who passes himself off as a composer, the diligent historian who believes he is a musicologist and the professional educator who confuses method with music. At the risk of oversimplification let us say at least that all of these diverse representatives of the field of music would seem to have one trait in common—a lack of musicality. And what do we mean by "musicality?" First let us note that the Harvard Dictionary of Music wisely skips from "Musical glasses" to "Musical offering," and then—again at the risk of oversimplification—let us pass on to Webster's Unabridged Dictionary where "musicality" is defined as "musicalness," a noun form of the adjective "musical" under which, at long last, definition number three may be quoted: "Fond of, or intelligently appreciative of, music; as, a musical coterie; having a natural aptitude for music."

Although at this point we may see some wisdom in the policy followed by the Harvard Dictionary, let us assume that a natural aptitude for music is essential to the musician.

The basic study and training which develops musicality is known by several names: musicianship, fundamentals of music, solfeggio. I have never heard a musician suggest that this sine qua non might be by-passed, that the beginner should start with musical analysis or criticism. The training of ears, eyes, hands and voice and fluency gained in these skills assure a real comprehension of theoretical studies, which in turn prepares the way for the professional activities of the performer, the composer, the musicologist and the music educator.

Perhaps it is not necessary to remind the reader that we are speaking of the world of music, that training in basic musicianship of one order or another is characteristic of cultivated music wherever it is found and to some extent is unconsciously present in the practice of ingenuous music. It may be of some comfort to the music student of the West to realize that the Chinese, Javanese or Indian student also must jump through a series of musical hoops. But if this kind of training is indeed essential, the Western musician who wishes to study Eastern music or the Eastern musician who is interested in Western music faces the challenge of "bi-musicality."

A considerable interest in the performance and composition of Western music in some Oriental countries indicates that the East has made more progress in facing this challenge than the West. In fact, in some instances, we might point to an "alternative musicality," i.e., an interest in Western music which has developed at the expense of the indigenous music. However, in Japan the musicians of the Imperial Household in Tokyo would seem to be truly "bi-musical." "[They] have undergone rigid training since childhood, not only in the Gagaku dances and instrumental techniques, but also in the performance of Western music of the Classical period. In their capacity as official court musicians, they are required to perform both Gagaku and Western classical music."[1]

Occidentals, on the other hand, have usually limited their interest in non-Western music to passive observation, working with informants and museum studies. There may well be a multiplicity of reasons why in this instance basic musicianship or the fundamentals of music have been by-passed; but keeping in mind the court musician of Tokyo we should eliminate the argument that an alien musical expression has cultural or racial characteristics which make it inaccessible. Rather than labor the point of what has not been done in the past, let us consider some of the specific problems which confront the student who is learning a foreign music. After understanding the nature of these problems we shall be in a better position to evaluate the realistic goals to which the student might aspire.

The following observations are based on personal experience and a constant association with the performance-study groups at the University of

*A paper read at the Fourth Annual Meeting of the Society for Ethnomusicology, Chicago, December 29-30, 1959.

California at Los Angeles which currently include: Javanese gamelan, Balinese gamelan, Balinese gendèr wajang, Japanese gagaku, Japanese nagauta, Persian music and South Indian music.

The initial challenge, of course, is the development of an ability to hear. The tendency of Westerners to "correct" unfamiliar intervals, usually without being aware of doing so, can itself be corrected only by repeated exposure to listening and by singing. This beginning stage of training is directed at aural perception rather than vocal production, the latter involving special problems to be considered presently. In liberalizing his aural perception the student who has had no previous musical training may have a slight advantage over the advanced music major; but the most important factor in this connection is probably Webster's minimal definition of "musicality"—a natural aptitude for music. The most difficult conditioned prejudice to overcome among Western musicians is the sense of perfect pitch. Such an individual must come to realize that in the world of microtonal inflections his sense of pitch is actually imperfect, and unless he manages to set aside this prejudiced standard, he will have to relinquish the field to those who can manage a more democratic approach to the world of sound.

In the early phase of training, traditional methods of imitation and rote learning are far more rewarding in both time and retention than the usage of notation. Even in Japanese gagaku where rather detailed part books are followed by the musicians a new piece is first learned by singing the instrumental parts. Javanese and Balinese gamelan is never performed from notation; the student sings and plays simultaneously as he learns a piece phrase by phrase. The person with no previous musical training again has an advantage over the music student who misses the printed page and who, in the beginning, finds it frustrating not to be able to "see" where he is going. In order to avoid psychological blocks in the acceptance of imitative learning, students new to these studies are given ample opportunity to demonstrate for themselves the validity of traditional methods. For example, at the beginning of the academic year when fifty per cent or more of the group is made up of newcomers, a piece is given to everyone in cipher notation. After an entire evening of rehearsal on this one piece, everybody (except the seasoned player) is satisfied that he knows it well. At the next rehearsal the notation is withheld, and then the fun begins. Characteristically, everyone makes a strong start, but after a few phrases memory fails and finally the piece falters and dies. At this point traditional methods are suggested. If a majority still prefers to use notation, the experiment is repeated. At the next rehearsal a confident beginning, a look of confusion when the tune suddenly develops variations, and finally everyone agrees that some other approach is worth trying. We musicians in the West are deficient in tonal memory and also unpracticed in memorizing parts from the printed page. By imitative methods a fairly complex and lengthy melody can be learned in one evening and retained for an indefinite number of years. Recently a former member of the Javanese gamelan returned after an absence of three years. To his amazement the old melodies were still fresh in his mind.

This type of training sharpens aural perception, develops tonal memory and begins to release the conditioned Western musician from his dependence on a visible conductor. Arm and hand movements are not used by the teacher but only the sound of metrical handclapping or basic drumming, so that from the beginning the student must rely entirely on his ears for a guide. Later when the single Javanese melody becomes only one thread in a polyphonic tapestry of fifteen to twenty different strata of sound, the student must be able to follow the basic pulsations which govern the entire ensemble.

The element of rhythm in non-Western music presents another challenge to the newcomer. In Balinese gamelan the ear must follow interlocking rhythms played by a pair of male and female drums, while the hand executes one part of a different pair of interlocking rhythms. The student must be able to perceive brief drum signals for abrupt changes in tempo or dynamics as well as follow a rubato executed by an ensemble of thirty players. In Javanese gamelan the principle of stratification produces many layers of cross rhythms; and when the dance drum and the keprak (a kind of wood block) are accompanying the dance, they produce a loud, clear and at times unmeasured rhythm against the regular pulsations of the rest of the ensemble. In Japanese gagaku the long time-spans of the taiko (a deep-toned drum) subdivided by the kakko (a small hour-glass drum) and the shoko (a small gong) will seem to the beginner like random sounds in the ensemble. An LP record of gagaku speeded up to 78 rpm will convince the novice that these instruments follow a regular metric structure. Persian music requires a good imitative ear to register the traditional spirit of its free meter. In the study of Indian music the student finds that he must learn a complex vocabulary of drum sounds, called bols, which forms the basis of improvisation on the tala.

The technical demands of oral or manual articulation vary in degree from one instrument to another, but even the simplest requires a surprising amount of study. It usually takes the beginner a few months to believe the experienced player when he says that it is no easy matter to learn to hit a gong or a single bronze slab in just the right way. The following account will illustrate this point. A Chinese-Indonesian friend of mine told me that before the Japanese occupation her family owned a beautiful, large gamelan. A member of her family most devoted to the evening gamelan performances was her blind grandfather, who could always tell at the first stroke of the big gong who, among several musicians, was playing it.

One of the most difficult instruments to master among the Javanese or Balinese idiophones is the gendèr. The Javanese gendèr has thirteen or fourteen thin bronze keys mounted over bamboo resonators and is played with two tabuh or beaters which have padded discs on the striking end. The right and left hands execute completely independent melodic lines, and in a refined style of playing the left hand sometimes carries two melodies. The keys increase in size from left to right, and the degree of melodic activity is greater in the right hand than in the left. For these reasons the two hands use different positions in holding the tabuh. In striking any idiophone the player soon learns that a blow which is strictly perpendicular to the sounding surface tends to damp immediately. Therefore, the slightest possible arc or "V" with a rounded vortex produces the best result. As the tabuh are swinging along in these almost imperceptible tight arcs or "V's," the same hand that delivers the blow must damp the key as the next key is struck or, in refined playing, a moment later. The Balinese gendèr uses two panggul or beaters with long handles and hard wooden discs on the striking end. In the large gamelan gong the two-handed gendèr has been replaced, except in a few of the older pieces like legong, by a slightly larger instrument which uses only one hammer-shaped panggul. However, the Balinese gendèr wajang, the two or four instruments which accompany the all-night puppet plays, are still very much in usage. The instruments have 10 keys and are tuned in male and female pairs which occur in two sizes an octave apart. The panggul used for this instrument has a small grommet mounted behind the wooden disc, and this little ring made of horn has just enough play so that it slides back and forth to produce a lovely "clacking" sound as the panggul rises and falls on the keys. The long handles on these beaters, unlike those of the Javanese, require similar positions for both hands. In my opinion, the music played by the gendèr wajang quartet is perhaps the most satisfying musical expression in Bali. The right hand tends to establish permutations on an ostinato often divided among three pitches while the left hand carries one or two independent melodies. In the course of one piece the parts played by the male and female instruments are sometimes interlocking, sometimes independent and occasionally the same.

One of the best illustrations of the challenge of mastering Oriental instruments of the aerophone family is Japanese gagaku. The chordal responsibilities of the sho (a kind of mouth organ), and the microtonal inflections of the ryuteki (the flute) and the hichiriki (a short oboe) demand an extremely sensitive ear and finely coordinated action between fingers and breath control. Accurate performance of these subtle embellishments can only be achieved through intense imitative practice and of course an aural perception that has been entirely freed from the twelve-tone tempered scale.

In the family of membranophones the challenge of hand drumming requires not only flexible fingers and hands but also a keen ear for discerning thirty or more different sounds which may be the vocabulary of one double-headed drum. The usage of mnemonics in teaching hand drumming may be taken as evidence that the proper sound is emphasized rather than the precise direction of finger and hand positions. Both are important, of course, but the physical difference between one person's hands and another's makes it necessary for each individual to experiment until he has found the proper adjustment of a given position that for him produces the correct sound. In Bali the pair of drums which leads the large gamelan in the accompaniment of the warrior dance called "Baris" uses a panggul or beater on the right head and only the hand on the left head.

The challenge of the chordophones may involve plucking, rubbing, striking or depressing in a particular way to produce microtonal inflections or ornaments. Among the bowed lutes the Javanese rebab is a good example of the kind of adaptability which may be required of the student. The rebab has two metal strings tuned a sléndro or pélog fifth apart in the approximate range of the D and A strings of the cello. It has a parchment head, a high thin bridge, a long slender neck but no fingerboard. Therefore too much or too little pressure from the fingers or the bow will produce the wrong intonation. The bow is loose-haired and must be tightened by the ring finger, which coordinates its movement with the hand and wrist to effect a slight "bite" at the beginning of each stroke. The rebab is the leader's instrument in the gamelan and must give directions for changes in tempo and dynamics as well as guide the instrumentalists and the singers in their improvisation.

In learning to sing in the traditional style the student faces a number of problems beyond the challenge of correct pitch. The sounds peculiar to the foreign language involved must be mastered; and related to this aspect of the study but more difficult is the appropriate quality of the singing voice. The quality of the Eastern singing voice varies in a marked degree from one musical culture to another. In the limited geographic area of Java and Bali there are three principal languages and three distinct qualities of singing voice: Sundanese in West Java, Javanese in Central and East Java and Balinese in Bali. Even the layman has no difficulty in recognizing that these three are quite different. Not only the melodic line, the style of ornaments, the use of vibrato and nonvibrato but also the very quality of sound itself set them apart. The student must imitate the proper shape of the mouth, the position of the tongue, the attitude of the head, the tension in neck muscles and even to a degree the revealing facial expressions which are an open window to the singer's unconscious muscular control. He must set aside Western notions of the bel canto voice and experiment with his own vocal production until he is able to perform feats in the control of intonation that a Western singer would have difficulty in hearing, not to mention singing.

The crowning achievement in the study of Oriental music is fluency in the art of improvisation. This is only possible after the student has become proficient in the technical demands of the art, so that he is free to follow the musical inventions of his own imagination. Needless to say, his inventions must be guided through the maze of traditional rules that govern improvisation. These can be consciously learned but can be artistically used only when the whole tradition has been assimilated. This means an understanding of and an insight into not only music and the related arts but also language, religion, customs, history—in other words, the whole identity of the society of which music is only one, but one very important, part.

At this point we might ask just how far a Western musician can go along the road of Oriental musical studies. My answer to this question is: "Just as far as his objective takes him." If his desire is to comprehend a particular Oriental musical expression so that his observations and analysis as a musicologist do not prove to be embarrassing, he will have to persist in practical studies until his basic musicianship is secure. If he chooses to become a professional instrumentalist or singer competing with others in the country of his chosen study (and this possibility seems to me remote), he will have to persist in practical studies considerably beyond the requirements of basic musicianship until he attains professional status. Perhaps the best answer to the question "How far can he go" is "How much time does he have?" The performance-study groups at U.C.L.A. are an extra-curricular activity. Considering the relatively small amount of time actually devoted to these practical studies, their understanding and performance is such that it would seem safe to say that the American student has a real potential in the study of non-Western music.

One question which seems to me implicit in the title assigned for this paper rises in connection with the term "bi-musicality." Earlier I mentioned

Western music which has displaced indigenous music as evidence of "alternative musicality." At UCLA there are several advanced graduate students who manage themselves quite capably in several different musical cultures. Here then are we to speak of "tri-musicality" or "quadri-musicality?" Perhaps we shall come close to the heart of the matter if we return to Webster's basic definition and retitle this paper simply to read: "The Challenge of Musicality."

NOTES

1. Robert Garfias, Gagaku, the Music and Dances of the Japanese Imperial Household, New York City: Theatre Arts Books, 1959, (not numbered) see second page under "Historical Development."

UNIVERSALISM AND RELATIVISM IN THE STUDY OF ETHNIC MUSIC

Leonard B. Meyer

It is remarkable with what persistent and single-minded intent human beings strive for inner security and psychic certainty. We cling tenaciously to familiar ways and accepted explanations, blandly disregarding or rationalizing away incongruities and inconsistencies, if only we may be permitted the tranquillity of a system and certainty of a set of principles. Only a few can tolerate ambiguity and its attendant tensions.

Perhaps it is this need for the reliability of order and regularity that compels the mind to obey the principles of pattern perception formulated by the Gestalt psychologists: the psychological organization will always be as good as prevailing conditions allow; a motion once begun will tend to continue in the simplest possible way; changes in memory traces will tend to improve shape; and so forth. In the realms of philosophy, science, and mathematics a similar need leads us to accept as "best" or "true" those explanations which are the simplest and most economical—as, for instance, in the principle of Occam's Razor.[1]

(Observe, incidentally, that in subsuming the theories of Gestalt Psychology and the principle of Occam's Razor under a single general concept, I am obeying the very tendencies which I am discussing.)

Not only does a principle of parsimony govern our perception of music, through the unconscious operation of principles such as those of simplicity and good shape, but it also influences the explanations we give of the nature of music, the development of musical styles, and the relations of music to the culture in which it arises. In short, it shapes both musical experience itself and our thinking about musical experience. And it seems possible that the operation of this principle is responsible for the strong tendency toward simplistic monism which has marked our thinking in the area of Ethnic music.

I.

Fifty years ago music was generally considered to be a universal language. Obvious differences between music of different cultures were explained away as being apparent rather than real. Beneath the profusion of seemingly disparate styles, it was argued, lay fundamental absolute principles which governed the structure and development of all music everywhere. It was only necessary to discover these basic underlying laws. But when these laws were not discovered, this form of monism was largely discredited and went out of fashion.

Then the warm winds of academic opinion began to blow in the opposite direction—toward an equally monistic relativism which sought to study each culture and each music "in its own terms" and which looked with suspicion upon any search for universal principles. Although scholars of this persuasion gathered much valuable data, for various reasons—perhaps above all precisely because it avoided cross-cultural questions such as those concerned with characteristics common to cultures that are unrelated ethnologically and geographically—relativism failed to produce fruitful hypotheses which might have led to new types of data and provided new insights into the nature of man, culture, and their interrelationships. As a consequence, this form of monism has come to seem less and less satisfactory.

There is, however, no transcendent logic compelling us to choose between these antithetical positions. Instead we can merely ask which features of music, if any, tend to be common to different cultures and which vary from culture to culture. The study and analysis of this material would presumably indicate which aspects of music are universal and which are culturally determined. Hypotheses might then be formulated to account for the findings and, of course, to explain the exceptions.

Unfortunately the matter is not so simply solved. Appearances are often deceptive. For instance, two cultures may appear to employ the same scale structure, but this structure might be interpreted differently by the members of each culture. Conversely, the music of two cultures may employ very different materials, but the underlying mechanism governing the organization of these materials might be the same for both. The possibility of such discrepancy calls attention to the importance of methodology and definition.

Strange though it may seem, such common terms as melody, mode, rhythm, form, and the like have been used in two different, though related, senses; and considerable confusion has resulted from the failure to keep these different uses separate and distinct.

Such terms have been used in a purely descriptive way to refer to sound stimuli and the objective relationships among them. Thus the tonal materials of a musical style can be analyzed, the relative frequency with which particular tones or intervals appear can be calculated, patterns of melodic repetition can be studied, minutiae of performance can be scrutinized, and so on. A descriptive method such as this treats music like a physical phenomenon—as something to be observed, measured, classified, and compared.

However, the interpretation of such objective data is not without difficulties. For interpretation and explanation involve the use of general laws or hypotheses which serve to order and make understandable the diversity and disparity of observed particulars. In physics the laws explaining, say, the behavior of masses are, like the empirical data itself, essentially descriptive. Thus the law of gravity is a formula which stipulates a constant relationship among mass, distance, and force of attraction. It does not posit causes, it describes.

Because of the number of variables and the complexity of their interaction, the data assembled by descriptive ethnomusicology yields relatively few observable regularities. Furthermore, music is so patently a human product that, even when they can be found, purely descriptive laws do not seem really satisfying. For we still want to trace these observed regularities to their human source and to correlate them with the more general laws governing all human behavior. Thus the initial descriptive data of music must ultimately be explained in terms of the mental behavior, needs, habits, and culture out of which it arises.

It is when such explanation begins that the meanings of terms become changed. They are no longer purely descriptive. Rather they refer to psychological experiences. A mode is no longer a constant set of individual tones. It is a set of subjectively felt tendencies among the tones. The scope of ethnomusicology has changed too. It now requires not only knowledge of the stimulus, but also knowledge of the responding individual—whether composer, performer, or listener—for whom the stimulus has significance; and such knowledge includes an understanding of mental behavior as it operates within the context of culturally acquired habits and dispositions.

Without belittling the importance and the many contributions of descriptive ethnomusicology, the nature and limits of the information it can yield need to be understood. For it has at times employed concepts and reached conclusions which were unwarranted because they rested upon unrecognized or untested assumptions of a psychological sort. For instance, descriptive data of a statistical nature has occasionally been made the basis for inferences about tonality. But tonality is a psychological phenomenon—a subjective sense of the tendency relationships among tones. And though I am inclined to believe that some sort of correlation exists between statistical frequency and felt tonal tendency, such a subjective response cannot validly be inferred from or correlated with descriptive data unless the relationship between them can be empirically demonstrated and theoretically explained.

In short, a purely descriptive method provides data rather than explanations (theory). In itself such data tells us little about music as a form of human activity—about its significance for the peoples who make and enjoy it. And when significance is, so to speak, thrust upon it, descriptive data is apt to be misleading because objective similarities do not necessarily give rise to correspondingly similar psychological responses and because, conversely, objective differences may be products of essentially similar psychological mechanisms.

This calls attention to a point of some moment. What we should ask about, when considering the problem of universals, is not whether the data itself is common to different cultures—anymore than we decide whether there are scientific laws on the basis of particular physical events. What we should ask is whether, beneath the profusion of diverse and divergent particulars, there are any universal principles functioning. Stated thus it becomes apparent that the descriptive method is less than satisfactory for dealing with the problem of universalism vs. relativism precisely because it ignores those psychological concepts which might provide common principles for interpreting and explaining the enormous variety of musical means found in different cultures.

II.

Understanding of the process of musical communication too has been muddled by the tendency of critics, theorists, and aestheticians to treat alternative modes of signification as mutually exclusive. Indeed, the monistic approach to the question of universalism vs. relativism is in part a product of this prior monism which sought to exclude as spurious or fortuitous all but one type of musical meaning. But communication is not thus limited. At least two basic modes of signification—the connotative and the kinetic or syntactic—can be distinguished.[2]

By connotations are meant associations—whether consciously intellectualized or unconsciously felt—made between the musical organization and some aspect of extra-musical experience, be it an idea, an object, a quality, or an activity. For our purposes the term will also include what has been called the "mood response" to music. As differentiated from the purely subjective, intrapersonal associations evoked by image processes, those involved in connotation are more or less standardized, having the same significance for, and producing the same attitudes in, all members of the cultural group. When a particular musical idea or pattern is used to refer to a specific concept, object or event—for instance, Wagner's Leitmotifs or the cannon in the 1812 Overture—it may be said to have denotative significance, though such denotation does not preclude the possibility of concurrent connotation.

It should be noted that few connotations are simple. What is communicated is a group of interrelated associations—a connotative complex.[3] For instance, night, winter, cold, death, solemnity, and sadness, constituting a kind of interwoven, inclusive musical metaphor, might be simultaneously signified by a single musical event.

Though any particular connotation is generally the product of both, two mechanisms of association can be distinguished: association by contiguity and association by similarity.

In the case of contiguity, some aspect of the musical organization—an instrumental timbre, a mode, a melody, etc.—becomes linked by dint of repetition with a concept, quality, activity, or mood. The organ is, for instance, associated for western listeners with religious concepts and attitudes; in Arabian music the strings of the lute were associated with actions of the soul, times of day, seasons of the year, and so on; the various Hindu ragas are associated with ethical concepts, moods, hours of the day, and seasons of the year.

Such associations by contiguity are culture-bound. A particular raga will not, for example, evoke the appropriate associations in a western listener unless he has learned its "meaning." The sound of an organ will not arouse religious associations in the members of a primitive tribe which has not been visited by missionaries—if such a tribe exists. Because contiguity creates associations which are contingent rather than necessary, they are subject to change and modification. Old associations die out and new ones arise.

However important associations formed by contiguity may be, their role in connotative signification is a relatively minor one. Most connotations arise as the result of similarities which exist between our experience of music, on the one hand, and our experience of concepts, objects, activities, qualities, and states of mind found in the extramusical world, on the other. Generally associations formed by contiguity modify and delimit those formed by similarity.

As Hornbostel has observed, perceptual experience is one.[4] Both music and life are experienced as dynamic processes—as motions differentiated both in shape and in quality. Such motions may be fast or slow, continuous or disjointed, precise or ambiguous, calm or violent, and so forth. Even experiences without literal, phenomenal motion are somehow associated with activity. Sunlight, the pyramids, a smoothly polished stone, a jagged line—each, depending partly upon our attitude toward it, is felt to exhibit some characteristic quality of motion and of sound.

The problem is not, as some have argued, whether music evokes connotations. An overwhelming amount of evidence proves that it does. Nor from the standpoint of ethnomusicology is the problem that of the propriety and aesthetic validity of connotative significance. The question is whether the processes of association are the same in different cultures; whether similar musical processes and structures give rise to similar or analogous connotations in different cultures. A modest sampling of the evidence indicates these processes are cross-cultural. The problem is an important one, of interest not only for ethnomusicology, but for aesthetics and psychology as well. It deserves thorough and carefully documented investigation.

One final point. It must be remembered that the musical characterization of an activity or concept depends upon the attitude of the culture toward the concept as well as upon the psychological mechanisms of association. Ostensibly similar concepts may be characterized differently in different cultures, or even within a single culture, not because the process of association is inconstant, but because the concept is viewed in different ways. In our own culture, for example, Death is generally considered to be solemn, fearful, and mysterious; but it has also been regarded as an expected friend or as the sardonic mocker of human pretensions. Obviously each of these views would give rise to a different musical characterization.

The kinetic-syntactic mode of signification refers to those essentially intra-musical experiences in which tonal stimuli have meaning because they are understood as the products of earlier musical events and point with varying degrees of probability to future events, creating a sense of movement toward and away from purely musical goals. Words such as tension, expectation, surprise, and delay are verbal descriptions of this mode of musical experience.

Note that, far from being antithetical, the connotative and kinetic modes of signification complement and qualify each other. Just as the behavior of an individual—his language, manners, decisions, and the like—play a part in shaping our opinion of his character, so the kinetic "behavior" of a piece of music (whether continuous or disjointed, expected or surprising) colors our feeling of its connotative significance. The converse of this also holds: connotations influence our expectations as to the way in which a piece will probably procede sytactically.

As was the case with connotation, two aspects of the process of kinetic communication can be distinguished: the grammatical and the psychological. In the grammatical are included the tonal materials of a musical style (its vocabulary) and the rules governing the ways in which these materials may be combined (its grammar). The grammatical aspect of music varies from culture to culture and from style to style within a culture. What remains constant are not scales, modes, harmonic progressions or formal procedures, but the psychology of human mental processes—the way in which the mind, operating within the context of a culturally established grammar, selects and organizes and evaluates the musical materials presented to it. For instance, the desire of the human mind for completeness and stability is a psychological constant. Consequently when a structural gap, such as a skip of an octave is perceived, the mind expects it to be completed, to be filled in. But the particular way in which it will be filled depends upon the tonal materials available and the rules governing their combination, that is, upon the grammar of the style. This will generally vary from style to style.

These observations too need empirical, cross-cultural confirmation. Such confirmation is difficult because, as Nettl points out, native informants find it difficult to verbalize about tonal organization, form, and the like.[5] But direct interrogation is not the only way to get evidence, nor the only way to discover what the norms and the permissible deviants of a style are and what rules and probabilities govern their use. Rather the ethnomusicologist, like the linguist, must learn to use the materials he wishes to study; he must learn to perform the music himself. For instance, by performing a group of carefully designed musical variants for an informant and asking questions such as: "is this a possible beginning phrase?" "which of these ways is better?" "can one do this?"—he can gradually discover the grammar and syntax of the style. Such a procedure supplemented by a statistical, descriptive study of the repertory of the culture should provide a reasonably detailed and accurate account of the kinetic features of the style being studied. It would also enable cross-cultural investigation to be more rigorous, more precise, and more revealing.

III.

Because the limitations imposed by an exclusively descriptive methodology have all but precluded an adequate analysis of signification, the problem of musical value, when it has been considered at all, has generally taken the form of an inventory of the uses made of music in a particular culture. Thus it has been observed that music is employed, and presumably valued, for its therapeutic properties, its magical powers, as an adjunct of ritual, and as a kind of recreation. Such observations, important though they may be, are relevant to the study of cultural choices and values rather than to the study of musical values. Treated thus, the problem of musical value is not logically different from that of the value of basket-weaving or of puberty rites. What is needed in addition to this data is an account of what constitutes excellence in the music of a particular culture—an account, that is, of the musical decisions made by musicians and audiences.

Although an adequate discussion of musical value is beyond the scope both of this author and of this essay, the problems involved are so intimately related to those of signification, that some tentative remarks may perhaps not be out of place.

It is possible, I think, to make a plausible distinction between cultural values and individual values. The former, which are analogous to the culturally dependent processes involved in association by contiguity and in the grammatical structure of style, determine the uses made of music in the culture, the emphasis placed upon connotative vs. syntactical signification, and the degree of conformity demanded (or deviation permitted) by the culture. Individual values, which are analogous to the mechanism of association by similarity and the laws of pattern perception, arise out of the psychological organization and needs of the individual. The satisfaction of these needs is controlled by, and takes place within, the context of culturally established modes of behavior.

Of special relevance to the understanding of individual values is the psychological need for novelty—or, as some have put it, for information.[6] Its importance as a basic human drive is implicit in recent studies of creativity, developmental psychology, and stimulus privation.[7] It seems possible that the need for information is in part responsible for the tendency of composers and performers to deviate from established stylistic norms. Or, to put the matter in a different way: exact repetition is dull, clichés are boring, and familiar tasks tedious—without value—because they yield very little information.

If the distinction between cultural values and individual values has merit and if the need for novelty can be shown to be a basic principle of individual value—as the need for good shape is the basis for the laws of pattern perception—then the study of musical value need not be confined to cataloguing cultural usage.

What follow from this are not infallible answers, but rather a myriad of intriguing questions. If novelty is a basic human need, why do some cultures place severe restrictions upon it? Can one discover any pattern between the type or the degree of restriction and other features of the culture? Is such restraint a function of cultural level? For instance, does the need for novelty act as a correlate of value only when music becomes differentiated from other aspects of culture as a special, aesthetic object? In what ways do the norms of a culture channel and govern the permissible modes of deviation?

These questions—and one can think of many more—might well lead to a more fruitful and enlightened analysis of the nature of value in western music as well as non-western music and at the same time help to clarify the correlative problem of universality vs. relativity of values.

NOTES

1. The search for mental security is not a product of psychological inertia or mental sloth. We are obviously willing to expend much effort and energy in order to simplify shapes and rationalize explanations. Rather the need for psychic certainty would seem to arise out of man's awareness of time and his consequent need to predict—to know the future.

2. These two types of signification are discussed at some length in my book Emotion and Meaning in Music (University of Chicago Press, 1956). However, in that book the term "embodied meaning" was used to designate what is here called "kinetic-syntactic signification."

3. See Meyer, op. cit., pp. 264-266.

4. E. von Hornbostel, "The Unity of the Senses," Psyche, VII (1927), 83-89; also see K. Koffka, Principles of Gestalt Psychology (New York: Harcourt Brace & Co., 1935), p. 303.

5. Bruno Nettl, Music in Primitive Culture (Cambridge: Harvard University Press, 1956), p. 59.

6. See Leonard B. Meyer, "Some Remarks on Value and Greatness in Music," Journal of Aesthetics, XVII (1959), 486-500.

7. See, for instance, Frank Barron, "The Psychology of Imagination," Scientific American, 199 No. 3 (Sept., 1958), 151-166; J. W. Getzels and P. W. Jackson, "The Highly Intelligent and Highly Creative Adolescent: A Summary of Recent Research Findings," The Third Research Conference (1959) on the Identification of Creative Scientific Talent, ed. Calvin W. Taylor (Salt Lake City: University of Utah Press, to be published in 1960); Woodburn Heron, "The Pathology of Boredom," Scientific American, Vol. 196 No. 7 (Jan., 1957), 52-56; John Rader Platt, "The Fifth Need of Man," Horizon, Vol. I No. 6 (July, 1959), 106-111; Morris I. Stein, "Creativity and Culture," Journal of Psychology, 36 (1953), 311-322; William R. Thompson and Ronald Melzack, "Early Environment," Scientific American, Vol. 194 No. 7 (Jan., 1956), 38-42.

INTRODUCTION

Japanese music, like the other Japanese fine arts, has gone through several marked stylistic changes. These extend over a period from approximately the seventh century to the present day. During the Nara and Heian periods Buddhist chanting and court orchestral music *(gagaku)* flourished while the Kamakura and Muromachi periods saw the rise of *biwa* lute accompanied narratives and a host of theatricals which culminated in the *noh* drama and its music. The Edo period luxuriated in music for the thirteen stringed *koto* zither, the end-blown *shakuhachi* flute, and the three stringed *shamisen.* The latter became an essential element in the *bunraku* puppet plays and the *kabuki* theatre. In the twentieth century, traditional musicians made several efforts to meet the challenge of western music, with varying degrees of success. Through all these periods of music history certain fundamental Japanese musical characteristics can be found. Their specific applications change with each period as, for example, in the West the concept of many-part (polyphonic) music in the thirteenth century varies vastly from that of the sixteenth, eighteenth, or twentieth centuries. The principles to be discussed have an importance to Japanese music analogous to polyphony in western music. Continuing the analogy, an awareness of the western fondness for several different lines of music sounding simultaneously is certainly one useful guide to understanding western music in general. With such knowledge one could go on to distinguish periods or styles of music in which a more vertical (harmonic) orientation is present such as early classical music, hymns, or modern folk singing, and traditions in which a more horizontal (contrapuntal) orientation dominates as in fugues, twelve tone music, and Dixieland. By this process, ideally, one becomes an "intelligent" music lover. The principles in Japanese music presented below can also be subjected to such a process of refinement. My intent in this article, however, is not to create a new body of Japanese music lovers, but rather to provide guidelines for an intelligent approach to Japan's various music traditions.

BASIC CONCEPTS IN JAPANESE MUSIC

The characteristics of Japanese music fall under three general headings; 1) the sound ideal, 2) the structural ideal, and 3) the artistic intent. In actual practice, of course, these three areas are difficult to separate.

The Sound Ideal

A basic concept in most Japanese music is to get the maximum effect from the minimum amount of material. Many times the full technical possibilities of an instrument have not been exploited in order to concentrate the player's and the listener's attention on a deliberately restricted sound spectrum. The *taiko* stick drum of the *noh* and *kabuki* theatres is a good example. It has two cowhide heads stretched over iron rings some twenty inches in diameter and lashed over a barrel-shaped body which is suspended off the floor by a special frame. One could play some brilliant solos on the *taiko* by banging away on its rim and heads, but the Japanese play it only on a small circle of deer skin set in the center of one head. The slightly muffled yet resonant tone that results is a musical equivalent of the *shibui* colors of Japanese fabrics and other materials. It is a brightness showing through a subtle dullness. Since part of art is, by definition, artifice, it is important to realize just how deliberate such effects can be. In the case of this *taiko* sound, one finds that it is capable of still further refinement. When the drum is used in pieces which contain dramatic dances the ropes that lash the skins to the body are tightened so that the pitch of the sound is higher while in more lyrical compositions the pitch is lowered. It is the combination of many such "little" things that creates artistry in the performance of any music, be it by Beethoven or Kineya Rokusaemon, the Sixth.

A restriction of the sound spectrum does not mean a sameness of sound. It means, rather, looking for variety in a microcosmos instead of a macrocosmos. Consider the sound of the thirteen stringed *koto* zither as an example. Its harp-like tone has often appealed to foreigners and, judging from personal experience, the soothing sameness of its sound apparently makes it an ideal background music for "oriental" parties. When one actually studies *koto* music it becomes apparent that its supposedly plain classical melodies are subjected to a large number of subtle variations. The strings of the instrument can be twisted, pushed down, or stroked in a variety of ways, each of which adds its own special color to the tones of the instrument. Of course, to be effective these techniques must in themselves be used with restraint. One can often judge the artistry of a performance by the player's sense of taste in the distribution of such ornamentations.[1]

Another aspect of the Japanese sound ideal is the chamber music approach. While this idea is partially an extension of the maximum effect-minimum material axiom, it has additional connotations. By a chamber music approach I mean that no matter how large the ensemble becomes, the individual instruments are meant to be heard. The antithesis to this is found in the orchestral music approach of the western romantic and impressionistic schools in which the sounds of individual instruments are merged into one massive musical color. The chamber music sound can easily be heard in such ensembles as the western piano trio (piano, violin, and cello) or in Japanese *sankyoku (koto, shakuhachi,* and *shamisen).* It is my contention, however, that the principle applies as well to the larger Japanese ensembles such as the *gagaku* court orchestra and the *kabuki nagauta* ensemble.[2] In *gagaku* the arpeggios of the pear-shaped *biwa* lute and the court *koto (gaku-so)* are clearly etched against the harmonic matrix of the *sho* mouth organ. The melody played on the *hichiriki* oboe differs slightly from that of the flute and those who have heard the *hichiriki*'s tone quality would agree that it would be unlikely to merge with any other sound. The sounds of the interpunctuating drums and gong are also distinct. In the *kabuki* ensemble, the stacatto-like notes of the *shamisen* are clearly separated from the vocal line. In very lyrical sections a bamboo flute is used which tends to merge with the vocal sound, but even in this case the flute's ornamentations help to separate its line from the voice and *shamisen.* When the *noh* flute *(nokan)* is used in *kabuki,* it differs from the voice and *shamisen* parts not only in melody but in tonality. The three drums of the *kabuki* (borrowed along with the *nokan* from the *hayashi* ensemble of the *noh* drama) also present contrasting sounds. Besides the *taiko* stick drum mentioned earlier there is a *ko-tsuzumi* shoulder drum and an *o-tsuzumi* side drum. Though both *tsuzumi* are played with the right hand, their tones are quite different. The *ko-tsuzumi* produces four different sounds, the most characteristic being a deep, trailing "pon." The *o-tsuzumi* by contrast produces a sharp, hard, cracking sound. Put all these *kabuki* sounds together and you have great variety but little coalescence. This is the essense of the Japanese chamber music sound ideal, distinctness versus coalescence. Such an ideal is not exclusively Japanese. It is found, for example, in most Near Eastern and Indian ensembles as well as in medieval and renaissance Europe performance practice. Nevertheless, it is a useful point of contrast between Japanese music and the western symphonic tradition as well as between Japanese music and the *gamelan* orchestras of Indonesia, similar ensembles in Southeast Asia, and the theatre orchestras of China.

The Structural Intent

In most music the basic structural unit is the melody. By extending the time span of our structural hearing we are able to recognize phrases, periods, sections, and entire pieces as coherent units. In the last three hundred years of western music there has been a general tendency to hear individual melodies in two parts and entire pieces in rounded or closed forms. The western two part attitude is often expressed in such terms as question and answer, arsis and thesis, or antecedent and consequent. Thus, for example, the first four notes of Beethoven's Fifth Symphony (G G G E flat) require for us a four note answer (F F F D). In addition, we presume that, if this theme is important to the work, it is likely to show up again somewhere near the end of the piece if not earlier. This is what is meant by a rounded approach to form, the feeling that material heard earlier should return.

In addition to being frequently used in art music, binary tunes and rounded forms are also characteristic of most western folk and popular music. In binary tunes like "Clementine," for example, we presume that a line like the one ending "...excavating for a mine" must be answered by a line like the one ending "...and his daughter, Clementine." As for rounded forms, one has only to think of the AABA form of such old standards as "Sweet Sue," "Blue Moon," or "Smoke Gets in Your Eyes" to realize that the rounded form has long been a way of life in tinpan alley, not to mention the "gay nineties" or Stephen Foster.

In Japanese folk and popular music there are many binary tunes and rounded forms. The two part melodies are also common in art music. There are, however, a very large number of Japanese examples which divide the melody into three parts and use what is called an open form, i.e., a form in which the material first heard does not return later.

Many examples of three part melodies can be found in the vocal music of the *noh* drama called *utaii* or *yokyoku.* For example, the standard 7-5 syllable division of a line such as "Sore kato omou, omo kage no" from the play *Hana gatami* would seem to require a two part division but, when set in the typical eight beat phrase of *noh,* it looks as follows (Gakudo 1922: 135):

JO			HA		KYU		
1	2	3	4	5	6	7	8
So — re	ka-to		o — mo-u		o — mo ka-ge no —		

In *noh* the terms used to describe these divisions are *jo-ha-kyu,* introduction, scattering, and rushing. These divisions are reinforced by the accompanying drummers who tend to place special vocal calls *(kakegoe)* before the third, fifth, and seventh beats. There also tend to be more drum beats played during the rushing *kyu* section just as, in the example above, there are more syllables at that point.

Larger applications of the *jo-ha-kyu* concept can be found by studying an entire *noh* drama for its many sections can be arranged in three large divisions (Tatsuo 1957: 181-200). Actually, the terms *jo-ha-kyu* first appeared in Japan as general divisions in the ancient court dances *(bugaku).* Since that time they have been used to explain both the minute and general meaning of pieces from many genre. The subdivisions of *nagauta shamisen* music, for example, have often been arranged like *noh* music in three parts (Malm 1963: 36, 40, 118). In *gidayu* music from the puppet theatre one can find acts divided into three sections called *kuchi, naka, and kiri.*

While some of the applications of a three part form on Japanese music have been artificial twentieth century superimpositions, the very fact that the Japanese musician turns to *jo-ha-kyu* or some equivalent tripartite term when he is forced to explain something shows that it forms part of his basic attitude towards music. It is his "natural" first reaction just as the binary approach is "natural" for the westerner. The term natural has been put in quotes because neither approach is really the result of natural laws. Both are the result of cultural conditioning. Both are valid, but their validity must be judged within their cultural context.[3] One should add that the general Japanese performer, like his western counterpart, is wont to play his part and not intellectualize about its meaning. An understanding of the three part approach in Japanese music, however, may prove useful to the intellectualized western listener.

The reader familiar with western music has perhaps by now evoked the famous three part sonata allegro form of western classical music (exposition, development, and recapitulation) to confound my generalizations. The entire approach of this form to the musical material, however, is totally different from that found in Japan. Indeed, it is very important to realize that one must not listen in Japanese music for returning themes or thematic development, at least, not as they occur in western symphonies and sonatas. There are, of course, Japanese forms in which material is repeated. In court orchestra music *(gagaku),* for example, melodies are often broken into three or more sections which are repeated in various ways (Harich-Schneider 1953: 49-74). In addition, *koto* variation pieces *(danmono)* display a kind of developmental technique in which a main melodic figure begins each section *(dan)* of the variations while the rest of the material relates to this "theme," some other earlier material, or is an accretion of new ideas which in turn may be varied in a later section.[4] The music of the *noh* flute displays a similar variation and accretion technique.

These various examples not withstanding, the western listener is generally more aware of a seemingly endless wandering in Japanese tunes rather than a repetition of previously heard material. Obviously some new orientation is needed if the ear is to follow the logic that must be there. To find this logic, one should really approach each kind of Japanese music as an individual case capable of a solution unique from other Japanese cases. The discussion that follows, however, will deal with a principle common to many Japanese genre. This is the principle of stereotyped patterns.

Stereotyped patterns are essential to communication, be it music or Morse code. In music they play an important role in the aesthetic enjoyment of a piece because the listener tends to anticipate the coming sounds through familiarity with the patterns of the particular music. This idea is, of course, not uniquely Japanese.[5] Its specific applications in Japanese music, however, can be quite different from those of the West. The drums of the *noh* drama are an excellent example. Their music consists almost entirely of named, stereotyped rhythm patterns, usually oriented to an eight-beat phrase.[6] A practice book for a *noh* drummer (notation is never used on stage) contains only the names of the patterns to be played. It is rather like the lead sheet of a jazz pianist or the figured bass of the Baroque harpsichordist, for in each case a single symbol or term stands for a musical complex. The crucial difference in the analogy is that the western examples both deal with vertical sound complexes called chords while the Japanese example deals with horizontal rhythmic patterns. Nevertheless, the analogy can be carried even further because these rhythmic patterns, like western chords, tend to appear in given orders. Thus, by cultural conditioning, the intelligent listener to *noh* music feels a sense of closure when, for example, the *taiko* pattern *uchikomi* is followed by the pattern *kashira*. It is the same kind of satisfaction a western-trained listener receives from the final chord of an "amen" cadence.

The puppet theatre music, called *gidayu-bushi*, offers a very different approach to stereotyped patterns. One singer and one *shamisen* player carry the full musical and narrative load. Musical research in this field has only just begun, but a preliminary study shows at least two kinds of stereotyped patterns in use. First, there are a set of repertory-wide leitmotives which are clues to emotions, actions, or the character of the puppets. For example, the pattern *naki* (crying) is played high for women's weeping and low for men's. Likewise, the entrance pattern *nori* will vary considerably in its tune depending on the age and sex of the character coming on stage.

The second kind of pattern in *gidayu* serves as a clue to the formal division of the play. If, for instance, in a concert of *gidayu* music the *shamisen* begins a selection with the tune called *sanju*, one knows, even though there is no scenery, that the next section represents a change of scene from the last. If the pattern *okuri* is played the setting is the same and if *sonae* is used the performance is starting at the very beginning of the first scene of a play.[7] There are other patterns which tend to show up only at certain points within sections of the form and thus signal a formal change just as, in western classical music, the return of the first theme in its original key signals the recapitulation in sonata-allegro form. In short, patterns are clues not only to what is happening but also to what might happen next. For example, if the crying pattern *naki* is followed by *shichome* one knows that the end of an aria *(sawari)* is approaching. If narration is to follow immediately after the tears the *shamisen* will play a short phrase that ends in a sudden "wrong note" in relation to the scale in which the previous pattern was played.[8] This leaves the ear suspended, the anticipation unresolved, and leads the listener into the narration smoothly. As yet I have not found a name for this song-to-narration pattern. There are many other such unnamed stereotypes, each of which guides the perceptive listener through some specific aspect of the music. The cumulative effect of all these patterns is a sense of logic in the musical form.

It is important to recall once more that stereotyped melodies are not uniquely Japanese. Renaissance madrigals have their mannerisms, Baroque cantatas and chorale preludes have their doctrine of affections, and romantic operas, particularly Wagner's, have leitmotives. In addition, every music in the world must have specific ways of indicating a stop, a start, or a moment of tension. It is as true for a Mozart symphony as it is for a Piphat orchestral piece from Thailand or a Chinese opera aria. In the study of ethnomusicology one is constantly reminded that the term art, as indicated earlier, is related to artifice and artificiality. The logic of music, while certainly influenced by the physical laws of sound, is basically man-made. The wonder is that we can still call so many pieces divine. Perhaps one of the great appeals of art may be that, as we struggle to find logic in other man-made structures such as history or sociology, the arts show us that man can create something which is both logical and beautiful. In any case, the western listener should approach unfamiliar musics with the expectation of logic, though the base from which this logic starts may be different from that of the music to which he is accustomed.

One of the more complex forms of Japanese musical logic is found in the main music of the *kabuki* theatre, *nagauta*. It combines principles from both the *noh* and *bunraku* traditions as well as adding ideas of its own. The standard *kabuki* ensemble, as mentioned earlier, consists of the *noh hayashi* (three drums and a flute) plus a line of *shamisen* and singers. A bamboo flute *(takebue)* is also used on stage while a whole battery of percussion instruments plus additional flutes and *shamisen* may be used by an off-stage *(geza)* group.[9] In addition, musicians from other genre of *shamisen* music such as *kiyomoto, tokiwazu, gidayu,* or *shinnai* may appear on or off stage. When a kabuki piece is derived from a *noh* play or has an "ancient" atmosphere, the drums make extensive use of the stereotyped rhythm patterns mentioned earlier. In *kabuki* dance pieces there is a greater tendency for the *tsuzumi* drummers to emphasize the rhythm of the *shamisen* in a style of drumming called *chiri-kara* after the mnemonics with which their part is learned. In addition, the *kabuki* has created its own stereotyped rhythm patterns to fit the needs of its more exuberant dance style. For example, in *kabuki* music there is a long rhythmic-melodic unit played by the *taiko* and *noh* flute called *sarashi.*[10] It is used specifically for that part of the dance *Echigojishi* in which two long streamers *(sarashi)* are waved by the dancer in imitation of a folk manner of drying dyed strips of cloth. The interesting aspect of this pattern is that it also is used in other dances in which this choreography does not appear. In such cases it evokes the same mood rather than supporting the same gesture. Thus, rhythm patterns can contribute to the mood and character of a piece as well as articulate its rhythm or its form.

The melodic stereotypes of *nagauta shamisen* music are of four types. First, there are melodies borrowed from other *shamisen* genre, many of which have ceased to exist as independent styles today. These borrowings evoke the mood of these other styles. A second type of borrowing is really a subtype of the first but its use is so specific that it is separated here. This is the so-called forty-eight *ozatsuma-te* derived from the now defunct *ozatsuma-bushi.* These patterns are all named and are used whenever there is a recitative or a moment of *kabuki-* or *noh*-style speaking in the midst of a *nagauta* piece. One need only think of a Mozart opera recitative to realize that the West has a similar stereotyped way of accompanying declamatory *vis à vis* lyrical sections in a vocal piece. *Nagauta* is classified as a more lyrical *(utamono)* than narrative *(katarimono)* genre. Therefore, there are few of the named patterns which stand for specific dramaturgical actions such as were mentioned in *gidayu.* There are, however, subtle reactions to the text in *nagauta* such as the depiction of a hot summer day in *Azuma hakkei* and a slight staggering rhythm whenever the drinking of *saké* wine is mentioned. The fourth type of stereotypes in *nagauta* indicates formal divisions. In *nagauta* they tend to be unnamed though they function just as clearly as the form-indicating patterns of *gidayu.*

One of the problems in approaching *kabuki* music is the fact that it does combine so many different techniques. When the drum rhythms of the *noh* and the *shamisen* melodies of the *kabuki* appear together there seems to be a kind of chaos. Sometimes the *taiko* rhythm doesn't match up with the *shamisen* and the *noh* flute, as noted earlier, is always in the "wrong key." From what has been said already about *noh* drum rhythms, however, we know that they operate much like chord sequences in western music with their sense of order and progression to a "tonic" pattern. A study of the *noh* flute shows that its melody is often inextricably linked with the rhythm of the seemingly dissident *taiko* drum. Put very simply, there seems to be a unit in *nagauta* ensemble music which serves neither a basically melodic or rhythmic function. Instead, it adds color to the music and creates tension against the melodic line which drives the melody forward to a goal at some cadence point.

In western music these are important functions of the unit called harmony. Harmony plays no significant role in *nagauta* and this unit of one drum and one flute obviously cannot play chords. I believe, however, that in lieu of harmony this third unit can perform harmony's functions. I have called this the dynamic unit, not in the sense of loud and soft dynamics but in the connotation of dynamism, that quality in things which gives them their sense of motion and action. Thus, if western music can be said to have melody, rhythm, and harmony, *nagauta* can be said to display melody, rhythm, and dynamism.

There are several additional structural intents in Japanese music that will be mentioned briefly. It has been implied that Japanese melodies tend to be non-harmonized and ornamented. In addition, they show a very careful use of melodic tension through notes that require further resolution. This is an important means of keeping up a purely melodic dynamism when rhythm is not prominent. All Japanese rhythm is not as metronomic as our earlier discussion might indicate. In fact, one of the most interesting aspects of Japanese rhythm is the frequent use of a rather elastic beat. The beginning rhythm of a court orchestra piece, for example, can best be understood by taking a deep breath before every fourth beat. The term breath rhythm, in fact, is most useful in discussing such situations. Likewise, one can seldom tap one's foot to the rhythm of a *noh* drama except in the dance sections. The great flexibility of *noh* rhythm is one of the reasons that the drum calls *(kakegoe)* are so important. It must be remembered that there is never a conductor as such in a Japanese traditional ensemble. Often there is not even eye contact between the musicians. The drum calls that startle so many westerners on first hearing are a vital part of the musical structure as well as a distinctive coloristic device. Similar calls are given by the *shamisen* players in narrative musics to assist the singers in timing their entrances on each phrase. Understanding the meaning of such calls is certainly an important step towards the appreciation of this characteristic device. Understanding the frequent flexibilities in rhythm should also increase one's enjoyment.

The Artistic Intent

So much has been said about stereotyped patterns that one might think, as some Japanese have said (Eishi 1952: 5-6), that Japanese music is nothing but a string of sterotyped patterns. When one looks at specific pieces, however, it is obvious that the arrangement of patterns and their linking materials are means to a very creative end just as the sterotypes of various periods of western music history are handled quite differently according to the individual genius of each composer. Japan has had its compositional geniuses as well. Most of the names that come down to us from before the sixteenth century are difficult to verify. A similar situation existed in the study of western music until the flourishing of musicology in this century. After the sixteenth century, the situation clears up in both Japan and the West. Thus one can speak of Japan's great composers such as Yamada Kengyo (1757-1817) in *koto* music, Takemoto Gidayu (1651-1714) in *bunraku* music, and Kineya Rokuzaemon, the Tenth (1800-1859) in *nagauta*. Our study of non-western art music has not progressed to the point where we discuss stylistic characteristics of individual composers as we do with Haydn or Mozart, but this is a result of the primitive state of our knowledge of non-western music, not the result any primitive state in the music itself.

It is true, nevertheless, that the relation of the composer to his creation in Japan differs from that relation in the West. For example, the names attached to *shamisen* pieces are always those of a singer. As far as we can tell at present, the singer creates the vocal line on the basis of a given poem. He is not always the creator of the *shamisen* accompaniment. In the puppet theatre, individual singers pride themselves on their special styles and hence adapt previous compositions in the light of their own talents. The *shamisen* player must then make the necessary adjustments in the traditional accompaniment by extending, shortening, or altering specific phrases as necessary. When larger ensembles are involved such as the *nagauta* group in the *kabuki*, other instrumentalists are called in to contribute their part. Thus, some pieces are truly cooperate compositions. While the composer whose name is attached to the piece is the main performer, the drummers, *shamisen* players, and flutists had their part in the creation of the artistic whole. When the music is connected with the theatre it undergoes occasional revisions to suit the requirements of new productions and new actors. In addition, the guild *(ryu)* system in Japanese music tends to encourage variant versions of the same piece. Thus, while there is a standard repertoire, there is not a standard version of each piece except as the standard refers to a specific group of performers. There is no improvisation involved here; rather there is variation. Once a given guild sets the piece they play it the same way every time. The variation comes in the guild interpretation of the piece plus the sylistic penchants of individual singers. Analogous situations can be found in purely instrumental forms by comparing various guild performances of, for example, the *honkyoku* pieces for the *shakuhachi* flute or the *danmono* of the *koto* tradition.

Variation in performances can extend beyond the notes. Many guilds have changed the construction of the instrument and use special playing techniques. Actually, such variations reinforce a very important characteristic of Japan music which can only be appreciate *in vivo*. In Japan it is not just what you play but how you play it. The co.rect posture, arm movement, gesture, and facial expression are as important as the correct pitches.

Perhaps the most stable performance tradition is court orchestra music because of its relatively limited repertoire and few number of performing groups. There is little belief that it is played today as it was centuries ago (Garfias 1960: 16), but the tradition has two stabilizing factors which are unusual in Japan: notation and a fixed pitch system. Since its importation from China in the Nara period, *gagaku* has used individual part books, some of which contained fingerings plus a vocal mnemonic for the instrumental melody.[11] The part books were arranged according to the mode in which the piece was played and the basic pitches upon which these modes were based were derived from pitch pipes of fairly fixed measurement.

Such details are seldom ours to enjoy in the music traditions that followed. The *noh* drama, as shown earlier, gave a fairly accurate picture of its drum accompaniment through the names of the stereotyped patterns being used but the actual performance of these patterns, if we can judge from contemporary practice, varied with the different guilds. Writings on *noh* singing from Zeami on give us many theoretical clues to style including some discussions of pitch and scales, but the form of notation used *(gomaten)* serves only as a reminder of a repertoire already learned. It cannot be sightread. There is considerable variation not only in the various schools of *noh* singing but also in the accompanying drum and flute parts. As with the *kabuki* music mentioned earlier, a given performance group will be consistent in its particular version of a specific piece.

There are a few notations of *koto* and other musics from the Edo period but, in general, *koto* and *shamisen* notations remain rare and, when existant, rather vague until the twentieth century. Since that time both traditions have developed rather detailed notations which give clear indications of rhythm, intervals, and instrumental techniques plus the vocal line when it is present. The only inconvenience of these systems is that, again, each instrument and each of the several guilds playing one instrument uses a different system.

It is important to note that while the intervals between notes are set in Japanese notations, the basic pitch (except for *gagaku*) is not. In vocal music, the basic pitch depends entirely on the range of the singer. Instrumental pieces are tuned to the best resonance of a given instrument. An analogous situation in the West is found in vocal music where, for example, one can buy a copy of a Schubert song in any one of several different key depending on the range of the voice. The difference in the Japanese case is that the notation does not show pitch but rather interval and thus one notation serves for all "keys." One need only tune the instrument to the proper starting pitch. Thus, there is no specific "key" for a given Japanese piece such as the western sonatas in B flat minor or symphonies in A major.

The word key has been put in quotes above because Japanese music is not in the keys of the western major-minor tradition. It has its own scale systems such as the *ryo-ritsu* pair of scales and the *in-yo* pair along with their modal forms.[12] Of course, contemporary Japanese music played on traditional instruments may make use of all tonal systems including an occasional brush with the Schoenbergian twelve-tone rows.

All that has been said above may seem to be somewhat remote from our subheading of the artistic intent. These attitudes towards notation, pitch, and variation, however, are all reflections of the artist's view of his own work. A composer with the idea of self-expression so hallowed in nineteenth century western art music or the concept of the social message popular in the twentieth century would, I believe, view these problems very differently. One has only to think of Beethoven or Verdi raging against the slightest changes in their pieces and the plethora of detail on performance practice which loads every page of late nineteenth century scores. Indeed, certain modern western composers have been dabbling with non-western principles in order to loosen up the tight hold western composers have had on their creations in recent centuries. A good performance of a Japanese piece needs all the accuracy of the performance of a Mozart symphony, but in Japan the model for accuracy is not necessarily that of the original composer. Within the limits of a given school and a given generation the standards of performance are exacting and provide solid ground for an appraisal of a given performance. Other schools or other generations may change the standard in its details. The general outline of the piece as seen in its form, text, and important melodic moments, however, tends to remain constant. The intent of the composer is to provide this framework.

Another aspect of the artistic intent of Japanese music is its tendency to be word-oriented. This is obvious in the great number of vocal forms found in Japan. However, purely instrumental pieces as well tend to be descriptive or to be the evocation of something poetical. This is seen, for example, in the repertoire of the *shakuhachi* where such titles as "The Sound of the Deers" *(shika no tone)* are common. Even the titles of *gagaku* pieces such as "The Barbarians Drinking Wine" *(Konju)* and their frequent use as dance accompaniment give this repertoire a literary tint. The first important exceptions to this literary tendency are the *koto* variation pieces with their abstract forms and titles.

A similar word orientation is found in much of the music of China and may have been part of Japan's Chinese heritage along with so many of her instruments and much of her theory. Indeed, there is always a tendency to lump the Chinese and Japanese musical cultures together since they have the same general roots. The end products of these roots, however, are quite different, though Japanese music in general has more relationship to Chinese music than to other Asian cultures. Again, *gagaku* seems to be the exception when one compares it with the present day instrumental ensembles of Southeast Asia. Its historical roots, however, are also primarily Chinese. Actually, the linking of various national musics depends to a large extent on one's point of view. If one chooses to study music as history, the high civilizations of the East and West provide ample written and archaeological material for the construction of chains of influence from one side of the world to the other.[13] If one takes simply the similarity of sound, the patterns of distribution become very different and intriguing.[14] If one takes the basic approaches to music as a guide, as this article has done, inter-cultural linkage becomes more tenuous. Each culture offers its own unique solutions to the aesthetic, creative challenges of art music, but each has to contend with similar problems such as tension and release, unity and variety, and meaningfulness to the members of the culture in which it is created.

CONCLUSION

Thus, while the actual sounds and some of the principles of Japanese music differ from those of the West, there are in the two musics a surprising number of approaches which serve analogous functions. As we learn more about other oriental traditions it becomes apparent that similar analogies can be made for their musics as well. Perhaps the term "oriental music" is becoming meaningless except in the geographical sense. Of course, there is still the problem of meaningfulness in music. It is primarily the private property of the cultural carrier. Nevertheless, I believe that the cultural outsider can at least learn to recognize the musical logic of a given genre with the proper clues and a musical ear. This can be a pleasurable experience. It also may provide new insights for the listener into the character and structure of the society as a whole. It is the hope of many ethnomusicologists that it can. In any event, the enjoyment of the arts has taken on an international potential. Non-western plastic arts have long been held in esteem. Non-western music may also now join the ranks of the respectful.[15] Music is not a universal language, but its many dialects are wonderful to hear. I hope the approaches listed in this article may prove useful when the reader looks for a meaningful experience in *hogaku*, the traditional music of Japan.

NOTES

[1] These differences can be heard by comparing various performances of the piece "Rokudan" on the Miyage Michio record (Nihon Victor JL 7), the Eto Kimio record (World 1428), and the Yuize Shinichi record (Cook 1132). The last is, in my opinion, overdone.

[2] It can also be applied to larger western ensembles such as the orchestra as used by Anton Webern. By the same token, western chamber works can sound orchestral, for example, the Ravel string quartet.

[3] In this context it is interesting to note that the academic discipline concerned with music outside the Euro-American art tradition was first called comparative musicology, but later changed its name to ethnomusicology, the study of music in culture.

[4] This technique can be heard clearly in the recorded piece listed in note 1.

[5] One of the best discussions of anticipation and patterning in the comprehension of music is found in Meyer 1956.

[6] For specific examples, see Malm 1958.

[7] See further *Bunraku* (in Japanese) 1959.

[8] For example, in a passage that has been using the scale A B C# E F#, the last notes will be F E D.

[9] The instruments and functions of *geza* music are discussed in Malm 1959.

[10] A transcription of this pattern can be seen in Malm 1963.

[11] This notation can be seen in Malm 1959.

[12] A resumé of Japanese scale systems is found in Peri 1934.

[13] For example, there have been attempts to link the *shamisen* with the *nefer* of ancient Egypt (Tanabe 1963: 13). A study of the movement of music along the East-West trade routes can be seen in Kishibe 1940: 261-304.

[14] For example, the sound of some Okinawan folk songs resembles that of the Tung people of China and also a folk style in Indonesia, while the female singers of Korea produce a sound similar to that found in Southwest Asia and among the gypsies of Spain.

[15] Respect will not come without a struggle. As late as 1960, Maraini said that the orient could claim equality in everything but science and music (1960: 13). The statement may be more a result of his Italian background than his Japanese insight.

REFERENCES CITED

BUNRAKU
1959 *Bunkazai.* Tokyo.

GARFIAS, ROBERT
1960 "Gradual Modification of the *Gagaku* Tradition." *Ethnomusicology.* IV, January: 16-9.

HARICH-SCHNEIDER, ETO
1953 "The Present Condition of Japanese Court Music." *Musical Quarterly.* XXXIX, Jan.: 49-74.

KIKKAWA, EISHI
1952 "*Samisen* and *Samisen* Music." *KBS BULLETIN.* June: 5-6.

KISHIBE, SHIGEO
1940 "The Origin of the P'ip'a." *The Transactions of the Asiatic Society of Japan.* December: 261-304.

MALM, WILLIAM P.
1958 "The Rhythmic Orientation of Two Drums in the Japanese *Noh* Drama." *Ethnomusicology.* II, September: 181-200.
1959 *Japanese Music and Musical Instruments.* Tokyo, Tuttle and Company.
1963 *Nagauta: The Heart of Kabuki Music.* Tokyo, Tuttle and Company.

MARAINI, FOSCO
1960 *Meeting with Japan.* New York, Viking Press.

MEYER, LEONARD
1956 *Emotion and Meaning in Music.* Chicago, University of Chicago Press.

MINAWAGA, TATSUO
1957 "Japanese *Noh* Music." *Journal of the American Musicological Society.* X, Fall: 181-200.

V

The Use of Music as a Technique of Reconstructing Culture History in Africa

Alan P. Merriam
Professor of Anthropology
Indiana University

Recent developments in the study of African history indicate that historians must begin to use a wider variety of analytic tools than has commonly been employed in studying history, even in those areas for which written records exist.[1] To this end, a number of aids to reconstruction have been suggested at various times by various authors: among them are archaeology used in conjunction with whatever historic records are available, oral literature, ethnographic distributional analysis, linguistic relationships, and botanical studies. The question of whether music can contribute to such studies has not, to the best of my knowledge, been seriously discussed, and there are some problems which must be carefully considered.

The first of these problems is to define what is meant by the phrase "reconstructing culture history" and to determine how we may use music to do so. The use of any special tool in such an investigation involves at least three separate possibilities. In the first place, part of the culture history of any group consists of a description of a way of life at a given point in time; that is, at any particular time the culture inventory of a people contains certain items, and these items, in turn, tell us something about the people and their way of life. Such descriptions, whether broad or narrow in terms of the number of items described, can be reached either through the use of historic accounts, which in the case of Africa seem to be of limited time depth, or through archaeology,

1. See Alan P. Merriam, *The Anthropology of Music* (Evanston, 1964), ch. XIV.

in which the time depth is theoretically unlimited. From such an approach we learn certain things about a way of life, subject, in the case of music, to the limitations to be noted below.

But inevitably, in considering the reconstruction of culture history, a dynamic is implied which involves the wider framework of development through time. In this case we look at culture change, and thus history, as a *process* of time, and we are interested in any theory which implies process and which enables us to reconstruct what has happened in the past. Music can be used this way too, though again only within certain limitations.

Finally, in using specific tools—in this case music—we must raise the question of whether there is anything unique or special about the tool which makes it particularly relevant to the problem of reconstructing history.

I should like to consider each of these approaches in turn; but it must first be clear that the potential importance of music to this kind of problem varies widely because of its special characteristics. So far as is known, no African culture ever independently developed a notational system for its organization of culturally-defined musical sound; this means there is relatively little hope of reconstructing the aural shape of African music with any accuracy. As will be noted below, some attempts have been made along this line, either through special archaeological techniques or through the application of a priori anthropological theory, but such attempts do not seem particularly effective or reliable. The tracing of the actual sound of music to any substantial time depth does not appear, therefore, to be a very fruitful avenue toward reconstructing culture history as a whole.

Of course, music is represented not only by sound but by musical instruments as well, and some of these instruments have survived over considerable spans of time. Thus, in dealing with music as a tool for historic reconstruction, we must consider the music and the instruments and be prepared to use either or both as the possibilities present themselves.

Finally, musical sound as an entity has three major characteristics which seem to make it potentially valuable to the reconstruction of culture contact; these characteristics, which culminate in the reliability of the reduction of sound to statistical terms, may in the future give us a particularly sharp tool for analysis. This aspect of music study will be discussed as the final section of this paper.

I have noted above that one approach to the culture history of a people consists in describing that culture at a given point in time. The question is whether this can be done with music, and if so what kind of information it can yield.

Though examples are few, there is some evidence indicating the use made of song texts in Africa to bring historical information to mind. Waterman and Bascom, for example, in commenting on the topical song in Africa, write:

> Topical songs have been known to persist for generations when they commemorate some historic event or when they treat with some incident of lasting interest. Thus, songs referring to battles of the 18th century are still current in Nigeria, just as calypsos were composed in Trinidad deriding certain slave overseers or commemorating the first visits of *The Graf Zeppelin* or *The Duke and Duchess of Kent.*[2]

Similarly, Herskovits notes the historic usages of song in Dahomey:

> Songs were and are the prime carriers of history among this non-literate folk. In recounting the ritual associated with the giving of offerings to the souls of those who were transported into slavery, this function of song came out with great clarity. The informant at one point could not recall the sequence of important names in the series as he was giving. Under his breath, to the accompaniment of clicking finger-nails, he began to sing, continuing his song for some moments. When he stopped he had the names clearly in mind once more, and in explanation of his song stated that this was the Dahomean method of remembering historic facts. The role of the singer as

2. R. A. Waterman and W. R. Bascom, "African and New World Negro Folklore," in M. Leach (ed.), *Dictionary of Folklore, Mythology, and Legend* (New York, 1949), 21.

the "keeper of records" has been remarked by those who visited the kingdom in the days of its autonomy.[3]

Further examples could be cited, although the study of song texts with the particular problems of African history in mind has not been frequently or exhaustively undertaken. The difficulty of this approach lies in the problem of the authenticity of the texts in terms of the accuracy of the message or description conveyed. This is a similar difficulty to that involved in the acceptance or rejection of the evidence of African oral literature. But we do have at least one example of a song text which has remained unchanged over the past sixty-three years. This is "Nkosi Sikelel' iAfrica" first sung publicly in 1899 at the ordination of Reverend M. Boweni, a Shangaan Methodist minister; more recently it was adopted unofficially as a nationalist anthem in parts of Central and South Africa, as reported by W. Rhodes.[4] It appears, then, that song texts are capable of existing unchanged in the folk idiom over substantial periods of time, although we do not know for how long. A study and analysis of this problem might well lead the investigator into some relatively important areas of historic information, though I personally doubt that the time span would be long, despite the Waterman and Bascom claim for what appears to be a period of approximately two hundred years. At the same time, historic reconstruction of relatively recent periods is in its way as valuable as that of great epochs of earlier history; given the limitations of the song text, it appears that music may be most useful in this way.

The use of music and musical instruments as described in historic accounts is a second kind of reconstruction of culture history in this same general category. Kirby, for example, reports information concerning the xylophone in East Africa dating back to 1586;[5] and considerable numbers of references since that time

3. M. J. Herskovits, *Dahomey: An Ancient West African Kingdom* (New York, 1938), II, 321.
4. W. Rhodes, "Music as an Agent of Political Expression," *African Studies Bulletin*, V:16–17 (1962).
5. P. R. Kirby, *The Musical Instruments of the Native Races of South Africa* (Johannesburg, 1953), 47.

give us rather remarkable information concerning African instruments over the past four centuries.

In respect to musical sound, the time depth is much shorter, although fragments of notated songs appear from time to time in the accounts of early travelers, explorers, missionaries, and others. The validity of these transcriptions, however, is in considerable doubt, and it was not until more recent times that large and reliable samples of African music, transcribed from phonograph records, began to appear. Thus in 1917, Erich M. von Hornbostel transcribed and analyzed songs collected in 1907–1909 by the Deutschen Zentral-Afrika-Expedition headed by the Duke of Mecklenburg. Various other bodies of song from a similar time period are now available to us.[6]

The question is whether such materials help us markedly in reconstructing culture history and, if so, how. It seems clear that we do not profit greatly from knowing that the Rwandese had music in 1907, or even knowing precisely what form that music took when reduced to notation by a European expert, although this knowledge is of considerable significance when cast in the framework of a theory of culture change. Yet, if we were to find an instance in which such early materials differed drastically from those we can record today, we would be faced with a problem of great importance; for given the generally conservative nature of music, we should be forced to conclude that historic events of considerable impact had taken place in the meantime. To the best of my knowledge, no such sharp differences exist between past and present music sound systems in Africa; but again to the best of my knowledge, no really detailed comparative studies of such materials have been undertaken.

Much the same sort of information is available from the study of historic records of musical instruments. We should expect to find, and so far as I know do find, cultural continuity in musical instrument forms; but again, the studies have not been exhaustive.

This kind of reconstruction from historic accounts tells us cer-

6. E. M. von Hornbostel, "Gesänge aus Ruanda," in J. Czekanowski, *Ethnographic-Anthropologie I, Wissenschaftliche Ergebnisse der Deutschen Zentral-Afrika-Expedition 1907–1908*, Band VI, Erster Teil (Leipzig, 1917).

tain things about the history of the people involved. The information gleaned is obviously primarily directed toward the history of music and musical instruments as things in themselves; that is, music is a part of culture, culture moves through time, and thus through music we can approach certain kinds of history. Further, as pointed out above, we expect the processes of change to proceed in a more or less orderly fashion; when the available record shows discontinuities, in this case in the course of music, we should expect to find reasons for the discontinuities.

A third approach to the reconstruction of culture history in terms of the description of a culture at any given point in time and through the use of music depends upon the findings of archaeology. Two kinds of problems have been approached in using this method in African studies. The first is virtually restricted to the field of Egyptian studies and has been carried on primarily by European scholars who combine interests and talents in antiquarianism and musical instrument studies. It has been pointed out by Curt Sachs that research in Egyptian instruments is particularly rich because of two major factors:

> The extreme aridity of the desert soil and the Egyptian belief in the magic power of painting and sculpture. Aridity has preserved hundreds of instruments from decomposition, and many musical scenes are depicted on tomb walls . . . Egyptian art works are explained by short, naive texts written between the human figures wherever an empty spot is left. "He is playing the harp," they read, or, "He is playing the flute." Thus, we know the authentic names of practically all Egyptian instruments.[7]

Because of these two factors, it has been possible to reconstruct not only the instrumentation of the early Egyptian orchestra but, according to the investigators, the kinds of scales and even possibly the orchestral sounds produced. Instruments themselves provide the student with measurable acoustic quantities which can give a high degree of precision; and where instruments are not themselves available, scholars such as Sachs and Hickmann, among others, have reconstructed both forms and probable musical

7. C. Sachs, *The History of Musical Instruments* (New York, 1940), 87.

sounds from finger positions of harpists, for example, as these are depicted in a substantial number of paintings and bas-reliefs.[8]

In African areas outside Egypt, the archaeological record is far less rich as most musical instruments are made of wood and the aridity of Egypt does not prevail. Even so, however, some instruments have been preserved and have come to form part of the archaeological record. The most notable examples are iron gongs and rock gongs, of which the latter can be discussed briefly here; the former will be discussed below.

A considerable number of publications has been devoted recently to what is sometimes called the "rock-gong complex." [9] These are ringing rocks characterized by so-called "chatter marks," which are small, cuplike depressions caused by repeated nonrandom striking of the rock with a hammerstone. Rock gongs have been located in Nigeria, the Northern Cameroons, Uganda, the Sudan, Portugal, Brittany, Wales, and England.

Interpretations of the rock gongs, rock slides, and rock paintings, which are sometimes assumed to be associated phenomena, vary widely. Fagg characterizes them as a megalithic, prehistoric complex, and calls attention to the common interpretation that stone instruments are among man's earliest musical modes of expression;[10] Conant, on the other hand, argues for a more limited interpretation:

8. C. Sachs, *Die Musikinstrumente des Alten Aegyptens* (Berlin, 1921); C. Sachs, *History of Musical Instruments; The Rise of Music in the Ancient World East and West* (New York, 1943); H. Hickmann, "Miscellanea Musicologica," *Annales du Service des Antiquités de l'Egypte*, LII:1–23 (1952); H. Hickmann, "La Flûte de Pan dans l'Egypte ancienne," *Chronique d'Egypte*, XXX:217–224 (1955); "Le problème de la notation musicale dans l'Egypte ancienne," *Bulletin de l'Institut d'Egypte*, XXXVI:489–531 (1955).

9. B. Fagg, "The Rock Gong Complex Today and in Prehistoric Times," *Journal of the Historical Society of Nigeria*, I:27–42 (1956); B. Fagg, "Rock Gongs and Rock Slides," *Man*, LVII:30–32 (1957); F. P. Conant, "Rocks that Ring: Their Ritual Setting in Northern Nigeria," *Transactions of the New York Academy of Sciences*, Ser. II, XXIII:155–162 (1960); J. H. Vaughan, Jr., "Rock Paintings and Rock Gongs among the Marghi of Nigeria," *Man*, LXII:49–52 (1962).

10. Fagg, "The Rock Gong Complex," 42.

May the use of rock gongs represent a substitution of abundantly available ringing rock for the double hand gong made of iron, a much more scarce material? The quality of notes produced by both instruments is so similar that it is sometimes difficult to tell them apart . . . In other words, it would be most suggestive if rock gongs and iron gongs eventually prove to have roughly the same distribution. The significance of rock gongs then might be largely in terms of the diffusion of iron metallurgy in Africa, associated by some prehistorians with the spread of Bantu-speaking peoples.[11]

Given the current state of uncertainty as to the antiquity of the rock gongs, it is clear that only further research will establish their usefulness in reconstructing Africa's culture history. At the moment, however, there appears to be a tendency to attempt to solve the puzzle of the uses of rock gongs in the past by describing current practice. Vaughan describes the current use of the rock-gong complex among the Marghi of Nigeria, and holds that the parts of the complex "should be viewed as distinct variables in a much larger behavioural context—rites of passage." He lists the following patterns which he feels may characterize the complex: social rebellion, symbolic death to childhood, birth into adulthood, fertility rites, and publicity. He concludes his discussion of the complex among the Marghi by noting:

Extrapolation from the Marghi materials to all other rock paintings in Nigeria would be unwise, but these data are suggestive of possible behavioural bases to rock paintings and gongs. More importantly they indicate that a shift in emphasis from antiquarian studies of material traits to studies of rites of passage may lead to new discoveries of paintings, gongs and associated phenomena, and could certainly lead to a broader understanding of just what these non-behavioural artifacts mean.[12]

All the approaches discussed so far are those which fall under the general rubric of description of culture at a given point in time. Song texts may preserve historic occasions and events; descriptions of music and music instruments in literate sources tell

11. Conant, "Rocks that Ring," 161.
12. Vaughan, "Rock Paintings," 52.

us much about change and development in forms as well as of continuities and discontinuities through time; and archaeological reconstruction, whether through the discovery of instruments or the discovery of paintings and carvings depicting instruments, can tell us the same kinds of things as historic records but presumably with a greater time depth.

Two major kinds of information emerge from materials of this sort. The first relates to the history of African music itself; here the emphasis is upon a single aspect of culture and its development through time. The second relates to music as an aspect of culture which is descriptive of one phase of culture and useful, primarily through extrapolation, for determining the relationship of that aspect to other aspects of culture. The last is a reconstructive process which depends not only upon evidence but also upon controlled comparative analysis and logical deduction.

The second major approach to the reconstruction of culture history involves the possibility of using music to establish theories of grand processes which operate throughout time. Anthropology has seen the rise and fall of many such theories in the past, and some of them will be discussed here. These are discussed, first because theories of evolution or *kulturkreis* form a part of the history of ethnomusicology; second, because such theories have all left their imprint, although we may be unwilling and unable to accept them as originally phrased; and third, because, though the broader patterns of such theories are now rejected, they contain some truths and some speculations which are clearly not without merit.

Least acceptable today are evolutionary theories of the development of music, particularly those which, through the use of what is now regarded as an invalid comparative method, array facts from cultures around the world into systems which "prove" a deductively formulated theory. We need not consider such formulations—which have devised systems of cultural stages through which mankind is said inevitably to move.

Of almost equal difficulty are theories of the particular and ultimate origin of individual music styles or instruments. Balfour, for example, held that the African friction drum originated from the stick-and-membrane bellows and found the two to have a roughly coterminous distribution on the continent.[13] While he may conceivably be correct, it is as logical to suppose that the stick-and-membrane bellows developed from the friction drum as vice versa, and there seems little that is useful in this kind of search for origin.

A more controlled, but still largely speculative kind of evolutionary analysis is found in the work of Kirby, who postulates a developmental sequence for the musical bow but restricts himself primarily to applying his analysis to the Bushmen. He speculates that the hunting bow is probably at the origin of a number of stringed instruments. The first stage is the twang emitted by the bowstring when the arrow is fired; the second appears when it occurs to the hunter "to tap his bow-string with an arrow, thus applying a new method of sound-production to the string." [14] The third stage comes when a number of bows are placed together on the ground and are tapped by a single person. Further evidences of evolution are postulated as the performer learns to use his own body as a resonating chamber, adds outside resonators, and so forth. It should also be pointed out that, according to Kirby, a Bushman rock painting exists in which the third stage is illustrated.[15]

Similar formulations have been made for musical sounds; for example, Phillips postulates a series of stages in the development of music in general and attempts to apply them to Yoruba music in particular.[16] One of the most determined formulations, though used in a cautious manner, is that of Bruno Nettl about Shawnee Indian music of North America. In this case, Nettl has put together historic data and music structural materials to reach conclusions about the history of the Shawnee. Basic to his work, however, and basic to all evolutionary schemes, is the assumption that culture develops chronologically from the simple to the com-

13. H. Balfour, "The Friction-Drum," *Journal of the Royal Anthropological Institute*, XXXVII:67–92 (1907).

14. Kirby, "Musical Instruments," 193.

15. *Ibid.*, 194–195.

16. E. Phillips, *Yoruba Music* (Johannesburg, 1953).

plex; thus Nettl postulates that the simplest songs are the oldest—simplest being those with "small range, simple form, and two or three tone scales." [17] Later in style are more complex songs, still later are those whose style appears to make it possible to postulate that they were borrowed from southern Plains tribes; newest of all are the Peyote songs whose origin in time is known.

Although the equation of old and simple is not, in my view, a fixed one, Nettl's study does indicate a possibility which will be discussed later in this paper. That is, he works from the basic fact that Shawnee style is internally diverse, with some songs showing certain constellations of traits and others showing other constellations. Given the diversity of the present repertoire, it is logical to assume that differing influences have come to bear upon it. In the case of the Shawnee, the various diversities of the style give clues to the influences which have shaped it; these in turn can be coupled with the historic record of the migrations of the Shawnee in order to help fix their history. In short, the diversity of style in the present Shawnee repertoire gives clues about contacts they have had with other peoples and enables us to buttress incomplete records. The scheme is not in itself evolutionary, except in the use of the "simple-old" syndrome.

The possibilities of using evolutionary schemes in reconstructing culture history are not particularly bright. In order to do so, we must make assumptions which do not seem tenable; for example, if one finds the stick-and-membrane bellows in one location, and the friction drum in another, it must follow, according to Balfour, that the culture of the first people is older than that of the second. Similarly, the culture of people who use the simple hunting bow as a musical bow must be older than that of people who use instruments of several strings. Or people who use two- or three-note melodies have older cultures than those who use six- or seven-note melodies. We can follow the logic of such propositions without difficulty; the problem is that logic and deductive theory are not substitutes for empiricism.

The same kind of criticism can be applied to *kulturkreis* theories

17. B. Nettl, "The Shawnee Musical Style: Historical Perspective in Primitive Music," *Southwestern Journal of Anthropology*, IX:284 (1953).

of the origin and history of various elements of African culture; but because music played such a large part in formulations of this kind, some discussion of these theories is necessary.

It will be recalled that Friedrich Ratzel established the first step in a series of speculations by drawing attention to the similarities between West African and Melanesian bows, in the cross section of the bow shaft, in the material and fastening of the bowstring, and in the feathering of the arrow. Leo Frobenius, however, took the idea a step further, calling attention to other culture elements which he considered similar in the two areas. Without going into detail concerning the arguments advanced by Frobenius, I should like to call attention to the fact that musical instruments (but apparently not music styles) formed the basis for a considerable amount of this speculation. In at least one instance Frobenius uses the drum as a primary piece of evidence:

> Our investigation of culture-anatomy may begin with African drum forms. By far the larger part of African drums consist of a log scooped out, one or both ends covered with hide. We need not enter into details here, and I do no more than state the fact that the Indonesian method of bracing drums reappears on the West African coast. Besides these commonest drum forms, others occur made entirely of a log, hewn round or with angles; in the latter case usually wedge-shaped, the broad surface resting on the ground. The logs are hollowed out within through a cleft, made always on the broad side. Often the cleft is enlarged at its ends, the enlargement forming a round aperture in the drums of the Congo, an angle in those of the Cameroons. The famous signaling or telegraph drums of the Cameroons belong to this class. The drums covered with hide are found throughout the whole of Africa, with the exception of its southernmost part, but the wooden drums occur only in the Congo Basin and in Upper and Lower Guinea. The hide-covered drums are a development of the famous millet mortar, which points to East India. The civilization of the Mediterranean shores has similar drums made of clay, and related to those found in Persia and in prehistoric tombs of Germany. Now, the wooden drums belong to the Malayo-Negrito elements of African culture. They recur in Melanesia and frequently in Poly-

nesia. Their home obviously must be the same as that of the lofty bamboo cane, for these drums are developed from the bamboo.[18]

Using musical instruments as one of his criteria for resemblance, Frobenius develops four culture circles in Africa: the Negrito culture, Malayo-Negrito culture, Indo-Negrito culture, and Semito-Negrito culture. In like order, each of these includes the following music instruments: (1) staff as music instrument; (2) bamboo lute, tangola and drum, wooden kettledrum, and marimba; (3) violin, guitar, earthenware base drum, iron kettledrum, tambourine; (4) gubo, gora, hide as drum, mortar drum, and pot drum.[19] Similar uses of music instruments were made by others, among them, Ankermann.[20]

Once established, the idea of the Melanesian–West African relationship, as well as of that of culture circles, was elaborated by other theorists, and musical instruments inevitably functioned as part of the schemes. Thus George Montandon devised a system of ten culture circles, postulated an original development in and near the Himalayan region which led through Oceania to Africa and, as usual, cited musical instruments as a major part of the reconstruction.[21]

For Africa specifically, he arrived at a series of five circles, as follows: (1) African primitive (15,000–20,000 years or more before our era) [including boomerangs, bull-roarers, whistles, trumpets, and other idiophones as instruments]; (2) Negrito period (15,000 or more years before the present era) [Pan pipes, primitive xylophones, wooden drum, musical bow]; (3) proto-Hamitic period (10,000 years or more before our era) [musical instruments developing out of 1 and 2]; (4) Hamito-Semitic period (7000–8000 years before our era) [same instruments plus those of

18. L. Frobenius, "The Origin of African Civilizations," *Annual Report of the Board of Regents of the Smithsonian Institution,* I:640–641 (1898).
19. *Ibid.*, 650.
20. B. Ankermann, "Kulturkreis und Kulturschichten in Afrika," *Zeitschrift für Ethnologie,* XXXVII:54–90 (1905).
21. G. Montandon, "La généalogie des instruments de musique et les cycles de civilisation," *Archives suisses d'Anthropologie général,* III:1–120 (1919).

India]; (5) Neo-Semitic (from about 700 A.D.) [instruments of Western Asian origin including the rebab, various lutes, etc.].[22]

These theories led to the postulation of further schemes involving similar principles but devoted exclusively to musical instruments. *In his Geist und Werden der Musikinstrumente* published in 1929, Curt Sachs, using the *kulturkreis* approach, laid out a worldwide theory of the history of all musical instruments which involved the creation of twenty-three strata; this was later to be "corroborated" by André Schaeffner among the Dogon and formed the basis for an extended study of African music instruments by Hornbostel.[23]

Hornbostel gave considerable attention to the comparison of his groups with Sachs strata, and found, in general, that they agreed, although there were differences on particular points. Using apparently the single criterion of extent of distribution of instruments, and assuming that the instruments with the widest distribution were also necessarily the oldest, Hornbostel arrived at a total of twelve groups, arranged as follows:

I. *Earliest Cultures.* 1. Universal: strung rattles, bull-roarer, bone-flute, scrape idiophones; 2. Universal—sporadic in Africa: end-blown conch trumpet; 3. Sporadic everywhere it occurs: percussion-rod. II. *"Ancient Sudan."* Extensive but not universal: gourd rattle? Cylindrical drum, mouth bow. III. *"West African."* W. and Central Africa, S. and E. Asia, South America: slit-drum, globular-flute, log-xylophone, nose-flute. IV. *"Mid-Erythraean."* E. Africa, S. and E. Asia—S. America: Pan-pipes, stamping-tube, central-hole flute, (gourd drum), single-skin hourglass-drum. V. *"Pan Erythraean,* Early." Indonesia—Africa: gourd-xylophone, iron bell, cup-shaped drum. VI. *"Pan-Erythraean, Late."* India-Africa: bow with gourd resonator, harp-zither with notched bridge. VIa. *"Hova."* Indonesia—Madagascar: flat-bar zither, tube-zither. VII. *Ancient Southwest Asia—Ancient Egypt:* 1. Proto-Hamitic? Animal

22. *Ibid.*, 93.

23. A. Schaeffner, "Ethnologie musicale ou musicologie comparée," in P. Collaer (ed.), *Les Colloques de Wégimont* (Brussels, 1956), 29–30; E. M. von Hornbostel, "The Ethnology of African Sound-Instruments," *Africa,* VI:277–311 (1933).

horn. 2. Pre-Islamic. Bow-harp. 3. Post-Islamic. Double clarinet, tanged lute. VIII. *Buddhism.* Buddhist Asia, sporadically in NW. Africa: double-skin hourglass-shaped drum. IX. *Pre-Christian, West Asiatic.* Arabia, E. Asia, Sudan: bowl-lyre. X. *Post-Christian, Pre-Islamic.* W. Asia—Indonesia, W. Africa: hooked drumstick. XI. *Islam.* NE. Africa, W. Asia—Indonesia; tanged fiddle with lateral pegs, kettledrum.[24]

Finally, Sachs later gave a concise explanation of his method and reduced his twenty-three strata and Hornbostel's twelve groups to three major ones. In respect to the method used both by himself and by Hornbostel, he noted as the chief axioms: "(1) An object or idea found in scattered regions of a certain district is older than an object found everywhere in the same area. (2) Objects preserved only in remote valleys and islands are older than those used in open plains. (3) The more widely an object is spread over the world, the more primitive it is."[25] In his three-part scheme derived from these principles, he reached the following conclusions:

The early stratum comprises those instruments which, prehistorically, occur in paleolithic excavations and, geographically, are scattered all over the world. These are:

Idiophones	Aerophones	Membranophones	Chordophones
rattles	bull-roarer		
rubbed shell?	ribbon reed		
scraper	flute without		
stamped pit	holes		

No drums and no stringed instruments appear in this early stratum.

The middle stratum comprises those instruments which, prehistorically, occur in neolithic excavations, and, geographically, in several continents, though they are not universal. These are:

slit-drum	flute with	drum	ground-harp
stamping tube	holes		ground-zither
	trumpet		musical bow
	shell trumpet		

24. *Ibid.,* 299–301.
25. Sachs, *History of Musical Instruments,* 62–64.

The late stratum comprises those instruments which, prehistorically, occur in more recent neolithic excavations, and, geographically, are confined to certain limited areas. These are:

Idiophones	Aerophones	Membranophones	Chordophones
rubbed wood			friction drum
basketry rattle	nose flute		drum stick
xylophone	cross flute		
jews' harp	transverse trumpet		

> This rough chronology, though established on the objective data of distribution and prehistory, gives satisfaction also to the mind concerned with workmanship and cultural level.[26]

How useful are theoretical formulations such as these? There seems, first of all, little reason for accepting the propositions forwarded by Frobenius and Montandon. This is partly because factual information is now available which did not exist some sixty years ago and which makes certain of their assumptions untenable, but mostly because both appear to have been dealing with a priori schemes for which they were intent upon supplying facts. The severest criticism must be directed toward assumptions of "layers of time." At the same time, the relationships between Africa and other parts of the world, in terms of migrations of peoples or of cultures, have never been clearly proven false or acceptable; and the criteria of form and quantity proposed by the Kulturhistorische Schule remain criteria better adapted to studying diffusion problems of more restricted scope.

The same strictures may be applied to the work of Hornbostel and Sachs, and yet it is clear that their formulations are based upon more reliable information more cautiously applied than those of Frobenius and Montandon. In both cases, one is struck by the extraordinary range of knowledge of music instruments brought to the theories; and it seems clear that the results may well be reasonably accurate in the broadest perspective. Logic is on their side, and in this case, logic is carefully buttressed by fact; the major difficulty, again, is in accepting the three premises regarding the diffusionary process; and if we cannot accept them

26. *Ibid.*, 63–64.

on the scale proposed by Sachs, then the theory must fall. The approaches taken by Hornbostel and Sachs appear more reasonable than those advanced by Frobenius and Montandon because they represent a step in the direction of far greater control of materials within the framework of diffusion studies.

There is no need here to summarize the increasing restrictions placed upon the study of diffusion and the reconstruction of culture history by a more rigorous methodology. But the result has been a controlled use of distribution and diffusion based upon certain principles which have been succinctly and simply expressed by Herskovits:

> It would seem, all things considered, that the effort is worth the return provided 1) *that the area selected for analysis should be one whose historic unity can be assumed,* and *the probability, not the absolute fact of historic developments, be recognized as the aim.*[27]

Under these conditions, we can examine one or two of the more recent diffusion studies of music instruments in Africa and assess their value in the reconstruction of culture history.

The concept of culture clusters as a taxonomic device for ordering cultures was suggested in 1952 by P. H. Gulliver, and further discussed by the present writer in relation to the cultures of the then-Belgian Congo.[28] In the latter article, I contrasted the cluster with the concept of culture area, and noted that:

> The cluster concept, however, adds a dimension lacking in the area concept in that it *suggests* generic relationship on the basis of historic fact and in what we have called commonality. In a culture area, diffusion from one or more centers is assumed and can often be traced, but in a cluster, by definition, we find not only diffusion but also the factor of commonality. Thus, for example, the fact that the Mongo say they are all re-

27. M. J. Herskovits, *Man and His Works* (New York, 1948), 521 (his italics).

28. P. H. Gulliver, "The Karamajong Cluster," *Africa,* XXII:1–22 (1952); A. P. Merriam, "The Concept of Culture Clusters Applied to the Belgian Congo," *Southwestern Journal of Anthropology,* XV:373–395 (1959).

lated and have myths and other means to 'prove' it, makes them quite different from the Flathead and Sanpoil Indians who are grouped together in the same Plateau area of North America but who deny any relationship to each other. The cluster involves an acknowledged historic unity, while an area shows unity, but of a descriptive nature only.

If the existence of the culture cluster can be accepted, and if it is further realized that music instruments inevitably are among the material traits characterizing a cluster, then it follows that instrument and cluster distributional boundaries should be very similar. This, in fact, turns out to be the case in the Congo where J. S. Laurenty in 1960 attempted to map the distribution of some musical instruments.[29] In reviewing Laurenty's work, the present writer attempted to draw attention to the correlations between clusters and instruments.

> In the first place, he [Laurenty] finds that in instrument distribution the peoples to the north of the Congo River and to the east of the Lualaba River are quite sharply differentiated from those in the Congo basin whose area is south of the Congo and west of the Lualaba: the differences are found in the form of affixing the drum head; the fact that the xylophone, zither and harp are found together in the north and somewhat to the east and not in the basin; and that the pluriarc is found in the basin and not to the north and east. Thus the boundary formed by the rivers makes a sharp distinction between harps and zithers on the one hand, and pluriarcs on the other. On the basis of ethnic divisions, this distinction is not particularly surprising; the pluriarcs are found among the Mongo peoples of the basin who form an enormous cluster of interrelated groups . . . while the harp, zither and xylophone belong to such well-defined clusters as the Mangbetu-Azande and the related Mamvu-Lese.
>
> It is generally felt that the Mamvu-Lese were pushed into their present location from the northwest probably before the 17th and 18th centuries, while the Mangbetu established themselves about 1750–1800 and the Azande about 1830, both com-

29. J. S. Laurenty, *Les Cordophones du Congo Belge et du Ruanda-Urundi* (Annales du Musée Royal du Congo Belge, Sciences de l'Homme, Vol. 2, Tervuren).

ing from the northwest and north. On the other hand, it appears that the Mongo have been in their present location for "several hundred years," having come from the northeast. The Mongo, then, must have moved through the present Mangbetu-Azande and Mamvu-Lese areas before the two latter clusters had arrived there, and thus the instrument distribution accords with what we know of the history of some, at least, of the peoples involved.

M. Laurenty's second conclusion is that there are some sharp distinctions between the Equator region north of the Congo River in the great bend of the Uele River, and those of Lake Leopold II: again evidence from the study of culture clusters accords with this conclusion. Further, Laurenty sees Ruanda-Urundi, the Lower Congo, and the Katanga as generally separated from each other and as distinct from all other populations as well in terms of musical instruments; again this is not surprising in view of what we know of populations and population movements. Ruanda-Urundi seems clearly to be East African in origin and affiliation, and thus separate from the Congo itself; the Kongo people in the Lower Congo are one of the earlier groups in the Congo region, having reached the Kasai about 500 AD, and thence moved into their present location by about 1150 AD; the Luba of the Katanga came into the area from the northeast while the Lunda peoples came from roughly the same area but before the Luba.

I am not trying to argue a necessary racial or even tribal correlation with musical instruments, of course, but it does seem logical that migrating groups would carry with them their musical instruments, which may or may not be like those of their earlier neighbors, and that thus we should expect some correlation to exist. But such correlation, it seems to me, can best be expected where culture clusters are involved, and not so much where we deal only with culture areas or even ecological areas. Thus the distribution of instruments noted by Boone and Laurenty and brought together by Laurenty, seem clearly to accord with what we already know about clusters in the Congo.[30]

I have quoted here at some length in order to make two points: first, that the culture cluster seems to be a valid concept which is

30. A. P. Merriam, Review of Laurenty, *Les Cordophones, Ethnomusicology*, VI:48–49 (1962).

much more precise than the older area concept in handling distribution of culture traits and the movements of peoples; and second, it appears that the presence and distribution of music instruments is predictable within a cluster. Reversing the latter point, it would then seem feasible to predict that the distribution of music instruments within limited African areas can be used both to establish clusters and to trace, either alone or preferably in conjunction with other evidence, the movements and history of the particular people involved. And the proposition as presented here seems to accord rather precisely with the restrictions on distribution and diffusion studies noted by Herskovits.

A second example of the use of music instruments in distribution and diffusion studies, as it applies to the reconstruction of culture history, concerns iron gongs. This subject is probably better known to prehistorians interested in African studies than it is to ethnomusicologists.

The first series of articles concerning the iron gongs was published by James Walton, and in it he established three gong classes: "double gongs joined by an arched link, single gong suspended from both ends, single gong with handle." [31] He found these gongs archaeologically distributed at Zimbabwe, Imnukwana, and Dhlo Dhlo in Southern Rhodesia, and from their distribution and development postulated that:

> Stratigraphical evidence at Zimbabwe shows that the arrival of these double gongs in Southern Rhodesia took place after the foundation of the Monomotapa Empire by Hima invaders at the end of the fourteenth century. The distribution pattern indicates that they spread from the Congo along the Kasai to Kazembe and thence southwards to Zimbabwe, and the Kazembe peoples, according to their own traditions, migrated from Mwato Yamwo on the Kasai to Kazembe.[32]

Barrie Reynolds raised some questions in a later article concerning Walton's descriptive typology and dating, as well as the

31. J. Walton, "Iron Gongs from the Congo and Southern Rhodesia," *Man*, LV:30 (1955).
32. *Ibid.*, 30.

diffusion route.[33] On the basis of this and other evidence, Walton changed his formulation both about the date and the means of introduction of the gongs into the Rhodesias:

> Studies subsequent to the publication of my original paper confirm that the iron gongs were introduced into Northern Rhodesia and further south by peoples who migrated from the Congo basin. This introduction took place sometime after A.D. 1500 when the first peoples began to migrate from the Congo into Northern Rhodesia and iron gongs may well have reached Southern Rhodesia by the middle of the sixteenth century . . . The people concerned could not have been the Lunda unless the gongs did not reach Southern Rhodesia until after A.D. 1740.[34]

Further studies on the problem were carried out by Brian Fagan, particularly in Northern Rhodesia, and he reached roughly the same conclusions.

> The Lusitu gongs open the question of the ultimate origin of these instruments, and the date of their arrival in Northern Rhodesia. It seems that they were introduced from the Congo by some reasonably early settlers, such as the Chewa/Maravi groups, who arrived in Northern Rhodesia from the Southern Congo about A.D. 1500 or earlier . . . It seems probable that gongs were introduced into Southern Rhodesia from the Congo by elements which entered the country around A.D. 1500–1600.[35]

And finally, using the gongs as well as other iron implements, Fagan was able to establish three phases of ironworking in Northern Rhodesia. "(1) The Earliest Period (*c.* A.D. 0 to ? A.D. 1000). (2) The Middle Period (*c.* ? A.D. 1000 to A.D. 1740) . . . and a few ceremonial objects including gongs are rarely found; at

33. B. Reynolds, "Iron Gongs from Northern Rhodesia," *Man,* LVIII:255 (1958).
34. Walton, "Iron Gongs," 30.
35. B. Fagan, "A Collection of Nineteenth Century Soli Ironwork from the Lusaka Area of Northern Rhodesia," *Journal of the Royal Anthropological Institute,* XCI:228–243 (1961); B. Fagan, "Pre-European Ironworking in Central Africa with Special Reference to Northern Rhodesia," *Journal of African History,* II:199–210 (1961).

Lusitu and in Southern Rhodesia, they are more common. The Chewa/Maravi migration brought in new ideas and tool forms around A.D. 1500. (3) The Late Period (A.D. 1740–1900)." [The source here is the Luba who came in repeated migrations.] [36]

In the case of iron gongs in Central Africa, then, a musical instrument recovered from archaeological sites and analyzed in stratigraphic and distributional terms has assisted materially in establishing dates and phases or periods of ironworking. Again the criteria proposed by Herskovits—for working in limited areas where historic unity can be assumed and for taking the probability rather than the absolute fact of history—have been clearly met.

It is clear that music instruments can be of considerable use in reconstructing culture history, both in connection with larger cultural units as in the study of culture clusters, and in archaeological investigations where musical instruments are part, or perhaps even all, of the materials recovered.

Up to this point three major uses of music in reconstructing the culture history of Africa have been discussed; the first of these is the reconstruction of the history of music and musical instruments through the utilization of various historic and archaeological techniques. It is assumed that such reconstruction for a particular aspect of culture is of value to the general historic picture since the analysis of a single complex such as music reveals patterns of change indicative of the culture as a whole. The second is the use of music and musical instruments as an adjunct to other kinds of investigations; and third is the role of music and musical instruments which, as in archaeology, point the way toward hypotheses which can be corroborated by additional information. All of these techniques are essentially additive, that is, they contribute to our knowledge of African history through analysis by methods which are basically non-musical—i.e., historic documentation or archaeological techniques.

A further question is whether music or musical instruments in themselves can present us with any unique method for reconstructing African culture history. The answer to this question is

36. *Ibid.*, 209.

positive, though many details remain to be worked out. If the method discussed below is rather highly technical, it is because of the nature of the materials to be presented. It would appear that music offers one extraordinarily precise way of reconstructing contacts between peoples as well as the migrations of cultures through time. If this is so, the diffusionists were wise indeed in their choice of music instruments to help to illustrate their theoretical culture circles; what was lacking was a precision of method which now seems potentially within our grasp.

It was noted previously that music has three special attributes which make it particularly valuable in the reconstruction of history. The first of these is that music is carried below the level of consciousness and therefore is particularly resistant to change. To the best of my knowledge, this aspect of music was first suggested by Herskovits who phrased it as follows: "The peculiar value of studying music . . . is that, even more than other aspects of culture, its patterns tend to lodge on the unconscious level." [37] What is meant by this is that patterns of music do not seem to be objectified by most members of most cultures, including our own, even though they are thoroughly learned. It seems to make no difference that most of us cannot make sharp definitions of consonance and dissonance, or speak with real knowledge of the perfect cadence; we recognize what is consonant and what is dissonant in our music, and we have learned the patterns of our music well enough to know when the closing measures of a musical composition are brought to a satisfying or to an "unfinished" end. Thus, we learn what kinds of sounds satisfactorily fit into our music without necessarily knowing anything at all technical about music; so music structure is carried subliminally, and it is resistant to change.

Two further points must be noted. First, this does not mean that music does not change; it does change, but except for cultural accident, it changes within what seems to be a culturally determined framework. In other words, barring unusual exceptions, we can expect music over a period of time to retain its general

37. M. J. Herskovits, "Patterns of Negro Music," *Transactions, Illinois State Academy of Sciences*, XXXIV:19 (1941).

characteristics. This is borne out in studies of New World Negro cultures whose music differs from the original African but retains the characterizing traits of African music.[38] The second point is that I am not convinced that music is unique in this respect; it may well be that other arts share the characteristic. In any case, it is clear that music operates in this manner.

The second attribute of music which makes it especially useful in studying culture contact is the fact that it is a creative aspect of culture which, through recording, can be frozen as it happens. Thus it can be repeated over and over and studied in detail.

Finally, and perhaps most importantly, music is one of the relatively rare aspects of culture whose structure can be transcribed to paper and expressed precisely through arithmetic and statistical means. While some questions remain to be answered in this connection, a number of such studies have been carried out with the result that there is a strong possibility of obtaining extremely fine and precise measurements of music pitches, as well as reducing song structure to a series of arithmetic measures which are subject to statistical analysis.

One of the earliest such studies was carried out by Hornbostel, who made comparisons between the absolute pitches of music instruments in Burma and Africa and in the Solomon Islands and Brazil.[39] In approaching the problem, Hornbostel set up three criteria necessary for significant comparison: these he refers to as exact determination, absence of purpose, and variability. Since the rate of vibration of various tones can be set out with what appears to be absolute precision, the first criterion, exact determination, is fulfilled simply in music. The criterion of absence of purpose is met by the fact that what is important in music is not the absolute pitch of any given note, but rather the intervallic relationships

38. A. P. Merriam, *Songs of the Afro-Bahian Cults: An Ethnomusicological Analysis* (Unpubl. diss., Northwestern University, 1951); A. P. Merriam, S. Whinery and B. G. Fred, "Songs of a Rada Community in Trinidad," *Anthropos,* LI:157–174 (1956); R. A. Waterman, *African Patterns in Trinidad Negro Music* (Unpubl. diss., Northwestern University, 1943).

39. E. M. von Hornbostel, "Über ein Akustisches Kriterium für Kulturzusammenhange," *Zeitschrift für Ethnologie,* XLIII:601–615 (1911).

among the various steps of the scale. That is, it does not matter (since it appears that some 70 tones can be distinguished within the octave) whether the first tone of a scale is at 236 or 250 vibrations per second; the human ear distinguishes both, and comparison on a world basis indicates that almost every possible absolute pitch is used by one or another culture. Therefore, absolute pitch seems to fulfill the requirement of absence of purpose. Finally, since pitch is infinitely variable theoretically, the criterion of variability is met. In sum, any single absolute pitch is an extraordinarily complex matter since pitch in general is theoretically infinitely variable and since it is intervallic relationship rather than any single pitch which is of vital concern in constructing a musical system. Thus, if absolute pitches are found in different musical systems, the possibility of coincidence, convergence, or parallel invention is very slight.

Hornbostel used the tones of four Burmese xylophones and two African xylophones, one from the Bavenda and one from the Mandingo. It is not necessary here to indicate the various computations made, but the result is a series of three figures, expressed in terms of vibrations per second, which represent the Burmese, the theoretical, and the Bavenda figures. These are as follows: 672, 669, 675; 738.5, 739, 735; 408, 408, 408; 450, 450, 453. These figures are almost incredibly close, and given the complexity of the event, as well as the coincidence of absolute pitch, type of instrument, and character of scale, the relationship is difficult, indeed, to contravene. Similar coincidences, it may be noted, were reached for Melanesian and Brazilian pan pipes.

More recently, A. M. Jones has made a similar study in which a somewhat broader range of musical characteristics has been used.[40] Jones, too, notes the almost exact similarity of beginning absolute pitch in comparing xylophone pitches of the Chopi, Malinke and Bakuba in Africa, with xylophones of Cambodia and Java. At one point he charts the pitches of the scale of six xylophones from these various regions and finds that in all cases the octave is divided into equitonal steps which are almost pre-

40. A. M. Jones, "Indonesia and Africa: the Xylophone as a Culture Indicator," *African Music*, II:36–47 (1960).

cisely the same size, and that the variations in no case exceed the smallest fraction of a semitone. Again, he notes the two Javanese scales, the *pelog* which is the seven-toned equidistant-stepped, and the *slendro,* an artificial pentatonic scale whose steps are either equitonal or nearly so, and finds examples of similar tunings in Africa. Finally, Jones adds information and comparisons of other kinds, i.e., the distribution of the techniques of singing in thirds as opposed to singing in fourths, fifths, and octaves, correspondence of physical form of music instruments found only in Java and West Africa, linguistic evidence, decorative patterns, game forms, and others. Jones closes his argument by saying:

> The thesis we have propounded alters our perspective of Africa; it calls for a map with the Indian Ocean in the centre—a basin whose rim is Indonesia on the east, Madagascar in the south, and Africa on the west, all, to a greater or less extent, sharers in a common sphere of influence. The theory calls for the collaboration of scholars working all round this rim. Perhaps African studies have tended to be too much confined to Africa . . . Let us all come into the open with evidence for or against. We would welcome discussion and criticism, but, as a musician, with one *caveat,* that those who would demolish the non-musical evidence must at the same time account for the musical phenomena if their argument is to stand . . . Perhaps all this is mere coincidence: but if so, will someone tell us what has to be its coefficient of frequency before chance coincidence changes overnight to become positive evidence? [41]

The single response to Jones' plea has come from M. D. W. Jeffreys who, however, does not argue the merits or demerits of Jones' evidence but rather confines himself to discussion of the point of view that Indonesia has not influenced Africa but Africa has influenced Indonesia through the Arab slave trade: "The similarities in music between Indonesia and Africa are due to the impress that African Negroes, imported into Melanesia by the Arab slave trade, exerted on the culture traits of Indonesia." [42]

41. *Ibid.,* 46.
42. M. D. W. Jeffreys, "Negro Influences on Indonesia," *African Music,* II:16 (1961).

Jones' final remark leads me to a last consideration of the potential use of music in the reconstruction of culture history. I have previously indicated that precision of technique and result can characterize the study either of music pitch or music structure as a whole; Hornbostel and Jones have used the former, but the latter is of equal potential importance.

The analysis of a music style depends upon breaking down a structure into its component parts and understanding how these parts fit together to form a coherent whole. Thirty or forty different parts can be isolated, measured, and expressed in arithmetic terms; for example, tonal range, melodic movement, melodic level, ascending versus descending intervals, proportions of wide, medium and narrow intervals, proportions of kinds of intervals used, and so forth. Given the fact that such measurements are significant, a problem to which I will return in a moment, it is clear that precise comparisons can be made between music styles. For example, the following figures were reached in a study in which Gêge (Dahomean-derived music of Brazil), Rada (Dahomean-derived music of Trinidad), and Ketu (Yoruba-derived music of Bahia, Brazil) were compared, and in which the three groups were contrasted to Cheyenne Indian music which was used as a control group. The figures below refer to the proportionate use of the intervals named, expressed as a percentage of the total number of intervals.[43]

Total	*Gêge*	*Rada*	*Ketu*	*Cheyenne*
Minor second	——	——	1.3 per cent	——
Major second	31.5 per cent	25.3 per cent	39	33 per cent
Minor third	35.5	39.6	22	28
Major third	12.3	14.3	13.5	10
Perfect fourth	13.5	14.3	21	15
Perfect fifth	4.4	3.9	2.3	5

It does not take a practiced eye to see that for this small number of measurements taken alone, the differences between the samples

43. Merriam, Whinery and Fred, "Songs of a Rada Community," 170.

are almost precisely what one would expect. That is, Cheyenne music stands apart in almost every respect, falling either above or below the Africa-derived figures. Further, the Gêge and Rada groups, both of which are Dahomean-derived, place themselves together in almost all respects, and are opposed to the Ketu (Yoruba-derived) music. I say that this is what we would expect because experience has shown that music does differ and also that a music system has continuity and integrity through time.

If we can accept figures of this sort, then it is clear that we have an extremely fine set of measurements which expresses a music style with great precision. If we can express a music style with this precision, and if the style does have individual integrity, we should be able to use the technique for the reconstruction of culture history. That is, given an unknown body of song in the New World, for example, we should be able to tell whether it is American Indian or African in derivation—common sense would tell us this, but through the application of this kind of analysis we can be more certain. But more important, it is apparently possible, once we know that the song body is African-derived, to know that it is Dahomean or Yoruba or Bakongo specifically. Similarly, if the method is correct, we should be able to take a Mongo group in the Congo, for example, and given the requisite quantity of comparative material, trace its antecedent forms in other parts of Africa, providing they still exist. And still further, given all the suppositions of the reliability of method and assuming refinement of technique, we should be able to disentangle the component parts which have contributed to the establishment of any given music style.

Since I have cited no examples from the literature concerning Africa, it is evident that none exists; and yet the technique has been used in New World Negro studies enough to indicate its high potential. It should be re-emphasized also that the examples noted above in connection with Gêge, Rada, Ketu, and Cheyenne music represent but a fraction of the items used for comparison, and that virtually all those used in the complete study give the same kinds of results.

There is, however, one set of problems which is still of concern, and this involves the questions of sampling and of which elements of music style are significant. The question of sample is universal in handling problems of this nature, and no further discussion of it need be undertaken here. The question of significance, however, is more pressing and more difficult.

Given thirty or forty items of music structure which can be isolated and expressed quantitatively, which of them are significant? Further, if we accept a particular trait as characterizing, do we have any right to assume that it is also unique? The answers to these problems lie in two directions, the accumulation of much more material than is presently available, and the submission of the results to tests of statistical reliability. The problem of the accumulation of further materials is a question of time, but there has been one case, at least, in which the arithmetic figures have been tested for reliability through the application of statistical means.

This test was undertaken by the present author and Linton C. Freeman, and the materials used were the interval counts for the Ketu and Rada materials noted above.[44] Without recapitulating in detail, the study is an attempt to discern the possible error in identifying the two song styles on the basis of the proportionate use of major seconds and minor thirds. The result, obtained through the application of Fisher's discriminant function, is that the probability of error in discriminating between the two styles is .09. That is, but 9 per cent of the cases in a distribution will be misclassified, and the authors note that "It is reasonable to believe that further reduction in error may be accomplished merely by adding more variables. In the final analysis it should be possible to reduce error in classification to less than one in one hundred." [45]

It would thus appear that the proportionate use of specific music intervals, calculated in relation to the total body of intervals in any given style, is both a characterizing and significant trait, and

44. L. C. Freeman and A. P. Merriam, "Statistical Classification in Anthropology: An Application to Ethnomusicology," *American Anthropologist*, LVIII:464–472 (1956).
45. *Ibid.*, 470.

given the large numbers of traits in a style which can be handled in the same way, it is clear that the precision of the tool is remarkably high. While its specific application to music styles within Africa has not as yet been carried out, its potential is enormous.

Music study, then, contributes in a number of ways to the reconstruction of African culture history. In certain uses it is corroborative; that is, its own history contributes to the knowledge of history in general, and both music sound and music instruments can be and are handled through techniques of historic documentation and archaeological investigation. It has reflected anthropological theory and history in that it has been widely used in evolutionary and diffusionist theories and, as with all other traits and complexes of culture, it can be used in diffusion and distribution studies. Its greatest potential contribution, however, lies in the fact that both music sound and music instruments, are subject to analysis of an extremely precise nature through the use of statistics.

METODOLOGÍA PARA LA RECONSTRUCCIÓN DE LAS DANZAS FOLKLÓRICAS EXTINTAS

por Flor de María Rodríguez de Ayestarán

1. Introducción

Los dos esquemas que presentamos para la reconstrucción de las danzas folklóricas extintas y sus correspondientes observaciones, no son hipotéticos o conjeturales, sino que están dictados por los "datos" con los cuales se inicia toda operación inductiva, que es la operación mental, casi diría natural, de toda ciencia. Este trabajo pretende ser la ordenación coherente de lo que me ha acontecido en mis viajes de recolección folklórica dentro del Uruguay, no es "lo que me hubiera podido acontecer." Se entiende, entonces, que pueden existir más datos o "casos" recogidos por otros investigadores - o por mí en el futuro - que aquí no están registrados. Bienvenidos sean.

2. Esquema de la Fuente Seca

A) Fuente Seca

- 1. Referencias escritas
  - 11. En la época en que la danza estaba en vigencia
    - 112. Libros de viajeros y cronistas
    - 113. Periódicos
    - 114. Cartas, cuadernos de baile y otros documentos
    - 115. Obras de ficción (narraciones, cuentos, poesías, novelas, etc.)
  - 12. En épocas posteriores, una vez que la danza se extinguió (puede subdividirse como el parágrafo anterior)
- 2. Referencias gráficas impresas o manuscritas
  - 21. En la época en que estaba en vigencia
    - 211. Dibujos, óleos, etc.
    - 212. Esculturas
    - 213. Grabados, bajo-relieves, cerámicas
    - 214. Daguerrotipos y fotografías (por excepción toma de cine cuando la danza estaba vigente)
  - 22. En épocas posteriores, una vez que la danza se extinguió. Información casi inservible (puede subdividirse como en el parágrafo anterior).

3. Observaciones sobre fuentes secas

A) Fuente Seca

1) El nombre de la danza aparecido en el libro de un viajero o cronista, es el testimonio de un hecho cronológico que no admite discusión y debe ser puntualmente registrado — y desde luego criticado — porque indica que el autor del documento lo fijó en una fecha exacta: por lo menos antes de esa fecha, la danza ya circulaba por tal o cual región.

2) Debe ser criticado implacablemente porque a veces el viajero lo tomó textualmente de otro viajero anterior que lo vió en otra región.

3) De todas maneras, aunque a veces puede ser una cadena de plagios como la que descubrió Carlos Vega con la Calenda de los negros de Montevideo del siglo XVIII, tomada de una danza que ve el Padre Labat casi cien años antes en Santo Domingo, hay que registrar este hecho, porque muy amenudo el viajero ve efectivamente una danza del país, pero cuando la va a describir recurre a un libro de su biblioteca y no al recuerdo de lo que vió su pupila.

4) Los periódicos son, a mi entender, una de las fuentes más ricas porque registran el acontecer cotidiano que puede facilmente ser impugnado por su propios lectores. Cuando un diario describe una danza del país, ya sea por medio de crónicas de costumbres rurales o suburbanas, es amenudo desmentido en números posteriores por sus ocasionales lectores y de esa confrontación surgen luces muy claras para los detalles de tal o cual danza. En los periódicos sudamericanos, aún la cartelera de teatros es muy esclarecedora: en los espectáculos populares, circos, etc. se anuncia frecuentamente "se bailará la danza del país titulada . . ."

5) Las cartas y documentos de archivo, son preciosos testimonios. Los primeros por el detalle familiar de una tertulia relatada con toda suerte de pormenores, de quien realiza un viaje al interior del país y cuenta a uno de sus familiares todo lo que le aconteció. Entre los documentos, debe atenderse a los "carnet de baile" del siglo XIX, donde uno ve aparecer el título de una especie que luego verá en los ambientes campesinos, y, sobre todo, a esos cuadernos familiares, donde se registran junto a poesías, recetas de cocina, ensalmos, adivinanzas y oraciones, las voces de mando de una danza con bastonero (o maestro de ceremonias) o aún el paso de determinado baile.

6) Las referencias escritas en obras de ficción (narraciones, cuentos, poesías) aunque son muy peligrosas de utilizar por la fantasía que puede impregnarles su autor, muchas veces nos traen por obra de la intuición creadora, los más recónditos detalles — a veces los más substanciales — de la coreografía.

7) Las referencias escritas que aparecen en obras concebidas una vez que la danza se extenguió son muy poco valederas. Por lo general el escritor es un investigador en potencia, pero sin las garantías profesionales del verdadero investigador.

8) Las referencias gráficas impresas o manuscritas en la época en que estaban en vigencia son importanísimas pero constituyen algo así como el cuadro aislado de una película cinematográfica que se recortó y se hizo ampliar. Se apresa en ellos una cantidad enorme de detalles, pero le falta la secuencia en el tiempo. A mi entender este dato sirve para corroborar; nunca para inicial afirmación positiva.

9) Cuando la referencia gráfica se produce cuando la danza está extinta, en todos los casos es "una proyección" del hecho folklórico y no la anotación científica del hecho en sí.

4. Esquema de la Fuente Viva

B) Fuente Viva

1. El informante ha bailado esa danza cuando estaba vigente
   - 11. Recuerda íntegra su coreografía
     - 111. Está en condiciones físicas de reproducirla ante el investigador
     - 112. No está en condiciones físicas de hacerlo (enfermedad, edad avanzada, timidez, etc.
   - 12. Recuerda fragmentariamente pasos y figuras
   - 13. Recuerda erróneamente y confunde detalles (demostrable por otros informantes que lo contradicen)

2. El informante no ha bailado esa danza pero posee testimonios personales o ajenos, de ella
   - 21. Esos testimonios son completos y verificados por otros informantes
     - 211. Ha visto bailar la danza cuando estaba vigente
     - 212. Otras personas del grupo folk se la han descrito
   - 22. Esos testimonios no son completos ni verificables por otros informantes (puede subdividirse como en el parágrafo anterior)
   - 23. Esos testimonios son erróneos simplemente porque el informante confunde:
     - 231. Una danza con otra (confusión de título), pero su testimonio puede ser valedero (véase 211)
     - 232. Un paso o una figura de una danza con los de otra (información escasamente servible)

5. Observaciones sobre Fuentes Vivas

B) Fuente Viva

1) La música de una danza vive, por lo general, más de 50 años después que ha muerto su coreografía. Se recoge en el Uruguay, por ejemplo, la música de más de 20 pericones distintos, pero el Pericón se dejó de bailar en los ranchos espontáneamente antes de 1920. El ejecutante de guitarra o acordeón que acompañó el Pericón — y que, además, en otras ocasiones lo bailó — es uno de los mejores informantes para la descripción de esta rica danza coral, porque, aunque no sabe notación, ello no obsta para que no ignore todos los períodos músicales de que consta y a cuales de ellos corresponde el desarrollo de las diferentes figuras.

2) A veces el informante ha bailado la danza y recuerda con claridad el paso y algunas de sus figuras, a veces solamente recuerdo el paso y asegura "que había figuras", otras recuerda solamente el "elemento" que había para embellecer dicha danza ya fuera el pañuelo, una flor, una silla (polca de la silla), la espuela, etc. Todos son datos de interés, eslabones rotos o sueltos que unidos a otros, entre fuente viva y seca, permiten al investigador reconstruir la cadena. El peligro estriba en apresurarse en el intento de reconstrucción cuando lo recolectado son pequeños retazos, porque puede crear una versión conjetural o monstruosa porque nunca funcionó como tal.

3) La moda impone períodos de vivencias a determinados grupos de danzas; naturalmente las danzas de cada época se parecen entre sí, Varían en su ritmo y en algunas figuras pero aún un principiante en el estudio de la reconstrucción, sabrá relacionar las generaciones de danzas a través de las épocas. Cuando la moda cambia y la danza declina para desaparecer luego, le ocurre otro tanto a casi todas sus contemporáneas. Muy amenudo convive una generación con otra y no es extraño que el informante que bailó las danzas de determinado período, confunda sus nombres y sus coreografías. Este es un punto cuya delicadeza preocupa mucho al investigador. Hay que estar preparado y alerta cuando la sinceridad del informante es manifiesta. Tal es el caso con danzas de países fronterizos en cuyos límites el informante aprendió la misma.

4) Cuando el área de difusión de una danza abarca la frontera de dos países, el informante de determinada localidad o pueblo fronterizo asegura que su recuerdo sólo se refiere a su pueblo; pero recordemos que los países folklóricos no coinciden con los políticos sobre todo en la América Latina de tan reciente creación (150 años) de existencia políticamente liberada. La información del bailarín

interesa a los efectos objetivos de saber en qué lugares se practicó dicha danza pero no su opinión sobre la procedencia o migración de la misma. El informante dar, como el enfermo, los síntomas; corresponde al médico (el investigador) diagnosticar cual es el origen del problema.

5) Insólitamente se recoge de labios de un informante el nombre de una danza y su correspondiente coreografía cuya trayectoria se desconoce. No aparece en documentos, ni otros informantes, en todo el área de la región investigada, la recuerdan. El dato se anota en espera de nuevas confirmaciones tanto de una fuente como de la otra, pero si no recibió confirmación, ese "dato" no lo incorpora a sus trabajos (es "danza en cuarentena"); tal vez otro investigador con nuevos aportes — o uno mismo — podrá más adelante develarla a la luz de seguros criterios o datos más precisos, porque con una o dos versiones aisladas nada avanza la ciencia tan fina y delicada de la verdad folklórica. Falta el criterio "de cantidad", como los antropólogos culturales.

6) En la reconstrucción de una danza vemos, pues, que los problemas se presentan en números mayores. En la referencia que aporta la fuente seca, no debemos descuidar que algunos viejos documentos de los siglos XVII y XVIII vienen cargados de "supuestos". Como el hilo de la vida de las danzas de esas épocas se ha cortado, los datos que aportan los hijos o nietos de personas que las bailaron, son fragmentarias e incompletas. La reunión del conjunto de datos da la luz, muchas veces, pero hay que ser cauto y no dejarse llevar de otro entusiasmo que el de la búsqueda de la verdad, sin olvidar que si a partir del descubrimiento de América hasta fines del pasado siglo, prolijos memorialistas y tradicionalistas americanos describieron con bastante precisión los pasos y figuras de las danzas nacionales, se ha de seguir su rastro en las fuentes europeas a través de las edades. Para lograr esto, el conocimiento académico de la danza es factor determinante. No hay que olvidar que la danza académica posee nomenclatura técnica que en la mayoría de las veces pasa al uso popular, y que aún sufriendo alteraciones esos términos son reconocidos por quien maneje con soltura o solvencia dicha nomenclatura. La danza, como todo hecho cultural, es el bien común de una colectividad y pertenece a su patrimonio. Se ha obtenido, como es lógico, por herencia y, además, por el acrecentamiento (o empobrecimiento) de esa herencia por parte del heredero que remodela las danzas en variantes notables. Pero cuidado de aferrarse a la idea de que una danza popular — como todo bien cultural — nace por generación espontánea o local. Este absurdo ha tenido éxito en épocas pasadas y aún perdura en mentes no adiestradas en

antropología cultural. En todo caso este proceso está muy bien esclarecido en el libro de Carlos Vega "El origien de las danzas folklóricas."

7) Cuando nos encontramos ante un informante que bailó la danza en plena vigencia de la misma y está en condiciones físicas de reproducirla ante el investigador en todos sus pasos y figuras, es conveniente interrogarle acerca del lugar donde la aprendió, y si recuerda los instrumentos y la música que acompañaron dicha danza. Si la danza es de pareja y hay dos informantes que la bailaron, el interrogatorio dará comienzo desde la forma de invitar a la mujer a bailar en qué lugar del salón comenzaban los primeros pasos. Es muy importante la "posición" al iniciarse la danza. Se investiga si el brazo cae a lo largo del cuerpo, si uno o ambos van flexionados, si las palmas de las manos van hacia afuera, adentro, vuelta hacia arriba o hacia abajo. Si las piernas permanecen derechas o bien si en la postura inicial se flexionan ambas o una de ellas. Si los pies se colocan juntos o separados; hacia dónde mira la punta, si una de ellas apoya en el suelo, si permanece en el aire; si un pie adelanta al otro, aclarar si es el derecho o el izquierdo. Si la danza es de pareja enlazada, se observa la forma en que lo hace: a qué altura del cuerpo se toman la mano, si se presionan toda la palma apenas se rozan con los dedos. En qué forma se apoya ella en el brazo (codo) del varón. A qué altura enlaza él el cuerpo de la mujer; si presiona la cintura femenina, observar si es con la palma entera y qué parte abarca con su mano (espalda, costado, etc.). También se estudiará si balancean los brazos al compás de la música o si los mantienen naturalmente flexionados o bien muy rígidos. La posición de las cabezas, es también punto importante. Observar si se inclinan hacia uno de los hombros, si se balancean, si permanecen en la misma posición durante toda la danza. Si se miran a los ojos, hacia los pies o hacia algún punto perdido. Al comienzo de la danza se anota con qué pie comienza el varón y con cual la mujer. Estudiar el paso y la duración del mismo. En cuanto a las figuras, se anotarán en la sucesión con que las presenta el informante y si al ejecutarlas hay combinación de pasos o si repiten el mismo durante toda la danza. Si aportan "elementos" para acompañar la danza cuales son y cómo los usan. Si en alguna parte de la danza los bailarines se sueltan, conviene anotar cuál mano se desprende primero y qué posición o giros realizan los bailarines durante la duración de esta figura. Caben las mismas observaciones con respecto a las danzas corales y omito todos los detalles que complementan el estudio porque sería fatigoso para los alcances de esta comunicación.

Montevideo, Uruguay

El informante bailó el "Chotis Figurita" cuando estaba vigente, recuerda íntegra su coreografía y está en condiciones físicas de reproducirla (Fuente Viva, caso 111). Piriápolis, departamento de Maldonado, Uruguay, 20 de enero de 1964: informante Juan Bonilla, 65 años, jardinero, nacido en Maldonado, explicando y danzando este baile con la recolectora Flor de María Rodríguez de Ayestarán.

CHARLES L. BOILES

sémiotique de l'ethnomusicologie

La semiosis est le processus qui implique que quelque chose fonctionne comme signe. L'étude des différentes dimensions de ce processus s'appelle la sémiotique, et, dans ce texte, nous proposerons l'application de la sémiotique à l'étude de la musique. Cette application exige qu'on considère la musique comme une forme de communication, parce que c'est grâce à l'utilisation de signes que la communication se fait. Seeger (1962, 1966) et d'autres ont décrit certains paramètres de la musique comme dotés de propriétés communicatives, et le concept de communication par la musique n'est pas tout à fait étranger au grand public. En effet, il n'est pas rare dans notre culture de faire des critiques sur des exécutions musicales, en se demandant si l'exécutant a communiqué quelque chose ou non. Soutenir qu'il y a communication au moment où se joue la musique, c'est affirmer que les phénomènes musicaux sont d'une façon ou d'une autre liés à la semiosis. Par conséquent, si l'on conçoit qu'il est possible de communiquer quelque chose avec la musique, on doit reconnaître qu'un certain aspect de la musique fonctionne comme porteur de signes *(sign vehicle)*, c'est-à-dire comme signifiant musical, et rend cette communication possible. L'utilisation de la sémiotique aidera à éclaircir ce qui, en musique, fonctionne comme signe.

Une courte explication de ce qu'est la sémiotique s'impose ici. La discussion qui suit se fonde sur les écrits de Charles Morris (1938). En premier lieu, un signe renvoie à quelque chose pour quelqu'un. On doit souligner qu'un signe ne renvoie pas toujours à quelque chose pour chacun. Assurément, il existe des signes qui ne renvoient plus à quelque chose pour tout le monde, et il en existe qui renvoient à quelque chose seulement pour quelques-uns. La personne pour qui le signe a un référent, s'appelle l'*interprète* du signe. Musicalement parlant, l'interprète est soit l'exécutant qui, consciemment, transmet le signe dans un acte de communication, soit l'auditeur qui perçoit que le signe est transmis, ou bien les deux à la fois. Il est important de bien se souvenir que le signifiant musical est uniquement l'aspect sensible du phénomène musical en vertu duquel il y a semiosis; le reste ne concerne pas la sémiotique.

Ce quelque chose que le signe indique à son interprète est le *designatum* du signe, et le designatum peut être un état ou un objet. On doit également faire remarquer qu'un designatum renvoie à une catégorie ou ensemble d'objets, dont les membres s'appellent les *denotata*. Une illustration musicale d'un designatum nous est fournie par l'*Affektenlehre* (théorie des sentiments) du XVIIIe siècle. Les compositeurs qui utilisent des *Affekte* dans leur musique, attribuent une émotion, comme le « tendre » ou le « triste », à une série précise de sons musicaux; ayant proposé ce système expressif, ils se sont trouvés en face de problèmes sémiotiques, et, pour eux, toute émotion formait le designatum indiqué par une série de sons donnée.

Si un phénomène donné fonctionne de telle façon qu'il montre qu'il a un designatum, on peut le considérer comme *signifiant* d'un signifié. Autrement dit, si un interprète prend conscience d'un designatum, c'est-à-dire par l'intermédiaire d'une troisième chose, les médiateurs sont des signifiants. Un exemple intéressant de signifiant musical nous est donné dans la forme théâtrale de Bali appelée *Gamelan Gambuh.* McPhee (1966) rapporte que quatre échelles sont utilisées pour accompagner quatre groupes différents d'acteurs. Il y a la « gamme *Selisir,* considérée comme idéale pour les *gending alus.* A cause de son aspect plus sombre, on considère que la *Tembung* s'adapte mieux aux *gendingkras* qui accompagnent les personnages principaux d'un type vigoureux, ainsi que les principaux antagonistes; tandis qu'on réserve la *Baro* aux entrées des personnages secondaires tels que les hérauts, officiers ou accompagnateurs de bouffons. La *Lebeng* est utilisée plus tard dans le spectacle, parfois pour les gending alus, mais tout particulièrement dans les scènes de récrimination et d'action dramatique » (*ibidem.*, p. 139). Dans le cas du Gamelan Gambuh, chaque échelle est un signifiant pour qui le designatum est une sorte d'acteur ou d'action, et on peut dire qu'au moyen de ces échelles, l'auditeur de Bali tient immédiatement compte des types de personnages engagés dans l'action aux différents stades des pièces.

Les *leitmotive* de Richard Wagner nous fournissent un excellent exemple pour expliquer ce qu'est le denotatum. On se souviendra que les denotata sont ces membres d'un ensemble que le designatum indique. Si l'on prend le motif de « l'anneau » (dans le *Ring des Nibelungen*) comme signifiant, on peut dire que le designatum de cette structure est l'anneau, et que les variantes de ce leitmotiv sont les denotata. Quand on examine les choses sous cet angle, il n'est plus important de se demander quelle est la version la plus authentique d'un leitmotiv, parce que chaque version sera, d'une façon ou d'une autre, reliée au designatum; de même, on devrait considérer les variantes mélodiques, harmoniques et rythmiques de ces motifs simplement comme des caractéristiques d'un denotatum particulier. La description sémiotique d'un leitmotiv se ferait sous la forme d'un exposé paradigmatique prenant en considération les diverses variantes qui tiennent lieu de *denotata*.

On verra que l'étude des signifiants musicaux se trouve liée à plusieurs dimensions de la semiosis, à savoir la syntaxe, la sémantique et la pragmatique. La syntaxe et la sémantique traitent des rapports des signes entre eux. D'un côté, la syntaxe s'occupe des types de rapports concernant les signes dont la combinaison se fait selon des règles de formation et de transformation. Les règles de formation précisent les séries possibles, ou chaînes de combinaisons, permettant n'importe quel groupe de signes; les règles de transformation déterminent quelles sont les autres chaînes que l'on peut dériver de la série originale.

Les règles de l'harmonie tonale européenne forment un des meilleurs exemples pour illustrer la syntaxe. Winograd (1969), entre autres, a démontré l'existence de cette dimension syntaxique en essayant d'appliquer l'utilisation de la linguistique à l'analyse de l'harmonie tonale sur ordinateur. Pour exposer les faits d'une façon syntaxique, l'ordre de présentation des enchaînements d'accords bien précis est soumis à des règles de formation, et les variantes de cette mise en ordre dépendent des règles de transformation. Dans le système européen, plusieurs accords ou leurs combinaisons jouent le rôle de signes, et ce rôle est d'indiquer le début et la fin des phrases, ou bien de mettre plus ou moins l'accent sur les éléments à l'intérieur des lignes mélodiques.

Dans la mesure où tel mouvement harmonique influence le mode de perception de la musique chez l'auditeur, on peut dire que, parfois, les accords spécifient des caractéristiques ou fonctionnent comme signes indiciels. Nous voulons dire qu'ils indiquent la localisation et les propriétés pertinentes des différentes parties des mélodies, comme les cultures européennes les reconnaissent dans un continuum musical. Une situation analogue existe dans les systèmes d'intonation utilisés par ceux qui parlent les langues européennes. Prenons l'anglais comme exemple : nous faisons une différence entre « Where are you *go*ing? » et « *whe*re are you going? ». Si l'on essayait de mettre le même genre d'accent sur les parties correspondantes d'une mélodie, on pourrait très vraisemblablement utiliser différents accords ou enchaînements d'accords pour chaque version de la même mélodie. Et puisque les langues européennes utilisent de tels systèmes d'intonation, on ne devrait pas être surpris de trouver un phénomène équivalent dans les systèmes musicaux européens. En fait, on devrait considérer les systèmes d'intonation linguistiques des langues européennes comme phénoménologiquement parallèles aux systèmes harmoniques des mêmes régions, et la syntaxe pourrait les étudier de façon profitable. Historiquement parlant, un accent plus fort mis sur les aspects syntaxiques de la langue a quelque peu éclipsé l'étude des autres dimensions de la sémiotique, et cette tendance se reflète également chez les musicologues qui consacrent une attention démesurée à l'analyse formelle et aux règles de formation. Ainsi, la syntaxe est une dimension de la sémiotique que la plupart des musicologues des cultures européennes comprendront plus facilement que la pragmatique ou la sémantique. Pour être précis, on en sait relativement peu sur les règles sémantiques qui existent dan^ les systèmes musicaux à travers le monde, et on peut attribuer cette situation en partie au fait qu'il n'y a encore aucune définition des paramètres musicaux fonctionnant comme signifiants. A l'intérieur de la sémiotique, la sémantique traite des conditions requises pour qu'un signe soit applicable à un objet ou un état. En sémantique musicale, le premier problème est de découvrir quels aspects de la musique constituent des signifiants et quels sont les designata de ces signes.

Il semblerait qu'en réalité il y ait beaucoup de types de phénomènes musicaux qui fonctionnent comme signifiants. Pour définir ce qu'on peut appeler à proprement parler un signifiant musical, le chercheur doit définir son contexte de référence; il doit délimiter l'univers dans lequel un signe musical donné est un constituant opératoire. Le terme *univers* est employé ici au sens de la théorie des ensembles, et il dénote une classe spécifique d'objets constituant un ensemble complet. Il est nécessaire de délimiter l'univers parce que, bien souvent, on donne une définition si large à un univers donné que les efforts pour les traiter analytiquement n'aboutissent qu'à de la frustration. Par exemple, il pourrait être assez difficile de faire des déclarations générales qui définissent les signes musicaux dans la musique japonaise kabuki. Mais si l'univers de référence était restreint à la musique de scène produite par l'ensemble *geza* du théâtre kabuki, il serait relativement plus facile de découvrir quels phénomènes musicaux sont reliés à leurs designata respectifs. De plus, on devrait peut-être éviter de faire des déclarations sur les signifiants dans l'art vocal européen en général, et limiter son univers à des mélodies ayant pour sujet l'amour éternel ou toute autre situation. En délimitant ainsi chaque univers, on ne nie pas les traits communs qui existent entre plusieurs ensembles de signes musicaux. Cependant, ce que signifie un signe musical dans un contexte, peut n'avoir aucun rapport avec ce qu'il signifie dans d'autres circonstances, et tout d'abord, on peut éviter la confusion si la recherche d'un signifiant et de ses propriétés se borne exclusivement à un univers très étroitement délimité.

Afin d'examiner une règle sémantique dans un système musical donné, prenons l'exemple d'un univers ainsi défini : « la musique de l'ensemble geza du théâtre japonais kabuki ». La musique de ce groupe *off stage* fournit ce qu'on a l'habitude d'appeler la musique de scène ou le fond sonore, et elle est une forme de ce que j'ai désigné ailleurs sous le nom d'accompagnement de barde. La musique de l'ensemble geza fonctionne sémantiquement au moins des deux manières suivantes: par l'utilisation du timbre, par l'utilisation de mélodies spécifiques. Du point de vue du timbre, les interventions musicales d'une signification donnée sont réservées à des instruments de sonorités bien déterminées. Ainsi, à un niveau général de significations, le timbre du *shamisen* est habituellement réservé à des interventions concernant les bruits naturels, les dispositions psychologiques ou un moment du temps. Dans le cas de cette musique de shamisen, le designatum est indiqué par un air bien précis ou *rubric*, afin qu'une mélodie telle que *yuki* évoque l'idée de la neige, la mélodie *tsukuda* indique que le fleuve Sumida fait partie de l'action, *Shinobi Sanju* établit une atmosphère mystérieuse et sombre, et *Kangen* implique une scène de cour d'autrefois (Malm, 1968, p. 210-226). D'autre part, le timbre du shamisen ne s'utiliserait pas d'ordinaire pour les scènes religieuses ou de combat. On indique habituellement les scènes religieuses par des métallophones, et on obtient une plus grande précision au moyen d'un instrument métallique bien défini. Ainsi, un petit gong appelé *hontsuri-gane* évoque une scène de temple, mais la *rei*, une clochette, indique des services religieux ou l'entrée d'un prêtre. Si le designatum de la musique était le combat ou la guerre, les instruments seraient de préférence un tambour comme le *gaku-daiko* ou des baguettes qu'on appelle *hyoshigi*. La liste exhaustive de ces timbres et de leurs designata est longue et Malm en a beaucoup parlé *(ibid.)*, mais d'après les exemples mentionnés ici, on voit que certaines conditions précises établissent un rapport entre un designatum et certains éléments de la musique de l'ensemble geza; une définition explicite des conditions établissant un tel rapport, s'appellerait la règle sémantique. En voici un exemple : « Quand la mélodie *yuki* du shamisen est jouée par l'ensemble geza dans le contexte d'une représentation kabuki, il faut que la neige apparaisse à ce moment-là dans la situation exposée sur la scène. »

Il devrait maintenant être clair que les conditions énoncées dans la règle sémantique ne peuvent exister si l'exécutant et l'auditeur ne les perçoivent pas comme telles. Ainsi, il s'avère nécessaire de faire un examen de la pragmatique, cette dimension de la sémiotique qui étudie la façon dont les signes sont reliés à leurs interprètes. La pragmatique étudie le processus de reconnaissance d'un signe, l'habitude qui fait que l'interprète perçoit qu'un signifiant désigne certains objets ou situations. Cette habitude s'appelle l'*interprétation* du signe.

Le problème de la pragmatique en ethnomusicologie est plutôt complexe, parce qu'il y a peu de cultures qui aient développé les moyens de discuter du comportement musical. On s'est aperçu que, la plupart du temps, ceux qui utilisent un système musical ne formulent pas d'ordinaire des règles pour l'utilisation des signifiants musicaux, ou, s'ils le font, ce n'est qu'en partie. De telles règles sont plutôt des habitudes de comportement, de sorte que ce sont seulement certaines autres combinaisons de signes musicaux qui en sont tirées, et ce comportement exige aussi que seuls certains signes musicaux soient opératoires dans des situations déterminées. Par conséquent, il reste pour le chercheur à étudier aussi à fond que possible la culture qui est à l'origine de ce comportement, afin de découvrir non seulement les propriétés pertinentes du signifiant musical, mais aussi le comportement qui permet son utilisation. Dans de très nombreux cas, sans faire au préalable une étude très poussée du comportement musical de cette culture, il est presque impossible de déterminer en priorité et avec précision quelles sortes de véhicules de signes musicaux elle a. A ce sujet, citons le cas de la musique de culte des Otomis que l'on trouve dans l'état de Veracruz au Mexique où j'étudie cette musique depuis 1966.

Comme beaucoup de groupes indigènes de la côte du golfe du Mexique, les Otomis affirment que la musique instrumentale de leurs genres religieux communique quelque chose. Désirant savoir ce qui était communiqué et de quelle façon ce l'était, j'ai dû utiliser la pragmatique afin de discerner quelles étaient l'habitude des interprètes, les signifiants musicaux et les designata. Il m'a fallu utiliser plusieurs méthodes pour établir les paramètres de ce comportement musical. La première consistait à déterminer le matériel du corpus et les contextes dans lesquels on le jouait. L'univers à étudier a été défini comme étant ces airs utilisés dans les rites de subsistance Otomis, appelés *Costumbres*; dans ces fêtes, il s'agit d'apaiser différentes grandes divinités pour assurer le succès de l'activité agricole des Otomis.

Le rite a été enregistré dans son intégralité au cours de cinq célébrations différentes et on a pris beaucoup de notes afin de relever tous les comportements associés à la musique. Dans le but d'interpréter ce comportement de cérémonie, il a fallu étudier la cosmologie Otomi et connaître à fond son système religieux manifeste. D'après cette étude, on a découvert que ces cérémonies de subsistance concernaient surtout les panthéons des divinités célestes et terrestres, et que des airs bien précis se jouaient en référence à un panthéon précis, et à un acte de cérémonie précis consacré à un membre de ce panthéon.

Il a fallu ensuite faire entendre les enregistrements des airs à des spécialistes religieux et à des musiciens et des adorateurs, et leur demander de raconter quelle communication ils saisissaient dans cette musique. La réponse à cette question fit découvrir une attitude qui allait de quelques commentaires serrés jusqu'à des observations très profondes de vie intérieure. Cet éventail de données plutôt déroutant fut soumis à une analyse comparative, et on appliqua le même processus à des manifestations de comportement que l'on avait relevées au moment de l'enregistrement des cérémonies. D'après ces modèles de comportement et de commentaires, on put alors arriver à une sorte de consensus au sujet de la désignation de telles divinités ou de telles situations par l'air en question.

Une fois que ces designata furent établis expérimentalement, il devint possible de soumettre la musique à une analyse comparative identique. Dans ce but, on étudia deux types de regroupements. Dans le premier, on groupe les mélodies en ensembles selon les designata communs à tous les airs d'un ensemble quelconque. Dans le second, les ensembles sont formés d'après une similarité musicale quelconque qui semble commune à n'importe quel ensemble. L'analyse de chacun des groupes de mélodies possédant des designata communs révéla certains phénomènes musicaux qui s'y rencontrent très fréquemment. La chance de découvrir des signifiants musicaux ayant un lien avec des designata fut plus tard renforcée par les résultats obtenus pour le deuxième regroupement. Ces ensembles de mélodies regroupées d'après des ressemblances musicales observables confirmèrent, non seulement l'association avec des designata connus, mais encore aidèrent à établir les denotata de tout designatum. Les résultats de ces analyses révélèrent le fait plutôt surprenant que, dans cette musique, trois types différents de phénomènes musicaux fonctionnent simultanément comme signifiants, à savoir une suite de hauteurs sonores ordonnées, le modèle rythmique et la structure formelle. En outre, tout type de phénomène musical semble se limiter à un genre bien précis de designatum : les suites de hauteurs musicales ordonnées désignent des entités, tandis que les modèles rythmiques désignent des actions, et que la structure formelle désigne un emplacement du monde Otomi.

L'utilisation Otomi de la suite des hauteurs sonores comme signifiant, aide à faire une différence non seulement entre les panthéons mais aussi entre les membres de chaque panthéon donné. Par exemple, la suite *mi-do-ré-do* désigne le Dieu Soleil, mais la suite *mi-fa-ré-mi* précise l'envoyé du Dieu Soleil, un personnel sacré laissé sur terre pour guider les prêtres fidèles. Sans tenir compte du modèle rythmique auquel ces hauteurs s'adaptent, chaque suite de hauteurs continue à désigner une entité précise. Les modèles rythmiques et les structures formelles conservent aussi leurs designata uniques dans n'importe quelle circonstance d'association avec les suites de hauteurs. Quand ces trois types de signifiants se combinent, ils constituent un signal complexe qui a un ensemble unique de référents ayant une signification pour l'interprète Otomi. En ce qui concerne ces phénomènes, une règle pragmatique de la musique Otomi affirmerait que, dans cette culture, les interprètes ont l'habitude d'établir une corrélation entre des suites de hauteurs et des entités, des modèles rythmiques et des actions, des structures formelles et des lieux, si, et seulement si, de tels phénomènes se produisent dans la musique qui doit se jouer lors des cérémonies de subsistance.

D'après les différents exemples présentés ici, on voit que les règles pragmatiques concernant les signifiants musicaux auront une latitude plus large que les règles identiques qui concernent les signes utilisés dans le langage parlé. Pour les diverses cultures mentionnées ici, il y a des signifiants musicaux assez variés, et on a démontré que dans le monde entier, les conditions auxquelles un véhicule de signes musicaux peut devenir un signe, sont différentes : les Japonais interprètent les sons en établissant une corrélation entre des gammes et des types de personnages et d'actions; on peut opposer à ce cas l'utilisation Otomi d'ensembles ordonnés de hauteurs sonores pour désigner des entités. On peut faire une autre comparaison intéressante entre le leitmotiv wagnérien et la musique de l'ensemble geza. Bien que les deux aient un but comparable, la musique geza comprend la corrélation d'un timbre avec un designatum, ainsi que l'utilisation nécessaire d'airs groupés en ensembles, même si les mêmes timbres et airs peuvent s'utiliser dans beaucoup de pièces kabuki. D'autre part, le leitmotiv wagnérien peut apparaître sous différentes formes, mais son utilisation se limite à un drame ou à un cycle déterminés. On a constaté que les autres genres de signifiants musicaux étaient des suites d'accords, des modèles rythmiques et des structures formelles.

Étant donné l'éventail effrayant des types de signifiants possibles dans toute culture, on voit que, à moins de chercher à découvrir la règle pragmatique d'un groupe donné, le chercheur peut très vraisemblablement passer des années à étudier des aspects d'une tradition musicale qui ne concernent pas la sémiosis du groupe en question. Cela ne veut pas dire que tous les autres aspects d'une tradition musicale ne soient pas des objets d'études, mais puisque une grande partie de l'analyse musicale se préoccupe de découvrir des traits classificatoires, la perspective de l'analyste est moins discriminante en ce qui concerne le choix des types de phénomènes à étudier. Quand l'analyse en traits en est le moteur, la musicologie est plus intéressée par la description pure, mais les traits stylistiques que le chercheur perçoit ne sont pas obligatoirement ceux qui sont pertinents pour l'interprète musical indigène. Très souvent il peut apparaître que, alors que nous nous occupons de cataloguer les structures formelles, le nombre d'intervalles et les types de gammes, la sémiosis de l'interprète, elle, fonctionne grâce au parallélisme des « formes » mélodiques, au dénombrement de la fréquence des hauteurs sonores, ou de leur succession qui se reproduit dans un ordre donné.

Du point de vue de la sémiotique, les phénomènes musicaux que nous avons étudiés prennent un aspect différent. Au lieu de poser comme but l'étude de la structure formelle pour elle-même, on demande de découvrir si oui ou non la forme est un élément pertinent pour la culture qui engendre cette musique, ou bien si la structure formelle est seulement un sous-produit de quelque autre genre d'acte musical. De même, une perspective sémiotique ne se contente pas de savoir seulement quelle gamme ou mode permet d'engendrer des signes musicaux. Du point de vue sémiotique, l'étude d'une gamme ou d'un mode exige de savoir si le type de gamme est plus vraisemblablement le résultat de règles syntaxiques, ou si le mode est important surtout parce qu'il a un designatum d'un intérêt considérable pour la culture qui en est à l'origine. On retrouve les mêmes exigences pour l'étude des intervalles. Un inventaire statistique des intervalles peut être ou non significatif pour caractériser la production musicale d'une culture, mais en tout cas, l'inventaire des intervalles en tant que tels n'est pas plus significatif que l'inventaire phonétique d'une langue fait par un linguiste. Précisément, une fois que le linguiste est arrivé à comprendre la phonétique d'une langue, il se trouve encore confronté avec le problème de l'analogie de ses morphèmes et de leurs designata, et d'un point de vue sémiotique, le musicologue est dans la même situation. Une fois ses intervalles classés, un musicologue travaillant du point de vue sémiotique désirera savoir si certains intervalles ou leurs combinaisons ont un référent sémantique, s'ils fonctionnent d'après une règle syntaxique, ou si la culture en question possède une façon d'interpréter ces intervalles comme des signes. Ainsi, la sémiotique met en doute la validité de toute analyse qui se contenterait de l'analyse formelle pour elle-même.

En appliquant les principes de la sémiotique à notre étude, une nouvelle perspective musicologique peut être exploitée. Au-delà de toutes les techniques classificatoires compliquées dont se servent à l'heure actuelle les analystes et les historiens de la musique, la sémiotique de la musicologie a la possibilité de développer des domaines de recherche qui permettent une pénétration plus profonde des dimensions cognitives du comportement musical. Bien que fascinée depuis longtemps par la syntaxe, la sémiotique, dans sa façon d'aborder la définition des rapports syntaxiques existant entre les signes musicaux, devrait apporter une meilleure connaissance des règles de formation et de transformation non seulement dans notre propre musique, mais dans tout système musical du monde. Pendant trop longtemps, les perspectives passionnantes de la sémantique ne se sont pas développées comme un des secteurs attirants de la communication musicale. Quand les musicologues auront sondé le riche symbolisme fourni par les signes musicaux et leurs designata, une des formes les plus absorbantes de l'expression intellectuelle humaine divulguera ses secrets immenses, l'essentiel d'une vision du monde étant évoquée dans la musique de chaque culture. Enfin, la pragmatique promet de sonder les profondeurs de la connaissance musicale, d'explorer les magnifiques sentiers du comportement qui unit un interprète à la plénitude de sens rencontrée dans un signe musical.

La sémiotique offre ces possibilités immenses pour développer une connaissance de la musique qui dépasse un travail d'expert technique et historique; elle offre une méthodologie qui est un premier pas vers ce recoin de la conscience humaine où la pensée musicale et le symbolisme musical attendent d'être déchiffrés, comme des livres qu'on ne lit pas attendent sur une table de bibliothèque, fermés et cependant prêts à divulguer leur contenu à l'esprit curieux. Le déchiffrage de ce conte que seule la sémiotique est capable d'opérer, devrait prouver que c'est une des aventures les plus stimulantes offertes à la musicologie, apportant avec elle une meilleure compréhension de la musique et, grâce à elle, une meilleure compréhension des cultures humaines.

RÉFÉRENCES CITÉES

W.-P. Malm, (1968), *Japanese Music and Musical Instruments*, Rutland, Cermont, Charles E. Tuttle Company.

C. McPhee (1966), *Music in Bali*, Hartford, Connecticut, Yale University Press.

C. Morris (1938), *Foundations of the Theory of Signs*, Chicago, University of Chicago Press.

Ch. Seeger (1962), « Music as a Tradition of Communication, Discipline and Play », *Ethnomusicology*, VI, 3 (sept.),

(1966), "The Music Process as a Function in a Context of Functions", *Yearbook of the Inter-American Institute for Musical Research*, vol. II, New-Orleans, Tulane University.

T. Winograd (1969), "Linguistics and the Computer Analysis of Tonal Harmony", *Journal of Music Theory*, 12, p. 2-49.

LINGUISTIC MODELS IN ETHNOMUSICOLOGY[1]

STEVEN FELD

"Cheshire puss," she began, rather timidly, "would you tell me please, which way I ought to go from here?"
"That depends a good deal on where you want to get to," said the Cat.
"I don't much care where," said Alice.
"Then it doesn't much matter which way you go," said the Cat.

Alice in Wonderland

1.0. LANGUAGE-MUSIC RELATIONSHIP

Discussions concerning the relationship of language and music are now commonplace. General or review papers, devoted entirely or partially to the subject have appeared in major linguistic (Harweg 1968, Springer 1956), musicological (Nattiez 1971), ethnomusicological (Bright 1963), and social science (Jackson 1968, Ruwet 1967a) volumes.

Interest thus far in the language-music relationship occurs at two distinct levels; one being the overlap of musical and linguistic phenomena, the other being the possibilities of applying linguistic models to musical analysis. Until recently, literature was weighed to the former concern. The current growth of the latter idea, has, no doubt, been spurned by the use of structural linguistic models in anthropology and folklore (Lévi-Strauss 1963), the development of transformational linguistics (Chomsky 1957, 1965), and the new popularity of semiotics (Morris 1938).

1.1. Language in Music and Music in Language. Continuing research into aspects of the language-music overl.p has looked at two types of relations, namely language in music (relations of text, poetics, and stylistics to song structure) and music in language (musical properties of speech).

In the investigation of language in music there stems from Herzog (1934, 1942, 1950) a number of studies of the coincidence of musical and textual structure (Robins and McLeod 1956, Bartok and Lord 1951, Laloum and Rouget 1965, Nettl 1964:286). In addition there is Bright's work on the relation of syllabic length to durational values in South Indian song (1957, 1963), and a number of discussions of the interplay of poetic language, versemaking, and song structure (Jakobson 1960, Rouget 1966, Sebeok 1956). A recent advance in this area is the formal demonstration of graded syntactic flexibility in Gujarati poetry, song texts, and prose (Durbin 1971).

Studies of the forms intermediate to speech and song have been undertaken by both linguists (Chao 1956) and ethnomusicologists (List 1963); there is also a well known joint study of Russian intonation (Buning and van Schooneveld 1961). More recently, Sundberg (1969) has attempted to deal with the problem in terms of articulatory phonetics. Finally, there are, again stemming from investigations by Herzog (1934, 1945), studies of the relation of speech melody of tone languages and corresponding song melody (List 1961), and instrumental "talking" (Alexandre 1969, Carrington 1949a, 1949b, Rouget 1964, Stern 1957; for a new methodological twist see Zemp and Kaufman 1969).

1.2 Linguistic Models in Ethnomusicology. There is another logical relationship of language and music quite distinct from that of their mutual overlap. Namely, language and music are the two principal ways by which humans pattern sound for social communication. For this reason it has been argued that language and music are both open to analyses of a general semiotic character, and, hence, that they may benefit from uniformities in analytic approach.

The largest body of literature concerning linguistic approaches to music derives from analogies to structural linguistics.[2] Most of the structuralist papers are highly programmatic and minimally empirical. Nettl (1958) for instance suggests starting with a defined corpus, moving on to identify significant vs. non-significant features, and then plotting the distribution of the distinctive elements in the total structure. Such a procedure may be applied to both melody and rhythm, building from minimal units (phonemes) to recurrent sequences (morphemes), noting allophonic and allomorphic variation, and finally isolating phrases and sections. Nettl sees the rearrangement of data into these levels as a means of objectifying musical analysis, thus minimizing subjective judgements about such things as "tonality" and "harmony." Portions of Nettl's suggestions have been echoed by both musicologists (Seeger 1960) and linguists (Bright 1963), but with little empirical advance. Aside from Lévi-Strauss' own structural analysis of Ravel's *Boléro*, (Lévi-Strauss 1971) the major attempts to demonstrate musical structuralism are provided by Ruwet (1966) and Arom (1969). Ruwet basically follows Harris' taxonomic distributionalism (Harris 1951); the notion of segmentation based on units of repetition is stressed, as is the formalization of such structural units as "motif" and "phrase." Methodologically, Ruwet advocates a procedure where musical segments are re-written one beneath the other such that formal similarities in structure (especially repetition) are isolated and distributionally plotted in relation to other segments; all of Ruwet's examples are from the Western art music tradition. Arom has applied

Ruwet's procedures to non-Western music, isolating the distributions and oppositions of a larger inventory of musical properties.

Recent excursions into musical structuralism are found in Nattiez (1972a, 1972b) and Asch (1972). The former discussions are programmatic and stress the structuralist paradigm as the logical model for the development of music semiotics. Nattiez's concern is principally methodological; he asserts that ethnomusicology will increase its scientific status if it adopts a "rigorous methodology" of discovery procedures ("working instructions") by which a music corpus may be transformed into a music grammar. Asch, in an opposite vein, begins by stating the necessity of an anthropological approach, but then resorts to an analysis which simply lists in prose rules the sound organization of Slavey drum dances. John Blacking (1972) has presented the single critique of musical structuralism; his concern is that structural analyses emphasize the isolation of logical units outside of their cultural contexts.

Transformational and other generative models for music have been used since 1967, when Boilés' transformational grammar of Tepehua thought-songs appeared. These songs are like spoken linguistic code in that specific meanings are assigned pitch sequences. Boilés' transformational grammar was written to show how the melodic and rhythmic sequences signal the semantic message (Boilés 1967). Unfortunately, Boilés does not comment on whether transformational grammars are applicable to music where the notes cannot be assigned specific lexical meanings. Moreover, the author does not discuss the extent to which his grammar makes the kinds of claims and predictions that a linguistic grammar makes.

Another type of transformational approach is illustrated by Sapir's (1969) grammar of Diola-Fogny funeral songs. Sapir uses both "emic" and "etic" approaches in his analysis by combining transformational notation with native song structure terminology. Phrase-structure rules are used to convey features common to all the funeral songs, and the transformational rules indicate ways that possible variations can be derived.

Other attempts at generative description range from purely mathematical melody-writing algorithms (Lidov 1972) to the three models for visualizing musical syntax presented by Chenoweth and Bee (1971). The flow diagram, formulas, and geometric model proposed by Chenoweth and Bee derive from applying Pikean descriptive linguistic procedures to music, and then restating the analysis in generative rules. The goals of this procedure are to allow foreigners to compose in a given musical system, and to help ethnomusicologists predict all the syntactically correct melodies that the system will generate.

The above transformational models do not share a basic feature with transformational linguistics; they are not derived from a deductive theoretical posture about the nature of music or the most adequate way to analyze music. Papers beginning from this theoretical problem are few; Lindblom and Sundberg (1970) discuss appropriate goals of a music theory in terms of the approach from natural science and develop a theoretical starting point for the generative description of melody. Two papers by Blacking (1970, 1971) deal with the theoretical notions of competence, performance, and deep and surface structure from an anthropological view. Blacking is asking: What is the nature of an ethnomusicological theory that best accounts for the interplay of musical structures and social categories? A final paper from a theoretical position is Boilés' outline of the semiotics of ethnomusicology (Boilés 1971). From Morris' characterization of the nature of sign communication (1938) Boilés discusses the possibility of approaching musical communication from the three pointed orientation of syntactics, semantics, and pragmatics. The goal of this perspective is to produce "a more profound penetration of the cognitive dimensions of musical behavior (Boilés 1971:13)" in ethnomusicology.

2.0. EPISTEMOLOGICAL DIMENSIONS

Since the application of linguistic models is increasing, it seems important that we now reflect critically on some epistemological dimensions of their usage. Specifically, it is necessary to isolate the factors which motivate the usage of the models, and to decide if these factors have been satisfactorily justified. The following arguments proceed from the view that if one uses formal models, then one is bound to formal criteria for their evaluation.

2.1. Assumptions vs. Explanations. The job of scientific inquiry is to delimit and solve problems in terms of general theories. Hence the job of the scientist is to collect evidence in order to advance explanations for problems. To explain means to account for observable phenomena in terms of their underlying regularities, or principles (Hempel 1966).

We might first note that one never explains something by previously assuming it. The difference between explaining and assuming lies in evidence. Explanations require empirical support, assumptions do not. It is always the case that a science does not assume what it seeks to explain.

Following this notion, we must differentiate between assuming that linguistic models adequately account for musical phenomena and explaining how and why linguistic models might do this. It is epistemologically silly to assume that linguistic models explain music without some demonstration of why this is the case. This would be like explaining V^7-I resolution by saying "it makes the music pretty" or subject-verb agreement by saying "it makes the language clearer."

To assume the correctness of linguistic models takes us away from science, that is, it makes a problem into a non-problem. To explain the correctness of linguistic models is to create some theoretical baseline for inquiry. An explanation of the benefits of linguistic models must derive from evidence that shows the models to account for the facts in the most powerful manner. The criteria of explanatory adequacy cannot be met by analogy or *a priori* notions, it must be met empirically.

2.2. Assertions vs. Demonstrations. The next logical point is that one cannot make a case for the adoption of a scientific procedure by asserting its essential goodness; one must demonstrate its essential goodness. The difference, again, is evidence.

Thus far the utility of linguistic models has been asserted rather than demonstrated. Proponents of the models have reasoned that an application of a model is, *ipso facto*, proof of its efficiency. But this is not necessarily true. One demonstrates the superiority of theory X over theory Y by comparative analysis; that is, by evidence showing that whereas theory X accounts for A, B and C, theory Y accounts for only A and B. One never demonstrates the superiority of theory X over theory Y by simply asserting the data in the format of theory X. Any clever author can rephrase any data into any notational conventions and then assert that a superior theory has been uncovered, but this is not science. Hence, while the application of a model is an assertion of its utility, it does not constitute an empirical demonstration of its utility. Simply increasing the volume of applications does not advance the case; one makes demonstrations with evidence, not with quantities.

2.3. Reasons vs. Justifications. We have noted thus far that the advantages of linguistic models have been assumed rather than explained, and that their adequacy has been asserted rather than demonstrated. The margin in both cases is evidence. Restated, the fault in the logical scaffolding beneath using linguistic models is that reasons rather than justifications have been provided in their support. A reason can be, and sometimes is no more than an excuse–momentary, faddish, *a priori*; a justification, on the other hand, requires some lasting empirical support, validation.

Reasons do not last long in science; procedures and claims must be justified. One adopts a new model when it is demonstrated that the model either (a) accounts for the observables in a more interesting way, or (b) accounts for more observables. It is usually the case that scientific breakthrough is characterized simultaneously by both (a) and (b) (Kuhn 1962). As one philosopher of science concludes:

> We are *justified* in placing the trust in [theories] that we do because–and to the extent that–they have proved their worth in competition with alternatives (Toulmin 1963:101-102).

Thus far, no justifications of this logical order exist validating the use of linguistic models in ethnomusicology. What exists are reasons, specifically three different reasons, of three logical types.

3.0. REASONS AND THEIR LOGICAL FALLACIES

The first reason for delving into linguistics is the simplest, namely, everybody else is doing it (e.g., film, folklore, visual arts, literature, etc.). This is the "everything is semiotics" position: language, music, magazines, clowns, breakfast, haircuts and all human behavior should be approached via a common science of signs.

The second reason stems from two different, though equally sincere attitudes towards the language-music analogy–treating the analogy as truth or treating it as a heuristic that must seriously be explored.

The third, and strongest reason offered, is formalism; it is argued that since progress in science is characterized by formalization, and since the models have proven their efficiency in the formalized science of linguistics, their usage in ethnomusicology is valid.

While the first and third reasons are logically distinct it seems fair to say that they come from the same kind of concern; hence I will lump them together for the purposes of analysis.

3.1. Analogy. The first reason for using linguistic models is the claim that language and music are similar enough that they deserve the status of "true" analogy.[3] Such a claim usually preceeds the application of a specific linguistic model, and is characteristically stated in non-explicit terms. For instance, in a recent paper we get these comments:

> ...musical systems are also semiotic systems, somewhat like language (Chandola 1970:135).
>
> ...tonal systems and linguistic systems are governed by almost the same theoretical principles (ibid:147).

Music is somewhat like and almost the same as many things, depending on how good your imagination is; while Chandola's phraseology is suggestive, it is hardly convincing scientifically.

Another way of analogizing is to claim that language and myth are alike, and music and myth are alike, hence music and language are alike. Nattiez follows this path as he attempts to bolster musical structuralism with the conclusions of Lévi-Strauss.

> . . .Lévi-Strauss is convinced that music and myth function the same way. To be more exact, his analysis of myth proceeds along the lines of an orchestral score (Nattiez 1972a:5).

Those who have read Lévi-Strauss surely know that his overtures to music are poetic and interesting, but, alas, the chapter headings of *The Raw and The Cooked* hardly constitute evidence for a theoretical posture.

Further attempts to validate analogizing derive from the attitude that linguists have managed to explain language more comprehensively than ethnomusicologists have explained music. This attitude has been raised most recently by Chase:

> Can the musicologist, using a method analogous to the method used in structural linguistics, achieve the same kind of progress in his own science as that which has taken place in linguistics (Chase 1972:5)?

That is a reasonable question; in the following I will show that while analogous reasoning is richly suggestive it has failed to produce clearer ethnomusicological explanations.

Preliminarily we must note the problem of metalanguage and notational conventions. Readers of the new ethnomusicology must now be fluent in linguistic as well as standard ethnomusicological terminology and notations. Given the nature of linguistic, musical, and anthropological specialization, this is certainly not a simplicity measure. But, of course, this is a rather weak criticism.

More problematic is that the use of the models introduces, by analogy, a whole set of slippery epistemological variables that must be resolved in order to understand what the music grammars actually explain, and how the explanations account for the facts. Consider for instance three such epistemological domains: (a) on the choice of models, (b) on the claims that the models make, (c) on the relation of the models to the nature of the phenomenon.

3.1.1. Analogy in the Choice of Models. Currently two linguistic paradigms, structural and transformational-generative have been used in ethnomusicological applications. Turning to linguistic history we must note that the groundstone of transformational linguistics was the empirical and metatheoretical demonstration by Chomsky (1957) that some linguistic constructions and facts unexplainable by the structuralist paradigm are adequately accounted for in the transformational model (also see Postal 1964). If it is the case that linguists accept the transformational paradigm as the more powerful, why should ethnomusicologists bother with structuralism at all?

One response is to argue that both models may comfortably be used since there are many European and American linguists who are structuralists, and since Lévi-Strauss' structuralism is popular in anthropology and folklore. The counter-argument is, of course, that now we are not clarifying anything about the most powerful way to explain ethnomusicological facts, we are simply allowing linguistic theory arguments to be transported *in toto* to ethnumusicology. Moreover, while the linguistic arguments are taking place on empirical and theoretical grounds, there is not one stitch of ethnomusicological evidence from which we may begin to evaluate the models in terms of how they explain what we want them to explain. Hence, the analogizing has backed us into a corner.

An even less satisfactory response to the structuralist vs. transformationalist issue is to misconstrue the linguistic facts and issues. Nattiez, for instance, has written:

> American linguistic structuralism [has] two main branches: the distributionalism of Harris and the generativism of Chomsky (1972a:1);

moreover the two are "rigorously equivalent" if confined to a finite corpus (ibid:10). Apparently Nattiez introduced this argument so as not to be open to criticism for ignoring transformational linguistics. But whatever the motivation, his characterization is inaccurate. In actuality, transformational grammar as proposed by Chomsky (1957, 1965) entails a radically different approach to language and science than does the structuralism of his teacher, Zellig Harris (1951, 1954).[4] As one linguist writes in a recent review:

> Chomsky denies the fundamental assumption of structuralism by arguing that an adequate linguistic description of grammar cannot be derived from applying sets of operations to primary data but rather must be viewed as a formal deductive theory whose object is to separate the grammatical sentences of a language from the ungrammatical ones and to provide a systematic account of the structure of grammatical sentences (Maclay 1971:163).

A serious question is raised by all of this: Why should ethnomusicologists sit around and wait for linguists to create and decide on the issues, and then copy their models and decisions? Linguistic arguments and analogies aside, I would suggest that the only sensible grounds for adopting models in ethnomusicology is theoretical-empirical, i.e., by demonstrating the explanatory adequacy of the model.

3.1.2. Analogy in the Claims the Models Make. An even more crucial problem than the choice of models is that of understanding the claims that a grammar is actually making, and how the claims are to be evaluated. Suppose for instance that a transformational linguistic model is adopted in ethnomusicology. Reasoning analogously we must at least resolve the following questions:

(1) Is a transformational grammar of music a theory of what it means to know a music; that is, is musical competence the domain of an adequate ethnomusicological explanation?

(2) Is a transformational grammar of a music a theory of how that music will be acquired by children? What claims does the grammar make about learning?

(3) When a transformational grammar specifies a deep and surface structure is it making the claim that the deep structure constitutes a formal music universal? Does the deep structure contain musical meaning?

(4) Do transformational grammars of music imply a philosophy of mind? Specifically, do transformational grammars of music follow from a Cartesian rationalist orientation to knowledge (see Chomsky 1968) and a rejection of Skinnerian behavioristic learning theory?

(5) Does a transformational grammar of music make the claim that musical syntax is autonomous of semantics and cultural assumptions? Is musical semantics interpretive, based on lexical meanings given to notes, motifs, phrases, and segments?

(6) Does a transformational grammar of music account for analogues to linguistic competence? Specifically, is the grammar designed to explain native (a) knowledge of synonymy, (b) knowledge of ambiguity, (c) creative ability to produce novel utterances? If not, why have deep and surface structures?

(7) What is the musical counterpart of the "ideal speaker-hearer?" Does this imply that all members of a culture share the same musical knowledge, and that the skills of musical specialists are like the skills of orators and public speakers?

(8) Does one write tranformational grammars for the entire musical output of a culture, or for styles, sub-styles, genres and the like? In fact, what is reasonable to expect a grammar to claim in regard to the relationship of these units?

(9) Finally, how are evaluation procedures to be developed, and what does it mean to construct the "simplest" or most general grammar of a music? Given two competing grammars of music X (i.e. two competing theories of the psychological reality of music X) we must be able to judge which is more reasonable on some principled grounds; if this could not be done, we would be making the claim that there is more than one psychological reality to the

music system. Or is it the case that it is not reasonable to expect ethnomusicological theory to make any claims about psychological realities?

Like those who have used transformational models in ethnomusicology, I find these questions interesting and provocative. But I would insist that they be dealt with in theoretically explicit ways, rather than be left in the air as a residue of papers that express musical data in linguistic notations. It must be understood that the significant part of a grammar (musical or linguistic) is not the abstractions themselves, but the claims that one uses the abstractions to make.

3.1.3. Analogy in the Nature of the Phenomenon. A final, and perhaps most crucial problem to be raised is that of whether the proposed models adequately capture the facts of ethnomusicological phenomena at all; here I refer to the curious fact that, thus far, the models focus only on music sound.[5]

To begin to understand this problem we might start with the current linguistic scene. The major upheaval in linguistic theory and practice today is in the areas of semantics and sociolinguistics, and the central issues are the empirical and theoretical validity of two of Chomsky's central notions: syntax vs. semantics, and competence vs. performance. Both dichotomies are at the root of Chomsky's contention that it is valid to study language code independently of its social context.

Since the appearance of Katz and Fodor's important semantic theory paper (1963), the problem of semantic description in transformational grammar has received much attention. Many linguists have provided counterexamples to Chomsky's claim (1965) that all relevant semantic data is contained in deep syntax. Now, generative semanticists claim that no principled boundary can be drawn between syntax and semantics; hence, there cannot be a distinct syntactic deep structure, and Chomsky's "interpretive" semantics are not adequate (G. Lakoff 1971, McCawley 1968; a recent defense of interpretive semantics is Jackendoff 1972).

Sociolinguists, in addition, claim that the competence vs. performance dichotomy is also wrongly construed; "raw grammaticality" is not all that native speakers intuitively know about their language.

> Rules of appropriateness beyond grammar govern speech, and are acquired as part of conceptions of self and of meanings associated both with particular forms of speech and with the act of speech itself (Hymes 1971:56).

Hence while

> transformational theory recognizes that what seems the same sentence may enter into two quite different sets of relations, syntactically: it must [also] recognize the same thing to be true, socially (ibid:58).

In short, the semantics and sociolinguistics movement is insisting that language structure cannot be properly understood in isolation from the context of language use (R. Lakoff 1972). As semanticist George Lakoff rather forcefully puts it:

> What we are trying to do is develop a linguistic theory that is rooted in the study of human thought and culture—the very antithesis of transformational grammar as narrowly construed by Chomsky (G. Lakoff 1972:34).

While I do not intend to use current struggles in linguistic theory as a justification for an ethnomusicological posture, I think it worth pointing out that the hot issue in linguistics is much the same as the central theoretical split in ethnomusicology—the split between those who think that the autonomous structure of code constitutes an explanation of a phenomenon and those who think that interplay of context with code is what needs to be explained. This is essentially the split between musicological and anthropological ethnomusicology (Merriam 1969).

Whether any of us like it or not, the fact is that people make music, and they make it for and with other people. Consequently, ethnomusicological theory must somehow attempt to account for such facts (Merriam 1964:17-36). Hence we are led to seriously question whether linguistic models, confined to sound structure, constitute adequate explanations of ethnomusicological facts.

If twentieth century anthropology has shown anything, it is that context is the single most crucial epistemological variable in ethnographic method and description. It seems obvious that the same must be true of the study of music in culture. As Blacking states so well in his critique of musical structuralism:

> Music is much more than a cultural game and the expression of the unconscious activity of the mind, and the most rigorous structural analysis of its sounds cannot be adequate without some attention to the social dimensions of music. The rules of any musical system begin with the categorization of music and non-music, and they may seem to be arbitrary. But they are also social, in that they can have no meaning without consensus. And because social behavior is also subject to rules, it follows that there may be relationships between the rules of systems of musical and social communication. This seems to me to be the essential justification for the existence of ethnomusicology as a separate discipline (Blacking 1972:4).

As is always the case in science, the power of a theory must be judged relative to the way the facts are circumscribed. I would join Blacking and Merriam in arguing that what is required of the most powerful ethnomusicological theory is the ability to formally account for the interplay of sound structure with the context and cultural assumptions of its creators/listeners.

To sum up 3.1, I conclude that until basic theoretical questions like the many raised above are explicitly dealt with, the use by analogy of linguistic models does not clarify ethnomusicological facts and does not clarify the task of ethnomusicological explanation.

3.2. Formalism. Now that the problems with analogizing have been noted, we will deal with the other reason, formalism. This is clearly the more sophisticated reason, and the more important to counter. The point I wish to develop is that while the property "formal" is an important part of science, its nature has been misunderstood by those using linguistic formalisms in ethnomusicology.

To begin, we must distinguish two senses of the notion "formal." The first sense is formal inquiry; this basically denotes three properties:(a) explicitness, via resolution of conceptual ambiguity, (b) standardization, via resolution of notational and terminological ambiguity, and (c) generalization, via elimination of the inessential. Hence formal inquiry would be synonymous with highly objective inquiry. This is the way philosophers of science use "formal"; both Kuhn (1962:15-18) and Hempel (1966:13) point out that a science is immature without a governing paradigm to give direction to inquiry; without such formalization the collection and interpretation of data is largely random and unscientific.

Such formalization is the foundation of modern linguistics; as Lyons writes:

> Chomsky's most original and probably his most enduring contribution to linguistics is the mathematical rigor and precision with which he formalized the properties of alternate systems of grammatical description (Lyons 1970:43).

Nettl (1958:37) has alluded to this property as a justification for linguistic models; in particular he is impressed by the fact that descriptive linguistics has had some relationship to natural science.

The second sense of formal derives from formal logic. This property enters into the discussion because music is frequently likened to mathematics and logic, as is language (for instance, in Whorf 1956:248). Also, there are a number of simple parallels between a system of formal logic and a generative grammar, and Fodor points out (1970:199-200) that linguistic rules function like logical inference rules; the former preserve grammaticality while mapping through syntactic transformations; the latter preserve truth while mapping through formulae.[6]

While there is some allusion to this latter sense of "formal" (formal logic) in the current literature, it is the former sense (formal inquiry) that concerns the proponents of linguistic models. Their argument, as stated before, is that linguistic models will formalize ethnomusicological description, a valid goal since all progress in science is characterized by formalization.

3.2.1. The "Hollow Shell" of Formalism. Surely none of us would deny that an increase in objectivity via explicitness, standardization, and generalization would enhance ethnomusicology. And it is certainly the case that many of these qualities characterize modern linguistics. But in envying formalism, proponents of linguistic models have failed to distinguish the theorectical task of formalizing ethnomusicology from the exploratory exercise of borrowing notational and terminological formalisms from linguistics. Many cases could illustrate this point; consider these two:

(1) In his discussion of Diola-Fogny funeral songs, Sapir summarizes musical mechanics in phrase-structure and transformational rules, briefly apologizes for using outdated conventions of transformational grammar rule writing, but concludes that the analysis

> serves our present needs, which are simply to illustrate that on a general level *bunãnsaŋ* song-phrasing can be subject, without much difficulty, to formal statement. Obviously, other techniques of formal statement could serve equally well (Sapir 1969:182).

Yes, obviously other techniques of formal statement could serve equally well; this is making the problem into a game where the object is to rewrite one set of abstractions (musical transcription) into another set of abstractions (transformational grammar). Any formal statement might work, but the aim of an ethnomusicological theory must be to find the best way to explain things, not just ways that work. The point is that formalism is treated here as if it were a value in itself–a value unrelated to the goals of developing ethnomusicological theory.

(2) In an even more abstract approach, Lidov makes the following statement at the beginning of his paper:

> My objective is not specifically ethnomusicological. It is rather the theoretical one of developing musical applications for formalisms of mathematical linguistics. . .My investigation is based on a very small amount of data, too small to certify any generalization as secure. The essence of the work is formal–*only* formal or *purely* or *merely* formal–your choice–and without further pretensions (Lidov 1972:1).

Despite Lidov's disclaimers I find the approach absurdly formal and totally pretentious, not because I can't appreciate his matehematics, but because he purports to do a theoretical task and then says nothing about what kind of ethnomusicological theory he is talking about. Yet worse, the music is considered as nothing more than one dimensional transcriptions–a set of abstractions which a mathematician may retranslate into other abstractions of another logical order. This method of analysis is based on the completely false assumption that transcriptions of music have some sort of objective reality, and are standardized to the extent that linguistic phonetic transcription is standardized. Moreover, the author is absolved from discussing what claims this type of "explanation" is really making and what (if anything) it has to do with music because the "essence of the work is formal" and because there was little data to begin with. When it boils down this is an "anything that's possible is interesting and/or feasible" approach, and it has little to do with the development of a scientific ethnomusicology; it merely exalts formalism as an end in itself. It does not use formalism for what it really is in science—a means towards expressing general theories in the most explicit way.

I have no doubt that the authors cited above, and the other ethnomusicologists utilizing similar approaches have good intentions; I simply want to point out that they are not formalizing ethnomusicology—they are just using the formalisms of linguistic notation and terminology. They have given analyses filled with tree diagrams, phrase markers, derivations, rules, binary oppositions, and the like—but hardly any of their discussion has taken place on a theoretical level. Only Blacking (1970, 1971) and Lindblom and Sundberg (1970) have dealt explicitly with basic theoretical issues like the approach to music from natural science, the differences between music and natural language, the concept of generative description, musical competences and performance, and deep and surface structure. The rest of the literature ignores issues like the empirical comparison of models, a metatheory of music, evaluation procedures, and the relation of the models to the phenomena they supposedly explain. This paucity of theory in the midst of a sea of applications makes it clear that the models are not scientizing ethnomusicology but playing games with abstractions.

In a recent article discussing the empirical and logical superiority of a transformational approach to language teaching, linguist Robin Lakoff notes the misuse of transformational grammar in some new grammar texts. She points out that rather than borrowing and using the significant conclusions of transformational linguistics (viz., the rationalist approach), these books are simply borrowing the rules themselves, the abstractions of transformational grammar, its "narrow shell of formalism (R. Lakoff 1969:129)." Just as the books cited by Lakoff miss the point of transformational grammar, linguistically based ethnomusicology has missed the point of formalism. By simply borrowing a hollow shell of formalism from mathematics and linguistics, rather than dealing with substantive issues in theory, proponents of linguistic models have not formalized ethnomusicology; they have thrown out rules and notations which in themselves do not clarify any significant ethnomusicological issue. Hence, I would join with Blacking in concluding:

Analytic tools cannot be borrowed freely and used as short cuts to greater achievements in ethnomusicological research as can electronic devices such as the tape recorder: they must emerge from the nature of the subject studied (Blacking 1972:1).

4.0. CONCLUSIONS

In evaluating models, linguists and anthropologists have sometimes distinguished between a "God's truth" and a "hocus-pocus" analysis (Householder 1952, Burling 1964). The difference is essentially between doing science and playing a game: the former explains facts inherent in the data, the latter re-organizes the data into a convenient statement. As an example of the difference, Burling, in his critique of componential analysis, raises the question of whether the rules postulated by the analyst really exist or whether they, as one of many possibilities, simply work to generate back some original data (Burling 1964).

I would conclude that thus far most of the activity involving linguistic models in ethnomusicology falls into the hocus-pocus category; the models constitute new and indeed fancier ways of expressing only that part of ethnomusicological data that concerns music sound. Moreover, the reasons advanced for using the models (analogy, formalism) involve basic misunderstandings of scientific epistemology.

Nevertheless, the conclusion should not be taken to mean that (a) justification of an ethnomusicological theory deriving in part from linguistic theory is impossible, or (b) that ethnomusicology has nothing to learn from linguistics.

On the first point we should note that linguistic theory and one major anthropological theory share a basic feature–mentalism. Linguistic analysis specifies the rules that a speaker knows which account for an actual speech performance. Ethnoscientific anthropological theory defines culture not as an inventory of the things a people make a..d do but has an inventory of the things that people commonly know. Hence, an explanation of cultural behavior is a theory of cultural knowledge (Werner and Fenton 1971). An adequate ethnography must then be seen as a statement of the things that people "have in mind,"–the tacit rules people know which generate acceptable behavior within their society (Goodenough 1957).

Looking at music as a domain of cultural knowledge, and using the notion of generative description from linguistics, it seems reasonable to conceptualize an ethnomusicological explanation as a theory of the things a people must know in order to understand, perform, and create acceptable music in their culture. Such a theory, like linguistic theory and ethnoscientific anthropological theory, attempts to capture the tacit rules that govern the domain of systematic behavior we call music. The central ethnomusicological question, What is music? is thus specifically approached via the problem, What does it mean to know a music? (Feld 1973).

On the second point, I think it obvious that ethnomusicology can learn from linguistics, just as it can learn from musicology, anthropology, aesthetics, philosophy, human biology, and physics. The real question is what ethnomusicology can learn from linguistics, and I find some current notions of that what to be very distressing. In particular, Nattiez's assessments of music semiotics (1971, 1972a, 1972b) constantly stress that linguistics is important because it can provide musicology with a mechanical and rigorous set of discovery procedures.

> Musical semiotics . . . must seek to develop not binding rules for analysis, but rather a set of procedures that will always be explicit and controlled (Nattiez 1972a:4).

I would argue that mechanical discovery procedures are the least interesting thing that semiotics can do for ethnomusicology or anybody else. It is wholly unreasonable to expect that a scientific theory be a list of rules which take the analyst from data to explanation in a mechanical sweep; such an expectation shows a fundamental ignorance of the nature of scientific theory and philosophy (on the death of discovery procedures in linguistics, see Chomsky 1957:50-56). In fact, what ethnomusicology might learn from linguistics is about the nature of theory in science—the relation of deductive theory to data and fundamentals.

The problem of scientizing ethnomusicology is the problem of building a metatheory of music through which one may deductively analyze music in culture: by "analyze" I mean to separate out the acceptable and culturally appropriate music of a society from the unacceptable and culturally inappropriate music of a society, and to isolate the cultural logic which underlies the acceptable and appropriate music (Feld 1973). Implicit in such an approach is the assumption that as evidence one collects sound and observes the conceptual and behavioral factors which produce it, and as an explanation one posits the principles of cultural knowledge which give rise to the manifestation. This is essentially the approach championed by Merriam (1964) and Blacking (1970, 1971, 1972); the latter writes:

> The central problem is to describe *all* the factors which generate the patterns of sound produced by a single composer or society; to explain music as signs and symbols of human experience in culture, and to relate musical form to its social and cultural content (Blacking 1970:69).

* * * * * *

Because the stance taken in this paper is sharply critical of several individuals, I feel compelled to explicity note that I have no interest in the petty business of personal attack. Rather, my concern has simply been to raise certain empirical and substantive issues that must be dealt with in the development of ethnomusicological theory. In doing so I have deliberately played the Devil's Advocate and voiced things in such a way that hopefully will provoke heated response, to the benefit of all concerned with epistemological refinement in ethnomusicology theory. As the Cat tried to explain to Alice, the problem of figuring out where to go is logically prior to the problem of how to get there; *mutatis mutandis*, the problem of conceptualizing an adequate theory is logically prior to expressing rules by means of the theory's notational abstractions.

FOOTNOTES

1. Written June 1973. Certain threads of thought presented here originated in two earlier papers: "Linguistically Based Formal Analysis vs. Communication Theory" and "Towards a Metatheory of Music": both were presented in Alan Merriam's classes in The Arts in Anthropology at Indiana University during 1972-3. For critical feedback on those ideas, as well as on the earlier draft of this paper, I am grateful to Prof. Merriam and especially to Jim Brink. My thoughts on the problems of dealing with symbolic forms as languages has benefitted greatly from conversations with Sol Worth on visual (especially film) communication, and with Carl Voegelin on linguistics.

2. This literature appears after the publication of *Syntactic Structures* (Chomsky 1957), which leads one to wonder whether the structuralist paradigm is more applicable (i.e. bears some inherent relation) to music than the transformational model or whether it is accidental that those applying linguistic models have a structuralist preference. Unfortunately, this question is not raised in the literature.

3. If this were the case, methods of musical analysis should be as applicable to linguistics as methods of linguistic analysis are to music. No proponents of linguistic models discuss this possibility.

4. Perhaps Nattiez's characterization derives from the fact that structuralism is the dominant paradigm in French linguistics. French readers might note that Nicolas Ruwet, whose structural studies of music (collected in Ruwet 1972a) are often cited by Nattiez, has authored an excellent French language introduction to transformational linguistics (1967b) as well as a transformational analysis of French syntax (1972b).

5. John Blacking's three papers (1971a, 1971b, 1972) are notable exceptions.

6. Transformational rules preserve meaning while mapping through syntax only if one is operating within the transformational grammar framework where all essential semantic information is contained in deep syntax.

REFERENCES CITED

Alexandre, Pierre
1969 Langages tambourinés: une écriture sonore? Semiotica 1(3):273-281.

Arom, Simha
1970 Essai d'une notation des monodies à des fins d'analyse. Revue de musicologie 55(2):172-216.

Asch, Michael
1972 A Grammar of Slavey drum dance music, paper presented at 1972 SEM meetings, Toronto.

Bartok, Bela and A. Lord
1951 Serbo-Croatian folksong. New York: Columbia University Press.

Blacking, John
1970 Deep and surface structures in Venda music. Dyn 1:69-98.
1971 Towards a theory of musical competence, *In* E. J. DeJager, ed., Man: Anthropological essays presented to O. F. Raum. Cape Town: C. Struik, pp. 19-34.
1972 Extensions and limits of musical transformations, paper presented at 1972 SEM meetings, Toronto.

Boilés, Charles
1967 Tepehua thought-song: A case of semantic signalling. ETHNOMUSICOLOGY 11(3):267-292.
1971 Semiotics of ethnomusicology, paper presented at 1971 SEM meetings, Chapel Hill.

Bright, William
1957 Singing in Lushai. Indian Linguistics 17:24-28.
1963 Language and music: areas for cooperation. ETHNOMUSICOLOGY 7(1):23-32.

Buning, J. and C. van Schooneveld
1961 The sentence intonation of contemporary standard Russian. The Hague: Mouton.

Burling, Robbins
1964 Cognition and componential analysis: God's truth or hocus-pocus? American Anthropologist 66:20-28.

Carrington, John F.
1949a Talking drums of Africa. London: Carey Kingsgate.
1949b A comparative analysis of some Central African gong languages. Brussels: Institut Royal Congo Belge, 43(3).

Chandola, Anoop C.
1970 Some systems of musical scales and linguistic principles. Semiotica 2(2):135-150.

Chao, Yuen Ren
1956 Tone, intonation, singsong, chanting, recitative, tonal composition, and atonal composition in Chinese, *In* For Roman Jakobson. The Hague: Mouton, pp. 52-59.

Chase, Gilbert
1972 Structuralism today: An outsider's report, paper presented at 1972 SEM meetings, Toronto.

Chenoweth, Vida and Darlene Bee
1971 Comparative-generative models of a New Guinea Melodic structure. American Anthropologist 73:773-782.

Chomsky, Noam
1957 Syntactic structures. The Hague: Mouton.
1965 Aspects of the theory of syntax. Cambridge: MIT Press.
1968 Language and mind. New York: Harcourt, Brace and World.

Durbin, M. A.
1971 Transformational models applied to musical analysis: theoretical possibilities. ETHNOMUSICOLOGY 15(3):353-362.

Feld, Steven
1973 Towards a metatheory of music, ms.

Fodor, Janet Dean
1970 Formal linguistics and formal logic. *In* John Lyons, ed., New horizons in linguistics. Baltimore: Penguin, pp. 198-214.

Goodenough, Ward
1957 Cultural anthropology and linguistics, *In* Paul Garvin, ed., Report of the seventh annual roundtable meeting on linguistics and language. Washington, D.C.: Georgetown University Press pp. 167-173.

Harris, Zellig S.
1951 Structural linguistics. Chicago: University of Chicago Press.
1954 Distributional structure. Word 10:146-162.

Harweg, Roland
1968 Language and music: An imminent and sign theoretic approach. Foundations of Language 4:270-281.

Hempel, Carl G.
1966 Philosophy of natural science. Englewood Cliffs: Prentice-Hall.

Herzog, George
1934 Speech melody and primitive music. Musical Quarterly 20:452-466.
1942 Text and melody in primitive music. Bulletin of the American Musicological Society 6:10-11.
1945 Drum signalling in a West African tribe. Word 1:217-238.
1950 Song, *In* M. Leach, ed., Funk and Wagnall's Dictionary of folklore, mythology and legend. 2:1032-1050.

Householder, Fred
1952 Review of Harris 1951. International Journal of American Linguistics 18:260-268.

Hymes, Dell
1971 Sociolinguistics and the ethnography of speaking. *In* Edwin Ardener, ed., Social anthropology and language (Association of Social Anthropologists Monograph 10) London: Tavistock, pp. 47-94.

Jackendoff, Ray
1972 Semantic interpretation in generative grammar. Cambridge: MIT Press.

Jackson, Anthony
1968 Sound and ritual. Man, n.s., 3:293-299.

Jakobson, Roman
1960 Linguistics and poetics. *In* T. A. Sebeck, ed., Style in language. Cambridge: MIT Press, pp. 350-377.

Katz, J. and J. Fodor
1963 The structure of a semantic theory. Language 39:170-210.

Kuhn, Thomas
1962 The structure of scientific revolutions. Chicago: University of Chicago Press.

Lakoff, George
1971 On generative semantics, *In* Danny Steinberg and Leon Jakobovits, eds., Semantics. Cambridge: Cambridge University Press, pp. 232-296.
1973 Deep language. New York Review of Books, February 8:34.

Lakoff, Robin
1969 Transformational grammar and language teaching. Language Learning 19 (1/2):117-140.
1972 Language in context. Language 48(4):907-927.

Laloum, Claude and Gilbert Rouget
1965 Deux chants liturgiques Yoruba. Journal de la Société des Africanistes 35(1):109-139.

Lévi-Strauss, Claude
1963 Structural anthropology. New York: Basic Books.
1971 "Boléro" de Maurice Ravel. L'Homme 11(2):5-14.

Lidov, David
1972 An example (from Kulintang) of a generative grammar for melody, paper presented at 1972 SEM meetings, Toronto.

Lindblom, Björn and Johan Sundberg
1970 Towards a generative theory of melody. Svensk Tidskrift för Musikforskning 52:71-88.

List, George
1961 Speech melody and song melody in central Thailand. ETHNOMUSICOLOGY 5(1):16-32.
1963 The boundaries of speech and song. ETHNOMUSICOLOGY 7(1):1-16.

Lyons, John
1970 Noam Chomsky. New York: Viking.

Maclay, Howard
1971 Overview, *In* Danny Steinberg and Leon Jakobovits, eds., Semantics. Cambridge: Cambridge University Press, pp. 157-182.

McCawley, James D.
1968 The role of semantics in a grammar, *In* E. Bach and R. Harms, eds., Universals in linguistic theory. New York: Holt, Rinehart and Winston, pp. 91-122.

Merriam, Alan P.
1964 The anthropology of music. Evanston: Northwestern University Press.
1969 Ethnomusicology revisited. ETHNOMUSICOLOGY 13(2):213-229.

Morris, Charles
1938 Foundations of the theory of signs. Chicago: University of Chicago Press.

Nattiez, J. J.
1971 ed., Sémiologie de la musique. Musique en jeu, 5.
1972a What can structuralism do for musicology? paper presented at 1972 SEM meetings, Toronto.
1972b Is a descriptive semiotics of music possible? Language Sciences 23:1-7.

Nettl, Bruno
1958 Some linguistic approaches to musical analysis. Journal of the International Folk Music Council 10:37-41.
1964 Theory and method in ethnomusicology. Glencoe: Free Press.

Postal, Paul
1964 Constituent structure: A study of contemporary models of syntactic description. Bloomington: Indiana University Research Center in Anthropology, Folklore, and Linguistics, Publication 30.

Robins, R. H. and Norma McLeod
1956 Five Yurok songs: A musical and textual analysis. Bulletin of the School of Oriental and African Studies 18(3):592-609.

Rouget, Gilbert
1964 Tons de la langue en gûn et tons du tambour. Revue de musicologie 50:3-29.
1966 African traditional non-prose forms: reciting, declaiming, singing, and strophic structure, *In* Jack Berry, ed., Proceedings of the conference on African languages and literature, April 28-30, 1966. Evanston, Northwestern University Press, pp. 45-58.

Ruwet, Nicolas
1966 Méthodes d'analyse en musicologie. Belge revue de musicologie 20:65-90 (reprinted in Ruwet 1972a pp. 100-134).
1967a Linguistics and musicology. International Social Science Journal 19:79-87.
1967b Introduction à la grammaire générative. Paris: Plon.
1972a Language, musique, poésie. Paris: Editions du seuil.
1972b Théorie syntaxique et syntaxe du français. Paris: Editions du seuil.

Sapir, J. David
1969 Diola-Fogny funeral songs and the native critic. African Language Review 8:176-191.

Sebeck, T. A.
1956 Sound and meaning in a Cheremis folksong text, *In* For Roman Jakobson, The Hague: Mouton, pp. 430-439.

Seeger, Charles
1960 On the moods of a music-logic. Journal of the American Musicological Society 13:224-261.

Springer, George
1956 Language and music: parallels and divergences, *In* For Roman Jakobson, The Hague: Mouton, pp. 504-513.

Stern, Theodore
1957 Drum and whistle languages: An analysis of speech surrogates. American Anthropologist 59: 487-506.

Sundberg, Johan
1969 Articulatory differences between spoken and sung vowels in singers. Speech Transmission Laboratory Quarterly Progress And Status Report 1:33-46.

Toulmin, Stephen
1963 Foresight and understanding. New York: Harper and Row.

Werner, Oswald and JoAnn Fenton
1971 Method and theory in ethnoscience or ethnoepistemology, *In* R. Naroll and R. Cohen, eds., A Handbook of method in cultural anthropology. Garden City: Natural History Press, pp. 537-578.

Whorf, B. L.
1956 Language, thought, and reality. Cambridge: MIT Press.

Zemp, Hugo and Christian Kaufman
1969 Pour une transcription automatique des "langages tambourinés" Melanésiens. L'Homme 9(2):38-88.

PROLEGOMENON TO THE STUDY OF SONG TEXTS

by Bonnie C. Wade

The study of song texts by scholars in various fields has taken many directions. Some of those directions have been the result of particular disciplinary methodology such as literary history and criticism, history, folklore, anthropology, linguistics, and musicology. Others have been the result of peculiarities of a language, such as the problems of song in tone languages. This article is an introduction to and analysis and reinterpretation of some of the approaches to the study of song texts which seem at this time to present fruitful avenues for future research.[1]

The approaches are divided here largely into two foci: 1) song text as a mode of discourse, i.e., a particular use of language, and 2) a song text as an item. Included in (1) is the consideration of song texts as one mode of discourse relative to the other modes of discourse in a culture, in terms of cultural conception and function. Under "function" the distinction is made between the ways in which song texts are used by members of a community and by scholars.

"Song text as item" encompasses a plethora of approaches. The classification of items as oral or literary is an extremely important one, as is the extension of that into the effect of oral on literary and literary on oral. Equally important are questions of composition, or the manipulation of materials, to create texts. Fresh perspectives are being developed with regard to oral formulaic theory, for example, including consideration of the role of the individual artist within his tradition. Considerations of structure extend to the meaning of structure and to the very meaning of performance.

For the purposes of this discussion, a song text is any vocable inseparable from its musical performance, whether or not that vocable has referential meaning. In other words, for this purpose there is no such thing as a song sung without text, but we can consider both linguistically meaningful and meaningless texts.

One of the most enduring of interests in song texts has involved the peculiarities of language when sung. In particular, some attention has been given to differentiating such language from other modes of discourse. George List's article (1963), for example, suggests a continuum from speech to song based on pitch differentiation. He and many other scholars seem to have made the basic assumption that in all cultures (except those with a tone language) the two are distinguishable modes of discourse. More recent scholarship has shown that it is necessary to be very cautious about that assumption, because different cultures regard speech and song in different relationships.[2] Judith Irvine, an ethnolinguist at Brandeis University, has pointed out that for the Maori all music is included in speech and there is no form of communication that is not considered speech (Irvine 1968).

Another example to demonstrate this approach is the Muslim's tuneful rendering of the call to prayer and "reading" of the Koran, which are not considered in Islamic cultures to be song. Clearly, the ideas which a culture holds are important—if not the most important factor—in distinguishing modes of discourse. If one makes the assumption, for example, that extensive pitch differentiation makes a song a song and he proceeds to examine the "reading" of the Koran as song, he is likely not only to reach some incorrect conclusions about the material under consideration, but also to commit a cultural offense. Thus, it is crucial to put the various modes of discourse in perspective with each other in the course of studying song traditions.

Once song is put into proper perspective as a mode of discourse within a culture, its function can be examined more carefully. Indeed, a particular function can be what distinguishes song from other modes of discourse. George Springer pointed this out in 1956 in his important article "Language and Music: Divergencies and Parallels": "The essential distinction between language and music lies in their social function as much as in their technical make-up" (1956:504). The function of song texts has been of major concern to American anthropologists and folklorists. In particular, content analysis has been a path for such research.

For members of a culture, for example, song can be a vehicle for social commentary. This could range from criticism of an individual for wrong-doing of some sort[3] to the purposeful utilization of song for dissemination of political or ideological philosophies. From the frequent publications of sociologist R. Serge Denisoff we have learned about folk song and the American Left. Denisoff is one among many scholars who have been fascinated with utilization of song in left-leaning ideological movements. A counterpart article is Marcello Truzzi's "The 100% American Songbag: Conservative Folksongs in America." The conflicting ideological view is denoted there as Truzzi considers the folksongs and "quasi-folksongs" of the historical Right, groups in the United States such as the John Birch Society and the Ku Klux Klan.

For folklorist John Greenway, one of the most important facets of this type of study of folksong texts is that it can reveal the lack of uniformity in sentiment on the part of "the folk"—a lack which he suggests might come as a surprise to those who have been educated with the rather unconscious assumption (reinforced by much folklore research) that "the folk" all feel the same way about things. Studies of North American protest songs, says Greenway, neglect "the other side," and topics such as inter-ethnic conflicts expressed in song have been left unexposed as they are socially rather taboo. Greenway feels that there is much to be gained from understanding conflicting points of view in song texts. The Denisoff and Truzzi studies illuminate Greenway's point that "the folk" do *not* all feel the same way about things. Studies of conflicting ideology in folklore further expand the functionalist argument on social function of song texts.

Another way in which song can function in a culture is the recounting of the culture's history. In a recent article, Gregory Gizelis speaks to the process of putting historical event into song, and one way a scholar should interpret the result:

> The folk singer materializes a historical incident, perceived in culturally determined style by giving it form bequeathed him by his culture, during the process of his performance. And despite the fact that the meaning which the finished product of this action conveys may not stand the requirements of a so-called scientific history, it shows how that society conceives its history. It casts light on how the members of a particular group feel that an event should have happened or probably did occur (1972:306).

The use of song texts as historical records has been a major issue among historians and folklorists. Historian-folklorist Richard Dorson, committed to the literary tradition, makes a strong case for the use of various types of folklore for learning about local history, while others insist it is folly to do so.[4] Gregory Gizelis's approach seems a particularly useful one, because it regards the text from the point of view of the person who transmits it.

What does seem to be agreed upon by scholars is that folksong texts can reveal a great deal about societal attitudes, about what social behavior is admired, hated, or taken for granted. Studies of such things concentrate, of course, not on the "artifacts" of man, but on man himself.

Function, then, is an important consideration in the subject of song texts—not only the way a culture uses song texts for its own purposes, but also the use to which scholars put the content of song texts. Furthermore, function is one means by which a culture can distinguish its modes of discourse; and by discerning that, we can ascertain how to deal with a culture's texts.

The other aspect of differing modes of discourse which has received a great deal of scholarly attention has been structure. For example, what is structurally different about poetry and prose, about poetry recited and poetry sung? What is structurally different about the various types of spoken narrative and sung narrative? Such questions lead to the next points of analysis.

Song Text as "Item"

The second major approach to song text to be discussed here considers the text as an entity: an item which belongs to an oral or a literary tradition and which is composed accordingly; an item which is both "of a community" and "of an individual"; an item which is structured in definite ways which are perhaps meaningful in themselves. Each of these aspects will be discussed in turn.

It has been deemed important in the study of song texts to distinguish between those of an oral tradition and those of a literary tradition. Folklorists have dealt primarily with repertoires that have been transmitted orally or song that is composed during performance. Examples of those two types of song are the repertoire of English and Scottish popular ballads that were collected by Francis Child and the Yugoslavian epic singing recorded by Milman Parry and Albert Lord.

One point in the oral versus literary distinction that has been bandied about by various scholars is the literacy of a performer who deals with an orally transmitted or orally composed genre. In his famous study *The Singer of Tales,* Albert Lord asserts that the illiteracy of that group of oral poets determines the particular form that their composition takes; he is referring to the oral formulaic epic narrative of Yugoslavian poets (Lord 1965:20). In a recent study of the spontaneous sermons preached by American ministers of certain Protestant sects, however, folklorist Bruce Rosenberg found that literacy had nothing to do with the style of spontaneous sermons which, like the tradition studied by Lord, is formulaic in some respects. In fact, the most heavily formulaic sermon recorded for Rosenberg's study was preached by a man who had three years of college education, two of them in a seminary where he would have dealt with the material used in the spontaneous sermons. Said Rosenberg, "Literacy becomes a deterrent to oral recitation only when the preacher tries to read his sermon" (Rosenberg 1970:18, see also Smith and Rosenberg 1975). That is a direct example of the effect of the literary mode of discourse on an oral one, a written tradition on a spontaneous one.

Folklorist Judith McCulloh would probably agree with Rosenberg on this point: "Often in British-American areas the liveliest song traditions can be found where there is a high rate of literacy. Evidently people who read develop a love and respect for language, sung as well as written. And many songs go into tradition from print. Someone sees a good set of words and puts them to music, generally to a familiar tune" (McCulloh, 1976). According to McCulloh, even "fancy language" is not a deterrent to a singer if he likes the text. Along somewhat the same lines, Wolfram Eberhard, in his article "Notes on Chinese Story Tellers," examines the use of prompt-books in oral performances, and shifts from oral to literary forms, utilizing the same material.

Infusion in the other direction—oral styles into literary song styles—is examined by Neil R. Grobman in "The Ballads of Thomas Moore's *Irish Melodies*." This article is interesting not because it speaks about a particular traditional body of songs but because it speaks to the potential process of change when a literary purpose is fulfilled while drawing on materials from an oral medium. Grobman believes that Moore could not consciously have tried to imitate traditional or broadside balladry since he was not familiar with those traditions, yet there is a remarkable degree of resemblance between some of Moore's ballad-like song and traditional balladry. Grobman suggests that it was probably unconscious on Moore's part, acquired naturally from his Anglo-Irish cultural heritage. "If this is true, one implication is that perhaps many other popular nineteenth century Anglo-Irish poets and song writers, not previously thought to have utilized genuine ballad techniques, have also unconsciously imitated traditional balladry" (1972:120).

The effect of the literary on orally transmitted materials is but one aspect of the larger question of means of transmission of various materials— specifically, *the change of the means of transmission* and *its effect on the item being transmitted.* It is taken for granted that when a novel is adapted to a film screenplay, changes are made that are in part dictated by the characteristics of the medium. It is also acknowledged that when a piece of music is notated it will not be exactly as it would be if performed. Similarly, when a song text is transcribed as poetry or prose without its melody and given in written form, it is being transmitted differently than if it were being sung. A text transcribed, a melody notated, even a text notated with the melody are only potentials for performance; they are not themselves performances. Nor must the change be from oral to written; it can be from written to oral, or even oral to oral, if, for example, a song text is spoken rather than sung. If a text is conceived to be sung rather than read or recited, it is certainly best studied in the form in which it was conceived. Of course, this kind of study is impossible with many historical materials; but by understanding what happens when the means of transmission is changed, and taking that into consideration when studying them in changed form, the conclusions could be quite different.

Keeping this in mind is more important in some types of studies than in others, and it is most important in structural studies. It is also important in functional studies, however, because the effects of performance can be quite decisive, changing, for instance, the entire emphasis within a text.

The textual material used in song texts has also been considered from the point of view of oral versus literary, whether found in a traditional song or used in oral composition. Parry and Lord's discovery that in Yugoslavian epic singing the artists drew on a repertoire of textual formulas in the process of composing their presentations led to myriad studies of other orally transmitted narrative song forms in which it was suspected that formulas might be found. The search was carried into the structures of English, Scottish, and Anglo-American ballads. However, in 1973 Eleanor Long stated: "It seems apparant . . . that . . . the conservative insistence upon the anonymity and oral-formulaic methodology of the 'true' and 'original' ballad singer has been fairly well laid to rest in the United States and elsewhere" (p. 226). Indeed, this would seem to be the case. Much recent work on ballads takes cognizance of oral-formulaic methodology but includes several fresh approaches that are potentially fruitful for the study of song texts in general. J. Barre Toelken, for example, joined those who were suggesting that in ballad tradition there are analogies to the metrical formulas and themes discussed by Parry and Lord. However, he cautioned that before one can search for types of devices used in oral composition, one must be sure that the product being examined is oral material. For Parry and Lord there was no question about "oralness," but applications of their formulaic theory have been made to bodies of material such as the Child ballads without first being sure of their "oralness." Toelken challenged the generally accepted assumption that all the ballads in the Child collection were (or are) traditional, i.e., culturally shared and orally transmitted.

Accordingly, Toelken formulated a canon by which to determine how many Child ballads were oral. The canon took into account both textual and melodic factors, and according to his criteria, only 44 percent of the Child ballads qualified as certifiably oral. For Toelken it is important to distinguish oral and nonoral ballads because such elements as usage, meaning, and rate of occurrence of folklore motifs differ rather sharply between the two groups (1967:93). Examining the Child ballads which qualified as oral according to his canon, he found that "the color green had a viable figurative utility in oral tradition which was never wholly perceived—or adopted—by the more sophisticated ballad writers" (1967:93). References to flowers and plants, too, are more symbolic in nature in the orally transmitted group of ballads: there is a consistent relationship between plucking fruits, picking flowers, pulling branches, and the like, and seduction in the oral ballads (1967:96), whereas *none* of the ballads he classified as nonoral used that motif in any way in any of the versions available to him. An audience unfamiliar with the symbolic motifs in the oral group would not understand their meaning. Toelken concludes that such figurative elements form a traditional (i.e., culturally shared) battery of poetic devices which may be seen as analogous to the metrical formulas and themes discussed by Parry and Lord.

In response to Toelken's idea of the oral canon, George Boswell examined syntax in the fourth stanza line of ballads in the oral and nonoral groups as delineated by Toelken. Boswell, too, found that a distinction could be made in the handling of the material that coincided with the oral versus nonoral groupings (1971).

The discussion of oral versus nonoral with regard to narrative texts, including song texts, is also the subject of a recent article by Bennison Gray, "Repetition in Oral Literature." Gray distinguishes repetition that occurs *within* a work from repetition that occurs *from work to work*; the former he terms "repetition in oral literary works" and the latter "repetition in oral tradition." The two basic types of repetition are: 1) verbal repetition (including verse and formulas) and 2) repetition of incidents. In sum, Gray asserts that the use of formulas and repetition of incidents within a work are peculiar to "oralness" rather than "literariness" (Gray 1971:297).

Yet another scholar who has tested the results of the oral-formulaic methodology in ballad tradition is Kenneth Thigpen, who focuses on the commonplace:

> If any cross-cultural analogy concerning narrative song could be made at this time, it would suggest that individual ballad singers or groups of closely related ballad singers had their own sets of commonplaces which may or may not have been applied in a formulaic method of constructing ballads. On the other hand, individuals may have employed commonplaces . . . only as memorized descriptions of specific scenes in a particular ballad (1973:388-89).

Thigpen suggests approaching this analogous application of the formulaic idea as Parry and Lord approach their study: through an investigation of specific repertoires. Thigpen suggests that it is possible to analyze the individual repertoires preserved by Child to determine how commonplaces are utilized by the individual singers, to examine, for example, patterns of repetition of phrases and themes from ballad to ballad. Indication of community (as distinguishable from individual) commonplace phrases and themes can also be considered (1973:389). Thigpen tested this approach in his article and concluded that the conception of the commonplace by scholars should be radically altered and that the ballads are oral formulaic only in a vague sense.

Several other scholars in the United States have studied individual singers and their repertoires (for instance, Bronson 1969; Fowler 1968). Their effort has been to elucidate the role of the individual artist in shaping the oral performance. In "Ballad Singers, Ballad Makers, and Ballad Etiology," Eleanor Long reviews the literature on those subjects and suggests a hypothesis of her own: that there are four basic types of folk artistry and that it is very important for scholars to recognize those types as inherent in personality rather than in either the traditional material itself or the immediate audience context. Her hypothesis and the typology of folk artistry that she establishes are based on the study of narrative texts of diverse traditions and groups.

A few other folklorists have focused their attention on personality and the individual artist. In her doctoral dissertation, Ellen Stekert treats the folksong repertoires of two traditional singers from western New York State and the Kentucky mountains. She shows how the collecting situation and the personalities of those performers affected the texts of their songs. One important aspect of Stekert's study is her focus upon the use of the songs texts by the performers as expressions of their emotional states, showing how the song texts reflect the singers' personalities. The change in their oral tradition over four and six years, respectively, resulted from the peculiar and unique intermixture of individuality and environment (the informants' reactions to the collector and their audiences), wherein the song repertoire of the two men was employed for the purposes of emotional expression.

Another approach within the comprehensive topic of song texts as "item" is that of structural studies: searches for structure in a song text, searches for structure in the performance of the song text, and, further, searches for the meaning of the structure.

One important assumption that can be made about structure is that *structure itself* might be meaningful. George Springer, speaking specifically of music, has asserted: "As in all art, the expressive power of music lies in its form. Form taken in its widest sense and embracing all features and their interrelationships is the only means music has of conveying meaning" (1956). Whether or not one agrees with that statement, it is important to ask not only what structure is there, but also *why structures are the way they are*. Perhaps the most eloquent spokesman for this approach to music is John Blacking. Blacking suggests that "music expresses aspects of the experience of individuals in society" and that "music is sound that is organized into socially accepted patterns, and music-making may be regarded as a form of learned behaviour" (1969:35, 36). This is, perhaps, because "some or all of the *processes* used by a society in the organization of its human relations are used to organize available musical sounds" (Blacking 1969:53).

If the organization (i.e., structure) of music is to be taken as meaningful, then one must be all the more careful to see that the form from which we study the structure is kept in perspective. Studying a song melody without considering the influence of the text of the song should limit the questions we ask about the melody. Likewise, studying the structure of a song text without considering the structural influence of the song's melody should limit the questions to be asked about the text.

One crucial element of structure which should be considered potentially meaningful is repetition. Repetition, for example, is an important factor in distinguishing British ballad form from Anglo-American ballad form because repetition plays a more prominent role in Anglo-American ballad. The question to be asked is why this would be so. This approach to repetition should, theoretically, be valid for both song texts and melodies. Judging from many song text collections, however, repetitions are not always considered important. We may ask: How *many* song texts presented as poetry, as literary items apart from their melodies, and being considered structurally have been relieved of their repetitions? We should perhaps then ask: Is repetition meaningless? Sebeok suggests that repetition be classed as either obligatory (occurring with regularity) or random, and thus to determine its poetic function (1959:39). We could perhaps look beyond that: If it is obligatory, why? If it is random, why? In any case we should consider the repetition as potentially meaningful rather than ignore it.

The first step in considering the meaning of structure, then, is to view the structure in as meaningful a form as possible. This is partially a problem of transcription. One aspect already has been discussed, that is, looking for the effects of change of means of transmission as in distinguishing "oralness" from "literariness." Perhaps the most crucial aspect is yet to be discussed: the effects of performance.

An example of this can be found in Anglo-American ballad texts, which are frequently said to be in poetic meter, many in iambic tetrameter. Given below are two scansions of such a ballad, "Edward" (Child 13), as sung by Mrs. Crockett Ward at Galax, Virginia, in 1941. The scansion of the performed version of the first five verses is done with rhythmic signs from the system devised by Egil Bakka of Norway.[5] The scansion of the poetic version indicates only the stresses that would be likely to fall in the recited language; the unstressed syllables are given no durational marks in order to avoid further rhythmic distortion.

KEY:	*Bakka's symbols*	*Wade's symbols*
	• = 𝅘𝅥𝅯	⌒ = rhythmic tie
	| = 𝅘𝅥𝅮	[ ] = approximate
	— = 𝅘𝅥	⌐3¬ = triplet

Several things become clear. In the poetic version the stresses do not necessarily fall where they would in ordinary speech. In the third line of the first four verses we would stress neither *it* nor *is* but in the poetic meter one or the other is put into a position of stress. Already someone could say, "Are you sure what the stress patterns would have been in speech or recited poetry in that dialect at that time?"

"Edward" (Child 13)*

How come that blood all over your coat?
My son, come tell unto me.
It is the blood that galligarry hawk
[gray]
That flies across the field.

That galligarry hawk's blood was never so red
My son, come tell unto me.
It is the blood that galligarry hound
[gray]
That hunts the woods with me.

That galligarry hound's blood was never so red,
My son, come tell unto me.
It is the blood that galligarry mare
I used to ride so gay. [prolonged breath here]

That galligarry mare's blood was never so red
My son, come tell unto me.
It is the blood my own dear brother
That used to go with me
[rushing]

What'd you and him fall out about
My son, come tell unto me
'Bout cutting down yon hazelnut tree
What caused it for to be.

*As sung by Mrs. Crockett Ward at Galax, Virginia, 1941. Recorded by Alan Lomax. Library of Congress Recording AAFS L57. Note: *Galligarry* is probably a "corruption" of *gallant gray*.

"Edward" (Child 13)*

How come that blood all over your coat,
My son, come tell unto me ___
It is the blood that galligarry hawk
That flies across the field. ___

That galligarry hawk's blood was never so red
My son, come tell unto me. _
It is the blood that galligarry hound
That hunts the woods with me. ___

That galligarry hound's blood was never so red,
My son, come tell unto me. ___
It is the blood that galligarry mare
I used to ride so gay. ___

That galligarry mare's blood was never so red,
My son, come tell unto me. ___
It is the blood my own dear brother
That used to go with me. ___

What'd you and him fall out about,
My son, come tell unto me, ___
'Bout cutting down yon hazelnut tree
What caused it for to be. ___

*Poetic scansion

With those considerations aside, a look at the performed versions shows the effect of singing on the poetic scansion. In the first place, the stresses do not all fall on the same syllables; in line two, the syllables *son* and *un* of *unto* consistently received the durational stress. In the second place, the durations of the stressed syllables and the durations of the unstressed groups in between are not regular enough to label this iambic tetrameter. In fact, Abrahams and Foss would not adhere to that labeling. They would call it isochronic because there are stresses but an irregular pattern of durations between stresses (1968). Furthermore, the number of beats in a line is irregular in the performed version.

We still cannot be sure where stresses are made in the text, because we have considered no musical factors other than rhythmic durations. Pitch and vocal emphasis also have to be taken into account. When these are considered, the second half of line one of each verse—when the mother is challenging the son—becomes very strong. Both of the mother's lines in the dialogue include the highest pitch in the melody (here transcribed as *g*), while the son's answers are consistently lower in pitch. The meaning conveyed in this text is clearly carried partially in the music to which it is performed. And the transcription of the performance must show the style of the rendition as closely as possible for that meaning to be transmitted in print.

One of the most enthusiastic proponents of the study of folklore and literature as performance is the American folklorist Roger Abrahams. Although he sees adequate historical reasons for what he calls the excessive concern in the last couple of generations with the analysis of specific works as well-formed and significant objects, Abrahams would argue for a performance-centered approach. To him, performance "is a demonstration of culture, one of the products of men getting together with other men and working out expressive means of operating together" (1972:75). Like Blacking, Abrahams asserts that "we may reasonably predict that once a group devises a system of order, the system will tend to reiterate itself in different realms of the group's life" (1972:77). Those realms include creative performances. Thus, in the search for the meaning of structure, Abrahams would include the meaning of the performance itself.

An important recent article, "Musical Style and Social Change among the Kujamaat Diola," by Judith T. Irvine and J. David Sapir, speaks to the connection of musical structure, including performance, to social structure, and how change in music is a result of change within the society. Aspects of their argument concern relationships among participants in a musical event and the ways in which the musical roles are differentiated and coordinated in the musical performance. One result in social change which they see is greater diversification of musical roles, to include, for instance, "virtuoso performances of individuals as musical specialists that would be incompatible with the strict conformity of the older Kujamaat way of life—as would the texts of most modern *esimben*, which consists of praise singing for individual patrons" (1976:79). In this one model article the matters of musical structure (including text) and musical performance as well as the meaning of both are drawn together in a significant way.

Up to this point, the discussion has been about songs and performance of songs with linguistically meaningful text. One further comment about such texts is pertinent here: intelligibility is not always of prime importance even when a linguistically meaningful text is present. John Blacking relates how the Venda of South Africa often said that they neither knew nor cared what the words of some songs meant: "Why worry? After all, it's [only] a song."[6] In the case of North Indian *khyal* or of opera performed in the Russian language in England (when no translations are made available), factors other than intelligibility of text seem to dominate. Those factors may be as much social or cultural as musical, and they are an important subject for research.

In her study "The Mundane and Prosaic in Bengali Folk Song," anthropologist Eva Friedlander points out that English language is frequently used in songs which are sung to audiences who will understand little of the English:

> Although many English words and phrases have been taken into Bengali, they need not, however, be understood literally to convey particular connotations. . . . Nildanta Das sings not only for those who are educated, who know and use English, but also for the uneducated, unskilled workers and cultivators for whom the English language can evoke very different kinds of imagery. Frequently the very use of English, the language of the more educated higher classes, takes on importance rather than the denotative meaning of the words employed (1975:141-42).

There are also texts without linguistic meaning, the so-called meaningless syllables. Those texts are likely to be meaningful in ways other than linguistic ways. Two studies of such syllables suggests they be considered as structurally important just as meaningful texts are. Bruno Nettl's article "Observations on Meaningless Peyote Song Texts" reveals clear patterns of occurrence which are obviously structurally important in the music. Francis Collinson discovered that distinctive phrases of such syllables in Scots waulking songs serve to distinguish songs from one another. Along these lines of investigation are the recent studies of referential and nonreferential texts combined in a song style by Szomjas, Shields, and Katz.

It might be that the very fact that the text in such songs or phrases *is purposefully nonreferential* has some kind of meaning. It is social, perhaps, or reveals a preference for the melody and/or rhythmic elements in the song. In any case, it would be more precise to refer to such syllables generically as "vocables" rather than as "meaningless."

This article has introduced and analyzed several ideas about song texts and approaches to the study of them which seem at this time to present fruitful avenues for future research. Those concepts and approaches are routes to learning about the lives and values of individuals and communities, as well as learning about the texts themselves.

NOTES

1. This article had its conception in a seminar at Brown University in the autumn of 1974, conducted by an ethnomusicologist (myself), a linguist-anthropologist, and a folklorist-historian-archaeologist. The seminar considered the subject of song texts from the viewpoints of the disciplines of musicology, folklore, anthropology, linguistics, and history. Some results of that seminar were presented at the IFMC meeting in Regensburg, August, 1975, as "Fresh Perspectives on Song Texts," with emphasis on possibilities for the study of North American song texts. This essay for the YIFMC presents concepts and methods, past and present, and suggestions for future song text study. I wish to thank my colleagues William Beeman, John Blacking, Susan De Vale Carter, Judith McCulloh, Bruno Nettl, Peter Schmidt, Charles Seeger, and Klaus Wachsmann, for their careful readings, advice, and constructive suggestions. My students at Brown University and the University of California, Berkeley, through seminars and several renderings of the course *Folk music in Europe and the Americas*, have helped me refine my ideas on this large subject.

2. In the seminar this became apparent from the biases generated from our own individual work with different culture groups. My major areas of culture concentration have been North India and urban Japan. The linguist-anthropologist works primarily with Islamic civilization, particularly Persia. The folklorist-historian-archaeologist deals primarily with African cultures, particularly those of the East African areas of Tanzania and Uganda. Students in the seminar included those working on Chinese K'un Ch'u operatic tradition; French-Canadian and French-American tradition; Afro-Amercian blues; Polish-American tradition; and South Indian (Karnatak) materials.

3. See, for example, the articles by Robert Black, cited in the bibliography.

4. A summary of the various approaches to the reliability of oral tradition for historical purposes is found in Dorson, 1968:19-35.

5. As given in Bakka, 1970. This system was devised as a means of dance rhythm notation. It proves to be fairly useful here, although rhythmic deviations had to be shown by other means.

6. Blacking cited his *Venda Childrens' Songs*, p. 30, in his "Value of Music in Human Experience" (1969:44). Blacking does give contrasting examples of songs whose texts are purposefully meaningful as well.

REFERENCE MATERIAL

Abrahams, Roger
1972 "Folklore and Literature as Performance," *Journal of the Folklore Institute*. 9: 75-94.
Abrahams, Roger and George Foss
1968 *Anglo-American Folksong Style*. Englewood Cliffs: Prentice-Hall,
Bakka, Egil
1970 *Danse Danse Lett Ut Pa Fosten*. Oslo: Noregs Boklag.

Beeman, William
1974 Personal communications.
Black, Robert
1967 "Hopi Grievance Chants: A Mechanism of Social Control," in Dell Hymes and William E. Bittle, *eds., Studies in Southwestern Ethnolinguistics*, pp. 54-57, The Hague: Mouton.
1967 "Hopi Rabbit-hunt Chants: A Ritualized Language," in June Helm MacNeish, *ed., Essays on the Verbal and Visual Arts*. Seattle: American Ethnological Society. 7-11.
Blacking, John
1969 "The Value of Music in Human Experience," *Yearbook of the International Folk Musical Council*, 1:33-71.
Boswell, George
1971 "A Note-Commentary on J. Barre Toelken's 'An Oral Canon for the *Child Ballads*,'" *Journal of the Folklore Institute*, 8:57-65.
Bronson, Bertrand
1969 "Mrs. Brown and the Ballad," in Bertrand Bronson, *The Ballad as Song*, Berkeley: University of California Press, pp. 64-79.
1958-1970 *The Traditional Tunes of the Child Ballads*. Princeton, N.J.: Princeton University Press.
Child, Francis, James
1882-1898 *The English and Scottish Popular Ballads*. Boston: Houghton Mifflin. 5 vols.
Collinson, Francis
1971 "Scottish Folk Music: An Historical Survey," *Yearbook of the International Folk Music Council*, 3:34-44.
Denisoff, R. Serge
1971 *Great Day Coming: Folk Music and the American Left*. Urbana: University of Illinois Press.
Denisoff, R. Serge, and Richard Peterson, *eds.*
1972 *The Sounds of Social Change: Studies in Popular Culture*. Chicago: Rand McNally.
Densmore, Frances
1943 "The Use of Meaningless Syllables in Indian Songs." *American Anthropologist*, 45:160-62.
Dorson, Richard
1968 "The Debate over Trustworthiness of Oral Tradition as History," in Fritz Harkort, Carel C. Peeters, and Robert Wildhaber, *eds., Volksüberlieferung*, pp. 19-35. Göttingen.
Dundes, Alan
1966 "The American Concept of Folklore," *Journal of the Folklore Institute*, 3:226-49.
1968 *The Study of Folklore*. Englewood Cliffs, N.J.: Prentice-Hall.
Eberhard, Wolfram
1970 "Notes on Chinese Story Tellers," *Fabula*, 11:32-53.
Foster, George
1953 "What is Folk Culture?" *American Anthropologist*, 55:159-73.
Fowler, David C.
1968 *A Literary History of the Popular Ballad*. Durham: University of North Carolina Press.
Friedlander, Eva
1975 "The Mundane and Prosaic in Bengali Folk Song," *Journal of South Asian Literature*, 11:131-46.
Gizelis, Gregory
1972 "Historical Event into Song: The Use of Cultural Perceptual Style." *Folklore* 83:302-20.
Gray, Bennison
1971 "Repetition in Oral Literature," *Journal of American Folklore*, 84:289-303.

Grobman, Neil R.
1972 "The Ballads of Thomas Moore's *Irish Melodies*," *Southern Folklore Quarterly*, 36:103-20.

Greenway, John
1960 "Folk Songs as Socio-Historical Documents," *Western Folklore*, 19:1-10.

Herzog, George
1935 "Speech Melody and Primitive Music," *Musical Quarterly*, 20: 452-66.

Irvine, Judith (Temkin)
1968 "Speech and Song in Two Cultures," manuscript.

Irvine, Judith T. and J. David Sapir
1975 "Musical Style and Social Change among the Kujamaat Diola," *Ethnomusicology*, 20:67-86.

Johnston, Thomas
1973 "The Cultural Role of Tsonga Beer-Drink Music," *Yearbook of the International Folk Music Council*, 5:132-55.

Katz, Ruth
1974 "On Nonsense Syllables as Oral Group Notation," *Musical Quarterly*, 60:187-94.

List, George
1963 "On the Boundaries of Speech and Song," *Ethnomusicology*, 7:1-16.

Long, Eleanor R.
1973 "Ballad Singers, Ballad Makers, and Ballad Etiology, *Western Folklore*, 32:225-36.

Lord, Albert B.
1965 *The Singer of Tales*. New York: Atheneum.

McCulloh, Judith
1976 Personal communication.

Nettl, Bruno
1953 "Observations on Meaningless Peyote Song Texts," *Journal of American Folklore*, 66:161-64.

Redfield, Robert
1947 "The Folk Society," *American Journal of Sociology*, 52:293-308.

Rosenberg, Bruce A.
1970 "The Formulaic Quality of Spontaneous Sermons," *Journal of American Folklore*, 83:3-20.

Sebeok, Thomas
1959 "Approaches to the Analysis of Folk Song Texts," *Ural-Altäische Jahrbücher*, 31:392-99.

Seeger, Charles
1966 "The Folkness of the Non-Folk and the Non-Folkness of the Folk," in Bruce Jackson, *ed.*, *Folklore and Society*, pp. 1-9. Hatboro, Pa.: Folklore Associates.

Seeger, Peter
1972 *The Incompleat Folksinger*. New York: Simon and Schuster.

Shields, Hugh
1973 "Supplementary Syllables in Anglo-Irish Folk Singing," *Yearbook of the International Folk Music Council*, 5:62-71.

Smith, John B., and Bruce Rosenberg
1975 "The Thematic Structure in Four Fundamentalist Sermons," *Western Folklore*, 32:201-16.

Springer, George
1956 "Language and Music: Parallels and Divergencies," in Morris Halle, *ed.*, *For Roman Jakobson*, pp. 504-13. The Hague: Mouton.

Stekert, Ellen
1965 "Two Voices of Tradition: The Influence of Personality and Collecting Environment upon the Songs of Two Traditional Folksingers." Ph.D. dissertation, University of Pennsylvania.

Szomjas-Schiffert, György
1973 "Traditional Singing Style of the Lapps," *Yearbook of the International Folk Music Council*, 5:51-61.

Titon, Jeff
1975 "Tonal System in the Chanted Oral Sermons of the Reverend C.L. Franklin," manuscript.

Thigpen, Kenneth A., Jr.
1973 "A Reconsideration of the Commonplace Phrase and Commonplace Theme in the *Child Ballads*," *Southern Folklore Quarterly*, 37:385-408.

Toelken, J. Barre
1967 "An Oral Canon for the *Child Ballads:* Construction and Application," *Journal of the Folklore Institute*, 4:75-101.

Truzzi, Marcello
1969 "The 100% American Songbag: Conservative Folksongs in America," *Folklore*, 28:27-40.

Welch, David
1973 "Ritual Intonation of Yoruba Praise Poetry (Oríkì), "*Yearbook of the International Folk Music Council*, 5:156-64.

The Contribution of Musical Semiotics to the Semiotic Discussion in General

Jean-Jacques Nattiez

While in the first portion of this century semiotic research, essentially theoretic in approach, was the achievement of a few pioneers—Peirce, Saussure, Morris, Hjelmslev—and while it was slow, following the postwar years, at measuring its strength against empirical descriptions and concrete applications, in recent years the number of works placed explicitly under the semiotic banner has suddenly proliferated. The present North American Colloquium is caught in an irreversible movement of institutionalization which follows from this expansion of our discipline and finds expression through the creation of national associations and international meetings.

In the light of the present situation, the author of these lines does not hide his disquiet as these manifestations, far from representing a consensus on the object, the methods, and the limits of semiotics, display the often radically opposed orientations of theories and practices which have little in common aside from the affixed label. We know that it is impossible to list here all the arguments and the intellectual prerequisites which have led us to adopt our present stand. Instead of hoping to convince our reader, we have decided on an approach in which our previous stands, if today superseded, are revealed in

I wish to thank Gilles Naud for his invaluable assistance in translating this paper into English.

the hope that, by laying bare the doubts that we have encountered, our present position may be more easily comprehended.

Since 1967, we have been working on the construction of a musical semiotics[1] and our investigations have always been related to the search for a specificity of semiotics:[2] a general semiotics or a musical semiotics *sans rivage* would only constitute a scientific imposture. Let us therefore proceed in the manner of negative theology and examine, in turn, what musical semiotics is not. To do this, we will examine critically some of the ideas currently acknowledged in the literature on general semiotics.

Musical semiotics is the study of the signs of music. The strict etymological definition of our discipline—the science of signs—could lead one into thinking that a semiotics of music should seek the types of signs of which music is constituted. This type of investigation is not new: to quote but one example, the *Recherches sur l'analogie de la musique avec les arts qui ont pour objet l'imitation du langage* is a work by the musicologist Villoteau, who, in 1807, made the distinction between the expressive or imitative-expressive means "which move our soul," and the "'meaningful signs' which cannot recall to us the idea or the memory of things without recourse to reason and to reflexion" (1807: 32–33).

Thus envisaged, a musical semiotics encounters a difficulty of general semiotics: the latter has never been able to provide any stable and universally accepted definition of the different types of signs. Why? From St-Augustin to Condillac, from Port-Royal to the Encyclopedia, from Peirce to Saussure, the *features* retained in order to define a semiotic category are not the same. With Saussure, the sign, properly speaking and by opposition to the symbol, is conventional and arbitrary, yet it is possible to dissociate these two aspects and show that there are signs established by convention where the link between signifier and signified is not arbitrary (as is the case of certain roadway signs); moreover, an arbitrary sign is not necessarily unmotivated, as Saussure himself points out: all the words that derive from the same root are, in some way, motivated.

This first difficulty, ascribable to the incapacity of general semiotics to recognize the semiotic difficulties inherent to the constitution of its definitions, invites yet another problem: a semiotic category, although defined with precision *in abstracto,* will not necessarily designate the same phenomenon in different fields of application. Take for instance the Saussurian symbol: the example, relating to language, given in the *Cours,* is the onomatopea. To distinguish, in music, between symbolic and non-symbolic facts amounts to a particularly delicate endeavor: the sequence of sounds which imitates the songs of birds, the crashing of waves can be considered symbolic, as can the evocation of movement, of feeling. But are the latter the result of a natural association—therefore conceivably understandable by anybody—or is it something acquired in the frame of a given musical culture? From a typological point of view, these sonic phenomena may be assigned to different categories according to these two alternatives. In fact the entire classificatory issue does little to help us comprehend how these musical references to movements or feelings function. And what more have we gained by calling the Wagnerian leitmotive a signal—after Prieto, for example—when we know that bugle or trumpet calls, which represent another semiotic genre, answer the same criterion of communicational intention?

We think, with Molino (1975:45), that a certain importance must be attributed to Roman Jakobson's remarks on the famous trichotomy of Peirce: "One of the most important features of the semiotic classification of Peirce resided in the perspicacity with which he has recognized that the difference between the three fundamental classes is nothing more than a difference of place assigned inside *an all-relative* hierarchy. It is not the absolute presence or absence of similitude or contiguity between the signifier and signified, nor the fact that the usual connection between these two constituents should be of the order of pure fact or of pure institutional order, which is at the basis of the division of the set of signs into icons, indices, symbols, *it is only the predominance of one of these factors over the others*" (1966:26).[3] As far as music is concerned, Molino has recently provided an illuminating illustration of this remark: "The sonic phenomena produced by music are indeed, at the same time, icons: they can imitate the clamors of the world and evoke them, or be simply the images of our feelings—a long tradition which cannot be so easily dismissed has considered them as such; indices: depending on the case, they may be the cause or the consequence or the simple concomitants of other phenomena which they evoke; symbols: in that they are entities defined and preserved through a social tradition and a consensus which endow them with the right to exist" (1975:45).

A semiotic approach to music made from the standpoint of sign typologies therefore seems ill-fated from the start, but the investigation is not lacking in positive facts:

1) first of all, it shows that the categories of semiotics are themselves symbolic constructions, in the general sense of the term[4]—i.e., an object which refers by association to some categories of thought which are not immediately given;[5] they are therefore appropriate to a semiotics;

2) the features that intervene in the definition of semiotic categories will change with the *hierarchical weights* conferred upon them by the theories and the various fields of application; it seems just to call such features *variables;*

3) what is true of the variables of semiotic categories could also be true of musical phenomena;

4) finally, if music can, in turn, be an icon, a signal, a symptom, a symbol, an image, or a sign, it is proof that music is first and foremost a *symbolic fact.*

If it is true that the sign—an "undefinable" category according to Granger (1971:72)—or, rather, the various types of signs have at least the common feature that they *refer to something else,* then we can envisage music as a symbolic phenomenon. In such a case, the goal of a musical semiotics is to inventory the types and modalities of symbolic references to which the music gives rise, and to elaborate an appropriate methodology to *describe* their symbolic functioning.

There cannot be a semiotics of music if musical meanings do not exist. The semiotic character of music has often been given a rather restrictive interpretation: a musical sign exists because it is a two-sided entity (signifier/ signified, expression/content); we must therefore unravel "what music is saying to us," and if, in the process, music is found to be an asemantic art, then we must concede the impossibility of a musical semiotics.

We believe that such reasoning harbors at least three major inaccuracies:

1) The musical signifier is conceived after the linguistic signifier. Now, perhaps, it is here that a study of music may bring a new element to our knowledge of other domains, linguistic or artistic. As Molino pointed out, "The root of the fallacy is, in fact, to believe that language constitutes the model of all symbolic phenomena. In this, the study of music brings forth a rectification and makes an essential contribution to our knowledge of the symbolic: there is more in the symbolic than just the phantasmal concept" (1975:45). By trying to reduce all forms of meaning to linguistic meaning alone, it is precisely the latter which we forbid ourselves to understand.

Works in experimental psychology have shown that in the musical domain we must take care not to identify the musical signified with the linguistic signified. When, in their experiments, Robert Francès and Michel Imberty ask their subjects to translate into verbal statements what the musical excerpts mean to them, they know quite well that the musical meanings reach their consciousness in the form of vague sensations which the verbal word exceeds, by and large: "While attempting to *say* what the music just heard means to them, the subjects add to its meaning some additional conceptualized and referenced meanings which exist only in verbal language" (Imberty 1975:91). It is interesting to note that these observations concur with the conclusions reached by René Lindekens from his research on the semiotics of the photographic image (1971). Insofar as the only way to find out how the semantic content of music is perceived is to proceed with verbalization, the musical signified, as such, can never be pinpointed accurately; but we may consider that the statistical character of the experimental methods allows for a good approximation of it.

2) We think that the position criticized here is also erroneous with regard to the conception it implies of the *symbolic nature* of music. At times music is considered an ineffable language, of divine essence, capable of expressing the inexpressible; at other times it is considered a purely formal game of sorts, and then it is judged capable of references to the exterior world. In order to understand a debate as old as philosophy itself, let us go back to Eduard Hanslick's famous essay, *Vom Musikalisch-Schönen* (1854). This author is often invoked when the issue is to deny music any power of evocation: "The beauty of a musical work is *specific to music,* meaning that it resides in the links between sounds, without any relation to a sphere of foreign extramusical ideas" (1854:10). Now, if we look more closely at the book, we find out that it is an "essay in the reform of musical aesthetics," in other words a booklet published after Richard Wagner's *Das Kunstwerk der Zukunft;* the purpose of Hanslick is *normative,* he defines what he thinks music must not be: as an art, it must not seek the essence of Beauty in the imitation and evocation of non-musical facts (think of the leitmotives!). But Hanslick does not deny for a moment that music can stimulate in us various impressions or feelings. It could even be argued that he anticipated the experimental approach to musical meaning: "Any feeling provoked by music must certainly be brought back to the manner—special to each feeling—in which the nerves are affected by an acoustic impression" (1854:85).

Also, we must not mistake a particular aesthetic conception, unique to an era or to a philosophy, with the *fact* that any music, once conceived, perceived, or analyzed, becomes the starting point for a series of symbolic *references*. Hanslick does not deny that music releases in us all sorts of associations; he asserts that musical Beauty *must* reside only in the sonic forms, and that the "pure and conscious contemplation of the musical work" will apply to nothing else but to that same formal organization.

Roman Jakobson sees in music a semiotic system in which the "introversive semiosis"—that is, the reference of each sonic element to the other elements to come—predominates over the "extroversive semiosis"—or the referential link with the exterior world (1973:99–100). It is our opinion that the concept of *dominance* used by Jakobson to characterize the semiotic specificity of poetry, figurative and abstract painting, pure and program music, must be extended to the aesthetic conceptions of these various artistic manifestations: then, the formal and asemantic theories of music proved in the works of Hanslick, Jakobson, Stravinsky, and Hindemith appear to be a cultural fact in which the extroversive semiosis has been minimized with respect to the internal interplay of sonic forms. This has not always been the case in music's history. When Fontenelle apostrophizes: "Sonate, que me veux-tu?" his question is symptomatic of the disarray in which the theorists of the classical period were thrown when they found themselves confronted with the dilemma of pure instrumental music[6]—and there are societies (like the African Dogon and the Mexican Tepehuas) where music plays the same role as speech in interhuman relations.[7] The symbolic character of music is a *semiotic fact* which can be ascertained everywhere, but to which the various aesthetic theories, the compositional concepts, or the strategies of perception bring a *variable or changing weight,* and assign it to various levels in the hierarchy of acoustic components, according to time and culture.

3) The position questioned here thus runs the risk of mistaking semiotics for semantics. If we refuse to identify the musical signified with the linguistic signified used at the time of verbalization, then what is our *general* concept of meaning?

We will say that an object, whatever (a sentence, a painting, a social conduct, a musical work . . .), takes on a meaning for an individual who perceives it when he relates the object to his *experience-domain,* or the set of all other objects, concepts, or data of the world which make up all or part of his experience. To be more direct: meanings are created when an object is related to a horizon or a background. Now is the time to use, in perhaps its more fruitful manner, the theoretic contribution of Peirce: in his *Essay on a Philosophy of Style* (1968:114), Granger describes this phenomenon by means of Peirce's semiotic triangle, which he schematizes as shown in Fig. 1.

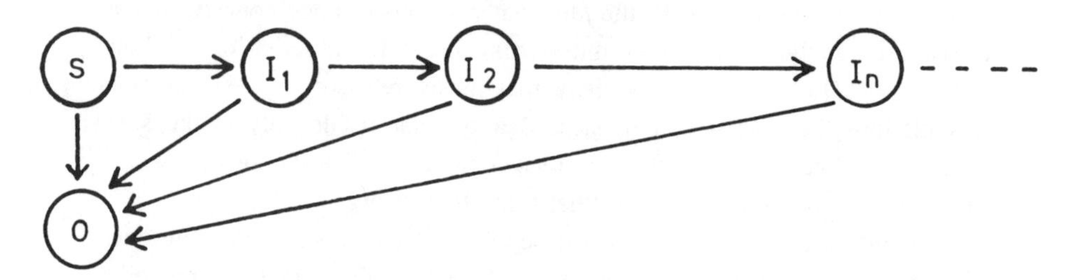

Figure 1

The sign S refers to an object O by means of an intermediate and *infinite chain of interpretants I.* These interpretants are the "atoms" of meaning by which we exercise our symbolic relation with the world.

The conceptual and verbalized meanings released in us upon listening to music are *but a part* of the interpretants associated with it. It is convenient here to use the expression "musical semantics" to describe the study of these interpretants are weighted. The objective of a musical semiotics is therefore sical experience—so long as we do not forget that a work of art is susceptible of many other types of references: when we analyze a musical score we favor such or such an aspect of the musical organization, we select this interpretant instead of that.[8] If we examine the Jakobsonian idea of a "musical introversive semiosis," a particularly positive idea will impose itself: when we establish relations of identity, equivalence, or contrast between the internal sonic phenomena of a work we are indeed calling into play a semiotic process—that is, an organization preferred by the composer, or by the performer, or by the listener, or by the musicologist, depending on the way in which certain interpretants are weighted. The objective of a musical semiotics is therefore not only to describe the semantic references *stricto sensu,* but to give an account of any type of symbolic association that takes place with the musical material.

Notwithstanding all of this, the fact remains that musical semantics represents an appreciable portion of the semiotic program in our domain. The perspectives in semantic research fall into three main categories.

The first of these we will call, after Spinoza, Granger, and Ricoeur, musical "hermeneutics." It is the *interpretation* of the meanings obtained from listening to music, the *exegetic* inspection of the proliferation of the interpretants, the establishment of subjective relations between the musical and individual experiences. As an example, think of the beautiful studies of Jankélévitch on Debussy (1968).

The second is *musicological reconstruction.* It deals with the construction of the relations between the meanings induced from the texts or situations in vocal or dramatic music, and the musical forms chosen. Such analyses tell us nothing about how the works are perceived; the musical lexicons developed in Lavignac's *Le voyage artistique à Bayreuth* (1897) or Chailley's *Passions de Bach* (1963) are typical of a composer's fancy. This type of research can be subdivided into more classes according to the methodology in use: the old studies of Pirro (1907), Schweitzer (1937), Lavignac, and more recently of Chailley, have in common that their authors conduct the analyses by going from the meanings to their musical embodiment; but it also proved necessary to proceed in the inverse manner, by going from signifier to signified, as in the works of Norma McLeod (1971) and Fritz Noske (1970). A synthesis of these onomasiological and semasiological orientations was proposed by Charles Boilès in his studies on Otomi music (1969). He later summarized the procedure as follows: "Two types of groupings were studied. The first grouping was arranged in sets according to designata common to all tunes placed in any given set. The other groupings were arranged in sets according to any musical similarities that seemed to be common to any set. Analysis of each group of tunes having common designata revealed certain phenomena that also occurred with great frequency in those tunes. The good fortune to discover musical vehicles that could be related to designata was further supported by results obtained from the second group'' (1973:39).

The last category is *experimental psychology,* to which we have already alluded; for Francès (1958) and Imberty (1975) it consists, among other things, in preferring free induction over guided induction in experiments on verbalization. This perspective has often been the object of some rather violent criticism: either all the interest—let alone its existence—of a musical semantics is denied, or else the claim is that it only leads to some already known results. But no experiment has ever brought out total agreement in the answers obtained, and for this reason the individual testimony, profound, rich, and subdued though it may be, cannot present the same scientific warranties as an experiment, however regional and limited.

Its overall epistemological validity is not a safeguard against some serious difficulties. The inquiries are usually conducted over fragments of musical works, some very short in duration, in other words *artifacts* extracted from the musical flux: we fear that the answers obtained will not correspond to a true listening situation, and as far as we can detect, there is still no complete experimental semantic analysis of a complete work.

In these researches, the correspondence between the meanings presented and the musical material as such is never abandoned, but it is an aspect which has never been tackled systematically. The works in experimental psychology have at least established an important principle: ''In the end, the features of the musical structures are pertinent to one determined (semantic) factor only, although they may also be observed in others'' (Imberty 1970:92). This means that there is no stable relation between a particular musical feature and a given meaning; the relation is always the result of some complex combinations of variables.

A semiotics of music is constructed with the help of linguistic models. During the 1960s and especially in Europe, the semiotic project, reactivated most visibly by Barthes in 1964—even if other scholars (Buyssens, Prieto, Mounin) were already working on it, albeit more discreetly—manifested itself in joint relation to linguistics. Today, it is not at all obvious that linguistics should be a determining factor in the construction of any particular semiotics, and in order to understand how this pertains to musical semiotics, it may be useful to go back in time.

It is quite independently from Peirce that Saussure places the semiotic project in line with semiotics with a few famous quotes from his *Cours de linguistique générale.* But we must not forget that when he writes: ''Linguistics can become the master-pattern of all semiotics, although language is only a particular system'' (1922:101), it is because he envisages a synchronic linguistics which depends on the *arbitrary* character of the linguistic signs, and because, according to him, semiotics should first of all attend to the arbitrary signs.

From Sechehaye, an authorized interpreter of Saussure since he was an editor of the *Cours*, we can see in the *C.L.G.* a true course in general semiotics: "*Language is only a particular case—albeit perhaps the most important—of a general case, and the problems concerning it must be considered before all as problems of semiotics* (. . . .) What is the special character of semiotics? . . . Any semiotics is essentially a science of values" (1917:13–14). Now this is the same notion of value[9] which, in the *Cours*, informs all the famous dichotomies: internal/external linguistics, signifier/signified, synchrony/diachrony, language/speech, syntagm/paradigm (Molino 1969: 341).

This interpretation of the *Cours* is similar to the semiotic conception of Hjelmslev. For him, the concepts of the *Prolegomena to a Theory of Language* "have a universal character and are valid for the system of signs in general (or for the system of figures which serve to form the signs)" (1943:130). For Hjelmslev, "language" is not limited to human language; it includes the set of *all* languages.[10]

With the publication of No. 4 of *Communication* (1964), Roland Barthes adds a new argument: semiotics constructs itself from linguistics because, in the past half century, the latter has developed tremendously while the former has remained essentially programmatic. The 1962 position of Mounin is more or less identical: "Even if not formally constituted, this semiotics of the future delimits and defines itself little by little with respect to the notional discoveries of recent linguistics. And as the latter brings into display, scientifically, the defining characters of natural languages, we can verify whether these same characters are valid or not with respect to the definition of systems of signs other than natural languages" (1970:68)—although an essential difference remains: in order to justify "the reversal of the Saussurian conception," Barthes does not hesitate to consider *a priori* all the systems of signs as languages, whereas, with Mounin, this comparative work is "propaedeutical," or preparatory to assessing the true importance of the functional linguistic model. But in both cases the objective is semiotic: the objects studied by Barthes are languages constituted of two-sided signs, those of Mounin are signals produced with an intent to communicate.

The question is whether, in this recourse to linguistics, the semiotic character of the object has been preserved. In much of the European research in semiotics, including our own articles on musical semiotics up to 1973, it seemed that the fact of using the abstract categories elaborated by linguistics in order to describe languages was judged enough to turn any object into a language. We thus ran the "ontological" risk, so well denounced by François Latraverse, which "consists of inferring the worth of a method from the nature of what it manipulates" (1974:70).

Gino Stefani's statement at the Belgrade Congress on musical semiotics in 1973, which bore a remarkable similarity to our thesis, defended in the same year, seems significant of this first stage in the development of musical semiotics: "The major influence on the new semiotic current in musicology can be imputed, up to now, to structural linguistics" (1975:12). "The more consistent contributions to a semiotics of music come from the application to music of linguistic methods and perspectives" (1975:13). Now, at the same time that general semiotics appealed to linguistics in order to free itself from the theoretical state in which it found itself, the linguistic models available in 1964 were perhaps not necessarily the best ones with which to analyze the linguistic and non-linguistic domains as symbolic facts. When Barthes asserted that "the development of mass media communications, today, contributes greatly to an actualization of this vast field of *meaning*, at the very time when the success of disciplines like linguistics, information theory, formal logic and structural anthropology provide *semantic analysis*[11] with new tools" (1964a:1), he was only deluding himself since:

a) While the concepts of signifier and signified, expression and content, can be used to operate a distinction in the domain, they are of little help in conducting a conclusive *analysis*.

b) The concepts of denotation and connotation, in the interpretation of Barthes, led him to a form of social psychoanalysis which certainly could do without linguistic concepts.[12]

c) The preferred linguistic model at the time in France was phonology, a model which did little to describe a particularly *symbolic* aspect of language.

d) As for information theory, Bar-Hillel has shown that it is inadequate to solve problems of semantics.

e) As for structural anthropology, today we can quote Dan Sperber: "In structural research the symbolic signifier, freed from the signified, is not much of a signifier except by a doubtful metaphor whose only merit is to elude the problem of the nature of symbolism, not to solve it" (1974:64). It seems difficult today to maintain an "identity of perspective between structuralism and semiotics" (Tremblay-Querido 1973:9).

f) There remains the question of the decomposition of the object studied according to the paradigmatic and syntagmatic axes: "These operations," Barthes claims, "represent an important aspect of the semiotic enterprise" (1964b:109). "Essentially, a semiotic analysis consists of distributing the facts inventoried according to these two axes" (1964b:116). Indeed, we think that this operation brings to light some fundamentally semiotic phenomena—

to which we shall later return—but if we re-read the context of these same two lines in *Eléments de sémiologie,* we realize that the semiotic justification is provided by recourse to the Saussurian model, not by the symbolic aspect which it brings into focus.

Then, the ontological illusion may well be succeeded by a sort of scientific illusion: the use of linguistics is no longer justified on the grounds that it effects a direct link with a semiotic fact, but because it fills a void (Barthes) and figures as a pilot science for the human sciences. In 1973, Stefani could say: "Any work on musical texts does not automatically belong to the realm of semiotics. Without mentioning other characters we feel that a dominant feature of our research is indeed the rigor which contributes to making semiotics into a science" (1975:9–10). We do not complain, but rigor alone cannot transform any musicological discourse into a semiotic object unless we identify science with semiotics, as Gardin suggested after Morris (1975:75) and as we thought for a time.[13] But in that case, as Ruwet pointed out (1975:33), there is no need for the term semiotics. In fact, there is a semiotic process in every scientific description (as we will show about music), but no science identifies itself with semiotics for that reason. The semiotic character must be *thematized:* this small difference is fundamental.

Now that the "dissemination" of semiotics is, today, at a maximum, a history of semiotic theories and practices should evaluate, for all the different domains, the manner in which the symbolic character of the objects studied has been brought to light and evidenced by recourse to linguistic models. Quite possibly, as we will see, such a venture may take place despite all facts and not because a linguistic model has been used. Today, the divorce between linguistics and semiotics is consummated; it is only unfortunate that this separation was made on account of fashion—structuralism, said Lévi-Strauss, died in 1968—and not for epistemological reasons. Whereas in 1966 Nicolas Ruwet could write: "I will treat music as a semiotic system which shares a certain number of common features—such as the existence of a syntax—with language and other systems of signs" (1972:100), a little less than 10 years thereafter he does not hesitate to say: "I don't particularly like the expression 'musical semiotics,' which I consider useless and perhaps even dangerous" (1975:33). This last assertion is undoubtedly excessive and unjust, but we ourselves have experienced this separation: when we set out to work, in 1967, by far the most vigorous example was the beautiful article by Christian Metz, "Le cinéma, langue ou langage?" First of all, we asked ourselves: "Is music a language?"—which is effectively a semiotic question—and this in turn led us to compare music and language; this "comparative semiotics," as we proposed calling it, thus served as a propedeutical or preparatory basis to control the transplantation, into musicology, of the linguistic models.

Later on, we will show explicitly how the use of a particular model can contribute to the specifically semiotic description of a musical work. Insofar as these borrowings have been more or less closely related to the semiotic project—at least in Europe[14]—our discipline can certainly benefit from their positive contributions:

1.) The comparison between music and language. On this subject, both the scattered (Dufrenne 1967, Schaeffer 1966) and the systematic (Springer 1956, Nattiez 1975e:2nd part) remarks available today favor a better understanding of the specificity of music and language. Besides the fact that it serves as a basis for the importation of linguistic models (Nettl 1958, Bright 1963, Becker 1973), this comparison contributes to a new form of classification of the Beaux-Arts (Nattiez 1973b:184). With the development of a systematic knowledge of music, we can hope, as Molino once suggested (1975:59), that the comparison will no longer be conducted one-way only (from language to music) but will also proceed from music to language. For example, it seems that what has been said of musical meaning could help examine in a different light the problem of linguistic semantics; of course, musical meaning is more connotative than denotative when compared to verbal meaning, but if we consider only the "core," or the "cognitive" part of meaning, the one which lexicologists set up with degrees of variations from one dictionary to the next, thereby indicating the existence of a certain laxity, do we not prevent ourselves from grasping the specificity of verbal communication, which, more often than not, remains an absence of communicaton?

2.) The functional models. First, the application of the functional models: given the analogy between the note and the phoneme brought about by comparative semiotics (Jakobson 1936), some phonological principles may be used in order to reconstitute extra-occidental music systems (Nettl 1958; Bright 1963), or to analyze the structure of a dance (Kaeppler 1972); up to this date, the best elaborated methodology is that of Vida Chenoweth (1973), based on Pike's tagmemic model. We agree with Stefani (1975:13) that the attempts to apply the Prague model to the analysis of musical works (Mâche 1971) remain rather vague.

Next, the functional point of view, in a more general way: this includes the attempts to apply Jakobson's grid of linguistic functions (1963) to music (Lévi-Strauss 1964, Stefani 1969, 1972), as well as what Stefani (1975:13) aptly calls the socio-cultural functionalism (Bogatyrev 1936, Kluge 1967, Sychra 1948), where the influence of Mukarovsky's functional aesthetics prevails. Finally, although their reference to the concepts of the Prague School is not always explicit, some American works (McLeod 1971, Boilès 1973) also enter this category.

3.) The distributional model. From the linguistics of Harris it can be said that Ruwet drew the fundamental principle of making explicit the analytical criteria (1966) and the idea of a taxonomic classification of a musical work (1962, 1966, 1967), which he relates to the paradigmatic procedures of analysis used by Lévi-Strauss in anthropology (1958) and by Jakobson in poetry (1963). Here we must distinguish between the parsing techniques, which are of linguistic origin, and the properly structural treatment of the units thereby obtained, which is of Lévi-Straussian inspiration—this being especially obvious in the analysis of the Prélude to *Pélléas* (but also in the recent analysis, by Lévi-Strauss, of Ravel's *Boléro* [1971:590–96]).

When we apply Ruwet's method of analysis to the analysis of monodies, we engage in the parsing of the musical syntagm into units which are paradigmatically associated, if identical or transformed according to a series of well-defined rules. If we look at it more closely, it will be seen that the procedure raises a number of questions, which have been tackled in various critical contributions (Arom 1969, Nattiez 1974c, Lidov 1975); these testify to the interest of the method. Being especially concerned with the question of making explicit every analytical gesture or criterion, we have developed this first aspect of Ruwet's enterprise[15] by applying it to the analysis of *Intégrales* by Varèse, the *Intermezzo* Op. 119 No. 3 by Brahms, *Syrinx* by Debussy (Nattiez 1975e: part 3, chapter II), and to *Density 21.5* by Varèse (1975d). The same perspective can also be ascertained in the works of Arom (1969, 1970) and Levy (1975) on non-European music, Stefani (1973) and Morin (1976) on J. S. Bach, Guertin on Messiaen (1975), and Hirbour-Paquette on Debussy (1975).

4.) The generative-transformational model. If we except a recent study, still unpublished, on the tonal harmonic system (Jackendoff and Lerdhal 1975) and a grammar of the melodic aspect of J. S. Bach chorales (Baroni-Jacoboni 1975), most applications of the Chomskian model are restricted to the analysis of folk and non-European music. We cannot fail, however, to note the number of works which indulge in the metaphorical use of certain Chomskian concepts: deep and surface structures (Blacking 1971), transformations (Herndon 1975, Cooper 1973), phrase or kernel sentences (Bent 1974:43, Treitler 1974:66). Generally, the generative ventures fan out in two directions: for generating pieces that belong to a given style (Sapir 1969; Lindblom and Sundberg 1970, 1973, 1975; Sundberg 1975; Asch 1972; Becker 1974), or to formalize musical theories verified according to an hypothetico-deductive procedure (Lidov 1975, Ruwet 1975).

Since the time of the first articles by Ruwet (1962), and given the influence of linguistics since then, we can consider that an autonomous current of research and musical analysis has abundantly developed, representing an original perspective in contemporary musicology.

A semiotics of music must be based on the acknowledgment of the symbolic character of the musical phenomena. It is still largely questionable whether the use of such linguistic models fosters a specifically semiotic approach to musical works, however. Speaking about "examples of semiotic analyses" Stefani specifies "analyses that are based on making explicit criteria rigorously adhered to" (1975a:15). If the explication of the criteria is indeed a necessary condition of scientific seriousness, is it enough to make semiotic objects out of musical works?

In the first paragraph, our conclusion was that a sign, or a symbolic fact, exists when there is some kind of *reference* or "renvoi." The very fact that a work or a human conduct becomes the object of an analysis implies that we have associated it with a certain number of interpretants. Simply put, the analyst is a specially attentive manipulator of interpretants, but one who, operating in the isolation of his workroom, should in principle be conscious of the fact that the scientific prehension of the object studied is not immediate, that in the passage from the work to its meta-language many aspects have been left aside. The composer, the performer, the listener also organize for themselves the interpretants of the work which is created, played, or listened to in a specific manner, and this without their being necessarily aware that a symbolic process is at work.

By making explicit the criteria of a musical analysis, the latter is transformed into a semiotic enterprise from the fact that it now enables us to describe and show, through such an analysis, just which interpretants have been retained, and how.

But the same enterprise is also semiotic in another way: created by an individual, the work is transmitted—at least in occidental music—by means of a written document, the musical score, to a performer who interprets it, translates it for the benefit of listeners. In this way, "a network of exchanges takes place between individuals" (Molino): the work cannot be dissociated from the one who produces it and the one who receives it. This is why "it is impossible to analyze, to reduce to units and organize a symbolic 'object' without going back to the three dimensions which the object necessarily presents" (Molino 1975:47). Molino calls these three aspects, after Gilson and Valery's terminology, the *poietic* (production pole), the *esthesic* (pole of reception), and the *neutral* (level of the *material* object, as heard and produced) aspects of a work.

As soon as an analysis explicates its own criteria, it cannot fail to encounter these three dimensions, because the reasons for considering particular units of a musical work to be paradigmatically equivalent are based on a phenomenon of perceptive association, on a knowledge of the equivalences allowed by the composer, or on both at the same time. One may wonder, then, about the necessity for a "neutral" description of the object, especially when the analysis is being referred constantly to the two extreme poles of the trichotomy. In fact, the poietic and the esthesic dimensions are not necessarily bound to correspond, and it is one of the contemporary myths of semiotics to conceive as normal a state of equilibrium between both. The aim of a neutral level is to inventory, as exhaustively as possible, the set of all possible configurations: bear in mind that a work is never perceived in the same manner from one time to the next, let alone by two individuals at the same time.

In this sense, Ruwet's principle of paradigmatic parsing, based on the dialectic repetition/transformation, is semiotic, less because it is inspired by linguistic procedures than because it helps inventory all possible relations between the units of the same piece. When he stressed the "impossibility of representing the structure of a musical piece by means of a unique diagram" (Ruwet 1972:134), he was not only raising a technical and material problem of analysis, but also showing that the multiplicity (properly infinite) of interpretants attached to a work forces us to present many different configurations or possible modes of organization of that work, *according to the explicit criteria that have been defined.*

Hence, when Stefani cautions us in a recent article (1976:49) to adhere to a monoplanar semiotics and deal only with the signifier, thereby leaving semiotics aside, he is only the victim of a semiotic concept still confined in the scheme expression/content, and even if the functional aspects of his analyses are not exactly comparable to concepts, they are not very far indeed from the Saussurian signified. Now, we think that Peirce's semiotic triangle breaks up the Saussurian dichotomy since, in the process of apprehending symbolically the musical material, the classical signifier is itself sprinkled with interpretants.

We will now give an example (Fig. 2) of the necessity for examining an object from the point of view of the three dimensions. The example is borrowed from an article by one of our collaborators, Gilles Naud, on Xenakis' composition: *Nomos Alpha*. The work was selected because Xenakis has published the mathematical program which served to compose the work. The following passage (Naud 1975:71) is poïetically divided by Xenakis into two objects: s2a and s3a. The neutral analysis, conducted on the basis of paradigmatic principles, identifies three distinct objects: α, β, and γ. The (esthesic) experiments on the auditive perception of this piece show that the same passage was categorized by a first category of listeners into objects (1), (2), and (3), which concur with the neutral segmentations. A second group of listeners identified objects (4) and (5), which coincide with the poietic data; a third group of listeners identified (6) only, and thus did not distinguish be-

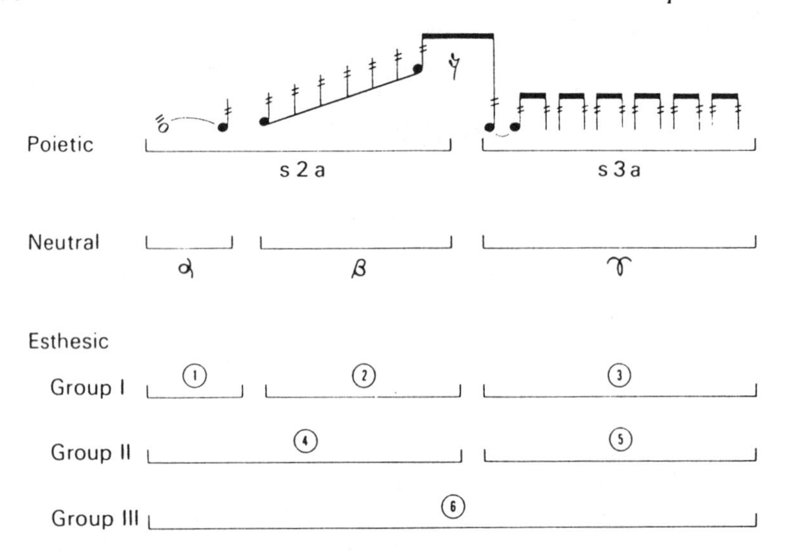

Figure 2

tween objects α, β, and γ. Had we preoccupied ourselves with only the poietic data, it would have been impossible to explain groups I and III of listeners, and a minimal neutral segmentation is also necessary in order to explain group I's perception.

This theory of the neutral level has met with much opposition, and, surprisingly, on behalf of researchers who should appreciate its necessity. During the past fifty years, linguistics has multiplied the modalities of an *immanent* description of languages. What happens today, after so many years of neutral descriptions, is that we can no longer remain at a stage where the phenomena are tackled "in themselves and for themselves," as Saussure would have it: they must now be envisaged in their relation to the poietic and the esthesic poles. An essential difference, however, with the reducing attempts (social character, psychology of the sign) denounced by Saussure in a famous page of his *Cours,* is that the only way to relate a poietic and an esthesic characterization to the works studied is through a neutral and immanent description of the object—this has been the fundamental attainment of structuralism—and for two principal reasons:

1) the musical works have an autonomous material reality which cannot be reduced to the poietic and esthesic aspects;

2) the *links* between the works and the strategies of production and of reception cannot be specified unless we first dispose of a *description* of the work itself.

Now, we may assign to their proper place in our semiotics the techniques imported from linguistics into musicology—not to mention the semiotic character of the inventories of paradigmatic equivalences: they provide models for inventorying, classifying, and organizing the constitutive elements of a work on the neutral level, such that the latter may in turn supply a basis from which the relations to the poietic and the esthesic dimensions can be effected. The external data supplied at these two extreme poles may then reilluminate or organize differently the combination proposed at the neutral level. It is easy to see that a work of art is never static, but is part of an unending process: and a semiotics of music must especially endeavor to bring out this *symbolic dynamism,* this swirl of interpretants.

Conclusion

Today, we can assess the attainments and perspectives of musical semiotics:

a) From the linguistic point of view, the essential comparison between language and music has been made. The task of reversing the perspective of comparative semiotics still remains, however.

b) Musical semantics will have to develop new methods in order to deal with musical works in their entirety, and make emphatically explicit the links between musical material and the meanings inventoried.

c) Ruwet's method had to be reevaluated on account of some difficulties it presented, but if it now can serve to classify and describe the units of a given work, it must also fulfill two further programs: it must be used in conjunction with the poietic and the esthesic poles of the analysis, as already mentioned; and it must set grounds for an integration of the isolated work to a series or corpus, by showing how it pertains stylistically to that series, while at the same time manifesting its own stylistic originality.[16]

d) We have shown why clarification of analytical criteria deserves a choice place in our semiotic project: it is equally important to reconstitute the criteria of already existing analyses.[17] Through a comparison of different analyses of the same work, we can extend the semiotic perspective on musical works to the discourse on the works themselves, and try to seek out and explain reasons for the differences between musicologists, or specify the non-explicated criteria which separate the various schools of musicology. The pedagogical importance of this perspective, at a time when musical semiotics is both the ferment and the symptom of a contest of the more uncertain aspects of the musicological discourse,[18] will escape no one.

NOTES

1. In its latest formulation: *Fondements d'une sémiologie de la musique* (1975e).

2. On this question, see our recent articles: 1974a, 1975b, 1975c.

3. Emphasis added.

4. Care must be taken not to mistake, in the remainder of this essay, *symbol*, a particular type of sign, for the symbolic function and facts, as defined here and which semiotics must study.

5. Let us give Ricoeur's definition of the symbolic function: "the general function of mediation by means of which the spirit, or conscience, builds up all its universes of perception and discourse" (1965:19).

6. Concerning this problem, see the article of Roland-Manuel (1963).

7. With regard to these two musical civilizations, cf. respectively Calame-Griaule (1965:527–43) and Boilès (1967).

8. Here we have an indication as to how a sociology devoid of allegorism could be created. Stefani's formulation concurs with our conceptions on this matter (Nattiez 1974b): "It would be important (and specifically semiotic) to establish through which specific mediations the semantic assertions (of musical sociology) are based on musical texts, or in other words, to find out how the interpretants of Peirce, which a musical work suggests to the receptors of the musical signs according to determinations which are specific to the given cultural systems (economics, language, politics, musical systems . . .), are articulated" (Stefani 1975a:16).

9. An unsolved problem which will not be examined here is the following: in order to account for the object as a symbolic fact, how important is it to make a description based on the notion of value?

10. Which is also a source of problems, for his definition of languages (1947) is based, quite evidently, on the characteristics of the human language.

11. Emphasis added.

12. Gardin has clearly shown how Barthes, in his article "Rhétorique de l'image," had used a certain linguistic vocabulary without subscribing to one of the requirements of phonology which confers most of its seriousness: to make explicit a procedure (commutation) by which we already know how the results of an analysis are obtained (1974: chapter II).

13. In the first version—today out of print—of our analysis of *Syrinx* (1975a), upon which Ruwet based his formulation of the criticism mentioned here. For our "retractatio," cf. Nattiez 1974a:5.

14. It is characteristic that the term of semiotics is never invoked in the linguistically-inspired works of American musicologists, much in the same way as Peirce and Morris develop their theories, not on linguistics, but on logic.

15. For a criticism of its Lévi-Straussian counterpart, cf. Nattiez 1973a:77–79.

16. We have often emphasized, elsewhere, the importance of stylistic characterization in our semiotic project (Nattiez 1971, 1975a, 1975e); we did not mention it here, but it is absolutely fundamental.

17. Concerning the theory of such a perspective, cf. Gardin 1974: chapter I; for musical illustrations: Nattiez-Paquette 1973, Nattiez 1975d.

18. Music analysis has become, lately, the *object* of musicological preoccupations, which is the sign of a certain disquiet. Particularly revealing is the publication in Germany of a history of musical analysis (Beck 1974) and a partially overlapping collection of music analysis (Schuhmacher 1974), and the article by Marcia Herndon (1974) in which she analyzes the same piece, belong to the music of oral tradition, in the manner of different musicologists.

REFERENCES

Arom, S. 1969. "Essai d'une notation des monodies à des fins d'analyse," *Revue de musicologie*, LV/2, 172–216.

———. 1970. *Conte et chantefables Ngbaka ma'bo*, Paris, Bibliothèque de la S.E.L.A.F., no. 21.

Asch, M. 1972. "A Grammar of Slavey Drum Dance Music: An Application of Linguistic Methodology to Music Analysis," annual meeting of the Society for Ethnomusicology (Toronto), mimeogr.

Baroni, M., and C. Jacoboni. 1975. "Analysis and Generation of Bach's Choral Melodies," *Actes du 1er congrès international de sémiotique musicale*, Pesaro, Centro di Iniziativa Culturale, 125–149.

———. 1976. *Verso una grammatica della melodia*, Bologna, Antiquae Musicae Italicae Studiosi, Università Studi di Bologna.

Barthes, R. 1964a. "Présentation," *Communications*, no. 4, 1–2.

———. 1964b. "Eléments de sémiologie," *Communications*, no. 4, 91–135.

Beck, H. 1974. *Methoden der Werkanalyse in Musikgeschichte und Gegenwart*, Wilhelmhaven, Heinrichofen's Verlag.

Becker, A. 1973. "A Grammar of Musical Genre: Rules for a Javanese Srepegan," communication at the annual congress of the S.E.M. (Urbana) (unpublished).

Bent, I. 1973. "Current Methods in Stylistic Analysis," *Report of the 11th congress of the I.M.S.* (Copenhagen, 1972), t. I, Copenhagen, Hensen, 42-3.

Blacking, J. 1971. "Deep and Surface Structures in Venda Music," *Yearbook of the International Folk Music Council*, III, 69–98.

Bogatyrev, P. 1936. "La chanson populaire du point de vue fonctionnel," *Travaux du Cercle linguistique de Prague*, VI, 222–234 (Neudeln, Krauss Reprint, 1968).

Boilès, C. 1967. "Tepehua Thought-Song: a Case of Semantic Signaling," *Ethnomusicology*, XI/3, 267–291.

———. 1969. Otomi Cult Music, Ph.D. dissertation, Tulane University.

———. 1973. "Sémiotique de l'ethnomusicologie," *Musique en Jeu*, no. 10, 34–41.

Bright, W. 1963. "Language and Music: Areas for Cooperation," *Ethnomusicology*, VII, 26–32.

Calame-Griaule, G. 1965. *Ethnologie et langage, la parole chez les Dogon*, Paris, Gallimard, Bibl. des sciences humaines.

Chailley, J. 1963. *Les Passions de Bach*, Paris, P.U.F.

Chenoweth, V. 1972. *Melodic Analysis and Perception*, Papua, New-Guinea, Summer Institute of Linguistics.

Cooper, R. 1973. "Propositions pour un modèle transformationnel de description musicale," *Musique en Jeu*, no. 10, 70–88.

Dufrenne, M. 1967. "L'art est-il un langage?" *Esthétique et philosophie*, Paris, Klincksieck, 74–122.

Francès, R. 1958. *La perception de la musique*, Paris, Vrin.

Gardin, J. C. 1974. *Les analyses de discours*, Neuchâtel, Delaschaux et Niestlé.

Granger, G. G. 1968. *Essai d'une philosophie du style*, Paris, Colin.

———. 1971. "Langue et systèmes formels," *Langages*, no. 21, 71–87.

Guertin, M. 1975. Analyse d' "Ile de feu II" de Messiaen du point de vue sémiologique, M.A. dissertation, unpublished.

Hanslick, E. 1854. *Vom Musikalisch-Schönen*, quoted from the 2nd French edition of 1893, Paris, Maquet.

Herndon, M. 1974. "Analysis: the Herding of Sacred Cows?" *Ethnomusicology*, XVIII/2, 219–262.

———. 1975. "Le modèle transformationnel en linguistique: ses implications pour l'étude de la musique," *Semiotica* XV/1, 71–82.

Hirbour-Paquette, L. 1975. Les Préludes pour le piano de Claude Debussy, Ph.D. dissertation, unpublished.

Hjelmslev, L. 1943. *Prolégomènes à une théorie du langage*, quoted from the French edition, Paris, Minuit, 1971.

———. 1947. "La structure fondamentale du langage," in *Prolégomènes à une théorie du langage*, Paris, Minuit, 1971, 179–231.

Imberty, M. 1970. "Polysémie et cohérence sémantique du langage musical: I. La polysémie dans les réponses verbales associées à la musique et la construction d'une échelle circulaire des expressivités musicales," *Sciences de L'Art*, VII/ 1–2, 77–93.

———. 1975. "Perspectives nouvelles de la sémantique musicale expérimentale," *Musique en Jeu*, no 17, 87–109.

Jackendoff, F. and F. Lerdahl. 1974. "Toward a Formal Theory of Tonal Music," colloquium Musique-Linguistique, I.R.C.A.M., Paris, unpublished.

Jakobson, R. 1963. "Linguistique et poétique," in *Essais de linguistique générale*, Paris, Minuit, 209–248.

———. 1966. "A la recherche de l'essence du langage," in *Problèmes du langage*, Paris, Gallimard, 22–38.

———. 1973. "Le langage en relation avec les autres systèmes de communication," in *Essais de linguistique générale II*, Paris, Minuit, 91–112.

Jankelevitch, V. 1968. *La Vie et la Mort dans la Musique de Debussy*, Neuchâtel, La Baconnière.

Kaeppler, A. 1972. "Method and Theory in Analysing Dance Structure with an Analysis of Tougan Dance," *Ethnomusicology*, XVI/2, 173–217.

Kluge, R. 1967. "Typ, Funktion, Bedeutung, Bemerkungen zur semantischen Analytik musikalischen Typen," *Beiträge zur Musikwissenschaft*, IX/2, 98–104.

Latraverse, F. 1974. "Théorie stratificationnelle et sémiologie," *Langages*, no. 35, 70–81.

Lavignac, A. 1897. *Le voyage artistique à Bayreuth*, Paris, Delagrave.

Lévi-Strauss, C. 1958. "La structures des mythes," in *Anthropologie structurale*, Paris, Plon, 227–255.

———. 1964. *Le Cru et le Cuit*, Paris, Plon.

———. 1971. *L'homme nu*, Paris, Plon.

Levy, M. 1975. "On the Problem of Defining Musical Units," *Actes du 1er congrès international de sémiotique musicale*, Pesaro, Centro di Iniziativa Culturale, 135–149.

Lidov, D. 1975. *On Musical Phrase*, Monographs on semiotics and musical analyses, I, Université de Montréal.

Lindblom, B. and J. Sundberg. 1970. "Toward a Generative Theory of Melody," *Swedish Journal of Musicology*, vol. 52, 71–87.

———. 1973. "Music composed by a computer program," *STL-QPS4* no 4, Royal Academy of Science, Stockholm.

———. 1975. "A Generative Theory of Swedish Nursery Tunes," *Actes du 1er congrès international de sémiotique musicale*, Pesaro, Centro di Iniziativa Culturale, 111–124.

Lindekens, R. 1971. *Eléments pour une sémiotique de la photographie*, Bruxelles-Paris, AIMAV-Didier.

McLeod, N. 1971. "The Semantic Parameter in Music: the Blanket Rite of the Lower Kutenai," *Yearbook for Inter-American Musical Research*, VII, 83–101.

Mâche, F. B. 1971. "Méthodes linguistiques et musicologie," *Musique en Jeu*, no 5, 75–91.

Molino, J. 1969. "Linguistique et économie politique: sur un modèle épistémologique du *Cours* de Saussure," *L'Age de la Science*, II/18, 335–49.

———. 1975. "Fait musical et sémiologie de la musique," *Musique en Jeu*, no 17, 37–62.

Morin, E. 1975. "Analyse sémiologique de la Fugue no 7 en mi bémol du ler livre du *Clavecin bien tempéré*," Université de Montréal, unpublished.

Mounin, G. 1970. *Introduction à la sémiologie*, Paris, Minuit.

Nattiez, J. J. 1971. "Situation de la sémiologie musicale," *Musique en Jeu*, no 5, 3–17.

———. 1973a. "Analyse musicale et sémiologie: le structuralisme de Lévi-Strauss," *Musique en Jeu*, no. 12, 59–79.

———. 1973b. "Quelques problèmes de la sémiologie fonctionelle," *Semiotica*, IX/2, 157–190.

———. 1974a. "Pour une définition de la sémiologie," *Langages*, no. 35, 3-13.

———. 1974b. "Sur les relations entre sociologie et sémiologie musicales," *International Review of the Aesthetics and Sociology of Music*, V/1, 61–75.

———. 1974c. "Problèmes de sémiologie musicale et de poétique structurale," *Semiotica*, XI/3, 247–268.

———. 1975a. "From Taxonomic Analysis to Stylistic Characterization: Debussy's *Syrinx*," *Actes du 1er congrès international de sémiotique musicale*, Pesaro, Centro di Iniziativa Culturale, 83–110.

———. 1975b. "Le point de vue sémiologique," *Cahiers de linguistique de l'UQAM*, no. 5, 49–76.

———. 1975c. "Sémiologie générale et concepts linguistiques," *Hommage à Georges Mounin pour son 65e anniversaire, Cahiers de linguistique d'orientalisme et de slavistique*, nos 5–6, 297-312.

———. 1975d. *"Densité 21.5" de Varèse: essai d'analyse sémiologique*, Monographs on semiotics and musical analyses, II, Université de Montréal.

———. 1975e. *Fondements d'une sémiologie de la musique*, Paris, 10/18.

Nattiez, J. J., and L. Hirbour-Paquette. 1973. "Analyse musicale et sémiologie: à propos du *Prélude* de *Pelléas*," *Musique en Jeu*, no 10, 42–69.

Naud, G. 1975. "Aperçus d'une analyse sémiologique de *Nomos Alpha*," *Musique en Jeu*, no 17, 63–72.

Nettl, B. 1958. "Some Linguistic Approaches to Musical Analysis," *Journal of the International Folk Music Council*, X, 37–41.

Noske, F. 1970. "Don Giovanni: Musical Affinities and Dramatic Structure," *Studia Musicologica*, XII, 167–203.

Pirro, A. 1907. *L'esthétique de J. S. Bach*, Paris, Fischbacher.

Ricoeur, P. 1965. *De l'interprétation*, Paris, Seuil.

Roland-Manuel, 1963. "Le classicisme français et le problème de l'expression musicale," in *Histoire de la Musique,* Encyclopédie de la Pléiade, t. II, Paris, Gallimard, 82–93.

Ruwet, N. 1962. "Note sur les duplications dans l'oeuvre de Claude Debussy," *Revue belge de musicologie,* XVI, 57–70; in Ruwet 1972:70–99.

———. 1966. "Méthodes d'analyse en musicologie," *Revue belge de musicologie,* XIX/1, 65–90; in Ruwet 1972:100–134.

———. 1967. "Quelques remarques sur le rôle de la répétition dans la syntaxe musicale," in *To Honour Roman Jakobson,* La Haye, Mouton, 1693–1703; in Ruwet 1972:135-150.

———. 1972. *Langage, musique, poésie,* Paris, Seuil.

———. 1975. "Théorie et méthodes dans les études musicales: quelques remarques rétrospectives et préliminaires," *Musique en Jeu,* no 17, 11–36.

Sapir, J. D. 1969. "Diola-Fogny Funeral Songs and the Native Critic," *African Language Review,* 8, 176–191.

Saussure, F. de. 1922. *Cours de linguistique générale,* Paris, Payot.

Schaeffer, P. 1966. *Traité des objets musicaux,* Paris, Seuil.

Schuhmacher, G. (ed.). 1974. *Zur musikalischen Analyse,* Darmstadt, Wissenschaftliche Buchgesellschaft.

Schweitzer, A. 1973. *J. S. Bach, le musicien-poète,* Lausanne, M. et P. Foetich.

Sechehaye, A. 1917. "Les problèmes de la langue à la lumiére d'une théorie nouvelle," *Revue philosophique,* LXXXIV, 1–30.

Sperber, D. 1974. *Le symbolisme en général,* Paris, Hermann.

Springer, G. 1956. "Language and Music: Parallel and Divergencies," in *For Roman Jakobson,* La Haye, Mouton, 504–613.

Stefani, G. 1969. *Communications sonores dans la liturgie,* Paris, Institut Catholique (xeroxed).

———. 1972. "Caro Mozart," *Nuova Rivista Musicale Italiana,* VI/1, 102–199.

———. 1973. *La ripetizione in Bach: i preludi "ad arpeggio" del Clavicembalo,* Centro Internazionale di Semiotica e di Linguistica, Urbino, Documenti e prepublicazioni E/22, 1973.

———. 1975. "Situation de la sémiotique musicale," *Actes du 1er congrès international de sémiotique musicale,* Pesaro, Centro di Iniziativa Culturale, 9–25.

———. 1976. "Analisi, semiosi, semiotica" in *Introduzione alla Semiotica della Musica,* Palermo, Sellerio Editore, 36–49.

Sundberg, J. 1975. "Linguistic Methods in Music Description," *Colloque Musique et Linguistique,* Centre Beaubourg, Paris (unpublished).

Sychra, A. 1948. "La chanson folklorique du point de vue sémiologique" (translated from Czech), *Musique en Jeu,* 1973, no. 10, 12–33.

Treitler, L. 1974. "Methods, Style, Analysis," *Report of the 11th Congress of the I.M.S.* (Copenhagen, 1972), t. I, Copenhagen, Hansen, 61–70.

Tremblay-Querido, C. 1973. "Vers une science des systèmes symboliques?" *Sociologie et sociétés,* V/2, 3–15.

Villoteau, G. 1807. *Recherches sur l'analogie de la musique avec les arts qui ont pour objet l'imitation du langage,* Slatkine Reprints, 1970, 2 vol.

TOWARDS A REASSESSMENT OF THE ETHNOMUSICOLOGIST'S ROLE IN RESEARCH

K. A. Gourlay

Ethnomusicology may or may not be, as Mantle Hood's "wag" allegedly observed, "what ethnomusicologists do," but it cannot be "done" without them. The aim of this essay is to examine the concept of the ethnomusicologist implied in certain theories of research method, to investigate the theoretical implications of alternative concepts, and to propose a research model which allows for Blum's contention that "any ethnomusicologist, like any of his informants, has lived through a specific 'learning process'," during which he is subject to "particular social constraints" (1975:208-9) which lead to adoption of one course of action, one set of interests, or one theory in preference to another.

My concern with research doubtless arises from the personal constraints of 11 years continuous experience in third-world countries, where the potential disappearance of traditional music induces a drive towards "preservation" and provides the opportunity for observation of musical activity impossible at a western university. Orientation inevitably moves from the "study of music as sound" to investigation of man as music-maker, while the opportunity to watch embryo ethnomusicologists in action increases awareness of both performers and scholars as human beings.

This opportunity is, however, subject to "constraints of situation." In formulating his theoretical position, the transplanted scholar finds himself caught between an academic colonialism which endowed third-world university libraries with Kobbé's *Complete Opera Book* and Hegel's *Aesthetics* and an inverted post-independence anti-colonialism embodied in all (48) volumes of the works of Lenin. If the resulting environmental constraints have led to the incursion of philosophy into ethnomusicology, the end-product should be judged by its value as a contribution to ethnomusicological theory.

Full investigation of the phenomenon of constraint implies the construction of a schema such as the following triad:

a) Personal Constraints, e.g. biological constraints such as deafness, absence or presence of perfect pitch, ability to distinguish an interval of three cents, or declining aural perception after the age of 50; character constraints, such as the inflated ego which inhibits one from ever seeing what happens, makes rapport with informants impossible, and results in creative accounts of musical behavior which exist only for the "observer"; or mental constraints, when we have to admit frankly that some matters are beyond our comprehension.

b) Situational Constraints, varying from the broadly economic, e.g. reduced availability of research funds or cut-back in teaching posts in the present crisis of western capitalism, to the more immediate as exemplified in the increasingly bureaucratic behavior of government departments and university administrations, or the specific field situation in which the ethnomusicologist as observer is himself a constraint on what he observes.

c) Universal constraints common to all ethnomusicologists in form, if varying in content, e.g. Blum's "learning process" and "the pertinent variables which shape our behavior" (Op. cit.), one result being that every ethnomusicologist adopts a "world view," which includes not only the way he looks at things but also how he thinks about them. In short, all ethnomusicologists operate within the constraints of the "ideology" which influences concepts held about the aims and methods of the discipline.

It is obvious that (i) an individual may be subject to more than one type of constraint simultaneously and that the relations between them require investigation: (ii) not all types of constraint are equally pertinent to ethnomusicological theory. The majority of personal and situational constraints are limitations on what one *can* do rather than on what one *should* do. Since theory assumes that its practitioners are not afflicted with physical or mental disabilities and that economic and administrative constraints are contingent rather than necessary, we propose to exclude them from what follows. This does not mean the postulation of an "ideal ethnomusicologist" to carry out an "ideal theory." The intrusion of the ethnomusicologist into a field situation which, by definition, includes both observer and observed, is, in its universality, qualitatively different from other situational constraints and, as will be argued later, crucial to the evolution of theory.

At the same time, the concepts underlying an ethnomusicologist's approach, which mediate between the universal phenomenon of experiencing a particular social reality and its individual expression, may themselves be neither overtly expressed nor consciously recognized, but so assimilated into his world-view that we can reach them only by reversing the process and approaching the concepts through expressions of the theory. This necessitates a historical approach and a naming of names. It should be made clear at the outset that we are not concerned with personalities, except to apologize in advance for any misrepresentation of views, but with individuals as *ethnomusicologists* whose integrity and honesty in holding particular concepts is unquestioned. Investigation into the constraints on an individual is *ultra vires* both the purpose of this essay and the writer's ability. How an individual ethnomusicologist comes to hold certain opinions while rejecting others, what in short is his "learning process," concerns the individual ethnomusicologist (or his biographer). Conversely, his views and the concepts embodied are matters of universal concern so far as they advance or retard accumulation of knowledge. The use of names is a matter of convenience to avoid unauthorized imposition of a label onto a theory.

THE MISSING ETHNOMUSICOLOGIST

Since, in the research process, the ethnomusicologist appears as subject investigating phenomena external to himself, the crucial question is that of subject-object relationship. The idea that research should be "objective" may result from a conscious philosophic stance, but is more likely to have been absorbed through the "learning process" as axiomatic to twentieth-century practice. Nettl, for example, appears to take the whole business for granted. "Needless to say, in all approaches, objectivity, avoidance of value judgments based on the investigator's own cultural background and acceptance of music as part of cultures are essential" (1964:11).

The criterion of objectivity presupposes *inter alia*:

1. The independent existence of data, which, objectively acquired, enable the formulation and subsequent testing of theory. Hence the development of recording techniques as means of providing accurate sound for transcription and analysis, the evolution of mechanical devices such as the Seeger melograph, and, in the theoretical field, insistence that "we must approach our data objectively" (Kaeppler 1971:175) or "submit all our preoccupations, assumptions and theories to the crucible of data" (Herndon 1976:220).

2. The communication of results intelligibly and without subjective bias, thus avoiding misunderstanding. Hence experiments with statistical or mathematical models (Freeman and Merriam 1956, Merriam 1967, Lomax 1968) or the demand for a metalanguage (Herndon 1974:250).

3. A methodology which enables the empirical testing of conclusions by others than their originators, as implied in Herndon's criticism of "descriptive models" whose "basic problem . . . is the impossibility of validating or invalidating them" (1976:219).

4. An overriding appeal to "science" or "reason" as the supreme court whose decisions are final. Hence in Feld's critique of the misuse of linguistics in ethnomusicology frequent references to "scientific inquiry," "scientific procedure," or the "more reasonable" (1974:200, 201, 205), and, in broader context, Merriam's demand for "sciencing about music" (1964:25).

Our concern is not to question the desirability of this approach as an objective but to examine the assumptions existing methods of achieving it make about the ethnomusicologist. If we accept Merriam's statement that "the ethnomusicologist seeks knowledge and seeks to communicate that knowledge" (1964:20), obviously the knowledge must be more than a subjective reconstruction and the means of communicating it ensure its passage from transmitter to receiver with minimum blockage. The difficulty is that the method he propounds to achieve this end involves a concept of the ethnomusicologist as both omniscient and non-existent, as subject to zero constraint and at the same time to absolute constraint.

This diagnosis is obvious as soon as we consider the prerequisites for his success in either the field or the "laboratory." In the field, he is *aware* of all variables, knows the types of music performed in the community, what percentage of recordings constitutes a representative sample even when the total is unknown, which questions to ask and how to frame them to elicit objective responses, where to place the microphone(s) to obtain an ideal recording, and whether informants are speaking truthfully or merely telling him what they think he wants to hear. At the same time, he wears a cloak of invisibility, is both there and not there, lives and works within a community without being seen, questions its members without taking up their time, attends secret rites and initiation ceremonies without being present, and records communal dances with an invisible microphone. In the laboratory he displays similar omniscience in transcribing music with absolute accuracy in perceiving pitch, duration, timbre and intensity, or makes a virtue of non-existence by letting a machine do it for him; in analysis he *knows* which successive tones constitute a phrase, how to designate melodic contour without ambiguity or bias, which features are significant and which not, and both how to relate the parts to the whole and musical sound to its context. In writing up results his omniscience enables him to choose a communicatory code that expresses precisely and without ambiguity what he wants to say, and from which all subjective bias and value judgments are eliminated as he reverts to final non-existence with a purely scientific presentation, dissolved in his own handiwork.

To challenge this analysis on the grounds that, as expressing an ideal rather than reality, its formulation serves little purpose, that the constraints implied are inherent in the human condition, that, while they cannot be eliminated, they can be minimized, and that theory can more usefully concern itself with advancing means towards this end than in demanding the impossible, is to miss the point—that these objections are inherent to the overall frame of reference. Either we admit that objectivity, at least in ethnomusicology, cannot be achieved through accepted empirical methods and the implied concept of the ethnomusicologist, that the discipline can never become "scientific," and that we must for ever be content with "second best," or we look for some other method to supersede the empirical framework. Our argument is that, confronted with the omniscience/non-existence contradiction, empiricism offers only a pseudo-solution; the ethnomusicologist is either omitted from its calculations or his ultimate and ineradicable existence obfuscated by postulating him as an abstraction existing only in its attributes. The converse is not to plead impossibility but to attempt to formulate a method which resolves the dilemma, not by suppression or abstraction, but through an approach which, by including the fact of contradiction, enables it to be superseded.

The empirical viewpoint, accepted as a *sine qua non* by many ethnomusicologists without recognizing it as a constraint and, in consequence, rarely questioned or formulated, is given systematic exposition by Merriam. In offering a critique, it is not my intention to belittle the importance of Merriam's contribution to ethnomusicology. His insistence that music be studied as part of culture, not solely as sound, his attempts to outline the principles of a coherent ethnomusicological discipline, above all, his concern to raise ethnomusicology to the level of a science, ensure him a permanent place in the development of ethnomusicological theory. In the 13 years since the publication of *The Anthropology of Music* we have absorbed its general aims and principles and can now view it in perspective as the product of a particular historical world view, which, through its failure to account for all the variables, is now in question. Ironically, the very thoroughness of Merriam's exposition enables us to see more clearly those lacunae which, in a lesser writer, would escape detection. Our object is not to reject Merriam's aims but to demonstrate the impossibility of their realization within his accepted frame of reference, and, by isolating the problem, advance nearer to its solution.

The crucial factor in any assessment of Merriam's contribution is his omission of the ethnomusicologist and, by extension, of the performer. This is no oversight but the logical and inevitable consequence of a consistent world view and its expression in deliberately impersonal language which, through the meritorious aim of avoiding the non-scientific and subjective, enables the user to conceal his omission of the personal, even when, as one of the totality of variables, it cannot be omitted. The root cause may be traced to Merriam's concern with a non-existent abstraction, ethnomusicology as an academic discipline, rather than with that existent, the ethnomusicologist, or with ethnomusicology as what ethnomusicologists *do.*

This is hinted at in the opening sentence of *The Anthropology of Music* which Merriam describes as "the result of some fifteen years of thinking and of discussion with colleagues and students in the fields of cultural anthropology and ethnomusicology, two disciplines . . ." (1964:vii), rather than as the result of working among the Basongye and the Flathead and trying to understand their music. In short, the emphasis is in the wrong place. The intrusion of linguistics, semiotics, proxemics and other current 'fads' have given his concept of the "dual nature" of a "discipline . . . compounded of two distinct parts, the musicological and the ethnological" (1964:17) an aura of pre-history, and this approach is worth recalling only as a pointer to a particular mode of thinking. It is this way of thinking, of viewing both the discipline of ethnomusicology and its practitioners, what we have called Merriam's "world view," which determines the later discussion on research method and technique (Ch. III). This opens with four assumptions, the first two being:

1) that "ethnomusicology aims to approximate the methods of science," by which is meant "the formulation of hypotheses, the control of variables, the objective assessment of data gathered and the grouping of results in order to reach ultimate generalization about music behavior which will be applicable to man rather than to any particular group of men," and

2) that it is "both a field and a laboratory discipline, that is, its data is gathered by the investigator from among the people he is engaged in studying, and at least part of it later subjected to analysis in the laboratory. The results of the two kinds of method are then fused into a final study" (1964:37).

These assumptions are "*essentially neutral* in nature; that is, they refer simply to the background out of which all ethnomusicologists work" (1964: 38, my stress).

Our concern is, first, with the underlying concept of the ethnomusicologist; secondly, the validity of these assumptions when applied to ethnomusicology. The framing of the opening sentence in terms of an academic discipline—"Ethnomusicology aims to approximate the methods of science"—rather than in relation to its practitioners—"Ethnomusicologists aim to approximate the methods of scientists"—is no accident but the result of a consistent use of abstract terminology in preference to the concrete. Admittedly we have to use words, and "Ethnomusicology" is a convenient "shorthand," but the cumulative effect of operating at this level is that "convenient" abstractions acquire an objectified existence, which, even when they begin by including the ethnomusicologist, too often result in his eventual exclusion.

This is apparent from the concepts of "science" and "anthropology" which, in both *The Anthropology of Music* and the later "Ethnomusicology Revisited," are treated as *entities* with recognized and accepted methods, and even attributes. "Science begins with observation and experimentation . . ., moves through repetition and verification . . . to classification of observations, formulation of hypotheses, prediction of further experimentation, testing of hypotheses, and the verification or modification of hypotheses" (1969:217), while anthropology, endowed with a sense of perception, "sees itself as a science, attempts to follow *the scientific method* and identifies itself with the goals and aims of science" (Ibid, my stress). Later, the "*systematic method-*

ology which grows out of anthropological theory" is referred to as the "*standard procedure* for the social scientist" (1969:224, my stress).

That many anthropologists and ethnomusicologists accept these methods and that much of the content of Merriam's remarks remains, and will remain, necessary in *any* method, serves only to disguise the conceptual constraints underlying their formulation, viz. that there is *one* scientific method, *one* systematic methodology, *one* standard procedure, because there is *one* science, fixed and eternal, to deviate from which is to be non-scientific, to lapse into solipsism and subjectivism. This conclusion may be challenged on three grounds:

1) Logically, it is valid only if the two possibilities–an objective "science" based on empirical method and a subjective "non-science," based on intuition, or at least ignoring the "standard procedure"–exhaust the universe of discourse. In theory there may be other methods of reaching objective results, which, in any total investigation of method, must be considered but which are excluded at the outset by framing the problem in terms of "either/or."

2) The "scientific method" of this conception is self-contradictory in its failure to include all variables, while achieving a semblance of authenticity through use of abstract expression which conceals their omission even from the writer.

3) The analogical reasoning that empirical methods which have produced objective results in the "hard" sciences are equally and directly applicable to the human sciences may or may not be valid. Statements of this type, as Feld pointed out (1974:201) require demonstration, not merely assertion.

The crucial factor in all three objections, and the "missing link" in any empirical exposition, is the ethnomusicologist, for the viewpoint is tenable only by his omission, or, what comes to the same thing, his elevation to an abstraction, in short, his de-humanisation. It is *not* "science" which "begins with observation and experimentation," etc. but the scientist, not "ethnomusicology" which "aims to approximate the methods of science" but the ethnomusicologist. By framing definitions in this way, the question of who formulates the hypotheses, controls the variables, assesses the data and groups the results, is not posed and the fact that these are not self-generating processes but require human agents, who, because of their humanity, embody varying conceptual constraints and are themselves variables in the total situation, is omitted.

To maintain that Merriam "omits" the ethnomusicologist when the opening quotation refers to "the investigator" and to "all ethnomusicologists" may appear as a contradiction. It will be argued that the whole of Merriam's subject-matter is what ethnomusicologists should aim at doing, both in the field and in the laboratory. As for the performer, is not a complete chapter (VII) devoted to the musician and another to his physical and verbal behavior? The point is that the approach adopted permits discussion of what ethnomusicologists should do without including them in the doing process, of musicians in all aspects of behavior, except the essential one of performance!

As an example we may consider Merriam's treatment of the ethnomusicologist in the field (1964:44-54), in which, after quoting Malinowski's criteria (including the need for "real scientific aims"), he cites other authorities, such as Paul on matters of "introduction, establishing a role, ethics of role playing, types of participation, the informant, interviewing," etc. and discusses four problems: "ethnographic truth," 'spot" studies, re-studies and comparative method. The basic issue, that the ethnomusicologist is *there* and exists as part of the total situation it is his task to investigate, is nowhere considered as a separate problem. Discussion of "ethnographic truth," which could have provided an opportunity for touching on the question, is framed in terms of "reporting the consensus of behavior with equal attention given to the limits of variation within that consensus" (1964:51) without mentioning the "reporter" or that it is the ethnomusicologist's "attention" and responsibility for deciding at what stage he has reached "equality." One of the merits of re-studies is their use in evaluating "the role of the personal equation, personality, and ideological or cultural variables" (Lewis 1953, quoted Merriam 1964:52), but this extract from Lewis is quoted without comment. To admit that ethnomusicologists operate with different "ideologies" would conflict with the concept of "neutral" assumptions, and that they are subject to "cultural variables" contradict the idea of a "common background out of which all ethnomusicologists work" (*supra*). Yet even here the ethnomusicologists is considered only in his attributes, reduced to a "personal equation" in the investigatory process, the object of which is his eventual elimination. Conceptually he remains an imperfect machine, less accurate in his hearing capacity than his Nagra, hampered in functioning by his humanity, an external recorder and observer, whose ultimate, if never realizable, aim is the removal of all constraints, the achievement of non-existence.

Turning to the ethnomusicologist's activities in the field, Merriam's prospectus for a "depth study in a single locale" includes six "areas of enquiry,"[1] but omits what, from the viewpoint of current interest in the "ethnography of performance," has become a central aspect of research, the actual process of music-making. The musician is considered from all aspects of behavior–specialization or its absence, professionalism, acknowledgment and rewards, role, status and training–except the very one by which he is what he is–performance. The "musical event" is mentioned, but only with reference to the behavior of a "non-musician," and even this is not followed up, only the behavior of non-musicians towards musicians *outside* performance. One is reminded of Laura Boulton's apologia to the Royal Anthropological Institute on behalf of African musical instruments that "they can be seen, handled and measured" and "are thus of great value in the material culture" (1937: No. 160), which omits all reference to the fact that they are intended to produce *sound*!

The word "performance" does not appear in the index to *The Anthropology of Music* and when it is eventually discussed in "Ethnomusicology Revisited" is listed as one of the differences between the musicological and the anthropological approaches. The only aspects mentioned are (1) providing "the artist with music to perform" (as a concern of musicology) and (2) "the act of performance," which turns out to be, not how local musicians make music, but the performance of non-Western music by ethnomusicologists as "an excellent methodological device in the field" (1969:22-3).

The end-result of this conceptualization is an ethnomusicological "discipline" which includes everything from synesthesia to symbolism and from composition to culture history but omits both the ethnomusicologist and the performer. The point we would stress, however, is not their disappearance but its *inevitability*, granted the world view within which the whole scheme is framed and which is epitomized in the word "behavior." The opening assertion, it will be recalled, included the possibility of "ultimate generalizations about music behavior"; "ethnographic truth" concerned "reporting the consensus of behavior"; Chapters VI and VII deal respectively with "physical and verbal behavior" and "social behavior," and Merriam's model for his study involves "three analytical levels–conceptualization about music, behavior in relation to music, and music sound itself" (1964:33), in which he rightly emphasizes that "the music product is inseparable from the behavior that produces it; the behavior in turn can only in theory be distinguished from the concepts that underlie it; and all are tied together through the learning feedback from product to concept" (1964:35). Is it pedantic or simplistic to suggest that "behavior" is also "inseparable" from men and women, including ethnomusicologists, who behave but who are lost sight of when conception remains permanently at this level of abstraction? That in attempting to "science about music" by eliminating the personal, the chosen terminology acquires a life of its own so that continual quantitative use produces a qualitative change into the non-scientific suppression of variables, whose inclusion is essential in any genuinely scientific approach? That, ironically, conceptualization in terms of "behavior" is as abstract and incomplete as conception solely in terms of "musical sound" which it is intended to supersede but which it can never do? Both are products of the same world view, formulated under similar conceptual constraints, and can be superseded only by an approach which recognizes these constraints and the resulting inherent antinomies and, taking these as its starting point, attempts to overcome them?

The assumption that there is only *one* scientific method results in analogous attempts to apply it in humanistic fields by eliminating the personal and subjective, as in anthropology or sociology, without fully considering whether it is applicable. This view has been challenged by a number of writers, but rarely in the name of science itself. The "either-or" syndrome, by which the alternative is conceptualized as solipsism, and the urge to remain "scientific" without being able to offer an "alternative science" result in a reluctance to allow healthy doubts to lead to a reassessment. Thus Herndon, quoting Bierstadt on *The Social Determination of Knowledge,* asks pertinently, "Are we reacting to the supremacy of mathematics and the 'hard' sciences in the same manner that earlier scholars tried to apply Darwinian principles to the data *whether those principles fitted or not*?" (1974:245, my stress). Her answer is disappointingly evasive: "wherever the fads and fashions of science . . . may be pushing us, we must still remember that our basic concern is with music and musical systems . . . and it is to music, not to fads, that we must turn for a source of theory." (Ibid.) Herndon is right to remind us that our basic concern is with understanding music, and that method is justified to the extent that it achieves this end; the "source of theory" is, however, no more "music" than it is "behavior," but the human mind acting in relation to music in all its ramifications. Preoccupation with science becomes a "fad" only when its methods are used from a desire to do something new without fully working out the relationship. The answer to a "scientific method" and "standard procedure" derived from the 'hard' sciences is not to dismiss them as "fads" but to devise methods and procedures which are more appropriate because they are more scientific. As Gramsci noted over thirty years ago,

> To think that one can advance the progress of a work of scientific research by applying to it the standard method (sic) chosen because it has given good results in another field of research to which it was naturally suited, is a strange delusion which has little to do with science (1971:439).

Feld's critique of the misuse of linguistic models in ethnomusicology, with its appeal to "science," remains valid because his epistemological differentations are appropriate and adequate at this level of argument, while his distinction between the notion 'formal,' as used by philosophers of science, and its 'hollow shell,' derived from formal logic, and "borrowed" (as a 'fad') in the application of linguistics to ethnomusicology, marks a positive advance in a scientific direction.

In considering the subject at a more general level, it is useful to begin by viewing it historically. The methods of the 'hard' sciences were not discovered as 'fads' but arose in particular historical circumstances. Bierstadt's examples (quoted Herndon 1974:245) demonstrate the preoccupation of the medieval world with matters totally alien to twentieth-century interests and ways of thinking, whose study was sanctioned and justified by the theological ideology of the time. Upholders of the concept of "a scientific method" tend to overlook the facts that (1) the process of history may render their methods and preoccupations as outdated as those of the medieval world; (2) the ideology by which it is justified is itself the product of historical circumstances; (3) it is human beings who pose the "questions that demand answers" in any society.

The effect of the circumstances under which the 'hard' sciences emerged to produce a particular form of constraint is aptly brought out by Lucien Goldmann.

> Since modern physics had to establish itself in the sixteenth and seventeenth centuries by a bitter struggle against *theological* and *social* pressures of all kinds, it stressed above all the necessity of *disinterested* research. In doing so, it contributed to the creation of a scientistic ideology which regarded *all* research and *all* factual knowledge as valuable in themselves and viewed with a certain contempt any effort to link scientific thought to any practical use or the satisfaction of human needs (stress in the original) (1969:24).

Goldmann is concerned with demonstrating that research can never be value-free, that "although it may be an *end in itself for the researcher,* scientific thought is only a *means* for the social group and for humanity as a whole" (1969:26). The physicist may split the atom as an "academic exercise," but the mushroom-shaped cloud continues to hang over humanity.

The notion of "disinterested" includes two aspects–that research has value in itself, i.e. it aims at acquiring knowledge rather than solving practical problems, and that its methods are free from subjective bias. Both aspects are present in the "scientistic ideology" which acts as a major constraint on our thinking. Before dismissing "interested" research as self-contradictory and the "practical" as somehow inferior to the theoretical, ethnomusicologists would do well to recall the embryo, if not always "scientific," interest in traditional and folk music of nineteenth and early twentieth-century "nationalist" composers whose aim, the creation of a national music, was far from disinterested, the concept of *Musica Humana,* so ably expounded by Walter Wiora (1976), and that ethnomusicologists in the third world are today in part concerned with the evolution of new music from the old or the marriage of diverse ethnic or local and external cultures.[2]

It is the second aspect, the analogous application of a disinterested "scientistic ideology" to fields other than the 'hard sciences' that is in question. Are there, as Goldmann suggests, two distinct fields, "the historical and human sciences" and the "physico-chemical sciences," different not merely in degree but in kind, which require not the attempted application of the method of one to the other, but the devising of appropriate methods for each? Has not this been obscured by the conceptual constraints imposed on us by an ideology whose success in combatting former theological constraints has in turn caused it to become, not a means, but a barrier towards understanding man's essentially human activities? Instead of forcing ethnomusicological method into a "scientific" mold, does not science itself suggest the devising of methods in which all variables are included?

The crux of any theory is the place assigned to man himself, in our own field, to the ethnomusicologist. In the 'hard sciences' the aim is to eliminate the "personal equation." Goldmann's starting point for research in the "human sciences" is the assumption that man cannot be eliminated and must be included in any theory for it to produce genuinely scientific results. The human sciences are "not, like the physico-chemical sciences, the study of a collection of facts *external* to men or of a world *upon which* their action bears," but "the study of *this action itself,* of its structure, of the aspirations which enliven it, and the changes that it undergoes" (1969:35). As a consequence, "when it is a question of studying human life, *the process of scientific knowing, since it is itself a human, historical and social fact, implies the partial identity of the subject and the object of knowledge"* (Ibid. Stress in original).

How far does this apply to ethnomusicology? Recorded tape may be considered a "collection of facts *external* to men" and thus suited to methods of study derived from the 'hard' sciences. In field recording, the ethnomusicologist is "external" to the men and women recorded. A moment's reflection, however, reveals the ethnomusicologist's subject matter as different from that of the physicist. Musical sounds are not things, aspects of an external world of nature (except in some societies where the wind in the trees makes music, and even here the sound is endowed with this quality only through human conceptualization), which form the subject-matter of the physico-chemical sciences, but products of *human* activity. Musical sounds can, of course, be studied as physical phenomena, but that is physics, not ethnomusicology. Performers are *external* to the recording ethnomusicologist and bear the relation of object (of study) to subject (investigator), yet the fact that both are human beings necessitates a "partial identity." The methods of the 'hard' sciences are applicable only on the assumptions that musical sound is made an object in its own right and that the human beings who produce it are down-graded to the status of things or the ethnomusicologist deprived of the humanity he shares with them through elevation to omniscience or reduction to non-existence. The basic antinomy of Merriam's argument is his insistence, on the one hand, that music be studied as human behavior and, on the other, the adoption of a scientific method which necessitates its study solely as sound. Ironically, those musicologists who concern themselves only with musical sound may, despite themselves, be more consistently "scientific," even if, for converse reasons, the results obtained bring us no nearer towards understanding music. The only solution is to bring back the ethnomusicologist as part of the total research situation implicit in the concept of a human science.

THE RETURN OF THE ETHNOMUSICOLOGIST

Theories based on eliminating the ethnomusicologist, of reducing the "personal equation" to zero, are paralleled by increased recognition of his existence, at first as a problem requiring solution, more recently as a "scientific fact" of cognition, or in the form of personal constraints; yet the formulation of a theory which incorporates objective aims with a subjective investigator is far from realization or even from recognition as a fundamental of research.

Almost twenty years ago Gilbert Chase, writing as a music historian, maintained that "History is a dialogue with the dead" and called for a "genuine dialogue" to replace the "pseudo-dialogue, in which the answers to the questions we ostensibly ask are prepared by us in advance in our own minds, conditioned by prejudice or by pre-established theoretical concepts" (1958:1). Despite its negative and emotive phraseology, Chase's argument that, since the historian or ethnomusicologist determines the questions posed in research, he is an essential factor in the research process, remains valid. To reduce this to a plea for "non-leading" questions or even for omitting questions and relying solely on observation does not eliminate his basic contention that our approach, and thus the results obtained, are conditioned by our "theoretical concepts." If modern terminology prefers "constraints" to "prejudices" (even in the non-pejorative sense of "pre-judging") and "unconscious" to "pre-established" (with its suggestion of conscious establishment which may be countered by conscious removal), these are differences in emphasis rather than in essentials. The importance of Chase's article is its attempt to solve the problem, not by eliminating the ethnomusicologist, or "removing" his theoretical concepts, but by recognizing these as inherent in the situation and attempting to decide where we go from there.

In quoting Woodbridge's dictum that "only *we* can answer the questions that we ask of the dead, . . . only *we*—each one of us individually, in a dialogue with his own conscience—can decide what answer, out of several that might be possible, should in a given instance be set down as the 'right' answer . . ." (Ibid.), Chase puts the responsibility firmly on the musical historian. Ethnomusicologists are fortunate in that, outside the fields of archaeology and ethnohistory, they can question the living, and, if not satisfied, rephrase the question; but it is the ethnomusicologist who frames the original question within his own conceptual constraints and decides when he is "satisfied" with the answers.

Compared with the interest aroused by Merriam's exposition of "the scientific method," Chase's proposed use of a dialectical approach produced little response, though its seminal influence may be detected in what future historians may call the Seeger-Wachsmann "thought-continuum." According to Chase, the first stage of "significant doubt" (following Russell's Cartesianism) leads to "that crucial moment when we make the decision to give a certain answer rather than another" and this "'moment of truth' can be attained only through the dialectical struggle of incessant question and answer" (1958:2). The "dialectical," as opposed to the "common sense," aspect of Chase's thought, appears in the suggestion that it is *we* who give the answers, whereas every ethnomusicologist knows that it is our informants, but Chase's concept of "dialectics" remains at the Platonic rather than the Hegelian level, and, while it includes both analysis and synthesis as its second and third stages, begins with the "preliminary phase" of the "mind talking to itself" (1958:2-3), a process which, even in Woodbridge's formulation of an individual's dialogue with his "conscience," is as likely to result in stupid answers being given to stupid questions as wise answers to wise ones, and which omits the essentially *social* nature of the Socratic dialogue. The overall impression, that "dialectics" as a method is little more than "dialogics" with the ethnomusicologist as Socrates is unlikely to appeal to those whose training has not qualified them for this role. Chase's article remains important for its recognition of the problem rather than for its "solution"; his inadequate exposition of dialectical method should lead not to its rejection but to more comprehensive reformulation.

In the following year Blacking advocated deliberate intrusion of the ethnomusicologist in the transcription of musical sound. Arguing that, "unless we are specifically studying interpretation, we want to know what a musician sets out to do each time he plays a certain piece of music, not *exactly* what he did play on a particular occasion" (1959:15), he produced transcriptions of Venda ocarina music which were "a synthesis of several performances of the same duets" and "intended to represent the musical patterns desired by any two Venda who set out to play the duets" (Ibid.). Our concern is not with the merits or defects of this method—the assumed existence of an ideal which the musician "sets out" to perform and the presumption that this is a kind of H.C.F. of several performances, in short, the equating of transcription with a "score" existing in "the mind of the composer" (n.3)—but with the elevation of the ethnomusicologist to an active role in the enterprise, for, in undertaking to distinguish the basic and structural from the interpretative and ephemeral, he answers the questions which he sets himself, guided by his knowledge of the total culture.

Blacking is concerned with a particular methodological problem rather than the place of the ethnomusicologist in research. Merriam's contention that

Blacking is "indeed reflecting ethnographic practice" and producing "ethnographic or ethnomusicological 'truth'" (1964:51) implies the possibility of wider application, even if to a layman the procedure is open to the objection that research results become an unverifiable construct of the ethnomusicologist in conflict with the canons of "scientific method" and elimination of the "personal equation." These contradictions may be attributed to the fact that, while Chase regards inclusion of the historian or ethnomusicologist as a logical necessity, Blacking and Merriam appear to regard it as accidental; the ethnomusicologist intrudes at a particular stage from deliberate choice rather than because he has no alternative, moving from non-existence in making "detailed transcriptions of every performance . . . heard or recorded" (Blacking: Ibid.) to omniscience in his knowledge of "the musical patterns *desired*" (my stress) by performers. This is consistent with Merriam's position, for Blacking's ethnomusicologist is superhuman rather than human and his relevance to a theoretical research model limited to those who share such abilities.

In contrast, more recent references have concentrated on the ethnomusicologist as subject to inherent constraints rather than as master of the situation, and often arise from consideration of the central problem of ethnomusicology, how to understand the music of another people. Seeger, for example, in discussing the "tactical devices" for implementing our strategy in talking about music, mentions the "ordering of the names of the percepts and concepts funded in the bank of ideation of the culture carried by each one of us, of which we form our own variant, determined variously by our genetic capabilities, the conditions of our individual life histories, and by our conscious effort" (1971:388-9); in short, in coming to terms with the biological and situational constraints under which we, as ethnomusicologists, work. In his concept of the ethnomusicologist as embodying individual variants of the cultural "bank of ideation" Seeger accepts his existence as a *sine qua non* of the research situation.

Towards the end of the same article, in explaining the inclusion in his chart of unnumbered boxes ["World View (outward) as Imagination" and "World View (inward) as Feeling"], Seeger comments on other possible views, adding that "Each of us has probably made up his World View, or had it made up for him, years ago. Can anyone fully define or describe what one's World View is? Many people are not interested in trying to" (1971:397). Both extracts concern the ethnomusicologist in relation to his "world," but the contrast between them in style and viewpoint is striking; the first, in familiar Seegerean phraseology, includes the possibility of "ordering" and "conscious effort"; the second, in simpler idiom, is more pessimistic, though the inclusion of "fully" before "define," with the implied perfectionism characteristic of Seeger's own world view, is little encouragement to those who are "not interested in trying to" define what their world view is.

The importance of Seeger's contribution is that he both recognizes and accepts the realities of the ethnomusicological situation *and* relates them to the central subject-matter. His whole article, including the excursions into philosophy and psychology, is an attempt to answer the hypothetical question posed by a person "well *indoctrinated* by school and college courses in music appreciation with a *concept* of a certain kind of music as one of the paraphernalia of social status" (1971:388, my stress), who, on hearing the music of another culture, asks, "But is it music?" Seeger points out how, in our answers, we rely upon our bank of ideation to find our way "through the thicket of ambiguity surrounding the familiar term 'music'" (Ibid.), just as the hypothetical questioner framed his question from a particular World View, whose only merit, in the present context, is that it is more easily recognized as "indoctrination." In relating the problem to the nature of music itself, Seeger extends his formulation to the whole ethnomusicological field. The ethnomusicologist does not divest himself of his bank of ideation when he moves from conducting a dialogue with his conscience to taking part in a Conference discussion or putting questions to informants in the field. Where Chase demonstrates the ethnomusicologist's responsibility in the question and answer process, Seeger extends the analysis to include the essential quality of the ethnomusicologist himself, his world view, particularly the bank of ideation that he carries.

Wachsmann's approach includes not only music in general but its realization as a particular communicatory event, a "relationship between psyche . . . and sound," which

> seems to present itself as an amalgam of relationships between (1) the physical properties of the sounds, (2) the physiological response to the acoustic stimuli, (3) the perception of sounds as selected by the human mind that is programmed by previous experiences, and (4) the response to the environmental pressures of the moment (1971a:382).

As he is concerned with "universal perspectives" in music, Wachsmann does not elaborate on the implications of his "tetradic schema" for the ethnomusicologist. His concept of a human mind "programmed by previous experience," despite the deterministic phraseology, which he would doubtless modify, extends Seeger's bank of ideation, which it resembles, both by placing it within the "historical" context of individual growth and experience, and following more recent findings of cognitive psychology, by including within it the process of perception itself. Music is not only made according to selected sound patterns acceptable to a particular group of human beings, but its perception is subject to similar constraints. We hear what we want to hear, or, rather, what our programming allows us to hear.

The significance of this for ethnomusicological theory appears when Wachsmann gives his "mind" a personal/individual body in the perception of music and, in considering the incidence of common parameters in different types of music, shifts his viewpoint from the check list of traits to the "receiver."

> I could say to myself that those phenomena outside my own immediate culture to which I now attach the label 'music' because I recognize and acknowledge them to be music, are merely so labelled because, rightly or wrongly, they seem to me to *resemble* the phenomena which I am in the habit of calling music in my home ground. I am used to thinking of a (more or less) certain group of phenomena as music; this group embraces a number of different properties which I cannot clearly define, yet I have no doubt that they belong to this group 'music' (1971a:384).

As examples, Wachsmann gives the *kulintang* music (performed before the discussion) and the early Heifetz recording of the Sibelius Violin Concerto. What one would like to know is whether he would include as belonging to the group 'music' the sound of New Guinea highland flutes or the bullroarer used by the Morwa of Nigeria for their *obwai* cult. Whether the answers would tell us more about "music" or merely reveal further details of the Wachsmann "programming" is another matter. But this singularly honest and remarkable attempt to face up to the problem cannot be dismissed as futile subjectivity—futile because its implication, that the inclusion of particular sound patterns as music or their exclusion as non-music depends on the personal decision of the ethnomusicologist in a dialogue with his own (programmed) conscience, would appear to make any genuine "scientific" approach impossible. To counter with Merriam's contention that ethnomusicological research must be conducted within the conceptual categories of the people under investigation, beginning with a distinction between music and non-music, or maintain, with Herndon, that "every culture has definitional boundaries which limit musical patterning in some way" (1974:274) is a neat and obvious answer to Wachsmann's "subjectivism"—until one realizes that things don't work out that way. Neither the Karimojong of northeastern Uganda nor the Hausa of northern Nigeria, for example, have a word for "music," and research shows similar results for 80% of the peoples in Papua New Guinea, though they all "sing" and group together certain sound phenomena. The existence of a speech-music continuum among many African peoples, pointed out by Wachsmann (1971:383) and found among others at a similar pre-'art'-music stage of development, means that, unless he intends to attempt the impossible and include *everything,* the final decision on where to draw the line (in all senses) remains the ethnomusicologist's responsibility. Even if he decides to go beyond what seems to him to "resemble the phenomena which (he) is in the habit of calling music in (his) home ground," in the very act of exceeding the "normal" boundaries of music he recognizes their existence and that of the determining conceptual constraints under which he works.

Herndon herself is aware of the ethnomusicologist's constraints for her experimental study with Fogelson of the Cherokee Ballgame Cycle was intended to present "an ethnographer's view" and "an ethnomusicologist's view," thereby presupposing the existence of (a) different "views" capable of designation in such terms, and (b) different "points of focus" and "theoretical stance" (1971:339). That both reached "much the same results" is attributed "in large measure to the fact that the Cherokee Ballgame Cycle is a cultural performance or occasion," i.e. an external factor so dominant as to be capable of negating the different "views" brought to its observation. While it is possible that the similarity of results arose from the fact that both Fogelson and Herndon approached the study as individuals trained in special skills but with a shared conceptual approach rather than as stereotype ethnographer and ethnomusicologist and were determined by relations *between* investigator (as subject) and activity investigated (as object) rather than by the object alone, this does not invalidate Herndon's contention that not "any ethnographer and any ethnomusicologist who study the same people will agree in conclusions, or *even in field observations*" (Ibid., my stress). Each will *see* different things, or ask different questions, according to the view/vision each brings.

In "Analysis: the herding of sacred cows?", Herndon goes a stage further and argues for the "active intrusion" of the ethnomusicologist in the construction of "cognitive" models. The aim is not to replicate

> the cognitive system of one's informants. On the contrary, it involves the active intrusion of the ethnomusicologist who states, to the best of his or her ability, what the variations and rules of occurrence are. The ethnomusicologist's model, then, is probably different from that of his informant. However, the methods of description are public and replicable; the results are predictive of the expectations of appropriate sounds and behavior, and to the extent that it will generate conceptual models approximating those used by a particular group, it is a model of their cognitive system. Conversely, if the model does not generate appropriate sounds and behavior, it will fall of its own weight (1974:248-9).

Superficially, this resembles Blacking's approach and may be regarded as a variant of the "ethnographic truth" method. The ethnomusicologist is viewed, not as an essential and non-eliminable factor in the total process, but as capable of active intervention at a particular point to solve a particular problem. The model is, however, an improvement of the earlier version in that it uses the methods of cognitive anthropology to construct "cognitive maps" in place of the vague ideal which the musician "sets out" to perform, overcomes objections to the subjective construct by incorporating a generative method which permits validation or invalidation by other investigators, and recognizes that variations may be as useful in understanding music as are rules.

While the proposal is important for its concept of the ethnomusicologist, who has not only returned but is now given a positive role, it immediately provokes a number of questions. Why, for example, is the ethnomusicologist only brought in at this point? If he is a product of his own culture, operating according to his own cognitive map, what is the relationship between his map, that of his informants, and the final model? Would it not be more logically consistent to admit that the ethnomusicologist intrudes, if not to the same active degree, throughout the whole investigation?

Herndon's concept of the ethnomusicologist appears more clearly, though again only incidentally in her reply to Kolinski. Asserting that "our basic orientation and the questions we pose about a subject matter influence our selection and treatment of the data," she adds, "whether our goal is descriptive or comparative, however, we must ultimately select a frame of reference in which to operate. That frame of reference affects the nature of our assumptions about music" (1976:218). Her model thus includes (a) an ethnomusicologist who is *active* in relation to his subject-matter, and (b) a research process in which investigator and subject-matter *interact* on each other. The ethnomusicologist affects results through choice of questions, selection of data and preferred "frame of reference," which in turn influences the ethnomusicologist's assumptions about music. One would like to see Herndon elaborate on this schema by clarifying the relationship between her "basic orientation" and Seeger's "bank of ideation" or Wachsmann's mind "programmed by previous experience," and by developing the dialectic of a frame of reference which appears both as a methodological device *within* the overall basic orientation (since the ethnomusicologist is able to *select* it) and as in some way equivalent to that orientation (since it has power to "affect our assumptions").

Still later, the ethnomusicologist's role appears as one of interpretation. "Whether one uses the term folk evaluation or native categories, however, it is expected that the ethnomusicologist will in some way interpret his data" (1976:221). The phrasing suggests a potential dichotomy between existing, objective data and the ethnomusicologist's interpretation of it, rather than the existence of data *as* interpretation which her previous statement that *selection* of data is influenced by "our basic orientation and the questions we pose" would lead one to expect.

These criticisms of phrasing in an article in which general principles appear only as incidentals are not intended to detract from Herndon's major contribution both to the present topic and to ethnomusicological theory. Her admission that she is "uncomfortable with the terms she uses," a debating point raised against her by Kolinski, is not only the beginning of wisdom in its refusal to accept a closed system (Wachsmann is "uncomfortable" about the term "music" and Seeger exhibits a permanent state of double discomfort by taking on speech as well!), but is symptomatic of our times and a hint that, viewed *sub specie aeternatis*, ethnomusicological studies are only in their infancy. Attempted integration of the ethnomusicologist into the research process inevitably leads to teething trouble before we can talk properly.

Blum's recommendation that ethnomusicologists should examine their own "social constraints," which this essay takes as its starting point, is supplemented by a call for diachronic examination of the ethnomusicologist in social context and synchronic investigation of him as a human being living in a certain historical period as ultimately inseparable aspects of the same process which affect research aims, interests and method.

> The contextual variables which determine the epistemology of a musician or scholar, as an agent who participates in more than one social group, must themselves limit the technique and options available for further intellectual (and musical) activity, including any interaction between one's own (socially produced) modes of operation and those exercised by 'informants' in a foreign culture (1975:208-9).

Seeger's bank of ideation, Wachsmann's programmed mind and Herndon's basic orientation are not only given bodies but the combined body-mind entity of the ethnomusicologist is conceptualized in its local (and social) habitation. Since understanding this implies investigating

> the past and present relationships between the European and American social structures which have generated such aims and the 'non-Western' societies placed under observation. . . . the development of a rational method must include continuing analysis of the historical process which has brought about the conscious desire for such a method (1975:209).

Applied at the more specific level of model-construction, this necessitates both

> a theory of the ways in which models are themselves altered according to circumstances [and] critical discussion of the history of various 'models' [which] will help us achieve a sharper awareness of the manner in which we ourselves have come to assign varying degrees of importance to particular aspects of communication (1975:210-211).

In this final statement Blum justifies Herndon's earlier "herding" and the successive critiques of this essay, the only proviso being that public presentation is validated by contributing to general theory rather than enabling the individual to discover his personal constraints in relation to theory.

To Blum the ethnomusicologist is both limited and necessary. A rational theory starts, not by attempting to eliminate him, or reducing him to a personal equation, nor, on the other hand, by allowing his deliberate and conscious intrusion at one stage of the investigation or endowing him with superhuman ability to decide what performers intend to sing as opposed to what they produce, all of which are contradictory to experience and demonstrate only the extent to which ideology can blinker all of us, but from acceptance of the fact that, whether he likes it or not, the ethnomusicologist is *there.* He is, moreover, no *tabula rasa,* no blank tape, but a human being limited by the constraints of his "learning process," the social nature of which Blum rightly stresses, even if his phrasing suggests a determinism rather than a reciprocal interaction between the unique and conscious individual product of the socio-economic structure and his environment, including other individuals.

How the ethnomusicologist operates at one specific level, that of perception, as opposed to the constraints affecting his operation, is revealed by recent findings in cognitive psychology, which add a further "scientific" dimension to our understanding of his role in research. Asserting that "all people 'construct' their worlds," that "we impose categories on our perceived environment, and this 'categorical perception' is as indicative of musical behavior as of vision, language–indeed, all human thinking" (1976:521), Harwood introduces two "widely documented" hypotheses on "information processing":

> 1) Humans 'chunk' information into meaningful patterns, attach labels to these chunks, and use them to construct a meaningful world. 2) Humans 'go beyond the information given' in understanding their world; we are active participators in how our world will look, drawing as much on hypotheses and conjecture as on data which impinge on our sensory systems (1976:531).

These

> successive levels of processing information about the world, therefore, involve both passive and active applications of abstract categories. In other words, we understand, or 'analyze' our world by 'synthesizing' it–constructing it the way we suspect it to be (1976:524).

In the present context, the obvious questions for the ethnomusicologist are: Where do we obtain the categories which we impose on "our perceived environment," and, as "active participators in how our world will look," what happens in inter-cultural research, when, surrounded by a "foreign" people, we perceive, not "our world" but *theirs*? Blum has already answered the first question; our categories are "socially produced" and arise from the "learning process." They are thus valid only for members of the same socio-cultural group. Is there then no escape from an irreducible subjectivism, or at most a narrow ethnocentricity, in which we interpret everything in meaningful "chunks" and, using them to construct a "meaningful world," impose our own, socially-conditioned patterns on the musical behavior we are studying because the *condition humaine* allows no alternative? To this central problem of research there is no simple answer (though Harwood's formulation contains a number of suggestions). In moving from past theories, from the concept of the ethnomusicologist as both omniscient and non-existent to the idea of his inescapable presence, to constructive theory, our starting point at least is clear–not to hope that, if we wait long enough, he will go away, but to begin with recognition of his existence.

ASPECTS OF A DIALECTICAL APPROACH

Recognition of the ethnomusicologist as non-eliminable necessitates the extension of previous models to allow for his inclusion. Schematically, the "ethnomusicological process" comprises:

1. A Preparatory Period, i.e. a "learning process," including both formal education and the broader aspects of socialization within a particular culture, during which the ethnomusicologist in one society and performers/informants in another acquire those particular skills which differentiate them from other people and adopt, through interaction between themselves and their respective societies, appropriate "world views" which, for the ethnomusicologist, affect his conceptualization of ethnomusicology, including its goals and methods, and his cognitive reconstruction of the external world through the "chunking" process, and for the performers determines the corresponding activity in performance.

2. The Research Process, during which ethnomusicologist and performers are brought together. Acting within the conceptual framework previously acquired, the ethnomusicologist applies his skills to investigating a particular facet of musical activity as supplied by the performers. Central to this investigation are the Musical Event and Musical Occasion (Herndon 1974 as amended by Asch 1975) which, to include the presence of the ethnomusicologist, may be redesignated Research Event and Research Occasion, leaving the terms "musical event" and "occasion" for activities at which he is not present.

3. The Presentation Process, which affects the ethnomusicologist in relation to a particular social network, either within his own culture, or, for the expatriate ethnomusicologist, within that of his employment, i.e. assessment, through "laboratory research," of results and feedback to an audience of academics or the general public through articles, lectures, record programs or a doctoral dissertation, etc.

The process is familiar to all and the only justification for setting it out is to allow it to appear as a totality, thus emphasizing the inter-relatedness of its components through the person of the ethnomusicologist. The "learning process" does not stop, though its emphasis may change, during the "research" stage, and both motivation and method in research are affected by foreknowledge of presentation. Within the same field situation the graduate student working for a doctorate and unconsciously aware of the world view of his supervisors operates according to a different set of variables and produces different results from the sponsored traveller aiming to obtain a balanced and vendable selection of recorded items for a commercial disc. The story of the novice in this field who asked, "How do you stop them singing after three minutes?", though possibly apocryphal, aptly illustrates the constraints imposed by questions of presentation on research method, and readers can doubtless supply their own examples of the working of academic constraints.

Both the Research Event, i.e. performance of an individual song, dance, etc. and the overall Research Occasion, i.e. sequence of Research Events, include two systems in relationship and may be approached at different levels. At the cognitive and conceptual level, they may be regarded as (a) on the part of the performers, "encapsulated expressions of the shared cognitive forms and values of a society" (Herndon 1971:340) as expressed through musical activity, including both the production of acceptable sound patterns and other behavior *in relation to* (b) the culturally different cognitive forms, values and methods of perception of the ethnomusicologist, as determined through his "learning process." At the communicatory level, both events and occasions include two simultaneously operating and interacting systems. Adapting Hymes linguistic model (1972:27) we may distinguish (a) participant members of the culture under investigation, i.e. performers and audience (even if the "audience" is only a man listening to himself) with recognized and intelligible channels of communciation, e.g. singing, instrument-playing, and shared codes for use in these channels, e.g. musical or verbal sounds, together with foreknowledge of the occasion of performance, i.e. shared expectancies, and (b) the ethnomusicologist as recipient of these aural and visual utterances which he hears, sees and interprets according to the extent permitted by individual modification of the pertinent variables to which he has been subjected up to this point, including both that part of the performance, or similar previous performances, which he has experienced, and foreknowledge of his own future expectations.

The crux of the matter, however, is that while, in constructing this model, "I" as the ethnomusicologist, remain outside it, in operating the model, "I" must both *enter* it *and* retain my independence in order to see if it works. In models "operated" by the investigator, e.g. in laboratory research in the 'hard' sciences, he appears as subject in relation to the object investigated; in the present model, as with other person-to-person investigations in the human sciences, he retains his external capacity in relation to the model, but as the "internal" subject of an (intra-model) research process in which members of another culture are the objects, he is at the same time the object of his own (extra-model) operations. Is not the model thus even more contradictory than one embodying that omniscience-non-existence contradiction inherent in the "scientific method" espoused by Merriam? The answer can only be that, if our model accurately reflects reality and is more genuinely "scientific," then reality itself must embody a contradiction, comprehension of which necessitates a methodology other than the formal logic by which A cannot be both itself and not-A, in short, a dialectical approach which accepts contradiction as an aspect of reality itself.

From this viewpoint it is both surprising and not surprising that ethnomusicologists have shown so little interest in dialectical method. Chase's dialectics (op. cit.) embody question and answer rather than contradiction, and even Seeger, whose denial that he is a philosopher only confirms his candidature for the Socratic role, while crediting Hegel with "seeding the conception" that enabled him to arrive at a "way of building a dialectic," cannot accept the "mystical notion" of Hegel's "interpenetration of thesis and antithesis" (1971:394). In practice both Seeger (see the explanation of his chart, 1971:392) and Wachsmann (e.g. in his "music-speech continuum" proposal, 1971a:383) adopt a dialectical approach because their insights happen to work that way, as does Herndon in her emphasis on interaction and Blum with his stress on historical process.

It is not our purpose to attempt an exposition of dialectical method, of which adequate accounts exist,[3] but to apply some of its basic tenets, particularly the concept of totality, to the operation of our model, (a) in a reassessment of presentation, (b) in the formulation of questions, and (c) as a hermeneutic device from the viewpoint of process.

The idea of totality, familiarized through the *Gestalt* and epitomized in Pascal's dictum that "it is impossible to know the parts without the whole, and to know the whole without knowing the parts" (quoted Goldmann 1969:128) offers both a solution, in that all contradictions are resolved in the whole, and a challenge, since it sets us an impossible task. We have already attempted to apply it through schematic exposition of a "total" research model in order to emphasize the inter-relatedness of its stages, and to show how the significance of each is realized only in relation to others and to the whole. Blum's proposed critical self-examination of "the pertinent variables which shape our behavior" must be interpreted in terms of the future no less than the past, of what we *exclude* as well as what is included. Since, for most of us, the ability to operate at this level, save in moments of exceptional insight, exceeds our grasp, the concept of totality may perhaps be best approached through deliberate mental "tacking" from one facet to another; critical examination of future aims, followed by investigation of the constraints operating in the choice of those aims and leading in turn to consideration of what we *exclude*, may not only enhance our awareness of each aspect but produce a reassessment that is both more scientific and more objective because it corresponds more closely to reality.

As an example, we may attempt a reassessment of the Presentation Process, i.e. consider results as embodied in the "end-product," as (1) what it appears to be, (2) the outcome of constraints on the ethnomusicologist, and (3) in terms of what it is not, in order to see it as it is or even as it might be. Limiting discussion to evidence available to all, the published article, investigation suggests that, considerations of theory apart, it has become axiomatic for presentation to be descriptive or comparative, for us to "science about music," and to express results in technical terms comprehensible only to specialists. In this respect ethnomusicological presentation resembles that of the "hard sciences," or the social sciences at their most inhuman, rather than that of other "arts," and rejects both evaluation and, in general, popularization. The effect on the research process is to direct it towards the "acquisition of disinterested knowledge" rather than, say, the practical possibilities of developing traditional music in a twentieth-century context.

This concept of ethnomusicology as non-critical, non-evaluative (performers' evaluation of their own music is permissible only as part of the "data"), is itself based on a value-judgment to exclude values, and arises historically from a combination of the constraints imposed on ethnomusicologists by musicological, anthropological or linguistic training; music is regarded as patterned sound, as an aspect of behavior, and as a means of communication (or all three in varying proportions), research into which, since its concern is with *how* things are done rather than with *what* is done, aims to be "scientific" and to express itself in the "language of science." Moreover, under present situational constraints the ethnomusicologist is usually a scholar working outside his own culture, who would not only consider it presumptuous to attempt the practical task of evolving a new music from the old, but whose prime concern is with other academics or with similarly-oriented students within his own culture.

Despite the predominance of this approach, there would appear to be general agreement that music, like poetry, painting or film is a mode of human expression, even if what it expresses is not so readily "identifiable," and thus a *prima facie* case for examining the aims and methods of presentation adopted by specialists in these media in relation to those accepted *or rejected* in the study of music. If we find that, within the common field of expression, these include topics normally considered outside the ethnomusicologist's sphere of activity, it is pertinent to ask whether this is due to differences between the media concerned (sight v. sound, or sound v. words) or whether, through constraints of training, ethnomusicologists are not neglecting essential aspects of their study or failing in presentation. Obviously, a full comparison is outside the scope of this essay, but a brief glance through ethnomusicological articles over the last fifteen years reveals an exclusiveness typified by the absence of any reference to literature between Archer's eclectic plea for an "ecology of music" (1964), which would include "consumer reactions" in the manner of I. A. Richards, and Blum's specific citing of Mandelstam, Proust and Mayakowsky.[4]

Graham Hough's statement of the goals of literary scholarship—

> Criticism... both pays tribute to the autonomy of literature and defines an area where it can speak with special knowledge. But the autonomy of

> literature is relative; and there is another requirement that seems to impose itself. Criticism should be able to give some intelligible account of the relationship of literature to the social order (1970:57)–

stresses the need for a special discipline and echoes Seeger's more succinct axiom that a well-organized musical study entails not only the "area *in its contexts*" and "that area in itself" but the "integration of the two" (1961:77). At the same time, through use of the word "criticism," it suggests a difference of approach. Further examination shows this to be more a matter of terminology than of aims. If the literary scholar calls himself a "critic" (while the term "music critic" has specialized connotations), he nevertheless seeks for knowledge and understanding of his subject and to increase the appreciation of others.[5] T. S. Eliot, arguing that knowledge of the genesis of Wordsworth's Lucy poems is unnecessary, asks, "Does this account help me to understand the Lucy poems any better than I did before? For myself I can only say that a knowledge of the springs which released a poem is not necessarily a help towards understanding the poem" (1969:111-2). The point here is not the validity of Eliot's argument but the similarity of his aims–knowledge and understanding of the expressive medium, to which he brings his specialist training, and which he then seeks to convey to others.

Both musical and literary scholars have at some period succumbed to the lure of numeracy in attempts to become more "scientific," as if this were a virtue *per se* and not a means to an end. The statistical approach of counting the number of major seconds or minor thirds in a musical performance (Freeman and Merriam 1956) had a one-time direct parallel in those literary scholars who counted the number of times the words "blood" and "bloody" occurred in Shakespeare's *Macbeth.* While such activities increase our "knowledge" of the works in question, and a repetition of a particular interval doubtless produces a particular effect, just as continued harping on blood contributes to the atmosphere of Shakespeare's play, one may query their contribution to "understanding."

One may ask further why scholars writing about one of the expressive arts (music) express themselves in a terminology incomprehensible to non-initiates, while scholars writing about other expressive arts (literature, film) use words (*vide* Eliot above) which a non-specialist can understand. Does this difference lie in music or in musical scholars? Obvious important determinants are the choice (or lack of choice) of a potential "audience" and Seeger's dilemma of having to use words to communicate about sound (music) as opposed to having to use words to communicate about other words (literature). Yet it was Eliot who produced Sweeney's agonized cry, "I gotta use words when I talk to you," and, twenty years later, was still "trying to learn to use words." Are contemporary calls for statistics or a metalanguage in ethnomusicology an escapist solution, an attempted negation of our inability to cope with language by rejecting it?

Perhaps the problem should be approached from the viewpoint of recipient rather than code. Ethnomusicologists have spent considerable time cogitating on the means of communication, while constraints inherent in the overall situation, together with a "scientific" urge to avoid a subjective Toveyian synesthesia (see Herndon 1974:227-8, 239), have resulted in an esotericism verging on the incestuous, scholars writing only for other scholars; yet the question of "audience" has received little attention. Applied to Kolinski's analysis of melodic movement of the Madagascan *Zaodahy* song, which opens with the statement that "most conspicuous among the seven recurrent movements are two returning line up-pendulums, one comprising the upper pentachordal area G-A-B-C-D . . ., the other the lower pentachordal area F-G-A-B-C" (1976:9), Eliot's question may be rephrased: "Does this account help me to understand the *Zaodahy* song any better than I did before?" Presumably it helps Kolinski, at least in providing a means for comparing this particular aspect of a song with similar aspects of other songs, and, in his own terms, this is a valid enterprise. But its utility in helping third-year music students in Papua New Guinea to appreciate their own music was not readily apparent when I experimented with its usage. To paraphrase Wachsmann, Kolinski's method of analysis of melodic movement may be of universal application, but it is not necessarily of universal interest, or, if our goal is appreciation, of universal use.

I am not suggesting abandonment of present approaches for a nebulous popularization but that we investigate the possibilities of other and different levels of presentation *within* the context of promoting understanding, and in particular examine the effect of our choice of level on the research process; in short, that we should be aware not only of what we do and why we do it but for whom it is done, recognizing that the ethnomusicologist enters the field guided by his "cognitive map," in constructing which ultimate, if non-explicit, notions of presentation are one of the determinants which affect not only what he chooses to see and hear but the "chunking process" of information gathering that follows perception. It would be interesting to stage a revised Fogelson-Herndon experiment by commissioning, not an ethnomusicologist and an anthropologist to investigate the same culture, but two ethnomusicologists of similar training and background, one engaged in producing a Ph.D. thesis for the music department of a western university and the other with the task of writing a textbook for local secondary schools, and to compare the two accounts of the music! Uncontrollable differences in the variables affecting the participants before research would doubtless exacerbate divergence, but in the evolution of a scientific discipline, comparative studies of the ethnomusicologist in action are a necessary counterpart to Blum's proposed critical discussion of the history of the theoretical models he employs.

Perhaps the most difficult task in a dialectical approach is to discover the questions we do not ask, not because we consider them irrelevant, but because the constraints on our learning process preclude their formulation. In investigating the phenomenon of praise-singing in West Africa, for example, a scholar whose world view is formed under the ideological constraints of regarding music as an "art" may come to recognize it as a craft dependent on patron-client relationships within a highly stratified society, yet, because his personal programming includes an aversion to such sordid aspects of existence as economics, fail to appreciate that, without the prospect of monetary, or other, rewards, "music" would not exist. Even if he overcomes this omission, the idea of music as part of a commodity transaction ultimately reducible to a bare cash nexus may be so repugnant to his sensibilities (or, since he chose this field for research, so debilitating to his self-esteem) that he fails to question the local justification of the process as a means for redistributing wealth, even when his contextual data include the patron's air-conditioned Mercedes and the client's hovel, where the roof falls in after each storm. All ethnomusicological research is partial, but some is more obviously partial than others. Adorno's assertions of philosophy that "the authentic question will somehow always include the answer" and that such questions must be "shaped by experience, so as to catch up with experience" (1973:63) are pertinent to ethnomusicology only in so far as, in the course of our experience, we have come to terms with our personal constraints and are able to pose authentic questions.

Discussion of the *relationships* between the different stages of our model—the influence of future presentation and the effects of constraints derived from the preparatory period on the posing of questions in research—must be supplemented by recognition of all stages as *processes*, whose significance is realized not only in relation to each other but to that larger process which we call "history." From this viewpoint, Wachsmann's interest in the historical approach to African music (1971b), Blum's plea for "comparative studies of the social and historical circumstances in which human beings (including scholars) devise meaningful symbolic structures" (1975:221) and its non-contextual embodiment in Herndon's "herding" (1974) may be seen as pointers in a cumulative process towards ultimate understanding.

Conversely, while the past affects the present, it exists only as seen from the present. All research is contemporary. The ethnomusicologist's "now" may be no more than a shifting point in the overall process, yet, even in movement, it remains the point at which he operates, for it alone includes his totality of experience. He may, however, utilize that experience to transcend time through the postulation of an "artificial present" as Adorno, in his critique of Schoenberg and Stravinsky, makes deliberate use of a device which many ethnomusicologists adopt unconsciously as an unrecognized constraint.

Wachsmann's suggestion that we take as "music" those sound phenomena which seem to resemble what we are in the habit of calling music on our home ground (*supra.*), with its implicit assumption of a boundary separating certain sound phenomena from others, is raised to a methodological postulate, the positing of what Jameson calls "the covert hypothesis of... a moment of plentitude,... so that... for Adorno the work of Beethoven stands as a kind of fixed point against which earlier or later moments of musical history will be judged" (1971:38-9). By intruding at the outset to impose his own standard, a standard he justifies on historical evidence, the musical scholar provides himself with a conscious viewpoint for linking his hypothesis with "a dialectical vision of historical change, in which the various moments are articulated according to the various possible relationships between subject and object" (Ibid.).

To the arguments that it is not the scholar's business to "judge" and that, as a young discipline, ethnomusicology lacks historical studies, at least compared with western musicology, Adorno would doubtless have replied that we cannot avoid making judgments. Our decision to accept certain sound patterns and reject others, our preference for the study of the Javanese *gamelan* or Ganda xylophone to Wogeo flutes or the Morwa bullroarer are acts of choice, implicit judgments, the major difference lying in the extent to which we are conscious of what we do. As for the dearth of historical studies, this is an excuse, not a reason, and it is time we did something about it.

In the operation of his model, the ethnomusicologist studying non-literate peoples might well consider the postulation of such a moment of plenitude as that point in the evolution of traditional society when, in the opinion of informants, their culture embraced those ideals, which, except for isolated examples, exist only in attenuated form where western or other outside influence has not destroyed them completely. Against this could be set, consciously instead of as an implied, if ever-present, concept, a second moment in the historical process, the ethnomusicologist's awareness of his own culture, in such a way that the relati^nships between the two "are articulated according to the various possible relationships between subject and object" (Jameson 1971).

The process of my own studies of the Karimojong of northeastern Uganda may serve as an example of how this stage may be reached. At the time of field research, eleven years ago, my main concern was the investigation of "correlations between music and social structure" (Gourlay 1971:18) by testing Nketia's assertion that problems of context "may... be reflected in the very structure of the music" (1967:26), more specifically in musical performance, following Wachsmann's suggestion that "thinking of the relationship between leader and group leads us closer to the character of the performance than thinking in terms of the analysis of musical forms"

(1953:55). The problem was simplified in that the Karimojong have no musical instruments and all types of music—young men's cattle songs performed at a beer party, traditional ceremonial music of the four generation sets, the music of women's groups or children's songs—are antiphonal. This overall simplicity of structure provides the basis for a variety of leader-group relationships appropriate to the type of music, demonstrates the values of Karimojong society, and, in more recent terminology, conforms to their "cultural cognitive map." In ceremonial music stressing loyalty to the age-group at the expense of the individual, the group-chorus is continuous but ends with a long sustained tone during which the leader squeezes in his solo as rapidly as possible, the contrasting leader-group relationship being emphasized by pitting one small voice against a surrounding group of a hundred or so male singer-dancers. Conversely, in the men's beer party, held in a man's hut in the company of a dozen close friends, the leader, introducing a song of his own composition, is dominant. In performance the soloist begins with an "opening lead" which is taken up by the group and used as chorus; at any point he chooses, the leader may interrupt the singing of this with a two or four phrase solo, the group stops immediately and, on completion of the solo, begins the chorus again, only to be halted by a further solo. The process continues until the leader runs out of inventiveness and allows the group to complete a chorus, thereby ending the song, or a member of the group, "moved" by the music to begin one of *his* songs, gives a verbal cue (Gourlay 1972) and usurps the leadership, the former leader becoming one of the group-chorus.

Interplay between leader and group reveals a further dynamic in that, as the song progresses, a confident leader interrupts the group at earlier points in the performance, reducing the full four phrase chorus to three, two or even one (except that he more frequently demonstrates his powers by entering mid-phrase), while the group, quickly realizing that the solos include phrases comprising an indeterminate variable (e.g. the name of a person addressed) followed by a constant ("Come and see my ox!") take their "revenge" by joining in the repeated portion, thus turning two-thirds of the leader's "solo" into a second "chorus."

This dialectical leader-group relationship was of interest not only in itself but as a microcosm of social practice. The Karimojong are a semi-pastoral people inhabiting a harsh terrain, where lack of rainfall necessitates that, for the greater part of the year, young warrior-herdsmen drive huge herds of cattle further and further afield through the overgrazed bush in search of water, occasionally indulging in culturally-sanctioned cattle raids on their neighbors, the Jie or the Turkana, to add to their stocks, or defending themselves when raided in retaliation. This mode of existence necessitates the development of qualities such as endurance, courage and individual initiative, with raids conducted under the leadership of an agreed leader, who, his brief moment of glory over, reverts, like his counterpart at the beer party, to a status indistinguishable from other members of the group. At the same time, since uncontrolled individualism can lead to anarchy, young herdsmen, as members of the junior generation group, are subject to the collective rule of the senior group, the elders. Egalitarianism within each group is thus counterbalanced by a hierarchical inter-group relationship.

The correspondence between leader-group relationships in social structure, devised as a means of coping with their environment, and song-structure, both in the dichotomy between ceremonial communal songs and young men's cattle songs and in the complex dynamics of performance of the latter, was sufficiently striking to suggest that it was more than coincidence, that one could in fact be understood only in terms of the other, and both as "projections" of the Karimojong "cognitive map." It now seems to me, however, that, important as this assessment may be as a step in the research process, the significance of musical activity among the Karimojong may be given a further dimension by viewing it in terms of what it is *not*, by seeing it as one aspect of the overall totality of music-making in relation to another aspect, the contemporary western musical scene. The problem of postulating a moment of plenitude for the Karimojong is easier than for many peoples for, as the result of almost total isolation, the idea continues to pervade their thinking even today. Whatever the reality, all agree that every young male composes and owns at least one cattle-song, and that his standing in the community increases with the number of songs a man "makes" and with his skill in performance, as evaluated through a shared aesthetic; in short, music is not the prerogative of professionals or even of a specialized craft group, but accepted as a natural attribute of the human condition. Women, too, have their individual songs and children who are not old enough to compose "borrow" one from their father to escape the ridicule of being "songless," while, as members of recognized social groups, all men, women and children share the songs appropriate to that group, more specifically to the age-group to which the fact of birth has assigned them.

The significance of every man, woman or child as music-maker is immediately obvious when we turn to our own society, where the specialist dominates and the making of music, on the level of individual performance, is aptly symbolized by Peter Sellers' bathroom vocalist, expending his creative energy in a lugubrious performance of "All the things you are" against a crescendo barrage of knocks on the door. Is it coincidence that the western folk revival centers its performance on those two essentials of Karimojong music-making–a group of "friends" and a supply of beer? It is not merely a question of comparison, of producing a balance sheet of loss or gain with the passage of history, but of seeing one in terms of the other *in order to see it as it is.* No one will dispute the greater complexity of the symphony orchestra or the possibilities of expression it offers compared with the Karimojong cattle song, in performing which even the ubiquitous African drum is absent, and no one is suggesting that we exchange our western clothes for a cowhide cloak and take to the bush. At the same time, as Jameson points out, it is impossible to deny that "western polyphonic music is 'unnatural' precisely to the degree to which it has no institutional equivalent in any other culture," that, through a difference in kind rather than degree, it

> has developed an autonomy of its own . . . and requires its participants to suspend their other activities in the exercise of some alert but non-verbal mental capacity . . . with the conviction that something real is taking place during fifteen or twenty minutes of practical immobility (1971:12-13).

"Primitive" he may be, even in the eyes of his fellow Africans, but in music-making no Karimojong is ever immobile.

The concept of a world in which everyone makes music is obviously not everyone's ideal (and may be viewed by musicians' unions as a threat to their livelihood) but it provides a viable moment in applying a dialectical approach. If we make yet a further shift of viewpoint–from a past ideal to an imagined future–the subject gains yet another dimension. Schiller's words about the objects of nature, dismissed as sentimental echoes of Rousseau's "noble savage" by a hard-headed "scientific" generation, may yet demonstrate Karimojong wisdom. "They *are* what we *were*; they are what we must *become.* We were Nature, just as they are, and our culture must lead us back to Nature along the path of Reason and Freedom" (quoted Jameson 1971:114).

Unfortunately, one cannot go back, only forward, even if, in the long run, one arrives at the same place, and it is not culture, but economics, not reason and freedom but greed and environmental exploitation committed in the name of pseudo-freedom, that may force us "back." When the oil runs out, coal reserves are exhausted and solar energy discovered to be pie-in-the sky, the seas polluted with atomic waste and the lands so overpopulated that there is no room for crops, the Karimojong may yet have the last laugh, as they trudge round the periphery of their land in search of water, driving their cattle before them, and entertaining themselves with a new song to celebrate the mounds of useless motor-cars, the unplayable tapes of their own music rotting in the archives of the West, and a people who have recovered the use of their legs but forgotten how to sing.

NOTES

1. The "six areas" selected by Merriam are (1) "the musical material culture," i.e. musical instruments, to be investigated "in terms of the *recognized* taxonomy" (my stress) ("recognized" presumably by *the* scientific method, if not by the local inhabitants;

the Kagoro of Nigeria, for example, have yet to learn their "Sachs-Hornbostel" for they insist on grouping both side- and end-blown horns as *gughwa*); (2) song-texts, including "linguistic" and "literary behavior"; (3) categories of music, in accordance with which "the student orders his recording program"; (4) the musician, especially his training and social behavior, including that "required of an individual non-musician at a musical event"; (5) "the uses and functions of music in relation to other aspects of culture"; and (6) "music as a creative cultural activity," especially "the concepts held in the society under investigation." This outline is expanded to fill the greater part of the book.

2. A full socio-historical-musical, i.e. an ethnomusicological, account of the subject is outside the scope of this essay but would include (a) the beginnings of the study of local folk music as part of nineteenth-century nationalism; (b) "disinterested" research into African and Asian musics as the result of colonialism and a period of relative stability in Western society; (c) the questioning of the value of disinterestedness along with other values in the present period of social upheaval and the attempt to find practical solutions to problems of cultural identity or overcome alienation, e.g. interest in "Black" music, protest music, and the "folk" revival, etc.

3. The most effective method is probably to grapple with examples of dialectical thinking, e.g. pondering on Wachsmann's "continuum" until one suddenly "grasps" what he is getting at.

4. Merriam's short discussion of the inter-relationship of the arts (1964:273-6), like his accounts of synesthesia and symbolism with which it is linked, is concerned more with the assessment of results than examination of method.

5. Nettl's comments on this point are suggestive. Pointing out that "many ethnomusicologists believe" that they are "conditioned to too many prejudices and personal associations to be properly objective" in studying Western music (1964:8), he adds later that "the historian of Western music, being a member of the culture which he is studying has not always had to be concerned with objectivity, and the approach of the critic rather than the scholar is still felt in many of his publications" (1964:12). While the recognition that we have "prejudices," i.e. operate under constraints, is to be welcomed, the suggestion that they are somehow cancelled out when studying a "foreign" culture is somewhat facile, and the distinction between "critic" and "scholar," with its implication that the former is not "scholarly," requires modification. Granted that journalistic criticism of a concert performance or first night of a play, dashed off to meet a deadline, is not always scholarly, this hardly applies to book or record reviews of, say ETHNOMUSICOLOGY! Neither can literary "critics" of Eliot's caliber be excluded from the circle of "scholars." One wonders, in fact, what conception Nettl holds of the "scholar"—except that his work should be value-free, useless and (preferably) anemic!

REFERENCES CITED

Adorno, T. W.
1973 (1966) Negative Dialectics. Trans. Ashton, E. B. London: Routledge and Kegan Paul.

Archer, W. K.
1964 "On the ecology of music," ETHNOMUSICOLOGY 8:28-33.

Asch, M. I.
1975 "Social context and the musical analysis of Slavey Drum Dance Songs" ETHNOMUSICOLOGY 19:245-57.

Blacking, J.
1959 "Problems of pitch, pattern and harmony in the ocarina music of the Venda," African Music 2(2):15-23.

Blum, S.
1975 "Towards a social history of musicological technique," ETHNOMUSICOLOGY 19:207-31.

Boulton, L.
1937 "Address to the Royal Anthropological Institute, London," Man 37:No. 60.

Chase, G.
1958 "A dialectical approach to music history," ETHNOMUSICOLOGY 2:1-9.

Eliot, T. S.
1969 On Poets and Poetry. London: Faber and Faber.

Feld, S.
1974 "Linguistic models in ethnomusicology," ETHNOMUSICOLOGY 18:197-217.

Freeman, L. C. and Merriam, A. P.
1956 "Statistical classification in anthropology: an application to ethnomusicology," American Anthropologist 58:464-72.

Goldmann, L.
1969 The Human Sciences and Philosophy. Trans. White, H. V. and Anchor, R. London: Jonathan Cape.

Gourlay, K. A.
1971 Studies in Karimojong Musical Culture. Ph.D. thesis. Makerere University, Kampala.
1972 "The practice of cueing among the Karimojong of north-eastern Uganda," ETHNOMUSICOLOGY 16:240-7.

Gramsci, A.
1971 Selections from the Prison Notebooks. Ed. and trans. Hoare, Q. and Smith, G. N. London: Lawrence and Wishart.

Harwood, D. L.
1976 "Universals in music: a perspective from cognitive psychology," ETHNOMUSICOLOGY 20:521-33.

Herndon, M.
1971 "The Cherokee ballgame cycle: an ethnomusicologist's view," ETHNOMUSICOLOGY 15:339-52.
1974 "Analysis: the herding of sacred cows?," ETHNOMUSICOLOGY 18:219-62.
1976 "Reply to Kolinski: *Tarus Omicida*," ETHNOMUSICOLOGY 20:217-31.

Hough, G.
1970 "Criticism as a humanist discipline," *In* Bradbury and Palmer, eds., Contemporary Criticism. London: Edward Arnold.

Hymes, D.
1972 (1964) "Toward ethnographies of communication: the analysis of communicative events," *In* Giglioli, P. P. ed., Language and Social Context. Harmondsworth: Penguin.

Jameson, F.
1971 Marxism and Form. Princeton, New Jersey: Princeton University Press.

Kaeppler, A.
1971 "Aesthetics of Tongan dance," ETHNOMUSICOLOGY 15:175-85.

Kolinski, M.
1976 "Herndon's verdict on analysis; *Tabula rasa*," ETHNOMUSICOLOGY 20:1-22.

Lomax, A.
1968 Folk Song Style and Culture. Washington, D.C.: American Assoc. for the Advancement of Science, Publication No. 88.

Merriam, A. P.
1964 The Anthropology of Music. Evanston: Northwestern University Press.
1967 The Ethnomusicology of the Flathead Indians. Chicago: Aldine Publishing Co.
1969 "Ethnomusicology revisited," ETHNOMUSICOLOGY 13:213-29.

Nettl, B.
1964 Theory and Method in Ethnomusicology. New York: The Free Press of Glencoe.

Nketia, J. H. K.
1967 "Musicology," *In* Brokensha, D. and Crowder, M. (eds.) Africa in the Wider World: 12-35. London: Pergamon Press.

Seeger, C.
1961 "Semantic, logical and political considerations bearing upon research into ethnomusicology," ETHNOMUSICOLOGY 5:77-80.
1971 "Reflections upon a given topic: Music in universal perspective," ETHNOMUSICOLOGY 15:385-98.

Wachsmann, K. P.
1953 "Musicology in Uganda" Journal of the Royal Anthropological Institute 83:50-57.
1971a "Universal perspectives in music," ETHNOMUSICOLOGY 15:381-4.
1971b (ed.) Essays on Music and History in Africa. Evanston: Northwestern University Press.

Wiora, W.
1976 "Volksmusik und Musica Humana," Yearbook of the International Folk Music Council, 7:30-43.

STRUCTURALISM AND MUSICOLOGY: AN OVERVIEW

Patricia Tunstall

The past decade has witnessed a growing interest among musicologists in the kind of inquiry known as structuralist. Although structuralism originated as a theory and methodology specific to certain limited disciplines, its relevance to other fields has become increasingly apparent, and its principles and assumptions articulated in increasingly general terms. One of the major trends of twentieth-century thought, it has significant implications for musicology; indeed, some major musicological debates have involved ideas central to structuralist theory, although these ideas are seldom expressed in structuralist terms. It is helpful, therefore, to explore the historical development of that theory at some length —not in order to have new labels to pin on old debates, but to better understand the intellectual history to which those debates are related.

The scope of the subject matter and the limitations of space imposed here will often necessitate somewhat cursory accounts of highly complex fields. The intention of this paper is not, however, an in-depth examination of any single aspect of structuralism, but rather an introductory overview of its basic definitions and procedures.

Structuralism, a theory generated and developed primarily by western European scholars who are the direct inheritors of the Western intellectual tradition, has its philosophical antecedents in the rationalist schools of thought prominent in the seventeenth and eighteenth centuries. Such theorists as Descartes conceived of the thinking human being as inherently rational, and thus as the determining locus of knowledge and truth. Kantian theory was an elucidation of the rational categories that constitute the human mind. French social theorists as diverse as Rousseau and Diderot discussed social functioning from the standpoint of an underlying assumption of the rational nature of man's cognition. The rationalist premises of such figures were reflected not only in the contents but in the formulation of their theories, which involved deductive and speculative rather than inductive processes.

The first challenges to rationalist thought came from within philosophical discourse: empiricists such as Hume and Berkeley argued that the mind has no inherent rational order, but is a repository of the impressions transmitted from the outside world. The nineteenth century, however, brought more formidable challenges. For the first time, the Western tradition of speculation upon the nature of the self was forced into extensive contact with foreign cultures with alien versions of objective reality. Within western European culture itself, radically different world-views became evident. Never before had such conflicting modes of thought and life demanded recognition; now, however, classes with different social experience were coming into increasing power, and nations with unfamiliar cultures were entering the world economic arena. The evident differences between cultures could not be accounted for by the rationalist assumption of a universal identity of mental categories. The new theories developed to explain these differences were based on a new assumption, that of the determining power of environment. In addition, developments in biological science had implications for every field. Emerging theories of evolution provided a new model for understanding human experience in terms of historical progress.

The challenge to rationalism from realms outside of formal philosophical thought thus developed into a powerful and eventually dominant critique. The rationalist assumption that the source of knowledge was the inherent, rational categories of the mind found itself in increasing conflict with theories locating this source elsewhere: in social and cultural experience, in political organization, in historical identity, or in biological nature. Freudian theory, while sharing the rationalist's emphasis on the discovery of universal characteristics of the human subject, implied, however, a refutation of a major rationalist premise: when Freud examined the self, he found not immutable mind but immutable drives—an unconscious which was the very antithesis of reason.

Theorists in all fields, then, rejected the idea of the rational mind and turned to the investigation of other sources of meaning and intelligibility. These theories differed in method as well as object: no longer relying upon deductive elegance, they were couched in the terms of empiricist inquiry and based upon claims of scientific validity. These changes occurred in the emerging discipline of musicology as well as in other fields. Theories that musical processes were determined by universal, invariant mental operations were challenged by explanations of musical activity as conditioned by social, cultural, or historical forces.

It is significant that the discipline of linguistics, in which structuralism first emerged as a systematic theory, has a particularly strong tradition of rationalist ideas. During the late eighteenth century, the French school of "philosophical grammar" had evolved a theory of language based on rationalist premises. Described by one commentator as "the linguistic equivalent of Cartesianism,"[1] this school postulated the existence of more and less abstract levels of language, and a transformational process by which less abstract levels were generated out of more abstract ones. Early in the twentieth century, a Swiss linguist named Ferdinand de Saussure revived and developed this line of thinking. Language, he claimed, is a system with logical and autonomous laws. At a level of organization more abstract than what we normally call grammar, a language can be investigated as a set of logical operations. Saussure's seminal distinction was between individual acts of speech ("paroles") and the universe of linguistic conventions upon which individuals draw when they speak ("langue"). Linguistic analysis, therefore, was the investigation of speech in order to discover the organizational properties of language. Saussure stressed that language as a system is not the conscious possession of any individual; rather it is the totality of linguistic rules available in a society, "a sum of impressions deposited in the brain of each member of a community, almost like a dictionary of which identical copies have been distributed to each individual."[2] According to a common formulation, language is a kind of "code"; each instance of individual speech is a "message" constructed with reference to the code. Although the code is not apparent in surface characteristics of speech, and its users are not conscious of it, it can be extrapolated through structural analysis of the relations among elements of a series of messages.

These concepts deviated significantly from many of the social-scientific ideas prevalent at the time. In contrast to the current emphasis upon social context, Saussure's method was to isolate language from its social functions on the assumption that within the elements of language itself could be discovered its essential qualities. Second, Saussure's thesis that these qualities were logically coherent implied the then unpopular premise that the ordering activity of the mind is systematic. Third, in contradistinction to linguistic theories stressing the historical development of languages, Saussure emphasized the importance of non-historical studies, since the system of language accessible to any speaker exists entirely in the present.

The task of the structural analyst, according to Saussure, is to organize a mass of data—a collection of individual utterances—in such a way as to clarify the logical system that comprehends all of them. This involves a process of dismantling and reconstruction, since, in specific utterances, linguistic elements are arranged and distributed so as to obscure the systematic nature of their relations. The linguistic code is thus never deducible from one message. A collection of messages, however, may be broken down into component parts; these parts may then be used to construct a logical model in which their interrelations are explicit. Through the orderly rearrangement of speech elements the fundamental order of a language can be revealed.

Saussure's reconstructive model—adopted by most succeeding structuralists—involves two axes, the syntagmatic and the associative. The horizontal, syntagmatic axis represents "contiguous" relations—that is, how elements are arranged sequentially in speech. The vertical, associative axis represents "thematic" relations, or how elements refer metaphorically or symbolically to other elements. Thus, reading horizontally, the analyst can discover the conventions by which words are combined into a series in speech; vertical configurations will reveal the categories of sound and meaning by which words are classified in memory. Linguistic elements related syntagmatically can occur next to one another; those related associatively can replace one another.

The significance of this model is that it embodies a basic structuralist view of mental ordering activity: the mind can link elements together linearly (and can follow rules for doing so), and it can associate them categorically (again, according to given rules). Crucial to the model is a conception of the mind as active and of mental categories as operations, not ideas. The structure of language explored by Saussure is a complex of operational capacities, not a constellation of images. And it is this feature that makes languages comparable; if the deepest structure of a language is not a set of rules about particular words and grammars, but a set of formal procedures for dealing with all words and all grammars, then this is a level at which all languages may be compared.

Saussure postulated other comparisons as well. Language, he suggested, is only one of several systems of signs operating in society—such systems having fixed correspondences between "signifiers" and "signifieds." In language, the signifiers are sound-images such as words and syllables; its signifieds are the mental concepts indicated by those sound-images. Although language is perhaps the most important system of signs, there are others: "Language is a system of signs that expresses ideas, and is therefore comparable to a system of writing, the alphabet of deaf-mutes, symbolic rites, polite formulas, etc."[3] Any systematic cultural phenomenon is a system of signs, according to Saussure, if it is characterized by a one-to-one relation between each signifier and its signified, and if that relation is not open to individual decision but is fixed by social convention. Linguistics is therefore potentially a field within a general science of signs, which he called "semiology."

The first to respond to this suggestion was the French anthropologist Claude Levi-Strauss, whose work was decisive for the development of an interdisciplinary structuralist theory and practice. A scholar whose training encompassed both Western philosophical tradition and modern anthropological techniques, Levi-Strauss found in structuralism a way to synthesize his speculative inclinations and his respect for scientific methods. "For the first time," he wrote of structuralism, "social scientists are able to form necessary relations."[4] Working from Saussure's premise that other cultural phenomena were organized like language, he applied the structuralist analytic techniques outlined above to various cultural systems, such as totemistic practices, kinship conventions, and myth repertoires.

In the course of these studies, Levi-Strauss added important dimensions to structuralist theory. First of all, he found that the specific organizational structures discovered in one system of a culture will be similar to those discovered in another. Studies of a Brazilian Indian society provided persuasive evidence for this idea. His structuralist investigation of their myths revealed strong systematic relations between the seemingly random elements of the myths: when analytically reorganized, the images, events, and characters of the myths fell into consistent thematic categories (such as honey and tobacco, raw food and cooked food). These categories, in Levi-Strauss's view, were symbolic expressions of a fundamental opposition between nature and culture; and the operations performed upon these symbols in the process of myth generation represented attempts by the culture to render the opposition intelligible. Myths, therefore, were not irrational explanations of natural phenomena; they were logic systems using a vocabulary of natural phenomena to explain the world. Exploring other systems within the same culture, Levi-Strauss discovered that the fundamental categories underlying the elements of myth also underlay other areas of cultural expression. The ways those categories were manipulated within the myths were typical of logical operations governing other kinds of mental activity and understanding. He concluded that the categories and manipulations themselves constituted the structural habits of the culture, the set of cognitive properties underlying all of its various sign systems. The particular value of structuralist anthropology, therefore, was that one could discern the logical structures of a culture in any of its semiological phenomena. The patterns of organization characterizing one system would be the patterns operative in any other, and all systems would be susceptible to the structuralist method of clarifying those patterns.

Levi-Strauss was interested in a still higher level of generalization. He theorized that logic structures were not only consistent among cultural phenomena, they were, at the most abstract level, universal. The ultimate importance of ascertaining such logic structures was that they reflected properties of the human mind itself. The formal procedures through which the mind structured reality were common to all minds; the content manipulated by these procedures was culture-specific, but the procedures themselves were universal in character. All aspects of human experience, then, were governed at the most basic level by a limited number of operational categories inherent in the structure of the mind. In Levi-Strauss's view, these categories were principally binary in nature, such as juxtaposition, inversion, and opposition. It was the task of ethnographers to refine such views: "Ethnographic analysis," he declared, "must try to arrive at invariants beyond the empirical diversity of the human species."[5]

In the work of both Saussure and Levi-Strauss, an analytical process that begins by restricting itself to an isolated object has as its eventual aim the extrapolation of the structures imposed on reality by the mind. The initial exclusiveness of focus is only a preparation for a conclusion at the most general level. This conclusion will not be a hypothesis of universal conceptual, linguistic, or thematic categories; rather it will be a formulation of the organizational properties of the mind that characterize all of its operations.

The connection of this premise to the rationalist philosophical tradition is unmistakable: basic to Cartesian and Kantian theories alike was the notion that all minds operate with the same formal properties, and that these properties are definitively logical. Yet the structuralist theories of Saussure and Levi-Strauss represent a distinctively modern reformulation of this notion.

Seen in the context of Western intellectual history, structuralism is a set of principles neither precisely rationalist nor precisely corresponding to modern ideas of environmental determinism. Like modern social sciences, it proceeds by examining cultural phenomena; like modern natural sciences, it isolates sets of phenomena for purposes of study; but in its ultimate goal—the formulation of cognitive universals—it is close to its heritage of rationalist philosophy. From this heritage it takes the basic assumption of an inherent mental structure that determines experience and knowledge. But it shares with modern social-scientific thought an awareness of the important role of culture in determining specific knowledge and experience, and so postulates universals far more abstract, less bound to specific concepts, than those of philosophical rationalism. Like many modern theories, structuralism postulates decisive limits upon an individual's conscious capacity to choose his forms of thought and action, but it defines those limits as innate to cognition, not as learned. This definition allows it to rely, as did Cartesian thought, upon speculative and deductive analytical techniques; but unlike Cartesian thought, structuralism first depends upon empirical data-gathering and verifying procedures. Structuralism, then, may perhaps be understood as a modern reemergence of rationalist ideas informed and tempered by the insights of modern social, political, and scientific thought.

What is the relation of structuralism to musicology? In recent years an increasing number of musicologists have taken an interest in this question. The answers they propose vary widely both in method and goals, and are thus difficult to classify or summarize. All, however, begin with the assumption that the methods of structural linguistics are relevant to musicological endeavors in some way. An interesting background to this assumption is provided in a recent paper by Howard Serwer,[6] which contends that modern linguistic theory is very close to older music theory in its rationalist emphasis on "rigorous abstraction." Heinrich Schenker, writes Serwer, was the last musical theorist to resist the rise of a relativist, superstructural approach to musical analysis, and his conceptual tools were similar to those of modern linguistics. Schenker's terms for differing levels of abstraction in music—"background, middleground, foreground" —correspond to the common linguistic terms "deep structure" and "surface structure"; his use of the term "Verwandlung" to account for relations between these levels is close to the linguistic concept of transformation, whereby surface structures of speech are generated from the deep structures of language. This concept is suggested by Schenker's statement, quoted by Serwer, that in music there is "nothing truly new . . . only transformations extending themselves."[7] Serwer's conclusion echoes Levi-Strauss's own goal: "Like linguistics, music theory was and should be concerned with the rigorous definition and abstraction of those elements common to all music, that is, with universals."[8]

Structuralist approaches to music may be roughly divided according to the type of theoretical model used. Two models have been of particular interest to musicologists in recent years. The first of these has been influenced by the concept of semiology, the second more by the anthropologically oriented procedures of Levi-Strauss.

The school of thought that, borrowing Saussure's term for the science of signs, calls itself musical semiotics, or semiology, has assumed increasing prominence during the past decade. Two congresses of the Society for Ethnomusicology have devoted considerable attention to this topic; several books and many articles have appeared; and a 1973 conference in Belgrade devoted itself to the exploration of topics in musical semiology.

Musical semiologists undertake the study of music as a system of signs. They link their efforts explicitly with semiologists in other fields, who have applied structuralist techniques to sign systems as diverse as newspaper photographs, advertising images, the conventions of high fashion, and the literary form of the narrative; thus they consider their investigations as contributions to the developing science of semiology first proposed by Saussure. The techniques of semiology, writes Jean-Jacques Nattiez, constitute a "procedure peculiar to the science of man [i.e., not the natural sciences]."[9] Musical semiology is linked as well with the particular tendency in semiology, popular in recent years, to consider not only social systems but also works of art as systems of signs. Implicit—and often explicit—in this tendency is the assumption that artistic works are not so much acts of free and spontaneous individual creation as they are assemblages of socially meaningful signs.

The basic premises of musical semiologists are those of structuralist theory. In the structuralist tradition, they insist upon the isolation of music from its social functions in the initial stages of study. They proceed on the belief that, although individual musical utterances may appear unsystematic or idiosyncratic, all utterances refer to a systematic universe of musical categories for their constructive properties. And they rely on structuralist techniques to disclose the underlying relationships between every musical element and every other; most operate with some form of the dual-axis model developed by early structuralists. Often this model is modified or supplemented by concepts borrowed from more recent developments in structural linguistics. Nicolas Ruwet, for example, makes systematic use of the "taxonomic distributionist" theories of Zellig Harris in his analyses of Debussy songs; the model he uses for reorganizing the components of these songs make particular reference to Harris's principle of repetition as a primary category. Through this process Ruwet is able to plot the distribution of structurally similar elements in relation to one another. Ruwet's analysis is an exemplary structuralist one, notes John Blacking, because it "takes essentially musical features as the basis of meaning and thus as the focus of analysis."[10] More recently, Gilbert Rouget, Charles Boilès, and Sinha Arom, among others, have followed similar procedures in analyses of non-Western music.

One of the foremost practitioners of musical semiotics is Jean-Jacques Nattiez, who sees semiological investigation as a critical task of modern musicology. Nattiez advocates the structuralist analysis of musical works along the general lines of Saussurian procedure. Three principles in particular are singled out by Nattiez as crucial premises for a semiology of music.[11] First, Saussure's emphasis upon the isolation of language from its social contexts for purposes of study is applicable to music as well: Nattiez proposes that musical analyses focus upon showing the relations among the internal elements of musical objects. Second, Saussure's advocacy of the synchronic approach should be heeded. Traditional musicology has been hampered, in Nattiez's view, by its consistently historical perspective. Finally, musical semiology must adopt Saussure's essential distinction between "langue" and "parole." Nattiez's semiological models are constructed within the framework of these three principles, using the conventional set of syntagmatic/associative axes. To standard Saussurian terminology he adds the linguistic concept of "transformation," using the term to mean formal operations upon musical elements to yield structurally related ones.

Nattiez suggests that further modifications of traditional structuralist methods are necessary to meet the specific exigencies of musical analysis. Every musical work, he postulates, has three manifestations: it is written, performed, and heard. Therefore each work constitutes not one but three "paroles"; and semiological investigation must acknowledge all three. Models must therefore be constructed not only of the work as it presents itself to the analyst, but also of the work as heard by the listener (the "aesthetic" pole) and the work as perceived by the composer (the "poietic" pole). Semiological analysis consists not of one reconstruction but of a series of rewritings. Only through such a series will the structural characteristics of a musical system be made clear. Nattiez sometimes seems to suggest that all three poles constitute the proper object of analysis for musical semiologists; at other times, he implies that the aesthetic and poietic dimensions should be assigned to other disciplines.[12] The latter view is reiterated by Otto Laske, who has proposed the development of another discipline, "psychomusicology," to account for these dimensions.[13]

Nattiez has argued that musical semiology differs from traditional music analysis principally in its degree of methodological rigor. In his view, traditional analysis is weak because it is not scientific; it is "merely intuitive and lacks organization; it cannot be considered a form of scientific knowledge."[14] The solution offered by semiotics is the development of a metalanguage, a collection of entirely abstract symbols with which to build structural models of music. Only with the establishment of such a language can musical analysis "acquire scientific standards: formulated on an explicit and repeatable division into units, it becomes exhaustive in a way that sets it apart irrevocably from the stylistic dissertations of traditional analysis."[15] Nattiez cites the theory of structural linguist Noam Chomsky that this model can be a kind of "generative grammar," exhaustive enough that an analyst can generate legitimate specific utterances according to its rules. With a comprehensive metalanguage and adequate models, believes Nattiez, semiology will have truly deductive verification procedures at its disposal.

Concomitant with the emergence of musical semiology has been a developing interest in structuralism among musicologists who do not use the term "semiology" to describe their work. These musicologists often refer to Levi-Strauss rather than directly to linguistic theories; their interests are often stimulated by Levi-Strauss's general anthropological orientation and by his specific hypothesis that music, like myth, is a supremely appropriate object for structuralist attention. Articles by Arden Ross King,[16] Gilbert Chase,[17] and Pandora Hopkins,[18] among others, have set forth descriptions and critical reviews of Levi-Strauss's expressed ideas on music. These articles outline his premise that music and myth are analogous because both are intelligible but untranslatable, and while each takes specific forms in specific cultures, both have fundamental structural characteristics that particularly illuminate cognitive principles of order. Hopkins and King express an uncertainty about the appropriateness of structuralist methodology for ethnomusicological analysis. Writes Hopkins, "Levi-Strauss has indeed found a convincing example [in "Bolero"] for proving the essential structural character of music. However, his contention that every musical work contains within it a resolution of conflicts is questionable."[19] But Hopkins concludes that Levi-Strauss "has made it possible to compare classificatory systems (and therefore patterns of thought) that have traditionally been considered . . . not comparable. . . . Thus Levi-Strauss's concepts are liberating."[20]

One of Levi-Strauss's most prominent musicological converts is Gilbert Chase, who finds the work of the structural anthropologist of central importance to the development of musicology. In a recent lecture,[21] Chase focused upon the structuralist assumption that the properties of an object must be analysed in terms of the relations among its elements, with the goal of understanding the operations performed on them; this focus, in Chase's view, is critical for all musical analysis. Chase is particularly interested in the work of Jean Piaget, who incorporates a notion of development and feedback through time into the static Levi-Straussian formulation. Piagetian structuralism allows for a cybernetic dimension to structuralist analysis—a diachronic as well as a synchronic model.

The work of John Blacking has been perhaps the most significant response to Levi-Strauss's recommendation for a study of music analogous to his study of myth. Blacking's understanding of the relation between universal and cultural determinants of knowledge is close to the structuralist view. "Artistic forms," he writes, "are produced by a synthesis of given universal systems of operation and acquired cultural patterns of expression."[22] Blacking's frequent references to "contextual" and "non-musical" phenomena do not signify a theory of environmental determinism; they express rather a conviction that musical principles of organization are the same as principles of organization in other areas. *How Musical Is Man?* is not an explicitly structuralist work, but it displays a strongly structuralist emphasis on the relation of internal musical structure to the internal structure of non-musical phenomena. "Attention to music's function in a society," he writes, "is necessary only insofar as it may help us to explain the structures."[23] The book shares with structuralist thought an ultimate interest in the implications of musical structure for human cognitive structure. Blacking criticizes the ethnomusicological tendency to "produce program notes outlining the context of the music" rather than an "analytic device describing its structures as expressive of cultural patterns."[24]

What sets Blacking apart from this tendency is, most clearly, a difference in goal: "functionalist" ethnomusicologists study the social context of music to illuminate the function of music in society, whereas Blacking studies this context to discover how it activates musical structures. Because the musical processes in a culture formally replicate others of its processes, the terms used for musical analysis should be logical and not specifically musical, applicable to other processes. It is ethnomusicology's responsibility to generate such analytic tools. Thus Blacking's emphasis on culture is a structuralist one; he is interested not in social rules about music, but in the "relationships between the rules of systems of musical and social communication."[25]

Both of the structuralist-oriented approaches to music outlined above share several basic premises and methods. They concentrate on the arrangements of internal musical elements and assume that these arrangements are systematic. They focus initial efforts upon the musical object itself, using logical categories as the terms of analysis. In the writings of both Nattiez and Blacking, the development of more abstract analytical language is emphasized as an essential task of musicology.

For several theorists, the tools and concepts of semiology have been considered useful as a model for a musical structuralism. However, the reliance upon semiology as it has been developed in other fields of analysis raises central difficulties. As a rule, semiologists take from Saussure the definition of semiology as the science of signs, and the definition of a sign as the existence of a one-to-one relation between a signifier and a signified. The application of the latter definition to music reawakens a long-standing issue in music aesthetics: what kinds of things are "signified" by the elements of music? Many hypotheses have been suggested by those interested in semiological research.[26] David Osmond-Smith writes that the term "semiotics" should perhaps be used in reference to the specific semantic meanings sometimes found in music, such as an instrumental imitation of a non-musical sound.[27] Sociological analyses offer a definition for the meaning of music closely allied with its social functions.[28] The semiologist Roland Barthes claims that the elements of aesthetic objects carry connotations as well as denotations: the signifieds of such objects therefore include both semantic and ideological meanings.[29]

However, no agreement seems to exist among musical semiologists about the definition of music's signifieds. Nattiez, for example, rejects all the kinds of meanings cited above. He declares that semiology is not the study of "the expressive, semantic aspect of music";[30] neither is it the determination of "the connections between certain sonorous combinations and certain social structures."[31] In Nattiez's view, these purposes rule out the level of scientific rigor that, for him, is the distinguishing feature of semiological inquiry. The work of Roland Barthes he finds particularly unscientific: "he gives the illusion of science to a procedure that is nothing other than the course of traditional hermeneutics."[32] According to Nattiez, semiotics must entirely disregard the question of music's meanings, and investigate only the internal arrangements of its elements.

If this is the case, however, the usefulness of semiological procedures as they have been developed in other fields is called into question. Semiological investigations of other art forms are usually undertaken with attention to the semantic as well as the syntactical properties of artistic elements. It is, in fact, precisely the existence of *both* kinds of properties that makes these investigations illuminating. A semiological analysis of a work of art or literature entails a structural reorganization of its formal elements, but that reorganization is accomplished with reference to semantic meanings; the reinterpretation of relations among elements depends partially upon the semantic associations of those elements. Works of literature or art are seen to involve meaning on several different levels—syntactical, semantic, connotative—and these levels must be considered in relation to each other. Semantic meanings may reveal implicit syntactical connections, for example; conversely, discovery of syntactical connections may reveal implicit semantic meanings. The analytic task is thus a charting of the structural relations among different levels of meaning. The organizational patterns of signifiers, in other words, are examined with reference to signifieds. The conclusions of semiological inquiries often rely upon such references.

Musical analysis, however, cannot rely upon a systematic reference to signifieds in its investigation of signifiers. Music seems to involve primarily syntactical, not semantic, relations; it does not exhibit a systematic one-to-one correspondence of each specific musical element with a specific non-musical meaning. According to Saussure's definition, then, music must be considered not a system of signs but a system of signifiers without signifieds. Therefore musical analyses can make only limited use of the particular virtues of the semiological approach.

This is not to say that musical structuralism is unviable, but that semiological models may not be its most useful tools. Although musical elements do not have semantic meanings, their organizational patterns may have extra-musical significance. The general goal of all structuralist endeavor is to examine the structural characteristics of objects in order to form hypotheses about the structural categories of cultures and the structural procedures of the human mind. Musical structuralism implies that such examinations do not necessarily have to involve semantic components; music's value for structuralism may lie precisely in the fact that it is *not* semantic. Its unique feature is that it lacks the kinds of meanings that semiological techniques are designed to investigate, but does not lack the kinds of significance with which structuralism is ultimately concerned. Its elements are not signs, but the relations between them are coherent and meaningful. It is these relations themselves, the formal operations performed upon sonorous elements, that are the essence of musical structure. Perhaps, then, that structure is a uniquely lucid and unmediated reflection of the formal operations of cognition.

Levi-Strauss was one of the first to suggest that music's "intelligible but untranslatable" nature makes it especially important for structuralism. As a sensuous manifestation not of concepts but of operations, music provides an unusually clear demonstration of the basic ordering processes of the mind. Unclouded by semantic associations, the procedures of music reflect not the mind's ideas but only its activities. It is thus an eminently appropriate object for an inquiry concerned with the nature of mental activity itself.

It is perhaps significant that Blacking does not invoke specifically semiological concepts and models; his work allows for the potential development of new concepts and models suited for the analysis of the uniquely abstract kinds of meaning found in music. Like Levi-Strauss, Blacking finds that music involves a synthesis of immanent, untranslatable structuring activity with culturally particularized forms. The analysis of musical structure may therefore be most fruitful for an understanding of mental structures and for the ways such structures emerge within specific cultures. Suggests Blacking, "Music may express the quintessence of a society's socio-conceptual structure and hence serve as a kind of litmus paper for structuralist analysis."[33] Blacking enriches structuralist thought with a new formulation of the concept of "transformation," suggesting that musical transformations reveal the precise connections between universal logical processes and culturally specific ones. Musical transformations occur, argues Blacking, in relation to social experience: the capacity for transformation may be universal, but is only activated under the stimulation of social phenomena. "By observing the patterns of social interaction which mediate between the innate structure of the mind and its extensions in culture, ethnomusicology can demonstrate the affective, social basis of musical transformations."[34]

In conclusion, musical analysis may be most enlightened by those structuralist principles that are *not* specifically borrowed from semiological endeavors in other fields. The application to music of a science of signs may eventually yield disappointing results: this science is oriented towards a kind of extramusical significance that music may not have and, when divorced from that orientation, may not yield substantially enlightening analyses. The structuralist interest in basic logical processes, on the other hand, invites a search for other kinds of extramusical significance, and this search may prove more rewarding. By bringing to musical analysis a desire to illuminate the rational character of musical processes, and to speculate upon the extramusical implications of those processes, a structuralist musicology will link its premises and goals to the traditions of its philosophical antecedents. This emphasis upon the cognitive dimensions of musical activity may provide new insights both about cognition and about music.

NOTES

[1] Howard Serwer, "New Linguistic Theory and Old Music Theory," in *International Musicological Society: Report of the Eleventh Congress; Copenhagen, 1972*, 2 vols. (Copenhagen: Wilhelm Hansen, 1974), 2:653.

[2] Ferdinand de Saussure, *Course in General Linguistics*, trans. Wade Baskin (New York: McGraw-Hill, 1959), p. 19.

[3] Ibid., p. 16.

[4] As quoted in Hayes, ed., *Levi-Strauss: The Anthropologist as Hero* (Boston: MIT Press, 1970).

[5] Ibid., p. 23.

[6] Serwer, pp. 652-57.

[7] Ibid., p. 655.

[8] Ibid., p. 654.

[9] Jean-Jacques Nattiez, "Sur les relations entre sociologie et semiologie musicales," *International Review of Aesthetics and Musical Sociology* 5 (1974):62.

[10] John Blacking, "Review Essay," *Ethnomusicology* 20 (1976):599. For Ruwet's analysis see his *Langue, Musique, Poesie* (Paris: Sevil, 1972).

[11] Jean-Jacques Nattiez, "Linguistics: A New Approach for Musical Analysis," *International Review of Aesthetics and Musical Sociology* 4 (1973):54-56.

[12] Nattiez, "Sur les relations," p. 63.

[13] Otto Laske, "Verification and Sociological Interpretation," *International Review of Aesthetics and Musical Sociology* 8 (1977):211-37.

[14] Nattiez, "Linguistics: A New Approach," p. 65.

[15] Ibid., p. 64.

[16] Arden Ross King, "Review Essay," *Ethnomusicology* 18 (1974):101-11.

[17] Gilbert Chase, "Review Essay," *Yearbook of the International Folk Music Council* 4 (1972):152-57.

[18] Pandora Hopkins, "The Homology of Music and Myth," *Ethnomusicology* 21 (1977):247-62.

[19] Ibid., p. 256.

[20] Ibid., p. 259.

[21] Gilbert Chase, "Structuralism and Music," in *Two Lectures in the Form of a Pair*, Institute for Studies in American Music, no. 2 (New York: I.S.A.M., 1973), pp. 20-37.

[22] John Blacking, *How Musical is Man?* (Seattle: University of Washington Press, 1973).

[23] Ibid., p. 26.

[24] Ibid., p. 30.

[25] Idem, "The Existence and Limits of Musical Transformations," paper delivered to the Society for Ethnomusicology Congress, Toronto, 1972, p. 4.

[26] For a thorough discussion of music and language as objects of semiological research, see Rose Rosengard Subotnik, "The Cultural Message of Musical Semiology: Some Thoughts on Music, Language, and Criticism since the Enlightenment," *Critical Inquiry* 4 (1978):741-68.

[27] David Osmond-Smith, "Music as Communication: Semiology or Morphology?," *International Review of Aesthetics and Musical Sociology* 2 (1971):108-11.

[28] See for example K. P. Etzkorn, "On Music, Social Structure and Sociology," *International Review of Aesthetics and Musical Sociology* 5 (1974):43-49.

[29] Roland Barthes, *Elements of Semiology*, trans. Annette Lavers and Colin Smith (New York: Hill and Wang, 1967).

[30] Nattiez, "Sur les relations," p. 61.

[31] Ibid., p. 71.

[32] Ibid., p. 67.

[33] Blacking, "The Existence and Limits," p. 6.

[34] Ibid., p. 9.

Alan P. Merriam

African Musical Rhythm and Concepts of Time-reckoning*

The thesis of this paper is that most scholars—both Western and African—who have studied rhythm in African music have consistently made several unacknowledged basic assumptions which have shaped the nature both of the work done and the results achieved. The most fundamental of these assumptions concerns the nature of time-reckoning as it is usually conceived in the West, as opposed to the way it seems to be conceived in Africa. I am thus simultaneously concerned with the assumptions, the "facts" of African musical rhythm as they are broadly accepted by the scholarly community, and the possible results of applying different concepts of time-reckoning in analysis.

I have elsewhere called attention to the four most important of these assumptions, and thus need repeat them only briefly here.[1] The first is the assumption of an "equal pulse base," i.e., the Western conceptualization of time as a linear structure consisting of an infinite series of equally spaced pulses; it is this notion of time which will be the focus of this essay. The second derives from the first; that is, such a conception of time leads us easily to the further assumption of an implied steady musical beat which provides the framework upon which rhythm is built. This, in turn, suggests the notions of meter, measures with their accompanying

*Grateful acknowledgment is made to Ivan Karp and Jean E. Meeh Gosebrink for bibliographic assistance, to Judith Becker and Wyatt MacGaffey for permission to quote from their unpublished works, and to Valerie C. Merriam for her constructive criticism.

[1] "Traditional Music of Black Africa," in *Introduction to Africa*, ed. Patrick O'Meara and Phyllis Martin (Bloomington: Indiana University Press, 1977), pp. 243-58.

bar lines, accent, and downbeat, and all this leads, finally, to the notion of multiple, or simultaneous meters. The third assumption arises from the nature of African musical rhythm itself; given its undeniable complexity, scholars have made the assumption that a basic organizing principle must be present, either tangibly or intangibly, which holds together the various rhythmic streams and centralizes them into a single, regularly pulsating unit. And fourth, most of these assumptions demand that we be able to locate a specific starting point for rhythmic groupings–in other words, some concept of "beat one" must be present. All these conjectures depend in one way or another upon the first one, which is the view of time as a coordinate straight line of equal pulses.

Effective discussion of the problems involved depends upon some knowledge of one of the most basic and difficult problems of cross-cultural research, whether musical or not. This concerns the distinction between the insider's and the outsider's views of a particular phenomenon, for the two are by no means the same, and the researcher looks for, and reaches, different kinds of conclusions depending on whether he is approaching his problem from one or the other viewpoint, or from a combination of the two. The distinction has been expressed in many ways, ranging from Bohannan's "folk organization" and "analytical organization"[2] to the now widely used "emic-etic" dichotomy. Harris is primarily responsible for the transfer of the latter set of linguistic concepts to ethnology; he defined the two as follows:

> Emic statements refer to logico-empirical systems whose phenomenal distinctions or "things" are built up out of contrasts and discriminations significant, meaningful, real, accurate, or in some other fashion regarded as appropriate by the actors themselves.[3]
>
> Etic statements depend upon phenomenal distinctions judged appropriate by the community of scientific observers.[4]

In other words, the two kinds of statements proceed from different premises and arise from differing obligations. The "folk" or "emic" evaluation is the explanation and rationale given by the people themselves for their actions, while the "analytical" or "etic" evaluation is applied by the outsider and based upon his broad comparative prior knowledge. Thus, in simple terms, an African musician may visualize a certain type of music in his society as

[2]Paul Bohannan, *Social Anthropology* (New York: Holt, Rinehart, and Winston, 1963), pp. 10-11; see also Alan P. Merriam, *The Anthropology of Music* (Evanston: Northwestern University Press, 1964), pp. 31-32.

[3]Marvin Harris, *The Rise of Anthropological Theory: A History of Theories of Culture* (New York: Thomas Y. Crowell, 1968), p. 571.

[4]Ibid., p. 575.

existing for its entertainment value, while the analyst views it as contributing to the cohesion and stability of that particular group of people.

It is not difficult to see both that confusion of the two approaches can lead to disastrous results, and that each involves its own sets of problems. Emically, the investigator is faced with a wide variety of interpretations of phenomena into which he hopes to be able to insert some kind of etic order and understanding, but the latter is according to his own interpretation which, in turn, is based upon suppositions of his own culture. Further, cross-cultural definitions are often particularly difficult to achieve in connection with the arts,[5] thus compounding the problems. But it is the nature of the distinctions with which we are concerned here: on the one hand, we may be attempting to understand African musical rhythm from the Africans' point of view or, on the other, we may wish only to understand it as we perceive it from the outside. Both approaches have been used, and it is in these two contexts that I will discuss African musical rhythm and concepts of time-reckoning.

Time from the Western Point of View

The intricacies of understanding time as a conceptual, physical, and phenomenological entity in Western terms are legion, and I have no intention of attempting to deal with them here.[6] Rather, I wish to explore briefly the general nature of one aspect of time as we commonly view it in the West. Time for us is essentially linear; that is, it is viewed as a series of equally spaced pulses which are thought to extend infinitely both backward and forward from the particular time point at which we are thinking. Thus, as Evans-Pritchard has put it:

> European time is a continuum. Whatever point we start at, each succeeding generation increases the distance from that point. Our grandfathers were nearer to 1066 than our fathers and our fathers were nearer to 1066 than we are.[7]

[5] Alan P. Merriam, "Definitions of 'Comparative Musicology' and 'Ethnomusicology': An Historical-Theoretical Perspective," *Ethnomusicology* 21 (1977): 189-90.

[6] See, for example, Leonard W. Doob, *Patterning of Time* (New Haven: Yale University Press, 1971); Dale F. Eickelman, "Time in a Complex Society: A Moroccan Example," *Ethnology* 16 (1977): 39-55; Martin P. Nilsson, *Primitive Time-reckoning* (Lund: C.W.K. Gleerup, 1920); and David F. Pocock, "The Anthropology of Time-reckoning," in *Myth and Cosmos*, ed. John Middleton (Garden City, N.Y.: Natural History Press, 1967), pp. 303-14.

[7] E.E. Evans-Pritchard, "Nuer Time-reckoning," *Africa* 12 (1939): 212-13.

In his remark, Evans-Pritchard has noted not only the linear nature of our time-reckoning but also our conceptualization of it in terms of distance—events move "toward" and "away" from us in time. Furthermore, we think of time essentially in terms of repetition, and Leach has noted in this connection that "whenever we think about measuring time we concern ourselves with some kind of metronome; it may be the ticking of a clock or a pulse beat . . . but always there is something which repeats."[8] This repetition, in turn, is evenly divided into equal units, and this equality is important—a second is a second and precisely equal to any other second which has ever occurred or will ever occur. This is not true, of course, in the relativistic notion of time introduced by Einstein, but most Westerners do not understand the Einsteinian concept of time and do not use it. A further point to be noted is the infinite quality of time, which is what makes it linear—so far as we know, these equal pulses of time have always gone on, and they will always continue. Finally, returning to Leach's comment, we are accustomed to measuring time, as opposed to counting time. Bohannan has commented:

> We in Western Europe have elicited an idea, or a medium, which we call "time"—or better, "chronology"—and have calibrated it into a standard gauge against which we associate single events or a series of events. The presence of such a time gauge . . . means that . . . we measure time.
>
> A minute and a day are qualitatively as well as quantitatively different: the difference is that between measuring and counting. Days are natural events and can be counted without a special apparatus; minutes and hours are artificial events . . . and can be counted only with the aid of special apparatus.[9]

The special apparatus, of course, began with the general 17th-century introduction of clocks and watches into Western society and has moved steadily since then toward more and more complex devices. Two quantitative processes have been used to measure time. One is the concept of dynamical time which is based on the laws of motion and gravitation published by Isaac Newton in 1687, while the other, electromagnetic time, is based on the laws of electricity promulgated by James Clerk Maxwell in 1864. Dynamical time involves the motions of material bodies, whereas electromag-

[8]Edmund R. Leach, "Two Essays Concerning the Symbolic Representation of Time," in *Rethinking Anthropology*, London School of Economics Monographs on Social Anthropology no. 22, ed. Edmund R. Leach (London: Athlone Press, 1961), p. 125.

[9]Paul Bohannan, "Concepts of Time Among the Tiv of Nigeria," *Southwestern Journal of Anthropology* 9 (1953): 262.

netic time does not, but both are measurements of linear time.[10]

I am aware that other ways of contemplating time do exist in Western society, but the linear system which views time as a repetitive succession of equally spaced pulses which have no beginning and no end and which function as a device for measuring is the most common among the most people. And this is also the way we view rhythm in music: a time framework exists for us within which we cast meter, pulse, isometric forms, and so on, and against which we cast syncopation, offbeating, "irregular" rhythms, and heterometric forms. Indeed, without the concept of an equal pulse base, the latter terms could have no meaning.

African Musical Rhythm Viewed From the Western Time Concept

Given this conception of time, what can be said about Western analyses of African musical rhythm? In the first place, an exception must be made for music in free rhythm, the presence of which is admitted by all scholars. It must also be noted that when speaking of "Western" analysis, I am including those African scholars, such as Nketia, Eno Belinga, Bebey, Cudjoe, and others, whose approaches, insofar as time is concerned, do not vary significantly from those of their Western colleagues.

With all this in mind, the fact is that the Western analytic, etic, or outside time concept fits very well with African music as heard and described by virtually all researchers.

Almost everyone who has written about African musical rhythm speaks in one way or another of a steady time pulse. Thus Blacking notes an "underlying 'pulse'," and "almost metronomic tempo" in the music of two girls' initiation schools of the Venda,[11] and A.M. Jones speaks of the "absolute exactness of his [the African's] time-keeping."[12] This steady pulse is described by more than one author as strictly duple, and thus Ekwueme writes: "We can then say that the background of the bulk of most African musical rhythm is a duple statement or pulsation"[13] and that we can speak of an "inherent pulse," for "... behind each rhythm pattern, lies a regular steady duple pulse dividing the whole pattern in a binary balance, whether or not the initial points of both

[10] *Encyclopedia Britannica*, 15th ed., s. v. "Time."

[11] John Blacking, "Tonal Organization in the Music of Two Venda Initiation Schools," *Ethnomusicology* 14 (1970): 5, 9.

[12] Arthur M. Jones, *Studies in African Music*, 2 vols. (London: Oxford University Press, 1959), 1:38.

[13] Laz E.N. Ekwueme, "Structural Levels of Rhythm and Form in African Music with Particular Reference to the West Coast," *African Music* 5, no. 4 (1975/76): 28.

halves are acoustically stressed."[14] Some years ago, Waterman introduced the concept of the metronome sense, which he explained as follows:

> From the point of view of the listener, it entails habits of conceiving any music as structured along a theoretical framework of beats regularly spaced in time and of co-operating in terms of overt or inhibited motor behavior with the pulses of this metric pattern whether or not the beats are expressed in actual melodic or percussion tones.[15]

Nketia has spoken of the "regulative beat"[16] and the "basic pulse,"[17] explaining that

> The listener or dancer must . . . be able to discover the regulative beat or basic pulse from the rhythmic structure that emerges in the performance.
>
> Because of the difficulty of keeping the subjective metronomic time in this manner, African traditions facilitate this process by externalizing the basic pulse . . . . The guideline which is related to the time span in this manner has come to be described as a *time line*.[18]

The "time line" is usually expressed by an instrument which has a penetrating or carrying tone, such as a gong, bell, small drum, or rattle, and as long ago as 1927, W.E. Ward spoke in such terms when he suggested that a single drum—the biggest if more than one were being used—played regularly in duple time: "This deep booming regular beat is the fundamental beat of the piece, and sets the time for all the other rhythms and instruments."[19] A.M. Jones pointed out handclapping, if present, as the indicator, and concluded that

> an African song which has a clap is constructed so that either 2 pulses or 3 pulses go to one clap right through the songs, irrespective of word division, word accent, or melodic accent. The claps do not indicate any sort of stress; their function is to act as an inexorable and mathematical background to the song.[20]

[14]Ibid., p. 30.

[15]Richard A. Waterman, "African Influence on the Music of the Americas," in *Acculturation in the Americas*, Proceedings of the 29th International Congress of Americanists, vol. 2, ed. Sol Tax (Chicago: University of Chicago Press, 1952), p. 211.

[16]J.H. Kwabena Nketia, *African Music in Ghana* (Evanston: Northwestern University Press, 1963), p. 64.

[17]*The Music of Africa* (New York: W.W. Norton and Co., 1974), p. 131.

[18]Ibid.

[19]William E. Ward, "Music in the Gold Coast," *Gold Coast Review* 3 (1927): 217.

[20]Arthur M. Jones, "African Rhythm," *Africa* 24 (1954): 28.

A considerable portion of the research on African musical rhythm has been carried out among peoples of the West African coastal area, particularly in the present country of Ghana, where a gong, usually identified as *gankogui*, "provides a background rhythm which keeps the whole orchestra in time."[21] The West African gong has also been described as "a common focal point,"[22] the "time keeper,"[23] and in other similar terms.

This assumption of a steady basic pulse is expressed in slightly different ways in tablature notation systems suggested for African musical rhythm by Serwadda and Pantaleoni,[24] as well as Koetting,[25] all of whom divide their graphs visually, and thus aurally, into segments of equal size which represent time. Koetting also makes the determination of "the fastest pulse" the keystone to his system,[26] and a "fastest pulse" requires a "steady pulse" for its conception: this idea has been picked up by a number of other writers such as Knight for use in their tablature systems.[27]

Pantaleoni has spoken of the basis of his notation system as the equal division of spans of time.

> Dividing a span of time may well be the fundamental orientation of the rhythmic process here transcribed. Certainly there is no evidence in our small sample to contradict such an interpretation . . . .
>
> To say we feel a pulse is to say we expect the equal spacing of a series of events to continue. It is not just a question of hearing or having heard such spacing; pulse involves the psychological state of anticipating its continuation. The play of *sogo* [a drum used among Ewe speakers of southeastern Ghana] . . . generated and sustained from beginning to end this kind of expectation.[28]

Only two writers seem to have deviated from this widespread endorsement of the presence of a steady and even pulse base, and in both cases the variations appear either to be minute or not to

[21]Jones, *Studies*, 1:53.

[22]Nketia, *African Music in Ghana*, p. 101.

[23]J.H. Kwabena Nketia, "Traditional Music of the Ga People," *African Music* 2, no. 1 (1958):21; and S.D. Cudjoe, "The Techniques of Ewe Drumming and the Social Importance of Music in Africa," *Phylon* 14 (1953):282.

[24]Moses Serwadda and Hewitt Pantaleoni, "A possible Notation for African Dance Drumming," *African Music* 4, no. 2 (1968):47-52.

[25]James Koetting, "Analysis and Notation of West African Drum Ensemble Music," *Selected Reports* 1, no. 3 (1970):116-46.

[26]Ibid., p. 125ff.

[27]Roderic Knight, "Towards a Notation and Tablature for the Kora and Its Application to Other Instruments," *African Music* 5, no. 1 (1971):31-32.

[28]Hewitt Pantaleoni, "Toward Understanding the Play of *Sogo* in *Atsia*," *Ethnomusicology* 16 (1972):8, 9.

affect the pulse base itself. Thus Garfias, in transcribing a musical bow song of the San, used electronic aids to measure the rhythm of the bow beats; he found "many minute differences in spacing between these bow strokes," but they appeared to him to be of no significance.[29] More important was the time spacing of the overall six-beat pattern, in which the last two beats were separated from the first four by the factor of about 1/20th of a second.[30] However, Garfias gives no indication that this affected the overall length of the time span of each six beats, and, in fact, it was apparently the deviation from an assumed equal pulse base that drew his attention to the uneven rhythmic patterning.

Kubik also found small variations in the basic pulse when he transcribed "a large number" of films of African xylophone music. He reports:

> In general, one observes that tolerance of slight rhythmic unevenness on the part of the musician is greater than one would initially expect. ... The distances between strokes which plainly ought to represent a beat or a regular basic pulse show considerable variation. While these strokes are clearly considered by the musicians as parts of a regular series of pulses, one cannot measure them with the regularity of a machine-made pulse.
>
> The listener's and the player's time perception "corrects" this physical irregularity and unconsciously bends the beats into a regular series. These deviations are only visible on the graph paper.[31]

Kubik's explanation of how the irregularities are resolved is reminiscent of Harwood's discussion of the theory of "chunking" used in information processing.[32] In any case, while he is careful to point out that some of the variation may be intentional and some unintentional, it is clear that the assumption of a steady pulse base is fundamental to Kubik's findings.

This assumption on the part of researchers is further emphasized by their concomitant assumption of meter. The tendency to group mechanically exact pulses is a well-known human phenomenon,[33] and thus it is perhaps no more surprising to find ascriptions of meter to African music than of an equal pulse base. Almost all students

[29]Robert Garfias, "Symposium on Transcription and Analysis: A Hukwe Song with Musical Bow. Transcription I," *Ethnomusicology* 8 (1964):240.

[30]Ibid.

[31]Gerhard Kubik, "Transcription of African Music from Silent Film: Theory and Methods," *African Music* 5, no. 2 (1972):33.

[32]Dane L. Harwood, "Universals in Music: A Perspective from Cognitive Psychology," *Ethnomusicology* 20 (1976):524.

[33]Daniel E. Berlyne, *Aesthetics and Psychobiology* (New York: Appleton-Century-Crofts, Meredith Corp., 1971), p. 238.

of African music assume metric organization, many without explanation or justification, such as Cudjoe,[34] Arom,[35] Knight,[36] and Nketia,[37] among others. Blacking points out that "for the Venda, the crucial difference between speech and song is that the words of a song are recited or sung to a regular metrical pattern,"[38] and Kolinski goes so far as to suggest that the African singer interprets what he is doing in specifically metric terms.[39] Only Eno Belinga seems to object, arguing that mensuration (which implies meter for him) is "hasardeux . . . parce qu'elle entraîne nécessairement l'existence de l'accent métrique dominant des temps faibles . . . ."[40]

The question of accent in conjunction with meter has apparently received little attention, although Blacking notes as a rule of the music of two Venda girls' initiation schools that "the basic tempo is expressed implicitly by accented performance or explicitly by a time-setter, such as the tenor drum."[41] For most students of music, accent and meter go hand in hand, but occasionally a definition of meter is proposed which eliminates accent as a necessary corollary. Such is the case of Kolinski's definition which was advanced in connection with a study of African music.

> *Rhythm is organized duration, meter is organized pulsation* functioning as a background for the rhythmic design. Contrary to the generally accepted concept which identifies meter with a more or less regular distribution of accents, it seems to me that neither accent nor stress represents a constituent element of meter.[42]

This definition makes the concept of meter slide almost imperceptibly into the concept of "pattern," a term which has frequently been used in connection with African musical rhythm and which functions as a successful explanatory principle. Once again, the concept seems clearly to fit the facts as perceived both by African

[34] "Ewe Drumming"; *An Approach to African Rhythm* (Legon: Institute of African Studies, 1971).

[35] Simha Arom, "The Use of Play-back Techniques in the Study of Oral Polyphonies," *Ethnomusicology* 20 (1976):486.

[36] "Notation and Tablature," p. 32.

[37] *African Music in Ghana*, p. 64ff.

[38] "Tonal Organization," p. 6.

[39] Mieczyslaw Kolinski, "Symposium on Transcription and Analysis: A Hukwe Song with Musical Bow. Transcription II," *Ethnomusicology* 8 (1964):251.

[40] Martin S. Eno Belinga, *Littérature et musique populaire en Afrique noire* (Paris: Editions Cujas, 1965), pp. 182-83.

[41] "Tonal Organization," p. 9.

[42] Kolinski, "Symposium," p. 249; see also idem, "A Cross-Cultural Approach to Metro-Rhythmic Patterns," *Ethnomusicology* 17 (1973):494-506.

and Western investigators. While no one has defined the term, it is consistently used in the sense of a set configuration of rhythmic pulses which is repeated either throughout a piece of music or through a significant portion of it.

Thus Cudjoe, for example, speaks of "rhythmic patterns appropriate to each dance" played by the gong,[43] and Jones writes that "what *Gankogui* plays is a rhythm-pattern. . . . There are several of these patterns whose length lies from 8 to 12 quavers."[44] Nketia speaks repeatedly of rhythm patterns of particular length and composition,[45] once again emphasizing the gong as the organizer of the ensemble, as in the following:

> Of the idiophones used in Ga society, gongs (*NoNo*) are the commonest. These are used both as "time keepers" and accompanying instruments. In the music of *Kple*, the principal cult of the Ga people, they may be used alone for providing the rhythmic basis of the mass stamping dance commonly called *obene Simo*.
>
> One or two gongs may be used, each one playing a different rhythm pattern.[46]

Koetting writes of the "twelve-unit pattern of the gankogui,"[47] Pantaleoni of the gong patterns among Ewe speakers in Ghana,[48] and many others have used the same language in describing African musical rhythm. Among the Basongye of Zaire, as among many other African peoples, mnemonic devices are used both to memorize and to retain rhythm patterns, as in the following, used by rattle players:

Further, the "bass" xylophone of the two-xylophone ensemble plays a rhythmic-melodic ostinato which has clearly defined beginning and ending points and which forms the background against which more complex melodies are played on the "treble" xylophone. Other terms have been used for the same phenomenon; thus Blacking speaks of "a 'pulse' group equivalent to 12 quavers"

[43] "Ewe Drumming," p. 282.

[44] *Studies*, 1:53.

[45] *Music of Africa*, passim.

[46] Nketia, "Traditional Music," p. 21.

[47] "Analysis and Notation," p. 129.

[48] "Play of *Sogo*," p. 7, passim.

as being "a fundamental unit in many songs,"[49] as well as the fact that "Venda music consists of repetitions of basic patterns. . . ."[50]

The concept of pattern in African musical rhythm thus goes hand-in-hand with the assumption of a steady pulse base and a steady musical beat; it also accounts nicely for the suggested presence of meter, since a patterned unit can be taken as the equivalent of an (unaccented) measure, repeats itself consistently, and has a definable starting point. But most important to this discussion is the point that once a steady pulse base is assumed for African music (except in the case, always, of songs in free rhythm), a basic explanatory principle has been adduced which, when elaborated, accounts for, and explains, the organization of African rhythm as viewed by the outsider. In other words, the theory fits the facts as we perceive, and thus conceive, them.

Time from the African Point of View

Concepts of time in African societies have not been widely discussed in print, but what is available indicates patterns which differ from those of the West. It is useful to preface a brief review of the literature, however, by noting that even in the West, time is by no means always regarded as being strictly linear. Leach reminds us, for example, of two other kinds of time experience. The first is the notion of "non-repetition" by which is meant that "we are aware that all living things are born, grow old and die, and that this is an irreversible process."[51] Thus time in this sense, while still a gross unit and while still countable in the steady even pulse represented by the unit of a second, is not infinite so far as the individual is concerned, though we still presume that in the abstract sense it will go on forever. The second reminder given us by Leach is as follows:

> Our third experience of time concerns the rate at which time passes. This is tricky. There is good evidence that the biological individual ages at a pace that is ever slowing down in relation to the sequence of stellar time. The feeling that most of us have that the first ten years of childhood "lasted much longer" than the hectic decade 40-50 is no illusion. Biological processes, such as wound healing, operate much faster (in terms of stellar time) during childhood than in old age. . . .
>
> Such facts show us that the regularity of time is not an intrinsic part of nature; it is a man made notion which we have projected into our environment for our own particular purposes. Most primitive peoples

[49]"Tonal Organization," p. 9.

[50]John Blacking, *Venda Children's Songs* (Johannesburg: Witwatersrand University Press, 1967), p. 17.

[51]Leach, "Two Essays," p. 125.

> can have no feeling that the stars in their courses provide a fixed chronometer by which to measure all the affairs of life. On the contrary it is the year's round itself, the annual sequence of economic activities, which provides the measure of time.[52]

The same argument concerning the potential importance of phenomena of nature as time-reckoning devices has been echoed by Pocock, who objects to Nilsson's idea that time is based upon a small number of natural phenomena. While Nilsson suggested that such phenomena could be divided into those of the heavens and the phases of nature,[53] Pocock argued that "... it is by no means inevitable that a given society should find the movement of the heavenly bodies useful in ordering its affairs."[54]

Yet it has been primarily on bases such as these, as well as on social activities, that observers have focussed in discussing time in African societies. Thus Bohannan says that "when it is necessary to place an incident in time ... Tiv do so by referring it to a natural or social activity or condition, using solar, lunar, seasonal, agricultural, meterological or other events."[55] He then enumerates Tiv divisions of years, months, the market-day week, and the day, but says of the last that "there is no notion of periods of the day which can be counted; nothing of which you can say that there are four or five between dawn and dusk."[56] Rigby speaks of the "reversal" of time which occurs during Gogo ritual,[57] and Evans-Pritchard summarizes Nuer time-reckoning as follows:

> ... strictly speaking, the Nuer have no concept of time and, consequently, no developed abstract system of time-reckoning.... there is no equivalent expression in the Nuer language for our word "time", and ... they cannot, therefore, as we can, speak of time as though it were something actual, which passes, can be wasted, can be saved, and so forth. Presumably they have in consequence a different perception of time to ours. Certainly they never experience the same feeling of fighting against time, of having to co-ordinate activities with an abstract passage of time. ... There are no autonomous points of reference to which activities have to conform with precision.

[52]Ibid., pp. 132-33.

[53]*Primitive Time-reckoning*, p. 2.

[54]"Anthropology of Time-reckoning," p. 305.

[55]"Concepts of Time," p. 252.

[56]Ibid., p. 257.

[57]Peter Rigby, "Some Gogo Rituals of 'Purification': An Essay on Social and Moral Categories," in *Dialectic in Practical Religion*, Cambridge Papers in Social Anthropology no. 5, ed. Edmund R. Leach (Cambridge: At the University Press, 1968), pp. 172-73.

> Also the Nuer has . . . few, and not well-defined, units of time. . . . They think much more easily in terms of activities and of successions of activities . . . than they do in units of time.[58]

Beidelman speaks of time-reckoning among the Kaguru in very similar terms.

> Kaguru time is essentially a vague sliding scale focused on the near present in which the past and future are of relatively little concern. Time is expressed in terms of the occurrences of various natural and social phenomena, not in terms of any abstract units of measurement, such as are utilized in Western society. No single type of reference point for charting time is used by the Kaguru, so that attention tends to focus not upon points in a time continuum separated by clearly defined distances in experiences but, rather, to be fixed alternately upon a number of different types of points in time separated only by a vague sense of the passage of many or few intervening events. Although the Kaguru have at least two abstract terms for "time," they do not reify time in the Western sense in which it sometimes seems to take on the attributes of a substance or a commodity, at least in the conversation and thinking of ordinary persons.[59]

The Basongye also reckon time according to the seasons and other natural phenomena, but they apparently use fixed points of reference more frequently than the societies referred to above, and thus approach, at least, a linear concept of time.[60] Over the life cycle, however, time is conceived as circular, since the individual spirit is reincarnated, returning in a different body at least twice after its first existence. This concept of time has strong consequences for Basongye social life since, for example, it obviates the need for elaborate explanations of an afterworld, and since it explains in part the strong desire for children in whom the spirits of departed ancestors are reincarnated.[61]

MacGaffey speaks of the BaKongo concept of time as spiral in nature,[62] since it "allows for the occurrence of similar but non-repetitive events,"[63] and notes also that "BaKongo . . . do not

[58]Evans-Pritchard, "Nuer Time-reckoning," p. 208.

[59]Thomas O. Beidelman, "Kaguru Time Reckoning: An Aspect of the Cosmology of an East African People," *Southwestern Journal of Anthropology* 19 (1963):18.

[60]Alan P. Merriam, *An African World: The Basongye Village of Lupupa Ngye* (Bloomington: Indiana University Press, 1974), p. 40.

[61]Ibid.

[62]Wyatt MacGaffey, "African History, Anthropology, and the Rationality of Natives," (Unpublished ms., 1977), p. 16.

[63]Personal communication.

think of history as a record of linear progress in the accumulation of material and moral goods, and indeed do not appear to think historically at all."[64] A "mouvement circulaire ou spirale du Cycle de Vie" is also ascribed to the Luba-Kasai by Tiarko Fourche and Morlighem.[65] Writing in such a manner as to include African societies, Leach summarizes as follows:

> Indeed in some . . . societies it would seem that the time process is not experienced as a "succession of epochal durations" at all; there is no sense of going on and on in the same direction, or round and round the same wheel. On the contrary, time is experienced as something discontinuous, a repetition of repeated reversal, a sequence of oscillations between polar opposites: night and day, winter and summer, drought and flood, age and youth, life and death. In such a scheme the past has no "depth" to it, all past is equally past; it is simply the opposite of now.[66]

Finally, Mbiti, generalizing specifically for Africa, stresses that the linear concept of time "is practically foreign to African thinking," that Africans organize time primarily in terms of the past and the present but have "virtually no future" concept, and that "numerical calendars . . . do not exist in African traditional societies . . . ."[67]

These accounts of African time-reckoning, while showing a considerable variety and while representing a tiny fraction of the societies of Africa, seem to hold certain things in common. Time-reckoning is thought to be non-linear; instead, it can be reversed, discontinuous, a "sliding scale," circular, or spiral. Time-reckoning is carried on in terms of referral to natural phenomena or, most particularly, social activity. Time is not reckoned as distance, it is not epochal, and it is not measured with special apparatus.

Although it does not appear specifically in the passages cited above, one further, and most important, point must be noted, and this is that the smallest time divisions cited by the various authors are divisions of the day; this is also true of the many general ethnographies of African societies. These divisions are usually based on natural segments encompassing fairly large time periods, such as

[64]"The West in Congolese Experience," in *Africa and the West*, ed. Philip D. Curtin (Madison: University of Wisconsin Press, 1972), p. 60.

[65]J.-A. Tiarko Fourche and H. Morlighem, "Architecture et analogies des plans des mondes, d'après les conceptions des indigènes du Kasai et d'autres régions," *Institute Royal Colonial Belge, Bulletin des Séances* 9 (1938):658; see also pp. 652-53.

[66]Leach, "Two Essays," p. 126.

[67]John S. Mbiti, *African Religions and Philosophy*, chap. 3, "The Concept of Time" (Garden City, N.Y.: Doubleday Anchor Books, 1970), pp. 21, 24.

the Basongye idea of "sunrise"; the period "when people leave their fields," which centers loosely around noontime; "sunset"; and night, which is loosely subdivided.[68] It seems to be generally agreed, then, that the smallest period in African time-reckoning is the division of the day, but it must be remembered that the divisions may or may not be reckoned discontinuously, that they are not measured with special devices, and that they are quite probably non-linear.

Discussion and Conclusions

What kinds of problems emerge from this seemingly paradoxical situation, and what, if any, conclusions can be drawn from it? It is clear that from the etic-analytic-outsider's point of view, African music is organized in such a way that the assumption of an equal pulse base seems perfectly reasonable. It makes no difference whether the assumption is right or wrong so long as we keep it constant; that is, the analysis works, given the assumption. Both African and Western scholars have carried out their studies on this basis, although it is stated implicitly rather than explicitly.

The problem is that the assumption seems to contradict the African conception of time as understood by Western observers. That is, while from the Western standpoint, African musical rhythm appears to demand a linear concept of time as well as measurement of time in small units, the scanty knowledge we have of African time-reckoning seems to point to the exact opposite, i.e., a non-linear concept and no measurement of time in small units.

Several possible resolutions of this conflict are available to us. The first is that we may simply be wrong about African time-reckoning, but this does not seem likely given the unanimity of those who have focussed attention upon it, as well as the facts that chronometers are not a part of traditional African life and that observers report no time units smaller than the rough division of the day.

This, however, leads to a second possibility, which is that African societies, like our own, may use more than one system of time-reckoning, i.e., one in general social and cultural life as described in previous pages, and a second made up of small units which operates most specifically in connection with music (and presumably with dance as well). This suggestion might be supported by the fact that most ethnographers are not interested in music past the simple level of describing music instruments, if that, and, further, that ethnographers seem clearly to have been interested in

[68]Merriam, *An African World*, pp. 61-62.

gross, rather than fine, segments of time. Once again, however, the explanation does not seem likely in view of the fact that no one who has focussed on African musical rhythm, including trained ethnomusicologists—both African and Western—has found or suggested such a dual time-reckoning system. This does not mean the idea is impossible, however, and the problem clearly needs investigation.

A third resolution of the conflict is simply that some other system may be operating in connection with the small units required in musical time, and this appears to be a distinct possibility. Involved is what can be called "learning or comprehension by unit," an idea which has been suggested by several investigators, though in different terminology and not in nearly enough instances or depth.

Blacking, for example, in dealing with "the metrical structure of Venda children's songs and its relationship to the words," has formulated a rule which states, in part, that "each 'line' of a song is in itself a total pattern," thus suggesting that the unit is learned as an entity rather than in terms of separate, counted out, parts.[69] Much more specific is Cudjoe's description of children's games which are used in the learning process. He writes:

> Music starts at an early age in Eweland. There are many games designed not only for amusement, but also for developing a strong feeling for compound rhythms. In one such game, the child is held between two adults by the arms and legs and swung to and fro, gently at first and violently later, to the following accompaniment:
>
> Devi mase no do'o da ne,
> Wlaya wlaya do'o da ne.
>
> What is most interesting here is the use of three different rhythmic patterns in a short piece of this kind. The vocal portion of the game consists of two sentences each of which ends with the phrase "do'o da ne." The rhythmic basis of this common phrase is broad triplets, whereas the rest of each sentence is based respectively on short triplets and semi-quavers. Note also that the main 2/4 pulse is maintained in the swinging as a background to the sharply contrasting triplets.
>
> There is another simple game which children play after a bath in the sea. They sit in a circle, gather as much sand as they can into their laps, and with each hand playing a different rhythm, beat out 6/4 against 4/4 on the sand.[70]

Pantaleoni has made the most direct and detailed assertions concerning the matter of learning or comprehension by unit, a theme he has reasserted in several articles. For example, in connection

[69] *Venda Children's Songs*, p. 159.
[70] Cudjoe, "Ewe Drumming," pp. 280-81.

with his forwarding of a new tablature system for African rhythm, he wrote, with Serwadda:

> Unfortunately, one drawback of Western notation remains inherent in our tablature, and that is the unavoidable fractionating of the total ensemble into its component parts. For instructional purposes this is undeniably useful, but it is a Western instruction. The African learns the whole simultaneously with the parts, which is why he has never depended upon stress for rhythmical precision . . . . The Westerner taps his foot to give himself a regular stress on which to hang his part; the African taps his foot to mime the motion of the dancers, or any other part of the ensemble he wishes to add particularly strongly to his own.[71]

Four years later, Pantaleoni expressed the matter even more sharply.

> This paper discusses only the matter of timing in *Anlo* drumming. The source of timing is a high, soft voice that gives out a repeating, asymmetrical pattern. The process of timing one's part to this voice is a process of creating correct polyphony with it. The players neither follow a beat nor build additively upon a small, common unit of time; they simply play in duet with the steady cycling of the bell. This relationship gives them both the correct timing for their strokes and the correct location for their patterns in the flow of the ensemble. Performers may derive from the play of the bell a feeling of pulse suited to their individual rhythmic needs, but this feeling of pulse is not the primary source of timing.[72]

The suggestions, then, are that Africans are neither counting nor learning their parts individually; rather, the basic conception is an entity, a single unit made up of several parts which are envisaged as a totality.

Even this, however, does not *prove* that Africans do not measure or that they do not have a linear concept of time in connection with music. The facts that an individual bases his pattern on that of the gong, and that he hears the ensemble as an entity, may indicate learning or comprehension by unit, but the units themselves may be counted or heard as a linear sequence. The question, then, is not finally resolved, for we have no real proof in either direction.

It is at this point that the emic-etic distinction becomes clearest, for the Western view points one way, the traditional African another, and the interpretation of both is necessarily being made from the Western standpoint—even those Africans who have tackled the problem of African musical rhythm have done so from the

[71] Serwadda and Pantaleoni, "Notation for African Dance Drumming," p. 52.

[72] Hewitt Pantaleoni, "Three Principles of Timing in *Anlo* Dance Drumming," *African Music* 5, no. 2 (1972):62.

foundation of their Western training. It has been pointed out that the analyses carried out to date have accumulated an impressive body of structured information by holding as a constant the Western assumption of an equal pulse base. From the strictly analytic point of view, the use of this assumption makes no difference so long as it *is* held as a constant. But from the emic or internal point of view, it may make a great deal of difference, for in this case it is not a Western analysis which concerns us, but rather the understanding of African musical rhythm from the African standpoint. From the African's outlook, our notions may be entirely wrong, his concept of rhythm may be very different from ours because his concept of time is different, and where we see rhythm in African music as a form of linear propulsion, he may well see it as circular or spiral or in some other form.

This forces us to take a fresh look at the phenomenon, but, alas, our information is so scanty that little can yet be achieved. We may, however, pose the question of whether a circular conception of time-reckoning could help us to account for any aspects of the structure of African music, and the answer is in the affirmative. If it is correct to assume that repetitive pattern is at the basis of African music structure, then a cyclical view of time may be its basis. *Within* the pattern, linearality of some kind must be present, but the broader music structure is not necessarily so viewed. The same point can be applied to the formal structure of African song, which is so often couched in the repetitive call-and-response form of litany, for this, too, could clearly be cyclical rather than linear in conception. Finally, it is germane here to point out that Becker has reached much the same conclusion but in connection with the music of Java; she holds that the Javanese time concept is cyclical, that in certain cases it is divided into halves, halves into halves, and so forth, and that this process is repeated in music both rhythmically and melodically.[73] The point is important because it reinforces the suggestion that concepts of time-reckoning do differ from society to society, and that they almost certainly must affect music.

Finally, I wish to pose a question to which I have no answer, and this is whether music for all mankind must have a steady pulse base, no matter how it is conceptualized and expressed. Certainly it is this assumption that for Westerners makes what we call rhythm possible. Can we conceive of a music without it? Even when we create music with free rhythm or deliberately attempt to

[73]Judith Becker, "Time and Tune in Java," in *The Imagination of Reality: Essays in Southeast Asian Coherence Systems*, ed. A.L. Becker and Aram A. Yengoyan (Norwood, New Jersey: Ablex Publishing Corporation, 1979), pp. 197-210.

destroy a regular rhythmic base through computer randomization, our efforts seem almost necessarily projected against an equal pulse base. In other words, without order, can disorder exist?

Again the question is unanswerable cross-culturally because of the paucity of our information, but it has often been suggested that human beings relate their sense of time to tne regular heart beat which, for most of us in any case, is an equal pulse beat (with obvious exceptions, such as change of tempo resulting from exercise). Kubik has analyzed the timing pattern of mallet strokes in Ugandan xylophone playing and discovered patterning of which the players are completely unaware.

> Triple subdivision of the space of time between two strokes is frequently to be found in Africa, the lifting of the striking medium taking two basic pulses, and the downstroke one. This is also widespread in work situations, for example pounding maize and millet, or using a hammer or mallet. The rhythmic organization of blacksmiths working the bellows has already struck many observers.[74]

Why such fundamental underlying patterns of organization should exist, and whether they are common to the human species, we do not know, yet regularity of pulse underlies much of human activity. We in the West are echoing it when we apply a linear, measuring, concept of time to the analysis of all music. If we employ the equal pulse base as a constant for analytic purposes, we are on one kind of firm ground, so long as we realize we are being arbitrary. But if the search is for how Africans conceptualize and organize their musical rhythms, and what it means to them, then we must also consider the organization, meaning, and application of time-reckoning in their cultural system.

[74]Kubik, "Transcription of African Music," p. 34.

ALAN P. MERRIAM

On Objections to Comparison in Ethnomusicology

> I have chosen to discuss the comparative method because I feel that anthropology ... can ill afford to give up a method, unless the method is proved to be without value. And this has never been done in the case of the comparative method. (Ackernecht 1954: 118)

In an article in 1973, Bruno Nettl discussed the general topic of comparison in ethnomusicology, citing major studies, problems, and achievements. In this paper, I wish to call attention to two specific aspects of the topic, both of which concern the objections made to comparison in ethnomusicology. The subject is important because the objections seem to me to be either half-truths or simply vague statements of the views of their proponents. Further, these anti-comparativist views have gained increasingly wide credence and influence among ethnomusicologists and by no means always with demonstrably positive results. Since the problems raised by comparison are complex and have long been the subject of pointed debate in anthropology, the literature is vast and can be only sampled here. In ethnomusicology, however, the same problems have been barely recognized in their wider context, and they badly need to be given more recognition and definition and to be the subject of clear discussion among us ethnomusicologists, for we are in danger of throwing the baby of comparativism out of the bath we are filling with the water of increasingly sophisticated methodologies. The basic argument of this paper, then, is that we should not abandon comparativism in favour of ideographic studies, no matter how great the methodological advances. Rather, we need to focus considerable attention and energy directly on comparativism in order to search for more feasible ways of making it a useful research tool in ethnomusicology.

Before pursuing the argument, I must clarify some basic positions. First, my purpose is not to annoy but to incite ethnomusicologists to a sensible discussion of how to deal with the problems raised by comparison. Second, my aim is not to scrap new methodologies for old; my aim is to call attention to the potential merits of ideas that have preceded those preoccupying us now, since I believe these older notions can assist us in our present work. And finally, in advocating new discussion on - and thus, by inference, respect for - a basically unpopular, and even disdained, approach in ethnomusicology, I realize that I risk misinterpretation of my own position. In order to avoid that complication, I wish to state that my basic position has not changed: I am still interested in the study of music as culture, and the study of music sound structure is a means to a more limited end than that which I usually wish to undertake. My purpose, then, is to remind us that structural studies clearly do have their place in ethnomusicology, that such studies lead naturally and inevitably to comparisons of structures, and that such comparisons can, under specific circumstances, lead to new and broadened knowledge of music.

ANTICOMPARATIVIST VIEWS

The two anticomparativist views I wish to use as a basis for discussion are quite different from each other, although in the broad sense their final results are the same. The first view, as phrased by Mantle Hood in several publications, is a denial of the past and present utility of any kind of comparison and, in the end, is an implication that there is no hope of future promise. The second, as propounded by John Blacking over a period of years, is a rejection of the utility of one kind of comparison - the comparison of forms - and an emphasis on the priority of another kind of comparison - that of meanings. Let us examine Hood's point of view first.

Some eighteen years ago, Hood stated his objection to comparison in the following terms: 'It seems a bit foolish in retrospection that the pioneers of our field became engrossed in the comparison of different musics before any real understanding of the musics being compared had been achieved' (1963: 233). Six years later, he expressed almost the same point of view: 'An early concern with comparative method, before the subjects under comparison could be understood, led to some imaginative theories but provided very little accurate information' (1969: 299). In both these statements the onus for the purported failure of comparison was put on past mistakes, as it was again in the following statement, which is both much stronger and much more explicit: 'I am convinced that the gross generalities that have confused and confounded comparative studies in the past ... will never expose ... [the] ... elusive universals of music' (1971: 349). And finally, this most recent word seems to be a denial of all possibility of the usefulness, or even the comprehensibility, of comparison: 'Comparative musicology? I no longer understand the term' (ibid.).

Hood, of course, is not alone in this attitude. Norma McLeod, for example, in discussin the work of Alan Lomax, wrote:

> Now, Lomax has taken another view ... He said ... that 'pieces of music relate directly to major cultural patterning.' For him, minute musical matters are symbols for major cultural patterns, such as incest, warfare, the extended family, or what have you. For example, in societies with extended families, you should

> have people singing in a certain way. He has related matters of internal form in music to what might be called context of culture: the major broad patterning of culture is, he says, reflected within the minute details of music. Well, now, this is fair if he can prove it, but I don't think he can. He uses a comparative technique ... I find myself unable to accept broad generalizations of this nature: I'm not comfortable with them. (Herndon and Brunyate 1975: 168)

Several threads seem to run through these statements. One is that comparison has earned its obscurity through the errors made and compounded by scholars in the past. But surely we do not discard a methodology simply because it has been misused or because its users reached what we now believe - in the light of the further accumulation of knowledge - to be faulty conclusions. Indeed, error is an important part of any kind of scientific method: failure is just as crucial as success. What is important is to learn how to use the methodology correctly and to advantage.

A second thread, which is sometimes an implication and sometimes a denial, is that although comparison in the past may have been premature, it may be possible in the fugure. But simultaneously a third thread - the most serious one - is the suggestion that comparative methods will never help us (Hood) or, put differently, that broad generalizations are neither acceptable nor, by implication, desirable in ethnomusicology (McLeod). This introduces the much broader question of the methodology used by ethnomusicologists, and particularly of the implied or actual role played by comparison in that methodology.

My assumption is that ethnomusicologists attempt to operate under a combination of methods borrowed from those used in both the humanities and the social sciences. Indeed, it is this mixture of borrowings, never reconciled with each other, that has led to so much of the confusion that marks ethnomusicology. The borrowings from the social sciences are at prime issue here, since comparison is at the root of many kinds of generalization and generalization is widely assumed to be the end result of scientific methodology. Moles, for example, remarked that 'after all, an objective of science is to generalize,' and that 'through generalization we gain order and, in addition, an explanation of that order' (1977: 236). In much of anthropology and in much of ethnomusicology as well, generalization has been assumed to be based upon the inductive method, and it is in this connection that even stronger statements of the aims of science have been made. Radcliffe-Brown, for example, saw a clear homology between the physical sciences and social anthropology:

> The postulate of the inductive method is that all phenomena are subject to natural law, and that consequently it is possible, by the application of certain logical methods, to discover and prove certain general laws, i.e., certain general statements or formulae, of greater or less degree of generality, each of which applies to a certain range of facts or events. The essence of

> induction is generalisation; a particular fact is explained by being shown to be an example of a general rule. (1958: 7)

If one of the basic goals of the ethnomusicologist is generalization, which he reaches at least partly through induction, it seems to follow that the use of a comparative methodology in some form cannot be avoided since 'comparison is a basic aspect of human thought ... In all analogy, classification, definition, and divisions, comparison is involved in one form or the other' (Śarana 1975: 12). Somewhat more formally, Murdock stated the matter as follows:

> Whatever other methods of investigation are employed ... the comparative method is indispensable. Without it, no combination of other methods can achieve scientifc results of universal application. At the most they can only produce culture-bound generalizations, approximately valid for a particular group of related societies during a particular segment of their history, but incapable of generalization to other societies except as highly tentative working hyoptheses, and equally incapable of predicting future developments in periods of rapid social change or even of comprehending them after they have occurred. (1965: 298)

Indeed, the process of formal comparison has been discussed repeatedly (among many others by Driver 1973; Naroll 1968; Ackernecht 1954; Schapera 1953), and it has often been suggested that its beginnings coincided roughly with the beginning of the eighteenth century (Radcliffe-Brown 1958: 144-52; Śarana 1975: 12-13; Ackernecht 1954: passim).

Besides its contribution to the inductive method, comparison has other uses. Lewis, for example (1961), suggested six specific applications, and Śarana (1975: 16 and passim) wrote that the possible end results included the establishment of inferential history, typology or classification, generalization, and formulation of generalized process. We shall return later to these matters, but it is the following string of assumptions that must occupy us here: one of the aims of ethnomusicology is to make generalizations; one of the ways of achieving generalizations is the inductive method; one of the important constituents of the inductive method is comparison. If generalization is not taken to be an aim of ethnomusicology, then comparison is not necessarily either useful or desirable. I do not believe this to be true, nor do I believe that either Hood or McLeod believes it to be true, for both have made numerous comparisons in their own work. Indeed, it is virtually impossible to conceive of a type of study that does not use comparison, if, for example, only on the simple basis of the mental opposition involved in the way 'I' make music as opposed to the way 'they' make music. Even description is based upon implicit comparison.

One final, if obvious, point remains: that induction is not the only kind of methodology employed by scientists. Indeed, deduction is equally important, although the fact does not seem to have been recognized clearly by ethnomusicologists. It is probably most accurate to say that induction and deduction go hand in hand in any investigation that operates from the initial basis of an organized problem. In writing of his approach to the study of economic anthropology Schneider expressed the basis of deduction as follows:

> In the nature of deductive reasoning the approach to the study of economic behavior is not through the ethnographic facts but by means of 'universal principles,' logico-mathematical in form, springing from the imagination. Generating the logical system necessary to deductive economics requires no cross-cultural data or facts from any system, except perhaps common-sense knowledge of the empirical realm to which the theory is to be applied. (1974: 23)

Deduction, in other words, is an artefact of the mind which is built up through the rigour of its own logic. When the ethnomusicologist creates a set of hypotheses, or a general proposition, that he wishes to test in the field, he is using deduction; in the process of testing them, he is using induction. The two are parts of the same general process, and each requires some form of the other, as Schneider observed: 'Conventional wisdom tells us that induction and deduction are concomitants of each other' (1974: 30).

But while deduction and induction are together at the basis of most field studies in ethnomusicology, neither is sufficient in itself for generalization. Deduction must be proved by induction or it leads only to the sterility of abstract and unproved theory; induction must be generated by deduction or it remains no more than pure description, no matter how inspired that description may be. I do not see the results of either Hood's or McLeod's work mired in either of these dead ends.

The second anticomparativist view, which denies the utility or the possibility of comparisons of form, has for a number of years been associated in my mind with a statement made some time ago by John Blacking:

> Statistical analyses of intervals ... are all very well, provided that we know that the same intervals have the same meanings in all the cultures whose music we are comparing. If this is not certain, we may be comparing incomparable phenomena. In other words, if we accept the view that patterns of music sound in any culture are the product of concepts and behaviour peculiar to that culture, we cannot compare them with similar patterns in another culture unless we know that the latter are derived from similar concepts and behaviour. Conversely, statistical analyses may show that the music of 2 cultures is very different, but an analysis of the cultural 'origins' of the sound patterns may reveal that they have essentially the same meaning, which has been translated into the different 'languages' of the 2 cultures. (1966: 218)

Blacking repeated this point of view in subsequent publications, though tying it ever more closely to the problem of deep and surface structures (1972: 108), and other scholars have followed suit. The point of view is an old one going back at least as far as the French sociologists (see Radcliffe-Brown 1958: 161); in ethnomusicology it was voiced at least as early as 1960 by Leonard Meyer: 'Appearances are often deceptive. For instance, two cultures may appear to employ the same scale structure, but this structure might be interpreted differently by the members of each culture. Conversely, the music of two cultures may employ very different materials, but the underlying mechanism governing the organization of these materials might be the same for both' (1960: 49-50).

One of the more recent statements of this point of view came from Johnston:

> An example of false analogy would be to compare the Uganda xylophone 4th to the Tsonga musical bow 4th. The former is produced by dividing the octave into five equal intervals of 240 Cents each and beating upon alternate xylophone slats tuned to these intervals, yielding intervals of 480 Cents. The latter is produced by inverting the natural 5th of 702 Cents, yielding 498 for the musical bow's 4th. Like or nearly-alike intervals cannot be compared cross-culturally as though the social meaning of the sounds were identical, regardless of cultural attitudes and the psycho-historical background of their production and use within the society (1973: 145).

The obvious question here is how Johnston can call both intervals by the Western term 'fourth,' given the facts that they do not encompass the same number of cents, that they are not derived in the same manner, that the use of a Western term inevitably introduces a comparison into the reader's comprehension, and that Johnston's point is that they are not the same thing. Nevertheless, this particular basis of objection to comparison is clearly delineated in these quotations.

Throughout the history of the discussion of comparativism in anthropology, and more recently in ethnomusicology, debate has centred on four basic problems. The first problem, emphasized by Blacking, has been put forward in the name of functional integration; that is, that one cannot take items out of context for comparison without knowing what each means in its own context, and that if the contexts or the meanings differ, comparison becomes impossible. Nketia (1967), among many others, made the same point, but a number of commentators have taken a contrary view. Śarana, for example, wrote: 'It may be argued that [because] the parts of a culture are functionally related ... to compare an aspect of culture with that of another means that both have been torn out of their respective cultural contexts. In some extreme cases this objection may hold good. But it can be overcome by a proper definition of the units and the items of comparison and by making clear also the level of abstraction at which one proposes to work' (1975: 76). Murdock made the same basic comment, though in rather more severe terms, in commenting on Ruth Benedict's views:

> She strongly implied that the abstraction of elements for comparison with those of other cultures is illegitimate. An element has no meaning except in its context; in isolation it is meaningless. I submit that this is nonsense. Specific functions, of course, are discoverable only in context. Scientific laws or propositions, however, can be arrived at, in anthropology, as in any other science, only by abstracting and comparing features observable in many phenomena as they occur in nature (1965: 146).

The antithetical views cited here do not, of course, resolve the problem but they do suggest that a second problem must be dealt with simultaneously. This is the problem of units, that is, how units are selected, what the proper unit for comparison should be, how to make certain that the units are indeed comparable, and so on. Once again, these difficulties have been the subject of considerable discussion and debate among anthropologists. The central point was expressed briefly by Naroll, who said that 'for anthropologists ... the most urgent need is a standard set of categories and terms ... [that] follow the most general and most nearly validated system at hand' (1968: 269). Leach discussed in lengthier terms the basic problems that he felt mitigate against this possibility:

> An essential part of this scientific procedure is the development of precisely defined concepts (such as species, elements, molecules, atoms, elementary particles, mass, energy, pressure, spatial dimension, temperature), which together provide an internationally agreed upon frame of reference in terms of which the particular phenomena observed by different investigators may be described. Scientific progress is possible only because all the specialists in a given discipline use units of description that are commonly understood and have precisely defined meaning ... These characteristics of natural science have been consciously imitated by leading theorists of the social sciences, but they have been reluctant to admit that the two fields are analogous rather than homologous ... The units of ordinary anthropological description - expressions like 'patrilineal descent,' 'uxorilocal residence,' ... are not in any way comparable to the precisely defined diagnostic elements which form the units of discourse in natural science. This is the heart of the whole matter (1968: 339, 340-1).

Such a general statement would be denied by many anthropologists whose interests lie in cross-cultural comparison (for example, Murdock 1949), and many scholars have worked intensively on solving the problems presented (for example, Moles 1977; Naroll 1968), but since these discussions are anthropological rather than ethnomusicological, they will not be presented further here. Attention may be called, however, to one of the most frequently cited methodologies, that of 'controlled comparison,' suggested by Eggan (1950) and further discussed in its application in ethnomusicology (Merriam 1964: passim).

Other scholars have suggested that certain kinds of phenomena are much more difficult to handle than others. This was emphasized by Osgood, for example, when he noted that 'comparisons across cultures are particularly difficult when what anthropologists term "non-material traits" are involved. I shall use the term "subjective culture." It is one thing to compare skull shapes, blood types or artifacts; it is quite another to compare peoples' values, stereotypes, attitudes, feelings or, most generally, meanings' (1967: 6). Presumably Osgood would include music in his 'non-material traits,' but would this classification, in fact, be accurate? It seems plausible to consider music as both material and non-material, depending upon which part is being studied; that is, the sound structure may well be regarded as made up of 'material' traits, and the meaning of music falls under 'subjective culture.' Whether or not this is true, some ethnomusicologists deny that any sort of comparisons can be made simply because 'you can't get comparable data.' This is the recent view of McLeod, who presumably intends to solve the problem by beginning again with the inductive method: since comparable data cannot be obtained, 'what we do instead is to say, "this society does this: does anybody know another one that does anything like it?" In other words, we take baby steps' (Herndon and Brunyate 1975: 178).

This in turn leads us to a third objection to comparison. In this argument it is held that one well-chosen example or one well-done experiment is all that is necessary to document a general principle. This approach seems to be animating much of ethnomusicological research today, not perhaps so much in the sense that a single example is taken to stand for all examples (which is the inevitable result of McLeod's statement that it is impossible to generalize), as in the sense of limited goals. Herndon, for example, expressed the view that 'the discovery of native categories should be a primary goal, a logical place to begin our investigations' (1976: 221), but it seems to me that this is rather precisely where many of us have already begun and, in any event, that it is by no means the only place to begin. Herndon was here apparently expressing her basic interest in goals that were 'limited, particularistic and pragmatic' (1976: 229), and although I see no possible objection to these goals, neither do I see them as the only possible goals. The idea of limited goals in anthropology today has been well expressed by Śarana: 'The contemporary anthropologists in general firmly believe that ... intensive field studies, aiming at tackling limited problems, are more useful for understanding the nature of human society and culture than aspiring for all-embracing generalizations covering the whole of mankind' (1975: 94). I believe this to be a reasonable statement of the situation as it exists now in both anthropology and ethnomusicology, but I would deplore the statement had not Šarana continued: 'We do not say that the latter are not at all worth pursuing. We all know, however, that at this stage of the development of our discipline we cannot attempt generalizations on a broader scale, with the same depth and authority, as we can do at the level of our microscopic and intensive fieldwork studies' (1975: 94-5). I am not quite sure I understand the self-contradiction in this statement but I am willing to take it at surface value as long as it is understood to mean that attempts at generalization are equally important as microscopic studies.

This recent emphasis on the particular leads us into the difference between two basic kinds of studies in both anthropology and ethnomusicology, as described by Naroll:

> Systematic comparative studies have long been carried out in cultural anthropology for two distinct ends. First, idiographic, historical studies have been carried out in an effort to reconstruct the specific culture history of certain regions or certain traits. Second, nomothetic, sociological studies have been carried out in an effort to discover or verify basic laws of society or culture, basic principles which presumably would hold good at least as tendencies in any society, anywhere, any time.
>
> Idiographic generalizations hold good only about the specific cultures compared. But nomothetic generalizations explicitly or implicitly hold good for the entire universe studied, at least as tendencies. Consequently, if valid, they permit predictions about cultures not yet studied, indeed about cultures not yet in existence ...
>
> This distinction has long been made between the purpose of idiographic and nomothetic studies. By an idiographic study is thus meant one whose purpose is to describe a particular sequence of events ... By a nomothetic study is meant one whose purpose is to discern a repetitive pattern which reflects a general characteristic of society or culture (1968: 236-7).

Selection of limited goals does not necessarily negate comparison per se (Harris 1968: 576, 579), but neither does it solve the question of comparable units. Rather it represents a choice of research strategy, a choice that may be made on the simple basis of preference or because one strategy seems to its user to be more powerful than another. It is this argument that animated the recent published debate between Herndon and Kolinski (Herndon 1974, 1976; Kolinski 1976, 1977), in which Herndon maintained that Kolinski's units were, in effect, imposed from the outside, and thus unverifiable on a cross-cultural basis. Her key observation was: 'Put quite simply, if we are going to compare musics, we must have testable, consistent units with which to compare; Kolinski's units, while consistent, are intuitive, rather than formal. Their utility as a classificatory device is not in question ... [but] ... their utility as a comparative instrument cannot be checked, and this is where one of the major problems with the system lies' (1976: 218). Herndon would presumably make exactly the same objection to Nketia's remarks concerning units of melodic organization and their utility in comparison:

> There are features of melodic organization which the concept of scale patterns enables us to handle, namely features of melodic movement - especially the choice of melodic patterns formed out of the steps of a given scale, patterns which constitute the basic vocabulary of the musician, or the building blocks that he uses in creating and re-creating music. Thus the patterns used in pentatonic melodies (whatever their pitch realizations) or those used in other scale patterns can be abstracted and compared where comparative stylistic analysis is required (1972a: 17).

The question at this point is whether the units that traditionally have been used in ethnomusicology, that is, Western units of analysis, are applicable to music of other cultures and, if so, whether they are suitable for use in comparative problems. At this point, the question of the meanings of such units is suspended; we are concerned for the moment only with the question of form. That form and meaning can be separated conceptually is also taken for granted (for example, Linton 1936: 403 and passim). Whether they should be separated is another kind of question to which I shall return later.

Surely there can be no argument about whether it is possible to abstract form from all other attributes of music and deal with it separately, for countless studies in musicology and ethnomusicology have done precisely that and have resulted in an accumulation of valuable information. In the simplest kind of example, suppose one were to select at random six songs of the Washo Indians of the Great Basin area and six songs of the Lakota Indians of the northern Plains, to present the figures on the tonal ranges alone to someone who had not heard music from either group, and ask that person to select which songs came from one group and which from the other. While this information alone would not enable the neophyte to identify which group was Washo and which Lakota, the chances are very high indeed that six tonal ranges would fall into one group and six into the other, and the chances are equally good that the division would be Washo : Lakota accurate. No reference is made to meaning, use, function, context, or any other variable: the sole criterion is form. Furthermore, it has been demonstrated through mathematical proofs that such formal distributions of elements of music are both constant and identifying (Freeman and Merriam 1956). The point is not that this is the best way of doing things, the only way of doing things, the best way of doing some thing, or that it is applicable in all cases, but rather that it _can_ be done, and that doing it produces certain kinds of verifiable results which do have worthwhile applications.

That this is so can hardly be of surprise to us. Similar procedures, with all the same advantages and disadvantages, have been applied, for example, in folklore with the concepts of motif and tale type, in dance with the elements isolated in Labanotation, and perhaps most notably in linguistics which, in certain of its operations, has relied exclusively and highly successfully on the level of form.

While we are well-advised to keep firmly in mind Feld's strictures (1974) concerning the applicability of linguistic models in ethnomusicology, it is clear that the linguist is in a better position to make much more powerful statements of form than is the ethnomusicologist. Again on a simple level, Fromkin and Rodman made the assertion, almost casually, that 'we find, for example, that the same, relatively small set of phonetic properties characterize all human speech sounds, that the same classes of these sounds are utilized in languages spoken from the Arctic Circle to the Cape of Good Hope, and that the same kinds of regular patterns of speech sounds occur all over the world' (1974: 69).

To the best of my knowledge, ethnomusicologists cannot make a statement like this, or even one analogous to it, for we simply do not have the requisite information. This is not to argue that a parallel statement about music would be a positive statement; rather, it is to say that we have not asked this kind of question seriously, that the present investigative mood in ethnomusicology seems to be precluding us from asking such a question, and that the same general mood makes us look askance at those who might like to ask it. It is perfectly evident that Kolinski has taught us some things, both positive and negative, about music, and so has Herndon; despite the polemics, neither is entirely correct or in a position to answer all our questions. Although the debate was useful, since it clarified basic problems, neither participant was the winner; rather, we all are winners if the result has been the widening of valid approaches to the study of music.

A final objection made to comparison is subsumed under the rubric of extreme relativism. The matter has been put clearly by Śarana:

> An anthropologist's exclusive concern with a single people at a certain period of their existence may give rise to a viewpoint opposing all comparisons. In such a case it is contended that every culture is unique and possesses a set of values which is not easy to define. But an anthropologist, with his long and close association with the people, may experience and understand it. The uniqueness of each culture is inviolable. So there can be no comparison of cultures or parts of cultures (1975: 75).

I have not seen this precise viewpoint in the published literature of ethnomusicology but I have discussed it in private and in correspondence with several of my colleagues. The philosophy, it seems to me, is essentially one of both particularism and despair, and I am inclined to agree strongly with Śarana when he writes: 'Extreme or arch-relativism, if accepted and practiced generally, becomes an impediment in the development of any scientific discipline. In its reasonably restricted form cultural relativism is one of anthropology's notable contributions' (1975: 76).

RESULTS OF COMPARISON

Assuming that comparison in ethnomusicology is possible, what kinds of results can we hope to obtain, and have any such studies been made? Among the suggested objectives is what Śarana (1975) calls 'inferential history,' and the ethnomusicological literature includes a number of such studies. Nketia, for example, begins his work concerning the sources of data on music in Africa by noting that 'our task is to discover what is old, to isolate it from the new by comparative methods, so that we can proceed from the present to the past' (1972b: 43). McLeod, in her study of musical instruments in Madagascar, tells us that 'this paper is presented in the hope that the materials from Madagascar will aid in a better understanding of one of the most puzzling problems of historical relationship: that between Africa and Indonesia' (1977: 189), and the method used is compartive. Wachsmann uses the same method for historical purposes in his study of music history in East Africa (1971: 97). Lomax both infers and postulates history directly upon a comparative method (1968), and many other examples could be cited. The utility of comparison for the establishment of inferential history in ethnomusicology can hardly be disputed.

Nor can we attack comparison as a technique for the study of distribution and typology. One of the uses of comparative data for this purpose has been the postulation of music areas, all of which have been organized on the basis of individual traits of music style, and all of which combine the two factors into distributional-typological schemes. What is interesting about this particular usage is that aside from inevitable slight modification, each successive area mapping shows not only continuity but also very little basic difference from one effort to the next. Thus Nettl's mapping of North-American Indian music-style areas (1954) is not strikingly different from that of Roberts, which preceded Nettl's by eighteen years (1936); nor, for Africa, are Merriam's (1959) from Lomax's (1970). Distributional and typological studies give us certain types of information and do not give us others. The point, however, is that they do give us reliable information of the type they are capable of giving, and this is attested to by the continuity and similarity of the successive results obtained.

A third objective of comparison is to suggest generalizations, and again ethnomusicologists have not failed. The work of Lomax (1968) comes readily to mind, and also the quite different sort of generalization by McAllester, who finds it possible to speak of what he calls 'near-universals' in music. While the units are stated far less precisely than in other instances, McAllester had to have engaged in comparisons of elements of style in order to be able to write:

> Almost everywhere there is some sense of the tonic, some kind of a tonal centre in music. Almost everywhere music establishes a tendency. It seems to be going somewhere, whatever its terms are, and the joy that the performers of that music feel has to do with the way in which that tendency is realized ... Music in almost every tradition seems to have a beginning and an end. Everywhere there is a development of some kind and form of some kind. There is pattern, there are formulae, there are special signs that all the practitioners of a particular music recognize ... (1971: 379-80).

Not every ethnomusicologist would agree with these generalizations, but none the less they are generalizations and they have been reached on the basis of comparison.

Other generalizations are made in flat assertive terms, such as Harwood's suggestion that octave stretching and four other identifiable aspects of musical sensation and perception are human musical universals (1976: 525-8). It is impossible to reach such conclusions without the use of comparison. Finally, potential generalizations are sometimes expressed as hypotheses, as in the suggestion that in Flathead Indian music slow tempo has a number of correlates, and that this may conceivably be true of other kinds of music, and even of all music (Merriam 1967: 323-4).

Closely related to the purpose of generalization through comparison is what Ŝarana calls 'generalized process' (1975: 48-51), that is, generalization about processes that show transition through time. This type of generalization has been applied in the use of Gluckman's theory of structural duration (1968) to explain change in music viewed as a social institution (Merriam 1977: 839-41). Other similar studies are to be found in the literature.

If we can easily cite comparative studies in ethnomusicology, and if we can accept the fact that they are solidly grounded and provide us with sound new information, then why are such strong objections to comparison voiced by Blacking and others? Two answers seem possible. The first is simply that the objectors feel other kinds of problems and procedures are more important and powerful in ethnomusicology than those suggested by a formal comparative approach. I will return to this point in a moment.

The second answer, also a matter of opinion concerning the relative merits of different kinds of approaches, specifically involves the question of levels of analysis. Blacking's urgent suggestion is that comparison is invalid unless it includes the component of meaning, that is, he would not study form alone but only form and meaning together. But intellectual endeavours are full of level-dichotomies, and the kinds of questions asked and the procedures used differ among schools, by preference, through conviction, and via other variables which are a matter of choice. Radcliffe-Brown, for example, referred frequently to the distinction between 'psychology and social anthropology,' which he saw as the extremely important difference between studying 'individual behaviour in its relation to the individual' and 'the behaviour of groups or collective bodies of individuals in its relation to the group' (1958: 17, passim), but I do not recall his suggesting that psychology be abandoned. Similarly, Hanson insists on a clear distinction between what he calls 'individual' and 'institutional' questions (1975); he does not suggest that we stop asking one kind or the other but rather that we understand the distinctions and their implications. Similarly we may study a group versus groups, the diachronic or the synchronic, or any one of a number of other possibilities. The point is that we can ask any set of questions of our data (though of course questions contemplated in advance will affect the ways in which the data are gathered). Are the questions valid? Of course they are, assuming that we know the basis on which the data were collected, that we hold that basis constant, and that the basis is not a palpably foolish one. Thus it must be concluded that we are entitled to ask questions about form as we are to ask them about meaning or about form and meaning combined. My objection arises when we claim that one kind of question is invalid merely because we believe that the kind of question we ourselves wish to ask is more important, feasible, or productive. While the latter may in fact be true, in itself it does not invalidate the utility of the former. We *must* ask different kinds of questions; catholicity of approach is the life-blood of intellectual investigation viewed large, and dismissal of valid methodology simply because it does not interest us is at best parochial.

It should be perfectly clear by this time that I am arguing here for the validity of a variety of techniques and applications in the field of ethnomusicology. If we are to learn as much as possible, in the most economical way, about music taken as a socio-cultural phenomenon, then we cannot cut ourselves off from any reasonable approach. Lest there be misunderstanding, I wish to reiterate that ethnomusicology for me is the study of music as culture, and that does not preclude the study of form; indeed we cannot proceed without it.

The most fruitful studies of music, I believe, will be of the kind that seeks broader goals than those that can be achieved by comparison alone; or, in the words of Blacking:

> More important to me than the possibility of comparing different styles of music is the prospect of knowing what music really *is* as an expression of human behaviour, and to what extent its generating processes are musical and specific to the human species ... we shall not be able to investigate these problems until analyses of music include the deep, as well as the surface structures, and we pay as much attention to man the music-maker as we do to the music man makes (1972: 108).

The proposition seems hardly arguable to me, and it has been accepted and stated by others, among them Meyer (1960: 50), Leach (1968: 341), and Harwood (1976: 531). But part of the process of reaching this kind of understanding has depended in the past, and will depend in the future, on careful, limited, controlled comparison. It does us no good to maintain that the comparison of form is to be abandoned because other problems are more cogent, or far-reaching, or interesting. We need the process of comparison as we need other techniques of analysis, and I suggest that instead of thinking of reasons for discarding it, we need to devote concentrated attention to making comparison a more workable weapon in the ethnomusicological arsenal.

REFERENCES

Ackernecht, Erwin H. 1954 'On the Comparative Method in Anthropology' in Robert F. Spencer, ed. Method and Perspective in Anthropology (Minneapolis, University of Minnesota Press) 117-25
Blacking, John 1966 'Review: The Anthropology of Music' Current Anthropology 7: 218-19
- 1972 'Deep and Surface Structures in Venda Music' 1971 Yearbook of the International Folk Music Council 3: 91-108
Driver, Harold E. 1973 'Cross-cultural Studies' in John J. Honigmann, ed. Handbook of Social and Cultural Anthropology (Chicago, Rand McNally) 327-67
Eggan, Fred 1950 Social Organization of the Western Pueblos (Chicago, University of Chicago Press)
Feld, Steven 1974 'Linguistic Models in Ethnomusicology' Ethnomusicology 18 (2): 197-217
Freeman, Linton C., and Merriam, Alan P. 1956 'Statistical Classification in Anthropology: An Application to Ethnomusicology' American Anthropologist 58: 464-72
Fromkin, Victoria, and Rodman, Robert 1974 An Introduction to Language (New York, Holt, Rinehart and Winston)
Gluckman, Max 1968 'The Utility of the Equilibrium Model in the Study of Social Change' American Anthropologist 70: 219-37
Hanson, F. Allan 1975 Meaning in Culture (London, Routledge & Kegan Paul)
Harris, Marvin 1968 The Rise of Anthropological Theory (New York, Thomas Y. Crowell)
Harwood, Dane L. 1976 'Universals in Music: A Perspective from Cognitive Psychology' Ethnomusicology 20 (3): 521-33
Herndon, Marcia 1974 'Analysis: Herding of Sacred Cows?' Ethnomusicology 18: 219-62
- 1976 'Reply to Kolinski: Tarus Omicida' Ethnomusicology 20 (2): 217-31
Herndon, Marcia, and Brunyate, Roger 1975 Form in Performance (Austin, Office of the College of Fine Arts, University of Texas)
Hood, Mantle 1963 'Music, the Unknown,' in Frank L. Harrison, Mantle Hood, and Claude V. Palisca Musicology (Englewood Cliffs, NJ, Prentice-Hall) 215-326
- 1969 'Ethnomusicology' in Willi Apel, ed. Harvard Dictionary of Music (Cambridge, Harvard University Press) 2d ed., 298-300
- 1971 The Ethnomusicologist (New York, McGraw-Hill)
Johnston, Thomas F. 1973 'The Cultural Role of Tsonga Beer-Drink Music' Yearbook of the International Folk Music Council 5: 132-55
Kolinski, Mieczyslaw 1976 'Herndon's Verdict on Analysis: tabula rasa,' Ethnomusicology 20 (1): 1-22
- 1977 'Final Reply to Herndon' Ethnomusicology 21 (1): 75-83
Leach, Edmund R. 1968 'The Comparative Method in Anthropology' in David L. Sills, ed. International Encyclopedia of the Social Sciences 1: 339-45
Lewis, Oscar 1961 'Comparisons in Cultural Anthropology' in Frank W. Moore, ed. Readings in Cross-cultural Methodology (New Haven, HRAF Press) 55-88

Linton, Ralph 1936 The Study of Man: An Introduction (New York, D. Appleton-Century)
Lomax, Alan 1968 Folk Song and Culture (Washington, DC, American Association for the Advancement of Science)
- 1970 'The Homogeneity of African-Afro-American Musical Style' in Norman E. Whitten, Jr. and John F. Szwed, eds. Afro-American Anthropology: Comparative Perspectives (New York, Free Press) 181-201
McAllester, David P. 1971 'Some Thoughts on "Universals" in World Music' Ethnomusicology 15 (3) 379-80
McLeod, Norma 1977 'Musical Instruments and History in Madagascar' in Essays for a Humanist: An Offering to Klaus Wachsmann (New York, Town House Press) 189-215
Merriam, Alan P. 1959 'African Music' in William R. Bascom and Melville J. Herskovits, eds. Continuity and Change in African Cultures (Chicago, University of Chicago Press) 49-86
- 1964 The Anthropology of Music (Evanston, Northwestern University Press)
- 1967 Ethnomusicology of the Flathead Indians (Chicago, Aldine)
- 1977 'Music Change in a Basongye Village (Zaïre)' Anthropos 72: 806-46
Meyer, Leonard B. 1960 'Universalims and Relativism in the Study of Ethnic Music' Ethnomusicology 4 (1): 49-54
Moles, Jerry A. 1977 'Standardization and Measurement in Cultural Anthropology: A Neglected Area' Current Anthropology 18: 235-58
Murdock, George Peter 1949 Social Structure (New York, Macmillan)
- 1965 Culture and Society (Pittsburgh, University of Pittsburgh Press
Naroll, Raoul 1968 'Some Thoughts on Comparative Method in Cultural Anthropology' in Hubert M. Blalock, Jr. and Ann B. Blalock, eds. Methodology in Social Research (New York, McGraw-Hill) 236-77
Nettl, Bruno 1954 North American Indian Musical Styles (Philadelphia, American Folklore Society Memoir 45)
- 1973 'Comparison and Comparative Method in Ethnomusicology' Yearbook of the Institute of Latin American Studies 9: 148-61
Nketia, J.H. Kwabena 1967 'Musicology and African Music: A Review of Problems and Areas of Research' in David Brokensha and Michael Crowder, eds. Africa in the Wider World (Oxford, Pergamon Press) 12-35
- 1972a 'The Musical Languages of Subsaharan Africa' in African Music. Meeting in Yaoundé (Cameroon) (Paris, La Revue musicale) 7-42
- 1972b 'Sources of Historical Data on the Musical Cultures in African Music. Meeting in Yaoundé (Cameroon) (Paris, La Revue musicale) 43-9
Osgood, Charles E. 1967 'On the Strategy of Cross-national Research into Subjective Culture' Social Science Information 6: 5-37
Radcliffe-Brown, A.R. 1958 Method in Social Anthropology edited by M.N. Srinivas (Chicago, University of Chicago Press)
Roberts, Helen H. 1936 Musical Areas in Aboriginal North America (New Haven, Yale University Publications in Anthroplogy No. 12)

Toward the Remodeling of Ethnomusicology

Timothy Rice

Ethnomusicology, like any academic field, is constantly being created and recreated through the research, writing and teaching of its practitioners. Direct action in the form of new data, interpretations, theories, and methods effectively defines the field. Modeling a discipline, on the other hand, requires a step back from direct engagement in research to ask the descriptive question, what are we doing?, and the prescriptive question, what ought we to be doing? The answer will surely depend on the intellectual and social matrix of the modeler (Blum 1975 and C. Seeger 1977) and the effectiveness of the model will depend either on the extent to which it captures simply and elegantly the current work being done in the field or provides a kind of "moral imperative" for future action.

Probably the best example of an effective model in the recent history of ethnomusicology is "Merriam's model" proposed in 1964 in the *Anthropology of Music*. His "simple model" . . . "involves study on three analytic levels—conceptualization about music, behavior in relation to music, and music sound itself (p. 32)." The model is essentially circular in form (see fig. 1) with concept affecting behavior which produces the sound product. And he continues, ". . . There is a constant feedback from the product to the concepts about music, and this is what accounts both for change and stability in a music system" (p. 33). This model was seminal in the history of ethnomusicology and to that date was the most forceful and cogent statement of anthropological concerns with respect to music. The model defined ethnomusicology as "the study of music in culture" and that view—even as modified to "music as culture" and "the relationship between music and culture"—has remained one of the core concepts in the discipline ever since.

We can of course argue about the extent of its influence during the last twenty years, but there can be no doubt that it continues to be influential. It is still frequently cited to contextualize particular research problems (for example, Yung 1984 and Sawa 1983), Bruno Nettl (1983) called it "definitive," not just of the study of music but apparently of music itself, and it provided the basic model for the recent collaborative textbook, *Worlds of Music* (Titon 1984). If that book's authors, coming from a very wide range of backgrounds, could agree on this model, then the continuing extent of its influence is clear—at least as an overall image or model of the field.

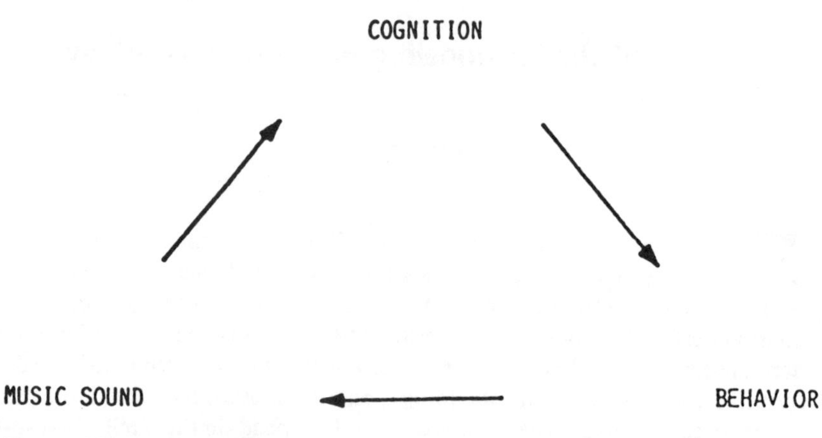

Figure 1. The Merriam Model

In addition to defining the field and being influential, Merriam's model also has three other attractive properties which make it a useful foil for the "remodeling" proposed here. First, it is a "simple model" with three "analytic levels." Part of the reason it has been influential is that it is easy to remember. Second, its levels seem to be relatively complete and inclusive. They cover a broad range of concerns. Third, it is a cogent model in the sense that its "analytic levels" are supposed to interrelate. In spite of these attractive properties, however, I acknowledge that not everyone has agreed with it, and we have certainly wrestled with it as much as we have embraced it. But because it is simple, inclusive, cogent, definitive, and influential, I am going to refer to it frequently in the "remodeling" that follows, partly because I hope the model proposed here has many of these same qualities.[1]

The first and most immediate effect of the Merriam model was to increase the amount and prestige of work done on social, physical and verbal behaviors associated with music. Its second effect was to set in motion a search for ways to relate these behaviors to the "music sound itself." Much of the subsequent work in "the anthropological study of music" (Blacking 1976b) can be interpreted as attempts to find the points of intersection, causation, or "homologies" between Merriam's "analytic levels."

In the search for those connections a number of social science paradigms have been borrowed and invoked over the last twenty years, including biological approaches (Blacking 1977), semiotics (Nattiez 1983), ethnoscience (Zemp 1978), ethnography of performance (Herndon and McLeod

1980) and communications (Feld 1984), structuralism (A. Seeger 1980), symbolic interactionism (Stone 1982), Marxism (Shepherd 1982), hermeneutics (Becker 1984) and an eclectic mix of a number of approaches (Feld 1982). Although these paradigms and methods are often seen as conflicting or mutually exclusive within anthropology and sociology, and certainly differ from the structural functionalism behind Merriam's *Anthropology of Music,* their application within ethnomusicology can be interpreted as an attempt to solve the central problem created by Merriam's model: how can we convincingly speak about the relationship between music and other human behaviors.

Although much of the "theory" developed in ethnomusicology over the last twenty years has addressed this question, there are obvious signs of resistance to the sought-after perfect union between so-called "musicological" and "anthropological" approaches. An incident from last year's annual meeting in Vancouver can serve to illustrate the divergence of opinion in the field and some of the continued resistance to anthropological approaches. During the discussion following Stephen Blum's paper, "The Ethnomusicologist vis-à-vis the Fallacies of Contemporary Musical Life," someone commented that in the paper and response and discussion to that point, he had not heard much reference to contemporary social theory, particularly coming out of anthropology, and worried that ethnomusicologists were perhaps twenty years out of date in their view of society and culture. The responses by prominent ethnomusicologists to this observation covered an astonishing range. Someone responded that she and probably others did keep up; someone else said she wished she could keep up but was so busy as a teacher covering "the whole earth" that she couldn't keep up; and two people responded essentially with, "Who cares if we keep up?" If anyone were laboring under the impression that ethnomusicology was a unified discipline or even that there was widespread agreement that it represented a union of anthropological and musicological approaches, this interchange would have been illuminating and perhaps discouraging.

In addition to this lack of agreement about the methods and disciplinary roots of our field, there is evidence of pessimism about what we have achieved in the way of a union between anthropological and musicological approaches even by those deeply committed to such a union.[2] Gerard Behague (1984: 7) recently wrote that "our analytical tools for establishing that relationship [between "social context" and "music sound-structure"] unequivocally lack in sophistication." Herndon and McLeod (1979: iii), in the late seventies, still complained that "the wholeness . . . which gives equal consideration to the music, itself, and the behavior surrounding its origin, production, and evaluation still eludes us." Ruth Stone (1982: 127), whose innovative approach to event analysis is designed to solve this problem, admits that "it is not yet possible to achieve the ideal unitary analysis."

Thus ethnomusicology seems to be in a rather odd position. On the one hand, we have an old model which continues to exert a fair bit of influence and to define the core problem for the field. On the other hand, there is pessimism about the extent of our achievements in solving the problem, continued open resistance to anthropological models,[3] and competition among a host of social science paradigms rushed into the breach in an attempt to solve all or some of our problems. In this context I think it is time to rethink the relationship between ethnomusicology and its cognate disciplines and perhaps, like an old house, remodel it along lines that describe and prescribe what we actually do rather than what particular scholarly traditions tell us we ought to do.

Some might argue that modeling a discipline is not necessary. Obviously research will continue largely along lines dictated by personal interest, intellectual training, traditions of scholarship, and social and institutional demands. Yet disciplinary models are attractive for a number of reasons.[4] They provide a kind of intellectual framework that helps us contextualize, interpret, classify and evaluate our work, and they can provide some sense of direction or purpose. Lewis Thomas (1974), the well-known essayist on biological topics, characterizes the scientific enterprise as analogous to the building of an anthill. He guesses that individual ants, like most scientists, have no idea of the shape of the anthill they are building. The combined intelligence of masses of ants and scientists achieves spectacular results even though individual ants and scientists cannot imagine exactly to what purpose their work is directed. Modeling is an attempt to imagine the shape—however hazy—of the metaphorical anthill that we are building.

THE MODEL

There are two immediate, personal sources for the model presented here. One comes from my teaching experience, the other from reading in the secondary literature. First, I teach an introductory course to all first-year students in a large conservatory-style music program at the University of Toronto. The course treats all kinds of music (Western and non-Western, classical, folk, popular and so on) as a prelude to a more detailed study of Western classical music. The course description, generated in committee, reads, "Formative processes in music cultures of the world." Thus, I have been forced to wonder in a very practical, pedagogical context just what the formative processes in music are. Are they melody, harmony, and rhythm as some of my colleagues at the Faculty of Music seem to imagine? Or are they the relationship between music and politics, economics, social structure, music events, and language as ethnomusicologists have claimed in the last twenty years? Was there a way to pull some semblance of order out of the long lists one could make? Was there a way of reconciling the music structural concerns of many music history courses with the anthropological concerns of many ethnomusicology courses?[5]

I developed various ways to deal with this problem, and then about four years ago, while rereading Clifford Geertz's *The Interpretation of Cultures,* I was struck by his claim that "symbolic systems . . . are historically constructed, socially maintained and individually applied" (pp. 363–364). Instantly I recognized these as the "formative processes" that I had been searching for. Here was a three-part model, analogous to Merriam's, that was easy to remember and that seemed to balance social, historical and individual processes and forces in ways that seemed immediately and intuitively satisfying. The Merriam model, or at least its working out over the last twenty years, has tended to lead to an emphasis on social processes and as a consequence alienated ethnomusicology from the concerns of historical musicology. How could one teach about all music when the perspectives brought to bear on different musics seemed so different?

I would like to examine the implications of a slightly modified form of this statement by Geertz as a "model for ethnomusicology." Simply put, I now believe that ethnomusicologists should study the "formative processes" in music, that they should ask and attempt to answer this deceptively simple question: how do people make music or, in its more elaborate form, how do people historically construct, socially maintain and individually create and experience music?[6]

It is hard to capture the overlapping strands of theory and practice as they currently operate in our field, but if this statement by Geertz struck a responsive chord in me, then it probably is because this sort of thinking is "in the air." When I looked more closely at recent literature with this model in mind I did indeed find "preechoes" of it in the writing of a number of our colleagues.[7] For example, Herndon and McLeod ask this same question, how does man make music, in their book, *Music as Culture,* but do not then go on to make the coherent series of claims that this model does. John Blacking has argued perhaps most persuasively for the emphasis on process, as opposed to product, that is modeled here.

Probably the place where the general emphases of this model are currently being worked on most clearly is in the area of performance practice or ethnography of performance and communications. Steven Feld (1984: 6), for example, argues for a focus on listeners "as socially and historically implicated beings"—a statement that captures the three poles of this model. Bonnie Wade (1984: 47) points out that "creativity in the performance practice of Indian art music . . . involves . . . the role of the individual performer, how he sees his own creativity in relationship to his musical tradition, to his fellow performers, and to his audience." Creativity as individual experience, history as tradition, and social processes involving musicians and audience represent one of many ways that the three parts of this model can be interrelated to tell an interesting story. That story gets at fundamental musical processes without belaboring points about homologies between musical and cultural forms, and yet manages to integrate the study of music into the study of history, society, and cognition.

Kenneth Gourlay (1982: 413) came very close to modeling the field along these lines. "Gourlay's A.B.C" calls for "a humanizing ethnomusicology with three distinct, if related, fields of inquiry." A, for Armstrong's affecting presence, involves the study of "how musical symbols operate to produce their effect or meaning, and what effects they produce." B stands for Blacking's model of change, and C, for condition, context, and conceptualization. He does not go on to show, however, how the three fields can be related.[8]

Thus, the general outline of the model proposed here is clearly "in the wind." But this relatively recent "atmosphere" in the field has yet to be developed into a simple, cogent and inclusive model, and to have its implications for the field examined.

THE PARTS OF THE MODEL

First, the model needs to be explained in terms of how it organizes the welter of "issues and concepts," to use Nettl's (1983) phrase, generated by ethnomusicologists.

"Historical construction" comprises two important processes: the process of change with the passage of time and the process of reencountering and recreating the forms and legacy of the past in each moment of the present.[9] In synchronic, "in-time" studies of music in a particular place at a particular time, the study of historically constructed forms as a legacy of the past finds a place here. Jean-Jacques Nattiez (1983: 472) has deplored what he calls the synchronic "culturalism" of much current ethnomusicology and argues for a greater emphasis on diachronic approaches to musical form. However, he concludes that "music generates music." I prefer this model's claim that people generate music at the same time that it acknowledges the formative power of previously constructed musical forms. Individuals operating in society must come to grips with, learn, and choose among a host of previously constructed musical forms. Although this process is normally acted out in specific instances of learning, listening and playing using the medium of music itself, analogous behavior in the speech domain requires musicologists to describe the intricacies of forms in words. Both operations—musician/performers making music for musician/listeners and musicologists writing or speaking to their readers or audience—require a sophisticated encounter with historically constructed forms.[10]

Historical construction can also be interpreted as the diachronic, "out-of-time" study of musical change or the history of music. In spite of the notorious difficulty of constructing music histories in many of the cultures we typically consider, ethnomusicologists have been fascinated by the issue of change. It would be descriptively accurate and therefore useful to have a model of our field that reflects the central importance of change, of historical processes. For us history or "historical ethnomusicology," to use Kay Shelemay's phrase, does not, in fact, seem to be one of many issues, but a primary issue, a fundamental process, a given of music making, and this model acknowledges that by elevating the study of change to the highest analytical level of the model.[11, 12]

Processes of social maintenance have been particularly well documented by ethnomusicologists in the years since Merriam's *The Anthropology of Music,* and it is easy to construct at least a partial list of the way music is sustained, maintained, and altered by socially constructed institutions and belief systems: ecology, economics and the patronage of music; the social structure of music and musicians; protest, censorship and the politics of music; performance contexts and conventions; beliefs about the power and structure of music; music education and training; and so on. The study of the processes by which these social systems impact music and, conversely, how music impacts these systems has been one of the most fruitful areas of research in the last twenty years, whether expressed in terms of context, causal relations, homologies, or deep-structural relations.

Emphasis on the individual is probably the most recent and as yet weakest area of development in ethnomusicology. While the study of individual composers and individual acts of creation is well-entrenched in historical musicology, such studies have remained until very recently suspect in ethnomusicology. The antagonism and even fear of humanistic, historical or individual approaches is exemplified in this statement of Judith and A.L. Becker (1984: 455):

> "A move toward the study of particularities nudges ethnomusicology away from the social sciences into the realm of the humanities where uniqueness is legitimate. Our discipline has historically been allied with the social sciences; we take our paradigms from the social sciences. Any step toward the humanities also feels like a step toward the approaches of traditional historical musicology with its outworn methodology and unexamined assumptions."

They then invoke another paradigm they call literary criticism, ironically an approach deeply rooted in the humanities but that has recently been taken over by social science. The interpretive anthropology of Geertz and others seems to move the social sciences in the direction of the humanities, and drastically reduces the need for the "fear and trembling" one senses on both sides of this apparently once formidable division. This model, in fact, does move ethnomusicology closer to the humanities and historical musicology (and might have the effect of moving historical musicology closer to ethnomusicology), but without giving up an essential concern for the social bases of musical life and experience or a general scholarly concern for generalization and comparison.

John Blacking has emerged as a clear advocate of approaches to the study of the individual in a number of recent articles, but he too betrays a fear of individuality when he argues that it is not Mozart's uniqueness but his capacity to share that is important (1976b). A balanced approach must be willing to acknowledge the extent and importance of individuality and uniqueness in particular societies, and finding a balance between historical, social, and individual processes should be an important part of "the interpretation of [musical] cultures." The recent work of Ellen Koskoff (1984), Dane Harwood (1976), Bruno Nettl (1983), Klaus Wachsmann (1982), Steven Feld (1984) and the writers of *Worlds of Music* (1984) has moved us substantially in the direction of increased consideration of individual creativity and personal experience as legitimate objects of scholarly enquiry.

Some of the issues that might be discussed under individual creativity and experience include: composition, improvisation and performances of particular pieces, repertories and styles; perception of musical form and structure; emotional, physical, spiritual and multisensory experience mediated by music; and individual cognitive structures for organizing musical experience and associating it with other experiences. If interest in the individual and individual experience continues to grow, then eventually the history of ethnomusicology might be interpreted as having moved successively through the three stages of this model from a concern with historical and evolutionary questions in its early "comparative musicology" stage to a concern for music in social life after *The Anthropology of Music,* to a concern for the individual in history and society in the most recent or next phase.

In fact the work actually being done in the field today is rather well balanced between these approaches. The articles in *Ethnomusicology* in the eight-year period from 1979 to 1986 contain a good balance among these approaches. The largest group predictably emphasizes social processes but a perhaps surprising number look at individual processes as well:

general theory and method	13%
surveys	4%
music analysis	10%
history/change	22%
social processes	34%
individual processes	17%
Total	100%

Thus it seems that this model rather effectively reflects not just the current theoretical atmosphere in the field, but the balance in the actual work we are doing. It is an accepting model in which virtually everyone in the field can find a place for his or her work.

INTERPRETATION IN THE MODEL

Perhaps the most exciting feature of this model is the richness of interpretation that it suggests, hardly surprising since it was originally sparked by a book entitled *The Interpretation of Cultures*. In fact, the model suggests four hierarchical levels of interpretation (see fig. 2).

To be effective a model ought to be dynamic or cogent, that is, it should imply or suggest ways to relate the parts of the model to one another. In fact, this model strikes me as particularly dynamic in the sense that its parts can so easily be shown to interlock and interrelate. If the levels easily interrelate, then the move from description to interpretation and explanation, which bedevils the Merriam model, should be straightforward and in fact a feature of this model.

The main interpretive problem set up by the Merriam model was to find ways to relate music sound to conceptualization and behavior, and I have already written about some of the pessimism about what we have

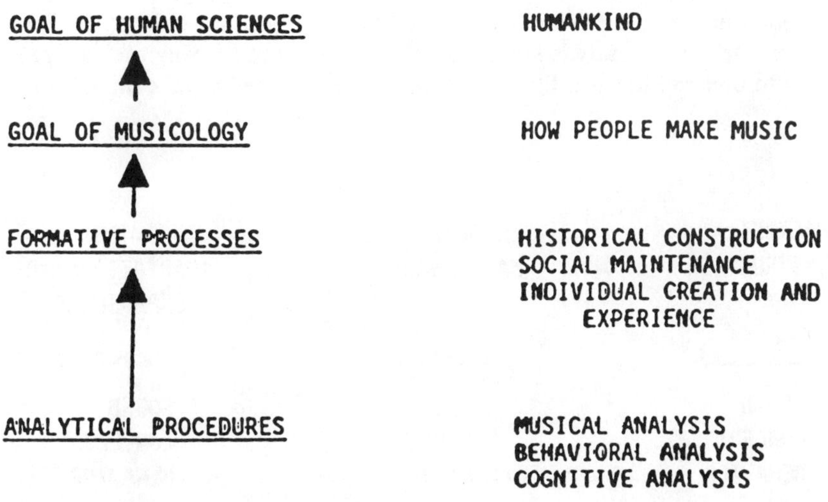

Figure 2. Hierarchy of levels in the model.

achieved. A striking recent statement of the difficulty of interpretation presented by the Merriam model comes from *Worlds of Music*, which uses it. Speaking of dividing music cultures into "parts" along the lines of the Merriam model, they write: ". . . At best, isolating parts of a music-culture for study is an oversimplification; at worst, an untruth. But given the limitations of courses and textbooks, it is our only recourse" (p. 9).

All of us sympathize with their dilemma precisely because it is not just a dilemma of courses and textbooks, but a dilemma for ethnomusicology as a whole. J.H. Kwabena Nketia (1985) recently called for "the development of an integrative technique that enables the scholar to group and regroup his data" (p. 15) and for "methods of synthesis that bring together the different aspects of music and music making in a meaningful and coherent manner" (p. 18). He called this a "challenge" for ethnomusicology, and this model is an attempt to respond to that challenge.

At the first and lowest level of interpretation, I suggest that instead of or in addition to seeking to relate the levels of Merriam's model to each other through cause, homologies, correspondences or what have you, that we embed them within the levels of this model and ask how they contribute to the formative processes we have identified (see fig. 3).

A rich story could presumably be told about how changes in sound, concept and behavior contribute to the historical construction of a particular kind of music (for example, Cavanagh 1982). Another story might revolve around the social forces that maintain sound structures, assign them meaning and value, and generate behaviors consistent across both musical and nonmusical domains. A third story might treat the range of individual variation in ideas, behaviors and music in a given musical culture. In this model, Merriam's analytic levels can still be used, but the way they are related to one another is a little more flexible and varied than a monolithic

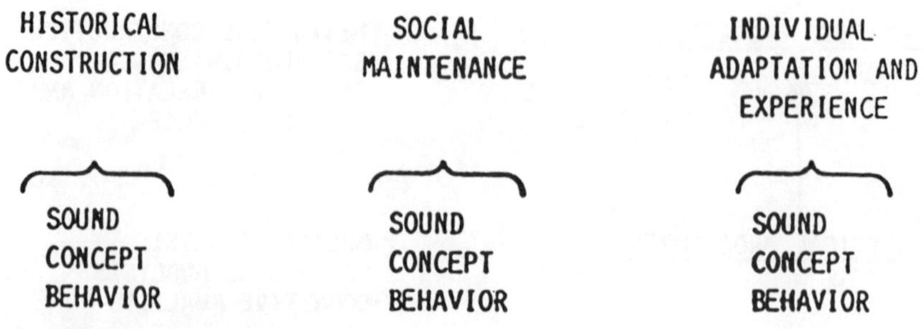

Figure 3. Merriam's levels embedded in this model.

search for causes and homologies, and thus easier to achieve. Furthermore, instead of sanctioning formal descriptions of either sound, cognition or behavior, as interesting as they might be, this model demands an interpretation of what our descriptions imply about our knowledge of fundamental formative processes. For example, a formal analysis of the "music sound itself" might yield interpretations of a piece's importance in the historical construction of the style, of individual creative processes as evidenced in the piece or performance, or of elements in the cultural or social system that affected elements of form. Good writing in ethnomusicology already does these sorts of things, and that is why I claim that the interpretations demanded by this model are relatively easy and enormously varied. It is a rich model allowing for a variety of perspectives, not a narrow model with a single perspective.

Moving to a second, higher level in this model, we can ask how its parts interrelate to generate interpretations. Two main structural problems with Merriam's model have led to problems of interpretation, whereas this model solves them. First, in the Merriam model music sound is directly contrasted to behavior and cognition. Having separated music from context in this artificial way, we have struggled ever since to put this particular Humpty-Dumpty back together again. In the model proposed here, the analysis of music, the study of the "music sound itself," is demoted to a lower level of the model, while people's actions in creating, experiencing, and using music become the goal of the enquiry. Instead of trying to find homologies between unlike things—sound, concepts and behaviors—this model tries to integrate and relate like things, namely three formative "processes."

The second structural problem with Merriam's model is that the relations between his analytic levels go only in one direction and relate one level to only one other (see fig. 1). In this model, on the other hand, each level is connected to the other two in a dialectical, or two-way, relationship. There are simply more relationships in this model and thus more possibilities for interpretation. Each process can thus be explained in terms of the other two (see fig. 4). Historical construction can be explained in terms of both changes in patterns of social maintenance and individual creative decisions. Individual creation and experience can be seen as determined partly by historically constructed forms as learned, performed, and modified in socially maintained and sanctioned contexts. Social maintenance can be seen as an ongoing interaction between historically constructed modes of behavior, traditions if you will, and individual action that recreates, modifies and interprets that tradition. Thus, the levels in this model are on a metaphorical "rubber band," which can be pulled apart to analyze, but which keep wanting to snap back together. This gives the model a certain dynamic, interpretive energy, to extend the metaphor, and allows the telling of many interest-

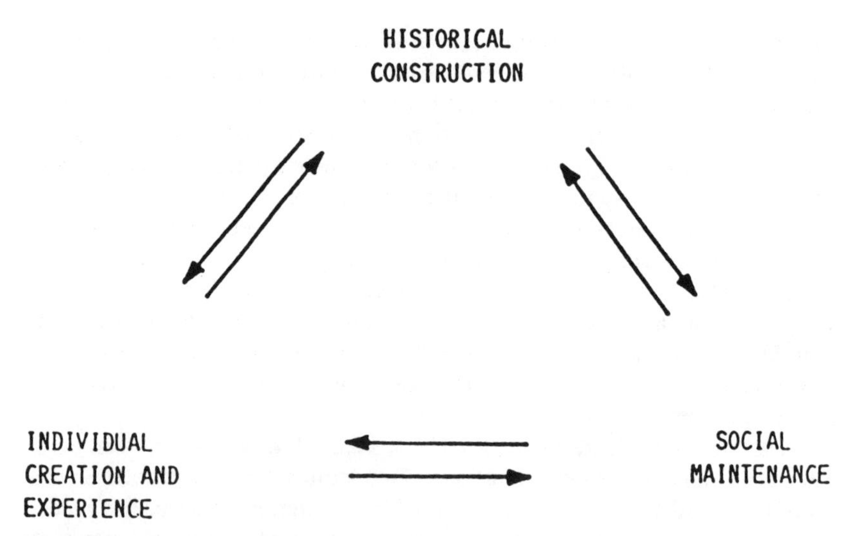

Figure 4. Relationships in the model.

ing stories. In general, application of this model demands a move from description to interpretation and explanation and provides a flexible, varied and rather easy way to do it, or at least to imagine how to do it.

If we are able to identify and relate fundamental formative processes in particular ethnographic situations, then this should lead us to the third level of interpretation in the model, which is a concern for general statements about how people make music. The model thus leads us to a comparative stance with respect to music. If we can keep before us an image of fundamental formative processes that operate in many cultures, this should lead us to create microstudies that can be compared to other microstudies, as opposed to the detailed, independent and insular studies that seem to proliferate in the ethnomusicological literature at present.

One example of how the model was used in a particular situation and had a comparative effect was a paper by Stephen Satory, a graduate student at the University of Toronto, who decided to use the model in his report of field work in the Hungarian community in Toronto for the 1985 Niagara chapter meeting of SEM. Subtitling his paper, "The role of history, society and the individual," he analyzed the musical life of Hungarians in Toronto, and particularly the position and importance of the dynamic revival movement involving improvised dancing called *tanchaz* or "dance house," begun in the early '70s in Budapest. Although he could have focused on any part of the model, he chose to address all three parts of it. Having committed himself to the model, he was constantly forced by it to move beyond a description of what he had observed to interpretations of broader processes. In his discussion of historical construction he periodized immigration patterns, discussed the rise of community social institutions in Toronto to support cultural expression and distinguished five types of transmission of the tradition, many of them involving specific individual actions. As for social maintenance he compared this tradition in three locales: in the villages of Transylvania where the forms originated, in Budapest and in Toronto. He interpreted its lack of popularity in Toronto, compared to its importance in Hungarian venues, as a consequence of the differing political, social and intellectual climate in the three places, concluding among other things that the unstructured, improvisational aspects of the tradition do not correspond to the goal and work-oriented values of Hungarian immigrants to Toronto. In spite of its lack of popularity and community support, however, the tradition lives in Toronto through the agency of a relatively small number of individuals who value it variously as a means of ethnic group identity, nostalgia for village life, a source of friendships, exercise, and the aesthetic pleasure of skill and virtuosity. Using the model allowed Stephen to rework his material from a number of different perspectives, and the interpretations he made of his particular data linked his work to the work of many others.

At the Niagara meeting his paper was one of four papers on immigrant musical traditions in North America. In the discussion that followed, Stephen's paper became the focus of comment not because it was the best researched, or had the richest data or concerned the most colorful tradition, but because it was the only paper that went beyond description to interpretation. The interpretations linked his specific research to wider issues that all of us were interested in and could discuss. Perhaps we should not ask much more from a model than that it increases the possibilities for communication among us.

The fourth level of interpretation would eventually identify what is shared and what is unique about music in the repertoire of human behaviors. Something like this level was suggested by Blacking (1976b: 11): "the aim of ethnomusicological analysis is to reveal what is peculiar to the process of making and appreciating music, as distinct from other social activities." At this level ethnomusicology would contribute to comparative studies in many cognate fields and to our knowledge of humankind in general. If the fundamental "formative processes" in music are conceived as historical, social, and individual, then the eventual identification of "musical processes" will connect music to the rest of human behavior and music study to the rest of the academic world.

RELATIONS TO OTHER DISCIPLINES

Finally, this model of an ethnomusicology that includes historical, anthropological and psychobiological components and concerns could be a model for a unified, rather than a divided, musicology. This is a satisfying conclusion because it reflects the direction in which some ethnomusicologists have wanted to move for years. Ethnomusicologists often possess a sort of missionary zeal that they have a corner on the best and most proper and widest perspective on music and that ethnomusicology is in fact musicology.[13] But it is not helpful to downplay or ignore the significant achievements of historical musicology in favor of a claim that we have all the right answers. Historical musicologists have much to teach ethnomusicologists about historical and individual creative processes, just as we have much to teach them about the powerful forces of contemporary culture on musical sound structures and the social and cognitive bases of musical experience.

When ethnomusicologists speak of musicology, they seem to regard its primary methodological stance as analytical and product-oriented (for example, Qureshi 1981), but at least some historical musicologists seem to work from perspectives not incompatible with those of ethnomusicologists. Anthony Seeger (1985: 349), in his review of the *New Grove* coverage of the many "ologies" of music, points out that Vincent Duckles, in his article on musicology, "at least raises the serious possibility that . . . all musicology becomes ethnomusicological in focus" and calls part of the article "an excellent summary of an important ethnomusicological perspective." As he points out, "no single perspective [on music] will ever be more than a perspective" (p. 351). The model proposed here may solve this problem of isolation and of unitary perspective by demanding the integration of perspectives at one level of interpretation.

The historical musicologist Richard Crawford likens his approach to that of a mapmaker in search of it all, as opposed to a prospector in search of a few treasures,[14] and Friedrich Blume, in his 1972 essay on "Musical Scholarship Today," defines a musicology that "embraces all fields of musical activity in all periods of history and all peoples and nations" (p. 16). He regards himself as a historian and musicology as a branch of history in much the way that many ethnomusicologists regard themselves as anthropologists, with ethnomusicology as a branch of that discipline. As a consequence of his view that musicology is a branch of a discipline with much wider social and cultural concerns, in his case history, he speaks about a musicology that has a broad reach, rather than a narrow analytic focus. Among other things, he calls for a study of "the mental processes shaping [sounds]" (p. 16) and regards as "dangerous" an isolated view of music that forgets "the impact of music in our social life and the role played by music in humanity" (p. 27).

If historical musicologists with deep roots in the discipline of history have such ethnomusicologically orthodox views, it would seem to follow that a complete musicology—one concerned with integrating our knowledge of music into our knowledge of mental, social, historical, and spiritual processes and with all the music of all peoples and nations—might best be imaged with roots in three far-reaching disciplines: history, anthropology, and psychology. Claims about whether the resulting discipline is humanistic or scientific in its orientation could perhaps be left aside once and for all. Blacking and Gourlay, in their search for what is life-enhancing about music, Feld in his search for the sources of emotional content in music, the Beckers, in their desire to interpret rather than explain musical cultures, have adopted value-based, personal, and difficult-to-compare orientations traditionally associated with the humanities. Some historical musicologists, on the other hand, perhaps taking their cue from developments in history generally and also in ethnomusicology, write about studying music "in the past" rather than "of the past" (Treitler 1982), the "vast masses" and their lives and music as well as the Great Heros and Great Masters, and the social life and mental processes of music—orientations traditionally associated with the social sciences. We seem to be living in an ecumenical age when the disciplines to which we are "sub" are moving closer together. Musicology must take part in that movement. We can both benefit from it and contribute to it. Such a musicology also has a much better chance than our present divided versions of making significant contributions to our knowledge of humankind.

If we are able to create a unified musicology willing to make bold interpretive statements about the nature of the "formative processes" in music, the result would be a new and stronger discipline.[15] Musicology, which now has a rather limited profile and impact in the wider academic world, could take its proper place alongside its cousins in the other humanities and social sciences as a discipline making engaging and coherent claims about people and their artistic, social and intellectual behaviors.

Acknowledgements

This paper and the accompanying responses were originally presented at the 1986 annual meeting of the Society for Ethnomusicology in Rochester, N.Y., October 19, 1986. I am grateful to the respondents for agreeing to participate in this "symposium" and to Bruno Nettl for both his able moderating of the panel and his helpful comments before and after the paper was delivered. To preserve something of the character of the event, the paper and responses are presented with only slight alterations from their original spoken form. At Rochester the responses were followed by comments from the floor, whereas here there is a short response from me.

Notes

1. For a recent list of "research models" in ethnomusicology, see Modir 1986.
2. Carol Robertson (1984: 450) complained recently of the "dozens of dissertations"

that comment on "ecology, geography and history without tying these introductory chapters into subsequent chapters on musical sounds."

3. Larry Shumway (1986) criticizes *Worlds of Music* for a "social science orientation" with not enough emphasis on aesthetics and the personal experience of music, a sign that he and others still resist the emphases of much recent research and writing.

4. While the best writers in any field probably have no need of simple models, it strikes me that models may be particularly helpful to students and others trying to find a context for their work. I did a casual survey of dissertations completed in the last seven years at U.S. schools of ethnomusicology and was surprised to find—perhaps naively—that few contextualized their work even perfunctorily within a general theoretical framework in ethnomusicology, but simply considered a particular musical tradition and previous scholarship on it. (The exceptions tended to be work on ethnicity and identity, for which there is a clear and identifiable body of literature.) In effect, ethnomusicology does not exist as a discipline in these dissertations. If they can be taken as an indicator of the field, then ethnomusicology is, as Blacking (1971: 94) has lamented, "little more than a meeting ground for those interested in the anthropology of music and in music of different cultures." A model, particularly an inclusive one of the sort being suggested here, might allow a higher percentage of students and scholars than at present to imagine the general shape of the field and the place of their work in it.

5. While the perspectives brought to bear on Western and non-Western music often seem different, that does not imply, as Kerman (1985: 174) has suggested, that, "Western music is just too different from other musics, and its cultural contexts too different from other cultural contexts" to allow ethnomusicological research to "impinge directly on the study of Western music." It is not the music and contexts which are so different as too preclude comparative study, so much as the mainstream approaches and values in the two areas that often seem to be at odds.

6. Another slightly more cumbersome way to articulate the question might be:

how do people {historically / socially / individually} {create/construct / maintain / experience} music?

The question might also be phrased, how and why do people make music, but the answer to the why question may follow rather naturally from a consideration of how. In any case, Herndon and McLeod and McLeod (1979), Erdman (1982) and Idries Shah among others have all retreated from asking why to asking how. Blacking (1976b: 4) has pointed out that there are important senses in which music makes man, but while this is an engaging aphorism, I prefer the notion that man is always the active agent in the creation, experience and maintenance of music.

7. J.H. Kwabena Nketia (1981, 1985) has recently struggled with the problem of defining the field in two interesting articles. Among other things he is critical of a shift of emphasis from musical experience to the behavior that surrounds music and the assumption "that there is a one-to-one correspondence and a relationship of causality between aspects of music and aspects of culture and society. . . . The assumption is not easily demonstrated even for individual cultures" (1981: 24–25). In his 1985 study he complains that "current approaches in ethnomusicology tend to be monistic or characterised by one dimension of music" (p. 12). He then goes on to call for "the development of an integrative technique that enables the scholar to group and regroup his data" (p. 15) and "developing methods of synthesis that bring together the different aspects of music and music making in a meaningful and coherent manner" (p. 18) —precisely the kind of approach being modeled here. He goes on to construct a categorization of the field based on "three cognitive dimensions of music" (p. 14), which really are more like three methodological stances vis-à-vis music: as culture; as the object of aesthetic interest; and as language. He claims that his cognitive dimensions provide scope for this integrative approach, but without demonstrating how this might happen, leaving it as a "challenge" for ethnomusicology. In fact, it may be precisely this sort of methodological classification, which seems to separate rather than unite us, that may have to be overcome or altered.

8. The thrust of this model may, at first glance, appear to be insular and academic, in comparison to Gourlay's simultaneously pessimistic and activist "humanizing ethnomusicolo-

gy." In fact, the model has as an important component of its social matrix the teaching enterprise. What are the important lessons about music that we want to convey in the course of a pedagogical process that, at its best and most optimistic, ought to be "humanizing"? I see a great potential for a model like this at least to "humanize" the environments in which we work and the students and colleagues whom we teach.

9. A third approach to historical issues is Kay Shelemay's (1980: 233) notion of "historical ethnomusicology," which involves "the potential that a synchronic study holds for illuminating the historical continuum from which it emerged," a remarkable reversal of the usual claims about the ability of history to illuminate the present. (For another recent reversal of the usual approach to history, see Yung's (1987) notion of "historical interdependency" as a process by which the new affects the perception, construction and revision of the past.) Shelemay thinks that "the lack of emphasis on historical studies is the result of the break with historical musicology." The lack of emphasis, however, may be more in theory than in practice. Although our methods rest heavily on field work and an implicitly synchronic approach to the "ethnographic present," a large percentage of our published work focuses on processes of change, either directly observed or reconstructed from previously available data. We have, in practice, identified change and historical processes not just as one of many processes, but as a fundamental one. Probably historical processes and interpretations have been resorted to as convenient interpretive gestures when social and cultural processes and interpretations were not observed or were more problematic.

10. Gourlay (1982: 142) objects that analysis is not an approach "to understanding what happens when men and women make music," but it may be a key to understanding what happened when people made music, to reconstructing past experience, and to understanding musical creativity (for example, Cavanagh 1982).

11. Bielawski (1985) attempts to develop a full-blown theory of historical perspectives in ethnomusicology and emphasizes them—perhaps not surprising for an Eastern European—in his statement of basic goals for the field: "To study music from various historical points of view should be the aim of contemporary ethnomusicology" (p. 14). He goes on to argue that systematic and historical perspectives are "supplementary and interdependent," but like so many other claims along this line, he does not go on to say how precisely this might work.

12. McLean (1980: 53): "The one means of compiling a 'history' of Oceanic music is to begin with music styles as currently practised." The study and description of musical styles on the modern map is the beginning of an attempt to reconstruct history (see Nattiez 1982 for an example of a theoretical map with historical density).

13. What will this discipline be called? Gilbert Chase (1976), in a pointed and delightful polemic on the relationship between history, anthropology and musicology, decries the divisions within the discipline and points out a terminological shift since the days of Adler (1885) and Haydon (1941), and a significant retreat from the promise held out by the Harrison, Palisca, Hood volume of 1963 entitled simply, *Musicology:*

> "We have not yet—unfortunately—reached that point in time at which the term *musicology* is generally accepted as signifying the *total* study of music in human culture . . . *musicology*, without any qualifier, has been tacitly appropriated by the historical branch of that discipline" (pp. 231-32).

The terminological situation since the mid-seventies has not improved, although one could cite the 1977 IMS meeting in Berkeley and the *New Grove* as evidence of a theoretical improvement. If usurpation of the term "musicology" was tacit in the mid-70s, it is explicit in the '80s with the publication of Kerman's *Contemplating Music* and the formation in 1982 of the *Journal of Musicology*, which, although it has an ethnomusicologist on the editorial board, pointedly ignores ethnomusicological concerns in its statement of purpose: "A quarterly review of music history, criticism, analysis, and performance practice."

14. Richard Crawford (1985: 2), speaking for the field of American music studies, also carves out an orientation very close to ethnomusicological principles: "For scholars of American music in recent years have more and more looked beyond the selective, aesthetically dominated perspective of the concert hall and begun to consider any kind of music made in America as potentially significant. They have broadened their focus from Music with a capital M to

music-making: in John Blacking's phrase, from product to process. . . . " He goes on to propose a journalistic who-what-where-when-how model, very similar to one proposed by Anthony Seeger (1980), that gets at issues dear to the hearts of ethnomusicologists.

15. Helen Myers (1981: 43) calls for a rigorous scientific approach based on Popper's notions of falsifiability. "What is required of us is to pose adventurous and imaginative conjectures and then strengthen them by systematically attempting to prove them false." While I share her enthusiasm for "adventurous and imaginative conjectures," the interpretive approach advocated here may not lead to directly falsifiable statements (Dentan 1984), but rather to complex "stories" that can only be compared using criteria such as completeness, cogency, inclusiveness and so on.

References

Adler, Guido
1885 "Umfang, Methode und Ziel der Musikwissenschaft," *Vierteljahrsscrift fur Musikwissenschaft* 1: 5–20.

Becker, Judith and A.L.
1984 "Response to Feld and Roseman," *Ethnomusicology* 28(3): 454–456.

Behague, Gerard
1984 "Introduction," *Performance Practice: Ethnomusicological Perspectives* (Westport, CT: Greenwood Press), pp. 3–12.

Bielawski, Ludwik
1985 "History in Ethnomusicology," *Yearbook for Traditional Music* 17: 8–15.

Blacking, John
1976a "Introduction," *The Performing Arts: Music and Dance*. The Hague, pp. xiii–xxi.
1976b "The Study of Man as Music-Maker," ibid., pp. 3–15.
1977 "Some Problems of Theory and Method in the Study of Musical Change," *Yearbook of the International Folk Music Society* 9: 1–26.

Blum, Stephen
1975 "Toward a Social History of Musicological Technique," *Ethnomusicology* 19(2): 207–231.

Blume, Friedrich
1972 "Musical Scholarship Today," in Barry S. Brook et al., eds., *Perspectives in Musicology*. New York: Norton, pp. 15–31.

Cavanagh, Beverley
1982 *Music of the Netsilik Eskimo: A Study of Stability and Change*. Ottawa: National Museums of Canada.

Chase, Gilbert
1976 "Musicology, History, and Anthropology: Current Thoughts," in John W. Grubb, ed., *Current Thought in Musicology*. Austin: University of Texas Press, pp. 231–246.

Crawford, Richard
1985 *Studying American Music*. New York: Institute for Studies in American Music, Special Publications No. 3.

Dentan, Robert Knox
1984 "Response to Feld and Roseman," *Ethnomusicology* 28(3): 463–466.

Erdman, Joan
1982 "The Empty Beat: *Khali* as a Sign of Time," *American Journal of Semiotics* 1(4): 21–45.

Feld, Steven
1982 *Sound and Sentiment*. Philadelphia: University of Pennsylvania Press.
1984 "Communication, Music, and Speech about Music," *Yearbook for Traditional Music* 16: 1–18.

Geertz, Clifford
1973 *The Interpretation of Cultures*. N.Y.: Basic Books.

Gourlay, Kenneth
1982 "Towards a Humanizing Ethnomusicology," *Ethnomusicology* 26(3): 411–420.
Harrison, Frank LL., Mantle Hood, and Claude V. Palisca
1963 *Musicology*. Englewood Cliffs, N.J.: Prentice-Hall.
Harwood, Dane
1976 "Universals in Music: A Perspective from Cognitive Psychology," *Ethnomusicology* 20(3): 521–533.
Haydon, Glen
1941 *Introduction to Musicology*. N.Y.: Prentice-Hall.
Herndon, Marcia and Norma McLeod
1979 *Music as Culture*. Norwood, Pa.: Norwood Editions.
1980 *The Ethnography of Musical Performance*. Norwood, Pa.: Norwood Editions.
Kerman, Joseph
1985 *Contemplating Music*. Cambridge: Harvard University Press.
Koskoff, Ellen
1982 "The Music-Network: A Model for the Organization of Music Concepts," *Ethnomusicology* 26(3): 353–370.
McLean, Mervyn
1980 "Approaches to Music History in Oceania," *World of Music* 22(3): 46–54.
Merriam, Alan P.
1964 *The Anthropology of Music*. Evanston, Il.: Northwestern University Press.
Meyers, Helen
1981 " 'Normal' Ethnomusicology and 'Extraordinary' Ethnomusicology," *Journal of the Indian Musicological Society* 12(3–4): 38–44.
Modir, Hafez
1986 "Research Models in Ethnomusicology Applied to the *Radif* Phenomenon in Iranian Classical Music," *Pacific Review of Ethnomusicology* 3: 63–78.
Nattiez, Jean-Jacques
1982 "Comparisons within a Culture: The Examples of the *Katajjaq* of the Inuit," in Robert Falck and Timothy Rice, eds., *Cross-Cultural Perspectives on Music* (Toronto: University of Toronto Press), pp. 134–140.
1983 "Some Aspects of Inuit Vocal Games," *Ethnomusicology* 27(3): 457–475.
Nettl, Bruno
1983 *The Study of Ethnomusicology: 29 Issues and Concepts*. Urbana: University of Illinois Press.
Nketia, J.H. Kwabena
1981 "The Juncture of the Social and the Musical: The Methodology of Cultural Analysis," *World of Music* 23(2): 23–31.
1985 "Integrating Objectivity and Experience in Ethnomusicological Studies," *World of Music* 27(3): 3–19.
Qureshi, Regula Burckhardt
1981 "Qawwali Sound, Context and Meaning." PhD Dissertation, University of Alberta.
Robertson, Carol
1984 "Response to Feld and Roseman," *Ethnomusicology* 28(3): 449–452.
Sawa, George
1983 "Musical Performance Practice in the Early 'Abbasid Era." PhD Dissertation, University of Toronto.
Seeger, Anthony
1980 "Sing for your Sister: The Structure and Performance of Suya Akia," in Marcia Herndon and Norma McLeod, eds., *The Ethnography of Musical Performance* (Norwood, Pa.: Norwood Editions), pp. 7–42.
1985 "General Articles on Ethnomusicology and Related Disciplines [in the *New Grove*]," *Ethnomusicology* 29(2): 345–351.
Seeger, Charles
1977 "The Musicological Juncture: 1976," *Ethnomusicology* 21(2): 179–188.

Shelemay, Kay Kaufman
1980 " 'Historical Ethnomusicology': Reconstructing Falasha Ritual," *Ethnomusicology* 24(2): 233-258.
Shepherd, John
1982 "A Theoretical Model for the Sociomusicological Analysis of Popular Musics," in Richard Middleton and David Horn, eds., *Popular Music 2: Theory and Method.* Cambridge University Press, pp. 145-178.
Shumway, Larry
1986 Review of *Worlds of Music, Ethnomusicology* 30(2): 356-357.
Stone, Ruth
1982 *Let the Inside Be Sweet.* Bloomington, Indiana University Press.
Thomas, Lewis
1974 *Lives of a Cell.* N.Y.: Viking Press
Titon, Jeff Todd, general ed.
1984 *Words of Music.* New York: Schirmer.
Treitler, Leo
1982 "Structural and Critical Analysis," in D. Kern Holoman and Claude V. Palisca, eds., *Musicology in the 1980s* (N.Y.: Da Capo Press), pp. 67-77.
Wachsmann, Klaus
1982 "The Changeability of Musical Experience," *Ethnomusicology* 26(2): 197-215.
Wade, Bonnie
1984 "Performance Practice in Indian Classical Music," in Gerard Behague, ed., *Performance Practice: Ethnomusicological Perspectives* (Westport, CT: Greenwood Press), pp. 13-52.
Yung, Bell
1984 "Choreographic and Kinesthetic Elements in Performance on the Chinese Seven-String Zither," *Ethnomusicology* 28(3): 505-517.
1987 "Historical Interdependency of Music: Case Study of the Chinese Seven-String Zither," *Journal of the American Musicological Society* 40(1): 82-91.
Zemp, Hugo
1978 " 'Are'Are Classification of Musical Types and Instruments," *Ethnomusicology* 22(1): 37-67.

ACKNOWLEDGMENTS

Helen H. Roberts, "Suggestions to Field-Workers in Collecting Folk Music and Data About Instruments," *Journal of the Polynesian Society* 40 (1931): 103–128. Reproduced by permission of the *Journal of the Polynesian Society*. Courtesy of the Library of Congress.

Erich M. von Hornbostel, "Über einige Panpfeifen aus Nordwestbrasilien," in *Zwei Jahre unter den Indianern*, ed. Theodor Koch-Gruenberg (Berlin: E. Wasmuth, 1910), Vol. 2, pp. 378–391. Courtesy of Columbia University.

Jaap Kunst, "Around von Hornbostel's Theory of the Cycle of Blown Fifths," *Mededeling* 76 (Amsterdam: Publication 76 of the Royal Institute for the Indies) (1948): 3–35. Reproduced by permission of the Royal Institute for the Indies.

Maud Karpeles, "Some Reflections on Authenticity in Folk Music," *Journal of the International Folk Music Council* 3 (1951): 10–16. Courtesy of Yale University Music Library.

Alan P. Merriam, "The Use of Music in the Study of a Problem of Acculturation," *American Anthropologist* 57 (1955): 28–34. Reproduced by permission of the American Anthropological Association. Courtesy of Yale University.

John Blacking, "Some Notes on a Theory of African Rhythm Advanced by Erich von Hornbostel," *African Music Society Journal* 1(2) (1955): 12–20. Reproduced by permission of the African Music Society.

Mantle Hood, "The Reliability of Oral Tradition," *Journal of the American Musicological Society* 12(2-3) (1959): 201–209. Reproduced by permission of the American Musicological Society. Courtesy of Yale University Music Library.

Mantle Hood, "The Challenge of 'Bi-Musicality'," *Ethnomusicology* 4(2) (1960): 55–59. Reproduced by permission of *Ethnomusicology*. Courtesy of Yale University Music Library.

Leonard B. Meyer, "Universalism and Relativism in the Study of Ethnic Music," *Ethnomusicology* 4(2) (1960): 49–54. Reproduced by permission of *Ethnomusicology*. Courtesy of Yale University Music Library.

William P. Malm, "Practical Approaches to Japanese Traditional Music," *Center for Japanese Studies Occasional Papers* 9 (1965): 95–104. Reproduced by permission of the Center for Japanese Studies.

Alan P. Merriam, "The Use of Music as a Technique of Reconstructing Culture History in Africa," in *Reconstructing African Culture History*, eds. Creighton Gabel and Norman R. Bennett (Boston: Boston University Press, 1967), pp. 85–114. Reproduced by permission of Boston University Press.

Flor de María Rodríguez de Ayestarán, "Metodología para la Reconstrucción de las Danzas Folklóricas Extintas," in *Music in the Americas*, eds. George List and Juan Orrego-Salas (The Hague: Mouton and Indiana University Research Center in Anthropology, Folklore and Linguistics, 1967), pp. 183–191. Courtesy of Yale University Music Library.

Charles L. Boilés, "Sémiotique de l'ethnomusicologie," *Musique en jeu* 10 (1973): 34–41. Courtesy of Yale University Music Library.

Steven Feld, "Linguistic Models in Ethnomusicology," *Ethnomusicology* 18(2) (1974): 197–217. Reproduced by permission of *Ethnomusicology*. Courtesy of Yale University Music Library.

Bonnie C. Wade, "Prolegomenon to the Study of Song Texts," *Yearbook of the International Folk Music Council* 8 (1976): 73–88. Courtesy of Yale University Music Library.

Jean-Jacques Nattiez, "The Contribution of Musical Semiotics to the Semiotic Discussion in General," in *A Perfusion of Signs*, ed. T. Sebeok. (Bloomington: Indiana University Press, 1977), pp. 121–142. Courtesy of the Library of Congress.

K.A. Gourlay,"Towards a Reassessment of the Ethnomusicologist's Role in Research," *Ethnomusicology* 22(1) (1978): 1–35. Reproduced by permission of *Ethnomusicology*. Courtesy of Yale University Music Library.

Patricia Tunstall, "Structuralism and Musicology: An Overview," *Current Musicology* 27 (1979): 51–64. Courtesy of Yale University Music Library.

Alan P. Merriam, "African Musical Rhythm and Concepts of Time-reckoning," in *Music East and West: Essays in Honor of Walter Kaufman*, ed. Thomas Noblitt (New York: Pendragon Press, 1981), pp. 123–141. Reproduced by permission of Pendragon Press.

Alan P. Merriam, "On Objections to Comparison in Ethnomusicology," in *Cross-Cultural Perspectives on Music*, eds. Robert Falck and Timothy Rice (Toronto: University of Toronto Press, 1982), pp. 174–189. Reproduced by permission of University of Toronto Press. Courtesy of Yale University Music Library.

Timothy Rice, "Toward the Remodeling of Ethnomusicology," *Ethnomusicology* 31(3) (1987): 469–488. Reproduced by permission of *Ethnomusicology*. Courtesy of Yale University Music Library.

c1

CATHOLIC THEOLOGICAL UNION
ML3799.G371990VOL.2 C001
ETHNOMUSICOLOGICAL THEORY AND METHOD NE

3 0311 00071 3169